Construction – Craft to Industry

Construction –
Craft to Industry

Gyula Sebestyén

E & FN SPON
An Imprint of Routledge

London and New York

Published by E & FN Spon
An Imprint of Routledge
11 New Fetter Lane, London EC4P 4EE

Simultaneously published in the USA and Canada by Routledge
29 West 35th Street, New York, NY 10001

© 1998 G. Sebestyén

Typeset in 10/12 Palatino by Saxon Graphics Ltd, Derby
Printed and bound in Great Britain by T.J. International, Padstow,
Cornwall, UK

British Library Cataloguing in Publication Data
A catalogue record for this book is available from the British Library

ISBN 0 419 20920 4

Contents

Preface

There are two questions that any author of a professional book should answer: what is the purpose of the book, and why is the author the best person to write it?

In relation to this book, the response to the first question is that during the twentieth century the construction industry and its products and technology have changed drastically. This metamorphosis has been insufficiently appreciated and is worthy of consideration. In answer to the second question, I have spent a lifetime working in research and development in the construction industry, much of it on an international level. Furthermore, as a third-generation professional in the industry and the father of a fourth-generation architect, I have had a front-seat view of the events of a whole century. I therefore felt the provision of an overview of the industry to be almost an obligation.

Construction technology has developed in a signal way in the last 100 years. In an increasing number of subsectors, the most up-to-date technology is used and more of the buildings to be constructed are really high-tech products whose design requires modern scientific methods. The internal structure of the building industry is also changing. An internationalization of the market goes hand in hand with the emergence of construction multinationals, which themselves promote technical progress. Despite this, several publications have claimed that construction lags behind other industries, that construction technology has been the least modernized, that productivity in building has developed at a lower rate than elsewhere, and that it is still a labour-intensive economic sector with accident-prone and health-endangering work practices. It is argued that most building materials, such as stone, timber and even brick, have been around since ancient times, and that their use is based on empirical experience in which the need for scientific research is limited. It has also been claimed that the construction industry's foremost concern in the future will be the maintenance and repair of existing stock rather than new construction.

However I wish to demonstrate here that this is an unrealistic and pessimistic picture, that the construction industry has been much transformed and that it does face a challenging future. This book reflects on the changes that are contributing to the transformation of construction from an ancient craft to a modern industry, while restricting its scope to selected trends that seem to be important in this process. This book also demonstrates that although there is relatively less research in the building sector than there is in other industrial areas, much of the progress in construction originates in the work of designers and manufacturers, so that the technical progress is not restricted to the result of formal building research. The book also points out that the enhanced performance of the buildings and construction sector is largely ignored by economic indices such as productivity, which, again, has the consequence that not all progress is reflected by statistical data.

Construction is becoming a modern industry, co-operating as an active partner with various scientific disciplines such as the medical and social sciences, psychology, mathematics, physics and chemistry. At its best, it has become an important contributor to global energy conservation, protection of the environment and sustainable development. Because it is such a vast field, many subjects, problems or trends have been discussed only briefly. Readers who wish to become acquainted with the subject to a greater depth should refer to the titles listed at the end of each chapter. Indeed, one important objective of the book is to draw attention to areas that may not be common knowledge to experts in other fields, and provide further avenues of information on those topics. It is unfortunate that this book pays relatively little attention to the small-scale sector of the market, and thus to vernacular building. But with the objective of analysing the most advanced forms of construction, this was unavoidable.

The book is not aimed exclusively at practitioners or researchers. On the contrary, it seeks to reach a wider audience. Nevertheless, it also hopes to help bridge the gap between practice and research in the profession. Although practitioners may do valuable work within a certain geographic area or professional field, they are often unable to find the time to follow trends outside their areas. I hope that this book may help to broaden their outlook with its succinct description of the global trends in the various professional disciplines. At the same time, it may identify problems of practice that are in need of solutions from the researchers. It is also to be hoped that the book will be useful for the students of professions such as architecture, civil engineering, real estate, building and facility management, housing, urban planning, building economics, environment and building services.

A brief comment on the use of the terms 'building' and 'construction' is worth while. In this book, the processes and products of both building and construction are discussed without specifically indicating in which sense the two terms are used; this should be obvious from the text. With regard to the products, selected buildings are as much discussed as civil engineering works. When discussing the industry itself, the whole construction industry is considered.

The chronology in the Appendix charts the technical progress, inventions and innovations in construction and innovative buildings. It also contains data not specifically included in the individual chapters. Understandably, the data collected from various sources are often conflicting or differing. I would therefore be grateful for any corrections that readers may like to forward to me.

Gyula Sebestyén
Rotterdam, The Netherlands
June, 1997

Acknowledgements

The book could not have been written without the contributions and assistance I received in various forms from many people, and no acknowledgement can sufficiently repay this debt.

The following people have helped with advice and information: W. Bakens, H.J. Blass, J. Blauwendraad, A. Cops, R.G. Courtney, K.H. Dekker, T.V. Galambos, K. Gertis, M. Groosman, J. Hogeling, H. Hens, L. Kollar, J.T.C. van Kemenade, P. Lenkei, C. McLeash, S.C.M. Menheere, A.W. Pratt, R. Rolloos, J.W.B. Stark, J. Szabo, T. Takeda, T. Tarnai, L. Twilt, J.N.J.A. Vambersky, P. van der Veer, L.G.W. Verhoef, G. Vermeir, A.C.W.M. Vrouwenvelder, J.C. Walraven, W. Wissmann, R.N. Wright. Several companies and organizations, including UNESCO, Philips, MERO and others, have also been most helpful. The constructive comments from the readers of the book appointed by the publishers have also been of great assistance. I wish to express my sincere gratitude to all.

Finally I would also like to express my thanks to J. Rudnay and C.E. Pollington, who were kind enough to read and comment on some parts of the book, and to Caroline Mallinder from E & FN Spon for her careful editing work. All responsibility nevertheless remains with the author.

The past up to 1945 1

CONSTRUCTION, FROM THE BEGINNING TO THE COLLAPSE OF THE ROMAN EMPIRE (AD 476)

Construction is an economic sector in the same way as, for example, car manufacturing or electricity generation. However, while modern manufacturing has only a short history, construction and its 'products' – buildings, villages, towns and cities – can be traced back several thousand years.

The first shelters and settlements were built from stone or mud and materials collected in forests, and provided protection against the cold, wind, rain and snow. The earliest buildings served primarily residential purposes, although some may also have had a communal function or been used for producing bread or ceramics or for the storage of grain and oil.

During the New Stone Age, several societies emerged, mainly on fertile plateaux with high rainfall, such as along the Nile in Egypt, along the Euphrates and Tigris in Mesopotamia, along the Indus valley in India and by the Hwang Ho in China. These people introduced dried bricks, wall construction, metal working and irrigation.

Gradually, people developed the skills to construct first simple villages and then towns and later cities. By the time of the great civilizations in Egypt, China, The Middle East and the Mediterranean Region some 4000–5000 years ago, considerable skills in building had been acquired. The pyramid of Cheops at Giza, in Egypt, built in approximately 2589–2566 BC, was originally 146.5 m high. Even today, without its cladding, it is still impressive at 127 m high. The text carved in the 2.25 m high stone slabs found in 1902 in the area that was ancient Mesopotamia defined the onerous responsibilities of the builder for his workmanship in the construction of houses. The stones were known as the Law Book of Hammurabi, King of Babylonia, and date from approximately 1792–1750 BC.

Fig. 1.1   The pyramids at Giza; original height: 146 m, aged 4500 years. *Source:* F. Pogány (1960) *Terek es utcák müvészete*, Müszaki Könyvkiadó, Budapest.

The expansion of Greek settlements around the Mediterranean after 2000 BC was preceded and strengthened by a population growth and migrations to and from Greece. Early Greek buildings were made of mud using timber framing. Later, temples and theatres were built from marble. The Greeks had considerable experience in stonemasonry and in using iron for tongs, clamps and plugs. The peak period of the ancient Greek societies was the fifth century BC. Subsequently, the Macedonians and the Romans came to pre-eminence. The Romans created a world empire reaching from what is now Great Britain to the Middle East. At its height, the Roman empire had a population of 60–100 million people. Rome itself developed into a world metropolis some 1500–2000 years ago, and became the leading centre of world culture which, of course, extended to construction.

Marcus Vitruvius Pollo, the first century BC military and civil engineer, published his 10 books (i.e. a book with 10 chapters) in Rome. This was the world's first major publication on architecture and construction, and it dealt with building materials, the style and design of building types, the construction process, building physics, astronomy and building machines. Even after 2000 years, Vitruvius's comprehensive treatment of construction remains fascinating. It is therefore not surprising that the

Fig. 1.2 The Pantheon, Rome, span of dome: 43.30 m, AD 118–28. *Source: Historia dell'Arte*, Salvat Editores, Barcelona.

book, which was thought lost until 1414, has seen very many editions since its first modern reprint in 1486. Among other details, Vitruvius describes the hypocaust, the heating system used in the public baths and the houses of important officials and wealthy citizens. Invented in the first century BC, the hypocaust consisted of a suspended floor supported by columns, and heated by hot flue gases produced by a furnace at one end and vented by a chimney at the other (Cowan, 1987). Later the flues were channelled under the floor and eventually through ducts on the walls so that the vertical surfaces could also be heated. The Korean *on-dol* and the Chinese *kang* were very similar, but whereas the hypocaust was abandoned after Rome collapsed, the *on-dol* and the *kang* are still very much in use today (Cowan, 1987).

Fig. 1.3   The Pont du Gard, France; height: 49 m. *Source: Historia dell'Arte*, Salvat Editores, Barcelona.

The collapse of the Roman empire marked the end of the period now known as antiquity, and also concluded a magnificent chapter in architecture and construction.

THE MIDDLE AGES AND THE FIRST PERIOD OF MODERN TIMES: 476–1800

The expansion of the Roman empire precipitated its demise, which was marked by the fall of Rome in 476. Meanwhile, Christianity, which had spread and consolidated, had been adopted by the whole of the west European world, although it continued to be threatened by the mounted peoples of northern Eurasia: the Huns, Avars, Magyars, Tartars and, later, the Ottomans (Turks). With the consolidation of the state in Germany, France and England, the medieval order was created.

From the demise of the Roman empire, construction in Europe stagnated for several centuries. During the three centuries between then and the accession of Charlemagne in France, many towns suffered from the effects of armed conflict: some were burnt, and others were abandoned and fell into ruin. Towns in Italy survived this period better than most, but elsewhere no balanced development could take place.

The Carolingian period witnessed the resurgence of urban development, although Aachen, a Carolingian centre, did not become a significant town (Saalman, 1968). When, in the eleventh century, the Norsemen settled in Normandy and England, building construction also profited from the greater calm in western Europe. A period of development in the medieval cities was assisted by the construction of churches and monasteries which, in turn, attracted more people to settle in their vicinity. Many cities enjoyed the protection of princes and lords, but at the same time fought for more freedom and independence (Pounds, 1974). For protection, cities girded themselves with walls and moats. Public buildings, such as hospices, hospitals, schools and town halls were also constructed. Around 1300, several cities in Europe had populations that exceeded 50 000; Florence, Milan, Venice, Seville, Cordoba, Granada, Constantinople and many more had a population of 25 000 to 50 000. The number of small and medium-size towns also increased.

The Medieval Age (476–1492) was a long period of history that is sometimes unjustly labelled as stagnant. In reality, much was achieved during those 1000-odd years. Improvements in agricultural and artisanal productivity, and exploration and the consequent broadening of commerce, provided an impetus to new population growth and an expansion of Europe to new regions in the east and north of the Continent. The Italian city states (Genoa, Venice, Pisa), cities in Flanders (Bruges, Ghent), and the Hanseatic cities (Lübeck, Bremen, Rostock) grew affluent at that time. It is true that progress was slow during the Romanesque period (approximately 1000–1140), but this was nevertheless the period of the construction of the magnificent German imperial cathedrals of Speyer, Worms and Mainz, as well as of other European marvels such as those in Pisa, Angoulême, Poitiers, Vézelay and Cluny. Later, as we shall see below, the Gothic period (1140–1600) brought many innovations to the construction of cathedrals.

The supply of building materials was critical. Landlords eventually gave permission for the felling of trees and the quarrying of stone for the construction of cathedrals and other buildings. In areas where neither timber nor stone was present, the firing of bricks and tiles was re-invented. Bricks were the main materials for construction in the north German plain. Lime burners either gathered in good locations or travelled from building site to building site. The supply and demand for timber, both for shipbuilding as well as construction, was high, and not surprisingly this led to the first complaints about deforestation.

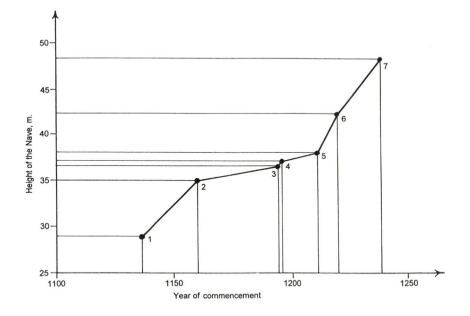

Fig. 1.4 Height of the main nave in French Gothic cathedrals. *Source:* author's diagrams.

The social stability of the late Middle Ages enabled elaborate craft training and education to develop, and these also helped to raise the status of the craftsmen. Building construction became a major industry (Phelps Brown and Hopkins, 1955; Spufford, 1988) and, as in other sectors, a structured approach to construction developed in the formation of guilds, also known as 'mysteries'. Craft guilds were European occupational associations for the protection and regulation of artisans working in a specific branch of a trade. The first guilds were formed at the end of the eleventh century and expanded rapidly during the twelfth. Their characteristics were remarkably alike throughout Europe. The guilds were hierarchical bodies, usually divided into the three categories of masters, journeymen and apprentices. Eventually, they divided further into special brotherhoods, which established a monopoly in a country or particular town in a certain trade.

The two most important building crafts were those of the carpenters and stonemasons. Their tools were made and sharpened by the black-

Fig. 1.5 Medieval scaffolding for a stone building. The poles are lashed together at the diagonals with tourniquets to tighten the binding. The master-mason greets a party of dignitaries. Stones are squared with mallet and chisel. Water for the mortar comes from a newly dug well. Note the stone-layer's trowel. *Source:* Ch. Singer *et al.* (eds) (1957) *A History of Technology*, Vol. II, Clarendon Press, Oxford, from a French manuscript, 1460.

smiths. Lead fittings were made by plumbers, and glazings by glaziers (Thomson, 1957). The stained-glass window, in which shaped pieces of coloured glass were fitted together by lead beads, was developed in the twelfth century in the Mediterranean region.

The master mason was totally committed to the building on which he was engaged. He not only designed it and led its construction, but in many cases he even lived on the site; indeed, it is no exaggeration to say that he lived for his building (Hamilton, 1958). Under the master mason worked the free- and roughmasons.

Although the account of the Medieval period has been confined primarily to Europe, contemporary civilizations on other continents deserve equal admiration: the various pre-Colombian (Maya, Aztec) cultures, the Mogul empire with its Taj Mahal, the Khmer empire with the Angkor temple complex, and the Arab and Ottoman worlds with their outstanding architecture in Granada, Seville, Samarkand and Bukhara, are all excellent examples.

The fifteenth century brought a 'renaissance' or renewal in architecture, building and science. Following a transition period in the sixteenth

Fig. 1.6   Medieval construction of a stone bridge and wooden fortifications under fire from the enemy. Trees are felled, squared by axe and cut into planks with a pit-saw. The planks are cut to length, jointed and pegged. Lying on the ground are a square, trimming axe, pair of pincers, brace and hand-saw. Masons square their stone with mallet and bolster, and the mortar is mixed and carried forward to the builders, who work behind screens to protect them from the enemy's fire. *Source:* Ch. Singer *et al.* (eds) (1957) *A History of Technology*, Vol. II, Clarendon Press, Oxford; from a French manuscript, 1460.

century, significant changes occurred in the seventeenth century (De Vries, 1976) and thereafter with the increasing transformation of construction and urban habitat.

Fig. 1.7   St Peter's Cathedral. Rome; span of dome: 42 m; fifteenth and sixteenth centuries. *Source:* F. Pogány (1960) *Terek es utcák müvészete*, Müszaki Könyvkiadó, Budapest.

More than 1000 years had elapsed since Vitruvius's book, when another ambitious and comprehensive publication appeared: four books on architecture by the Italian Andrea Palladio (*I quattro libri dell'architectura*), published in 1570. He created the new style of Palladianism, which subsequently found applications in many other countries including what is now the UK (Inigo Jones) and later in the USA, where Thomas

Jefferson, the country's third president and also an architect, followed the Palladian style (Guinness and Stadler Jr, 1973).

There were few remarkable architectural innovations during the seventeenth century, but the mansard roof, popularized (not invented) by the French architect François Mansard (or Mansart), is noteworthy, Another innovation, also related to roof carpentry, was that of Philibert de l'Orme, who built curved roofs out of short lengths of light timber for roof spaces with longer spans (Briggs, 1957a).

Metallurgy profited from the introduction of the waterwheel as a prime source of mechanical energy. The blast furnace was originally introduced in the Middle Ages, but larger furnaces operated by water power, were now built. Between 1750 and 1850, coke and coal were substituted for charcoal as fuel, and water was gradually replaced by steam as a source of motive-power. The quality of iron gradually improved as its consumption increased as a result of the mechanization of armies. This, and the increasing production of coal and iron in the seventeenth and eighteenth centuries, broadened the use of hammered wrought and cast iron in construction. In St Paul's Cathedral (built in London between 1675 and 1710), two iron chains were used to counter the outward thrust of the dome, while in the old House of Commons (built in London in 1714), iron columns were used. Concealed iron cramps, cross-ties and reinforcing bars became common practice in eighteenth century English masonry.

The traditional medieval monopoly of the construction guilds (masons, carpenters) began to be eroded with the introduction of new construction methods. Decrees and acts abolished craft (guild) associations in France (1791), Rome (1807), England (1837), Spain (1840), Austria and Germany (1859–60), and Italy (1864). Eventually, the demise of the guilds resulted in the introduction of professional designers and contractors.

THE NINETEENTH CENTURY

The scientific revolution of the seventeenth and eighteenth centuries gave birth to the great industrial developments of the eighteenth century. After some delay, construction followed these developments in the nineteenth century. Cast iron, wrought iron and later steel were important materials that enabled new structures such as bridges, railways and building frames to be introduced. Henry Bessemer, an Englishman, invented a new steel-making process in 1856. This was improved by another Englishman, Sidney Gilchrist Thomas, the German Karl Wilhelm Siemens and the Frenchman Pierre Émile Martin. By the end of the nineteenth century, the steel kings such as Andrew Carnegie, Eugène Schneider, Alfred Krupp and Vickers dominated the industry. The increasing demand for energy was at first catered for by the steam engine, and, later, by the internal combustion engine and the electromotor.

Glass, manufactured by modern methods (Hamilton, 1968) was used for steel-framed buildings with large glazed envelopes. The shopping arcades covered by glazed steel structures that are found in European cities such as London, Paris and Milan were built during the second half of the nineteenth and early twentieth centuries. Alexandre Gustave Eiffel is known throughout the world for his Eiffel Tower, built between 1887

Fig. 1.8 The Eiffel Tower, Paris, 1889; height: originally 300 m; with the added antenna: 327 m. *Source: Historia dell'Arte*, Salvat Editores S.A., Barcelona, Spain, Vol. 9

and 1889 for the World Exhibition of that year. Originally 300 m high (now 320 m), it was the world's tallest building until 1930.

Portland cement was invented in 1824, and with it concrete and later reinforced concrete structures were introduced. In the second half of the century modern factories of building materials (cement, lime, gypsum, glass, steel, bricks and roofing tiles) were established (Hamilton, 1968), and by the beginning of the twentieth century, a new industrial sector producing building equipment (elevators, boilers, radiators, pipes and sanitary appliances) was emerging.

Over the centuries, the transportation and lifting of heavy building materials had required the physical effort of many labourers and the use of simple, or sometimes elaborate, equipment, tools, scaffolds, ropes and winches. Although the processes of construction were mechanized later than those of manufacturing, manual work in the building industry has been increasingly replaced by machines over the past 150 years. Indeed, some of the present-day processes in construction are only possible because of machinery.

The steam mechanical digger or shovel originated in the USA in the 1830s. The Frenchman Couvreux registered his patent for a steam dragline-excavator in 1859 (Perrot *et al.*, 1979), which subsequently found successful application. Rotative steam engines could be used to drive such machinery as the steam hammer or the pile driver. The large-scale mechanization of construction took a major step forward with the invention of the internal combustion engine towards the end of the century.

The extensive projects in housing, industry, transport and city development of the nineteenth century formed the background to what emerged as the modern construction industry. However, most building construction remained in the hands of small and medium-sized local contractors, whereas civil engineering projects required much larger-scale operations.

Railway construction in Great Britain, which began in the 1830s, was another launching pad for the emergence of large international contractors. At first, these were only British, then French, and during the second half of the century German, Belgian and US contractors joined the league. During the early railway era, British railway engineers (George Stephenson, Robert Stephenson, Joseph Locke, Charles Vignoles, Isambard Kingdom Brunel, John Hawkshaw) dominated design and execution (Linder, 1994). The first British railway contractors were mostly self-taught practical men who learned by experience. The success of their initial contracts gave them a significant edge over others in competitions for subsequent assignments, even if those others were, at least formally, better educated (for example, the French already had excellent engineering educational facilities). When the railway fever subsided in Great Britain at the end of the 1840s, British contractors sought and won contracts abroad. Some of these contractors, such as Thomas Brassey, Samuel Morton Peto and Edward Bettes, were, at the peak of their activities, among the largest employers in Great Britain, providing work (directly or indirectly) to tens of thousands of people. Brassey, for example, employed or supervised 80 000–100 000 workers at his peak (Linder, 1994).

At about the turn of the century, Pearson built up a major international construction company in Great Britain. When he accepted a 1 million acre oil drilling concession in Mexico as part payment for his services, he showed an early example of diversification, which later became more common among large construction firms. Another international venture was the construction of the Suez Canal from 1859 to 1869 under the leadership of the Frenchman Ferdinand de Lesseps. It is interesting to note that by the end of the 1880s Germany still did not have a single construction company of international status. It was then that the Deutsche Bank launched the international career of Philipp Holzmann & Co. With the support of the bank, Holzmann built the first section of the Anatolian (Baghdad) railway at the end of the 1880s.

In the USA, the internationalization of contractors began somewhat later because there were plenty of domestic civil engineering projects, which nevertheless provided valuable expertise, allowing US contractors gradually (and successfully) to penetrate the world market, at first in the Americas and later worldwide. Several US construction companies were founded around the turn of the century. Warren A. Bechtel worked at first as a railway employee. Then he established his own firm, which, together with others such as Kaiser, Utah and Morrison-Knudsen, grew rapidly by executing railway, road and infrastructure construction.

The appearance of international contractors was the first wave in the globalization of construction. The twentieth century witnessed further developments in this process.

THE FIRST HALF OF THE TWENTIETH CENTURY

Optimism was the dominant sentiment at the turn of the century in the industrial countries. Progress in science and technology, and increasing affluence gave the illusion that peace would persist and that wealth would increase and spread. The half-century that followed was indeed a period of spectacular scientific and technological progress, and also of affluence in several countries, but major adverse political and economic disasters (two world wars and the great economic crisis of 1929–33) had a

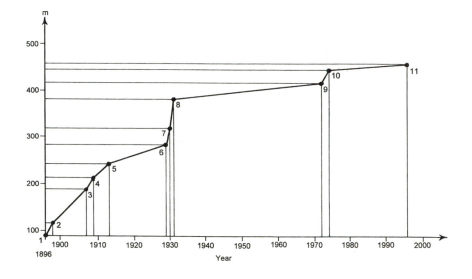

Fig. 1.9 Height of skyscrapers.

negative overall impact on social and economic conditions, including construction. Nevertheless, the construction industry became an important sector throughout the world, employing many workers. The construction of the Panama Canal during the decade preceding the First World War (1914–18) was one of the largest civil engineering projects in history. Although contractors from many countries participated, (including Lesseps's Canal Company) it was primarily a US-sponsored project, employing 45 000 workers at its peak, together with much excavating and dredging machinery (Linder, 1994).

Most building contractors, however, continued to work for the home market, constructing buildings of various types. The demand for new buildings was drastically reduced in most countries after 1929. The high unemployment rate brought about by the world depression prompted governments to launch labour-intensive projects. In the USA, dams and irrigation projects such as the Boulder/Hoover/Grand Coulee and TVA Projects were started. Some of the construction companies that participated (Bechtel, Morrison-Knudsen, Kaiser, Utah) gained strength as a result. Warren, Bechtel, Fluor, Kellogg and other large US contractors acquired experience in the construction of highways and oil extraction and petrochemical plants, and became well placed to handle complex projects, not only in construction, but also in industrial engineering.

The world economy revived to some extent after 1933, and the state itself became an important client for public works such as roads, railways, military facilities, prisons and offices, influencing production through new laws, financial regulations, interest rate policies and assistance for social housing. Altogether, the period between the two world wars saw a further strengthening of the construction industry into a modern sector of the economy. The overall development of the world economy, science and technology also had a positive impact on construction.

Inevitably, the growing economy required more energy. Coal was needed for steam engines, for the production of steel and machinery, and for heating, but it began to give way to oil as the leading energy source at the end of the nineteenth century, and in the first half of the twentieth century it came to play a major role in the affairs of the building industry. Transport and travel by train, car, aeroplane and boat, and telecommunication by telephone, radio and telegraph were expanded. All this made trade and commerce more mobile and more global, providing new tasks, such as the construction of highways and airports, for the building industry. Research and invention introduced new materials such as plastics and other new technologies. The introduction of steel welding reduced the risk of brittle fracture and the sudden consequences of metal fatigue. Also, welding made the manufacture of steel structures more economic.

After the First World War, the housing shortage prompted the use of industrialized methods for house production (the Waller, Dorlornco and Atholl houses), although these were mostly abandoned during the late 1920s. Even so, some prefabricated systems survived until the Second World War (Strike, 1991). Cast concrete enabled designers to make use of its 'jellymould' characteristics. The possibility of constructing curved forms gave birth to romantic structures, such as the buildings by Antonio Gaudi and Erich Mendelsohn. The original structural reinforced concrete was enhanced with the appearance of pre-stressed, lightweight and decorative concrete. Steel and reinforced concrete allowed the introduction of framed structures, often to replace load-bearing walls.

Following the period of the 'Liberty' style (or *Art nouveau* or *Jugendstil* as it is known on the Continent), modern architecture was assailed by a cry for functionalism, which led to pure geometric forms with none of the decorative elements of the historic styles. Several other styles alternated (New Brutalism), but these finally amalgamated into an 'International style'. In recent times new styles (Post-Modernism, de-constructivism, etc.) have emerged.

All these changes in architecture were made possible by the use of new materials and structures, new types of façade, glazing and other factors. Especially notable are the changes that occurred inside buildings. The partitions and ceilings were separated from the load-bearing structure, while the initial equipment was expanded and new services were provided. Specialization in building components led to specialization in the professions. The design process now called for co-operation between architects and engineers with differing professional expertise. Equally, the construction process demanded that the contractor engaged on the structure of the building should co-operate with the specialist firms responsible for the services to the building.

Meanwhile, technical progress continued. Structural design and the design of services gained sophistication. Contractors mechanized more readily, and excavators, scrapers, bulldozers, cranes, mixers, vibrators, pile-drivers and so on became more widely used.

With the advent of the Second World War in 1939 (1939–45), however, the focus inevitably switched from construction – basically a peaceful activity – to the requirements of war. Residential construction was reduced, and further developments in the industry had to await the end of the war in 1945.

THE PRODUCTS: STRUCTURES AND BUILDINGS

Construction comprises both the products of construction – buildings and structures – and the industry that produces these products. Any history of construction must therefore equally encompass the history of the industry as well as that of the development of buildings and structures. There is a vast stock of published information on various types of building and structure, but we will restrict our discussion here to selected types. The products of construction may also be dissected according to their components, such as foundations, walls, floors, roofs, and the services: heating, water supply, elevators and others. Once again, it would be impossible to discuss them all here, and we must limit ourselves to a selection.

With this in mind, let us start the discussion of selected products by taking a brief backward glance at arches, vaults and tall buildings. These have been chosen because they have always posed a technological challenge, and their development has always marked the progress of construction. Some building types, such as hotels and offices, are discussed in more detail in Chapter 6.

ARCHES AND VAULTS

Stone and brick domes

The arch and the vault seem to have been invented independently in many parts of the world in the late Neolithic period and early Bronze Age. Our earliest evidence of vaults stems from the fourth century BC, from Chaldea (vaulted drains, tomb chambers, probably halls and palaces) and Egypt. Both the arch and the vault were able to span a greater distance than any stone or timber beam.

The most spectacular result of Roman vaulting, with its 43.5 m diameter dome, was the Pantheon, completed in AD 128 by Hadrian. Investigations have concluded that heavy basalt was used in the foundations and the lower part of the walls, brick and tufa further up, and light pumice towards the top centre of the vault (Sandvik and Hammer, 1995).

The principal Byzantine contribution to vaulting was the support of the dome on pendentives, which could in turn be supported on four arches, so that the entire weight could be brought down upon piers at the corners. This allowed a remarkable degree of freedom in planning a building. One outstanding example of this is the Hagia Sophia in Istanbul (Constantinople). It was built for Justinian between 532 and 537 by two Byzantine architects, Anthemius and Isidorus, but the dome had to be rebuilt on several occasions because it collapsed repeatedly.

Vaulting was more or less forgotten after the demise of the Roman empire and had to be reinvented during the Romanesque period. Vaulting of naves (i.e. of longitudinal spaces) was also learnt. Later, in the Gothic period, ribbed and groined vaults were combined with pointed arches. French, German and English Gothic styles each developed specific features.

The main contribution of the Renaissance to vaulting was the lanterned dome on a drum. In the fifteenth century, Brunelleschi's dome in the Santa Maria del Fiore in Florence, with a diameter of 42.5 m, came close to that of the Pantheon. Brunelleschi won the commission for this dome in 1417 because of his proposed innovative method of construction, which did not require expensive falsework. The construction of St Peter's Cathedral in Rome, with a dome of 42 m diameter, was begun in 1506 by Bramante. It was continued by Michelangelo, and was finally completed in the sixteenth century.

At about the same time, domes of a characteristically different form were built in Samarkand (Gur-i-Mir), in Bukhara, in northern India by the Moguls (the domed sepulchral mausoleums of Humayun in Delhi and the Taj Mahal in Agra), and in Persia.

Reinforced concrete domes and shells

The use of reinforced concrete permitted a leap forward in the spanning of spaces. The ribbed reinforced concrete dome of the Breslau (now Wroclaw) Jahrhunderthalle (designer Max Berg), with its span of 65 m, was completed in 1913. Later, a new solution was devised and patented as Zeiss Dywidag. It was used on the first spherical dome of the Planetarium in Jena built by Dischinger, Finsterwalder and the company Dyckerhof-Widman (Dywidag).

The use of concrete ribbed domes (and, later, shells) gained popularity as it could span further and required less concrete. Such domes were built with the use of prefabricated wire mesh reinforcements, on to which

Fig. 1.10   Breslau, Century Hall (Jahrhunderthalle), ribbed reinforced concrete dome, span: 65 m, 1912–13, Max Berg. *Source: Knaurs Lexikon der modernen Architektur* (1963) Droemersche VerlagsAnstalt.

the concrete was sprayed under pressure. The theory and practice of shells made remarkable progress between the two world wars. Much was achieved by the German engineers Franz Dischinger, Ulrich Finsterwalder, Hubert Rüsch, and Anton Tedesko (the latter working from the 1930s in the USA), by the Spaniard Eduardo Torroja, and by the Italian Pier Luigi Nervi. Flat, concrete domes on round and rectangular spaces were also built (Schott-Domes). In essence, these were transversally cylindrical shells.

In the search for lighter reinforced concrete long-span structures, spherical domes, cylindrical shells, folded plates, shed roofs, conoidal and hyperbolic paraboloidal shells (conoids and 'hypar' or HP shells) were developed. This development started some years later in the USA; the rib supported reinforced concrete barrel of the Hershey Stadium, completed in 1936 with a span of 68 m, was one of the first.

Concrete shells evolved further during the years of the Second World War, mainly for military purposes. Hangars with spans exceeding 100 m were built for the US Air Force, first with an elliptical cross-section in order to limit building height and later with a shape that followed a more natural flow of forces.

TOWERS, CATHEDRALS AND SKYSCRAPERS

Masonry structures

Towers were built even in ancient times, e.g. the Tower of Babel (562 BC) and the Pharos of Alexandria (c.280 BC), and Islamic minarets have summoned Moslems to prayer since the ninth century. Bell towers performed a similar function for Christians during the Middle Ages. A subsequent technological marvel was the Gothic pointed vault, which enabled large openings to be constructed in the walls of cathedrals. Glass, which was known to ancient Rome, was not universally used in windows. Cathedral windows were only glazed from the twelfth century, after which the marvellous coloured glass windows of the cathedral at Chartres and of the Sainte Chapelle in Paris, among others, were created.

To build higher and higher was the ambition of the Gothic style. Abbot Suger built St Denis, and each subsequent cathedral exceeded the previous one in height. Table 1.1 shows their sequence. The highest point in the tower of Beauvais Cathedral was 153 m; after thousands of years, taller than the Cheops Pyramid and yet half the height of the future Eiffel Tower! The quest for height, which was halted by the collapse of the nave at Beauvais, was resumed in the nineteenth century. The heights of some of the world's tallest church towers are given in Table 1.2 (Heinle and Leonhardt, 1989). In Asia, minarets, temples, pagodas and stupas were built as tower-like structures.

Table 1.1   Sequence of heights achieved in Gothic cathedral construction

Place	Date of Commencement	Height of nave, m
Saint Denis	1137	29
Paris, Notre Dame	1160	35
Chartres	1194	36.55
Bourges	1195	37
Reims	1211	38
Amiens	1220	42.30
Beauvais	1238	48.50

Table 1.2   Examples of church tower heights achieved

Place	Height of tower, m
Ulm Munster	161
Cologne Cathedral	157
Rouen Cathedral	148
Srasbourg Munster/Cathedral	142
Vienna Stephansdom	137

With the introduction of new materials such as steel and concrete in the nineteenth century, a new era of tall structures was ushered in. The Frenchman Auguste Perret was a pioneer of concrete towers and buildings. One of his towers was the Tour d'Orientation in Grenoble, France. Completed in 1925, it had a height of 100 m.

Fig. 1.11 Tour d'Orientation, Grenoble, France: one of the early reinforced concrete towers; height: 100 m, 1925, Auguste Perret. *Source:* E. Heinle and F. Leonhardt (1989) *Towers*, Butterworth Architecture.

Skyscrapers

About 100 years ago, a new type of tall building called the 'skyscraper' appeared, first in Chicago and subsequently (when Chicago set limits on the height of office buildings) in New York (Douglas, 1996). For this development to occur certain other innovations were necessary. One of these was the perfection of the passenger elevator, essential in all tall buildings. The first (hydraulic) passenger elevator was installed in New York in 1857.

In practice, masonry walls permitted only a limited height: the Monadnock Building in Chicago (completed in 1891) may have had 16 storeys, but to achieve this it had to have 2 m thick walls on the lower floors! Wrought and cast iron columns had already been used. A major step forward was the use of rolled mild steel sections, which had greater strength. The first all-steel framed building was the nine-storey Rand-McNally Building built in 1891. From then on, tall buildings were built in increasing numbers and to increasing heights (Stafford Smith and Coull, 1991). Chicago and New York led the way, subsequently followed by other US cities and other countries. In 1913, the Woolworth Building in New York was the world's tallest at 242 m high. It was superseded by the Chrysler Building, also in New York, built in 1930 to stand 319 m tall. This was in turn superseded by the Empire State Building, completed one year later in 1931. At 381 m in height, it still ranks among the tallest buildings in the world, although having relinquished its premier position. The construction of skyscrapers ceased during the Second World War, but was resumed after 1945 (Chapter 6).

FROM SHELTER TO MODERN SETTLEMENTS: TECHNICAL DEVELOPMENTS

Human settlements (cities, villages) are the result of construction. They are seldom produced 'instantaneously', as it were, but rather grow organically and change continuously.

The first human settlements consisted of groups of huts built without any recognizable order, but some sort of pattern eventually came to be applied to the arrangement of the living quarters. In principle, any structure built for human habitation is a 'house'. The first houses that were actually constructed were open or closed wind-breakers, long or block houses, depending on the climate, location and social structure. The house with an atrium found favour in ancient Greece and Rome and is still used in Islamic countries. Traditionally, domestic buildings were low-rise (with one to three levels); in some regions and during some periods, however, multistorey arrangements were realized (e.g. Yemen, Rome).

Although large cities like Babylon, Athens, Alexandria, Rome and Xian already existed in ancient times, the bulk of the population lived scattered throughout the land in small villages and in remote houses and huts. Towns were established in several regions around the Mediterranean, first by the Greeks and later by the Romans (Briggs, 1957b). The ancient civilizations developed sophisticated city infrastructures. For example, the Palace of Minos at Knossos, Crete, had a drainage system in 1500 BC, and Pompeii had stone-paved streets.

Although styles changed over time, houses did not change much between the Middle Ages and the nineteenth century. Comfort was improved to some extent by modest initiatives, such as the glazing of windows, which had become universal by about 1870.

Sanitation and the supply of water were perhaps the biggest and most significant changes to houses from the earliest times to the nineteenth century. Some Greek houses must have had simple latrines, perhaps flushed with water, and a water supply and sewers certainly existed in ancient Rome, but their use disappeared until the eighteenth century. Although a very elementary form of water closet was invented in 1596, sanitary conditions in most cities in the Middle Ages were deplorable. It was common to discard all household refuse and human excreta on to the streets. Even Paris, Europe's largest town at the end of the fifteenth and beginning of the sixteenth centuries, was ill-planned, overcrowded and insanitary. These poor conditions prompted Henri IV and Louis XIII to attempt to improve the sanitation of Paris. The Industrial Revolution in Great Britain had a positive impact on the development of more sanitary conditions in London and the industrial towns. By 1780, the water closet had attained widespread use in the houses of the wealthy, and by 1800 most middle-class homes in London and other English towns had at least one privy, although it was still usual for the poorer classes to share a common privy among a number of houses. The washdown closet in the form we know it today was introduced around 1890.

Connected to the issue of the disposal of sewage was the supply of clean drinking water. The main source of water in Paris in the Middle Ages was the water-carriers who sold their wares on the streets. The supply of water was also a problem elsewhere in Europe at that time. It was solved first in Germany, were there were already 140 central waterworks by 1770. By the middle of the nineteenth century, all but the very poorest houses in London had a water cistern that was filled at set times. Central waterworks were introduced in England in the 1830s. Most sewage was initially discharged into cesspools rather than sewers, but these were seldom emptied and consequently overflowed frequently. Even sewers, when they were first built, were not always effective and frequently contaminated the ground. In 1849, 1853 and 1854, serious outbreaks of Asiatic cholera in London were traced by physicians to the drinking water supply which had become contaminated by excreted matter (Kennard, 1958; Rawlinson, 1958). As a result, the provision of a clean mains water supply and an efficient sewage disposal system became a priority, representing an almost continuous task for construction.

As we have already seen, the houses of the well-to-do in Rome had heating for cold periods in the form of braziers or hypocausts, the very first 'central' heating. Although the first steam heating system was developed in the eighteenth century, it was not used as a practical system until the early twentieth century. Hot water systems were developed alongside steam systems. In 1927 the circulator, which forced water through the system, was added. Cast-iron boilers have been used since the eighteenth century, initially for cooking. The heat pump was introduced by General Electric in the mid-1930s.

Electricity was introduced into buildings following the invention of the incandescent lamp by Thomas Edison in 1879. It was used only for lighting at first, but later found application in building services (such as pumps) and domestic appliances (Wilson, 1979). These all required small electromotors, which made their appearance around 1890. The first electric domestic appliance was the rotary fan, followed by the electric cooker, the electric heater and the vacuum cleaner. This latter was invented in 1901 by the English engineer H.C. Booth. It was the first electric machine to be put into the hands of simple uneducated people. It is therefore no surprise that it initially encountered opposition. In the UK, this resistance disappeared after the First World War, however, as domestic servants had all but vanished by then, and those still engaged in such work quickly grew accustomed to the machines. The use of domestic appliances spread even faster in the USA. By the 1920s, washing machines, spin dryers and refrigerators had found universal acceptance there. Apart from freezers and dishwashers, a broad range of other small electric appliances also gradually gained universal application in industrialized countries (e.g. electric iron, mincer, grinder, mixer, knife sharpener, carving knife, tin opener, electric blanket, tea-maker, hairdryer and so on).

Electricity was first carried by wires mounted on poles above the ground. When electricity started to become a widespread municipal service, the electricity cables were placed underground. The initial underground urban networks of water pipes, sewerage, and electricity cables were gradually joined by the telephone network and, more recently, in certain cities, district heating networks, and cable television.

Traditionally, shops were sited in cities and, for everyday shopping, in residential areas. Large department stores were built in big cities from the nineteenth century onwards.

At the turn of the century there were 8000 motor vehicles in the USA, whereas the motor car was still a comparative rarity in Great Britain: the horse-drawn tram was still the principal means of transport in London. Roads were untarred and dusty in the country and suburbs, and although stone-paved roads did exist in towns, 'the mud scraper for boots was a necessity outside every front door' (Berridge, 1978).

Despite the advent of the motor car, the growth of a village or a small town required a number of changes, including the provision of public transport. City authorities were established, municipal codes were devised, methods for the granting of planning permission were introduced, and certain building rules became mandatory in certain areas. The central areas of large cities gradually became unattractive for higher-income families, and so began an exodus to the so-called suburbs. The consequent need to travel further from home to inner-city workplaces was fulfilled by the development of tramways and, later, by commuter trains and cars. As a result, cities expanded still further, and the increasing suburbanization meant that more and more people commuted daily to work in the inner city. A poor population in dilapidated houses with reduced security was left in the city centres in North America. In large European cities, the abandoned flats were often taken over by small offices and handcraft workrooms.

After the First World War, the housing shortage and social pressure led to rent restrictions in several west European countries. While this policy did help low-income families to some extent, it distorted the normal economics of housing by reducing the profitability of renting out houses. Private investment in rented housing was therefore reduced, and so local councils and other public or semi-public organizations took over the sponsoring of new housing for the rented market. The problem of affordable housing for low-income families was simply deferred to after the Second World War.

At the beginning of the nineteenth century, fewer than 2% of the world's population lived in cities with 100 000 or more inhabitants. By 1945, urbanization had advanced worldwide, particularly in industrialized countries, and the growing skylines of the cities constituted a challenge to the construction industry, as we shall see in Chapter 2.

MILITARY AND CIVIL ENGINEERING CONSTRUCTION

FORTIFICATIONS

Since ancient times, military and civil engineering tasks such as the building of roads, bridges and aqueducts have been a most important, sometimes the most important, element of the construction industry.

Fortifications were the earliest means of protecting communities from attack, and the Great Wall of China is perhaps the best known example. Blockading a fortified settlement, resulting in food and water shortages inside, or using a ruse, such as in Troy, to gain entry were early means used to conquer such protection. But the introduction of gunpowder allowed the strategy of the attackers to change, and the competition between growing firepower and ever stronger fortifications began.

In the seventeenth century Sébastien Le Prestre de Vauban, the Marshal of France, perfected the design of fortifications (Pujo, 1991). At the age of 22 he became *ingénieur du roi* and later, after successfully rebuilding several fortresses, *commissaire général des fortifications*. At that time there was no distinction between the work of military engineers, civil engineers and architects. To conquer a fortress built according to the most advanced design of Vauban, the attacking army had to march up a slope straight into the defensive fire from the parapet. The cross-fire against an assaulting army from the fort's bastions protected all walls and left no easy target for the enemy's siege guns. Because the effective range of a musket was short, frequent bastions and 'counterposts' (free-standing bastions) were needed to protect the walls of the main fortification.

In more recent times, a series of major constructions were built in France with the intention of defending it against any attack from Germany in the case of the Maginot Line (built between 1919 and 1934), and against Allied invasion on the Atlantic coast. However, the Germans simply used a different route into France when they advanced, bypassing the fortifications, and the 'Atlantic wall', as it was known, was finally broken.

AQUEDUCTS AND BRIDGES

Aqueducts are artificial water courses and, in a more restricted sense, they are bridges formed by arches that span a valley to allow the free-flowing movement of water. Aqueducts such as Hezekiah's at Jerusalem (725 BC) were famous features of the ancient world, and there are surviving descriptions or remnants of early aqueducts in the Mediterranean and Middle East, such as the aqueduct with a tunnel on the island of Samos. Later, the Romans also built many aqueducts throughout the Roman empire. Particularly well known examples are the Pont du Gard in France and that in Segovia in Spain.

Bridges repeatedly took on a historic role: the first pontoon bridge across the Bosporus (493 BC, Darius), the bridge at Lodi in Italy (Napoleon), the bridge across the gorge of the Tatu River in China (Mao Tse Tung's crossing in 1935), the bridge at Arnhem (Second World War) and others. Rome's high priest was named 'pontifex' (bridge builder), and the Pope is the 'pontifex maximus', the greatest bridge builder (between God and man). Until the end of the eighteenth century, bridges were built from timber (one in Lucerne only recently burnt down), suspended on ropes, or made of stone arches. Between 1750 and 1800, bridges with flat arches were built in France and contractors tendered for a set fee for the entire work. A new type of centring was devised by Robert Mylne for the Blackfriars masonry bridge in London. His centring embodied multiple wedges and was more rigid despite using less timber. The exposed voussoirs of the bridge abutted against the spandrel walls.

The first cast-iron bridge was built over the River Severn between 1776 and 1779. It had a span of 30 m, and was designed and constructed by Abraham Darby III and attributed partly to Pritchard. Bridges with cast-iron arches and lattice-work to support the paving were an innovation of the time. Later, cast iron was replaced by wrought iron, and subsequently by steel. The bridges built by Thomas Telford, such as the Craigellachie Bridge (span 54 m, 1814) and the Menai Suspension Bridge (length 176 m, 1826) were among the most important structures built during the first part of the nineteenth century. In the USA, James Finley from Pennsylvania obtained a patent for suspension bridges as early as 1808. Isambard Kingdom Brunel designed the Clifton Suspension Bridge, several other bridges and structures (Paddington Station), and the London–Bristol railway, with a 3 km long tunnel.

Although many bridges were built, many also collapsed – 40 in the USA during the 1870s alone; half of these were railway bridges. Technical know-how did progress, but it was a somewhat bumpy road. One of the most exciting stories was that of the construction of the bridge across the Mississippi at St Louis (Gilbert and Billington, 1970). James Buchanan Eads, a self-taught, strong-willed US engineer, succeeded in completing this bridge in 1874 despite bitter opposition from several influential professionals and competitors. It was the world's first steel bridge with arch spans of 156 m and 150 m, longer than any previous structure, and it rested on caisson foundations that were deeper than any previous work. The structure itself consists of three steel arches made from ribbed and braced trusses, and vertical, equally braced, columns supporting the two levels of the bridge. Also worthy of special note was the development of steel suspension bridges. In 1855, John Roebling built the world's first railway suspension bridge at the Niagara Falls. It had a span of 250 m. He designed the Brooklyn Bridge in New York, but died before its construction (1870–1883); his son, Washington saw the project to its completion. Its main span was 486 m. Spans of suspension bridges first exceeded 500 m in the early part of the twentieth century.

The Frenchman Alexandre Gustave Eiffel was among those who developed arched-trussed steel bridges (such as the Pia Maria Bridge in Portugal with a 160 m span, built in 1877, and the Gabarit Viaduct in France, with a span of 165 m, built in 1884). It took the whole century (and some more collapses, such as the railway bridge over the Firth of Tay in Scotland in 1879) to reach a span of 521 m for the trussed Firth of Forth railway bridge. Competition remains fierce to this day between the different methods adopted for steel bridges: the trussed, arched, plate-girder beam (at first riveted, later welded), suspended and cable-stayed constructions.

Chain bridges such as the one by Thomas Telford across the Menai Straits in Wales, built between 1819 and 1826, and the Chain Bridge in Budapest, completed in 1849 by Clark, were among the earliest of their type. The last major chain bridge, the Elisabeth Bridge in Budapest, was built in 1903. Following its destruction during the Second World War, the bridge was rebuilt as a modern suspension cable bridge.

The first bridge with a span of over 1000 m was the George Washington Suspension Bridge across the Hudson River, built by Othmar Ammann. It was completed in 1931 and had a span of 1067 m. Ammann also designed the Golden Gate Bridge in San Francisco Bay in 1937 (span 1260 m) and the Verrazano Narrows Bridge (Billington, 1983) in 1965 (span 1278 m). To keep cable stress within certain limits, tall pylons were built; those of the Golden Gate Bridge, for example, are 227 m high. The cables were given great sag in order to resist earthquakes.

Electric arc-welding, torsionally superior steel box girders, better bolt fasteners and other innovations contributed to modern bridge building achievements prior to 1945, yet despite the knowledge available, bridges continued to collapse. For instance, the Tacoma Narrows Suspension Bridge in the USA succumbed to wind flutter in 1940.

Reinforced concrete was invented in the nineteenth century, but its widespread application for bridge construction did not come until the twentieth century. Pioneers of the technique were François Hennebique, Züblin, Mörsch, Marie Eugène Léon Freyssinet and Robert Maillart. Prior

Fig. 1.12   Chain Bridge across the Danube, Hungary: still in use, with new chains, Adam Clark. *Source:* Courtesy of the Museum of Transport, Budapest.

Fig. 1.13 Elisabeth Bridge across the Danube, Budapest, Hungary: the last major chain bridge (1903), rebuilt after the Second World War, with suspension cables. *Source:* Courtesy of the Museum of Transport, Budapest.

to pre-stressing, the arch provided new elegant solutions, as in the case of the Salginatobel Bridge in Switzerland, completed in 1930. Designed by Maillart, it had a three-hinged arch with a span of 88 m (Billington, 1979). The spans of arched reinforced concrete bridges soon exceeded first 100 m and than 200 m: the Sandö Bridge over the River Ångermanälven in Sweden had a span of 269 m. Construction began in 1938 and was completed in 1942 after its first centring collapsed. Although the first pre-stressed concrete bridges were built before 1945, this technology was not perfected until after 1945 (Chapter 6).

ROADS AND RAILWAYS

As with fortifications, roads and road networks have been built since ancient times. The Roman empire's military roads and the medieval commercial roads acquired great importance in their time.

The École Nationale des Ponts et Chaussées, founded in Paris in 1747, created the first civil engineering school. Modern Tarmac(adam) dates from the 1830s when tar was first used in Nottinghamshire to bind stones into the road surface. Later asphalt, bitumen mixed with powdered rock and concrete, evolved for various road surfaces. On the whole, however, the nineteenth century was considered to be the century for the construction of railways. The first operational railway line was opened between Liverpool and Manchester in 1830. During the rest of the century large railway constructions were carried out throughout the world. In 1840, the total distance of railway track in England and Wales was 1300 miles (2080 km). By 1870, this had exceeded 10 000 miles (16 000 km), and in 1900 it had reached 15 000 miles (24 000 km). Nearly 34 000 km of railways were built in the USA between 1850 and 1860, and a similar trend prevailed in most other industrialized countries.

Later on, the increase in the production and use of cars prompted the construction of motorways. The first half of the twentieth century was characterized by large-scale highway constructions, with railways being built primarily in developing countries only. The Avus Autobahn in Berlin was a much admired novelty in 1919, but by the end of the 1930s some 4000 km of motorways had been built in Germany. Roads were built by a high-capacity specialized road-construction industry, and machinery was developed exclusively for this purpose, such as the road roller, bulldozer, excavator, scraper, grader, mixer and others. As a result of this trend, by the middle of the twentieth century, most industrialized countries had well developed road and rail networks.

TUNNELS

Tunnels are underground roads or conduits and have also been built since ancient times. Tunnelling technology was developed in the seventeenth and eighteenth centuries, including that for tunnelling under rivers. The 460 m long tunnel under the River Thames, from Rotherhithe to Wapping, was the work of Sir Marc Isambard Brunel and was built between 1825 and 1843 using the tunnelling shield he had patented in 1818. The Mont Cenis tunnel, built between 1857 and 1871, was the first to be built through the Alps. Compressed air drills were used from 1860, their first large-scale application. Blasting gelignite (nitroglycerine plus nitrocellulose), invented by Alfred Nobel in 1875, was the next important contribution to tunnelling in hard rock. The 16.3 km long St Gotthard tunnel through the Alps, constructed between 1872 and 1881, was the first tunnel to be built using it. The compressed air hollow drilling machine (invented in 1897) also increased tunnelling speed in hard rock. Tunnelling shields and prefabricated tunnel linings were further technical developments, with specific adaptation for working in hard rock or soft ground (West, 1988; Burger, 1993). The Simplon tunnel, also through the Alps, consists of two 20 km long single-line railway bores, the first of which was built between 1898 and 1906, the second between 1912 and 1921.

Underwater tunnels are built by immersion: sections are prefabricated in de-watered basins, provided with temporary end bulkheads and then floated to the tunnel site and submerged (Rasmussen, 1995). The first successful large-scale application of this technique was the construction of the Michigan Central Railroad tunnel in Detroit, completed in 1909. Here, and elsewhere in the USA, the sections were built as single or double steel hulls, with some concrete stability as keel. Following immersion, non-structural concrete was added. This was the 'American' or 'steel' technology of submerged tunnels, and is still in use. The 'European' or 'concrete' tunnelling technology was first applied under the Maas River in Rotterdam. Its sections were made as reinforced concrete structures, and it was completed in 1942 (Vos, 1992). Both technologies have been applied in many countries throughout the world. At 10 km, the Californian Bay Area Transit system is currently the longest underwater immersed tunnel. The New York Delaware water supply tunnel is the world's largest tunnel (169 km).

CANALS

The concept of canals goes back a long way, and there are early examples in Ireland, England and France. The Suez Canal was built between 1859 and 1869, the Panama Canal between 1904 and 1914. Both acquired importance as a means of rationalizing global shipping. The construction of major canals and harbours required great efforts and new technological skills.

The building of embankments to gain land from the sea by draining low-lying lands and marshes ('polder' formation) originated in what is now The Netherlands sometime before the eleventh century. With time, technologies developed for protecting the face of embankments or dikes. The drainage-mill was perfected with the invention of the rotating mill cap in the fifteenth century, which made it possible to turn the sails into the eye of the wind without rotating the body of the mill (Harris, 1957).

SUMMARY

Construction, which has a history spanning several thousand years, has produced wonderful buildings and structures all over the world. Although built in different styles, their construction was based largely on empirical experience and the skill of master builders, masons and carpenters, as traditional building technology developed slowly. The transformation of construction into a modern industry began in the eighteenth century with the increased use of iron, among other factors. The technological change in construction accelerated in the nineteenth century when Portland cement and reinforced concrete were invented, steel replaced iron, and glass became mass-produced. Railway construction, industrial development and urbanization led to the appearance of large contractors, and a global market for the building industry emerged.

In the first half of the twentieth century, skyscrapers, long-span domes, shells and bridges were developed to satisfy new requirements, and marked the continuing progress of construction techniques. The provision of services such as heating, air-conditioning, electric lighting, mains water and elevators, to buildings became common. The twentieth century has seen the transformation of the construction and building industry into a major economic sector.

BIBLIOGRAPHY

Berridge, P.S.A. (1978) Civil engineering. In T.J. Williams (ed.), *A History of Technology*, Vol. VII, Clarendon Press, Oxford, 871–906.

Billington, D.P. (1979) *Robert Maillart's Bridges, The Art of Engineering*, Princeton University Press.

Billington, D.P. (1983) *The Tower and the Bridge*, Basic Books, Inc.

Bradford, J. (1954) Building in wattle, wood and turf. In Ch. Singer *et al.* (eds), *A History of Technology*, Vol. I, Clarendon Press, Oxford, 299–326.

Briggs, M.S. (1957a) Building-construction. In Ch. Singer *et al.* (eds), *A History of Technology*, Vol. II, Clarendon Press, Oxford, 397–448.

Briggs, M.S. (1957c) Building-construction. In Ch. Singer *et al.* (eds), *A History of Technology*, Vol. III, Clarendon Press, Oxford, 245–68.

Briggs, M.S. (1957b) Town planning from the Ancient World to the Renaissance. In Ch. Singer *et al.* (eds), *A History of Technology*, Vol. III, Clarendon Press, Oxford, 269–99.

Building for Tomorrow: Global Enterprises and the U.S. Construction Industry (1988) National Research Council/National Academy Press, Washington, DC.

Burger, H. (ed.) (1993) *Options for Tunnelling*, Elsevier.

Cameron, R. (1993) *A Concise Economic History of the World from Paleolithic Time to the Present*, Oxford University Press, New York.

Chapin, F.S. (1955) *An Experimental Design in Sociological Research*, New York.

Cowan, H.J. (1987) A note on the Roman hypocaust, the Korean on-dol, and the Chinese kang. In *Architectural Science Review*, 30(4), Sydney, Australia, 123–7.

De Vries, J. (1976) *The Economy of Europe in an Age of Crisis. 1600–1750*, Cambridge University Press.

Douglas, G.H. (1996) *Skyscrapers*, McFarland & Co.

Gilbert, R.W. and Billington, D.P. (1970) The Eads Bridge and nineteenth-century river politics. In D.P. Billington and P. Mark (eds), *Civil Engineering: History, Heritage and the Humanities*, Princeton University.

Guinness, D. and Stadler, Jr. F.T. (1973) *Mr. Jefferson, Architect*, The Viking Press, New York.

Hamilton, S.B. (1958) Building and civil engineering construction. In Ch. Singer *et al.* (eds), *A History of Technology*, Vol. IV, Clarendon Press, Oxford, 442–88.

Hamilton, S.B. (1968) Building materials and techniques. In Ch. Singer *et al.* (eds), *A History of Technology*, Vol. V, Clarendon Press, Oxford, 466–98.

Harris, L.E. (1957) Land drainage and reclamation. In Ch. Singer *et al.* (eds), *A History of Technology*, Vol. III, Clarendon Press, Oxford, 300–23.

Heinle, E. and Leonhardt, F. (1989) *Towers: A Historical Survey*, Butterworth Architecture.

Kennard, J. (1958) Sanitary engineering: water-supply. In Ch. Singer *et al.* (eds), *A History of Technology*, Vol. IV, Clarendon Press, Oxford, 489–503.

Linder, M. (1994) *Projecting Capitalism: A History of the Internationalization of the Construction Industry*, Greenwood Press.

Mainstone, R.J. (1979) Building and architecture. In L.P. Williams and H.J. Steffens (eds), *A History of Technology*, Vol. VII, Clarendon Press, Oxford, 930–57.

Perrot *et al.* (1979) *Les Techniques de la civilisation industrielle. Tome V*, Presses Universitaires de France, Paris.

Phelps Brown, E.H. and Hopkins, S.V. (1955) Seven centuries of building wages. In *Economica* XXII (1955); repr. in E.M. Carns-Wilson (ed.), *Essays in Economic History*, II (1962), London, 168–178.

Pounds, N.J.G. (1974) *An Economic History of Medieval Europe*, Longman.

Pujo, B. (1991) *Vauban*, Albin Michel.

Rasmussen, N.S. (1995) Immersed tunnels, *Structural Engineering International*, November, 213–15.

Rawlinson, J. (1958) Sanitary engineering: Sanitation. in Ch. Singer *et al.* (eds), *A History of Technology*, Vol. IV, Clarendon Press, Oxford, 504–19.

Saalman, H. (1968) *Medieval Cities*, George Braziller, New York.

Sandvik, M. and Hammer, T.A. (1995) The development and use of high performance lightweight aggregate concrete in Norway. In *Proceedings of the International Symposium on Structural Lightweight Aggregate Concrete*, 20–24 June 1995, 617–27.

Speer, A. (1985) *Architecture 1932–1942*, Aux Archives d'Architecture Moderne.

Spufford, P. (1988) *Money and its Use in Medieval Europe*, Cambridge University Press.P

Stafford Smith, B. and Coull, A. (1991) *Tall Building Structures: Analysis and Design*, John Wiley & Sons.

Strike, J. (1991) *Construction into Design*, Butterworth Architecture.

Thomson, R.H.G. (1957) The medieval artisan. In Ch. Singer *et al.* (eds), *A History of Technology*, Vol. II, Clarendon Press, Oxford, 383–96.

Vos, C.J. (1992) Submerged tunnels, examples of marine structures, *Post-Congress Report of IABSE*, 1–6 March 1992.

West, G. (1988) *Innovation and the Rise of the Tunnelling Industry*, Cambridge University Press.

Wilson, G.B.Z. (1979) Domestic appliances. In L.P. Williams and H.J. Steffens (eds), *A History of Technology*, Vol. VII, Clarendon Press, Oxford, 1126–49.

Initiatives and trends after 1945

2

THE YEARS OF OPTIMISM AND AFTER: 1945–95

The euphoria at the end of the Second World War soon gave way to stock-taking: 20 million people had lost their lives; a great part of the world's accumulated wealth had been dissipated; and in many countries much of the built environment – residential and other buildings, bridges, railways and public works – had been destroyed. In the Soviet Union, 70 million m² of living area in over 1700 cities and urban settlements was destroyed during the war along with 70 000 villages, and 25 million people had lost their homes as a consequence. Among the totally devastated towns were Kiev, Smolensk, Vitebsk, Voronezh, Sevastopol and Chernigov. Germany lost 2.4 million dwellings; Yugoslavia lost 25% of its pre-war dwelling stock; Poland 22%; and Greece 21%. Many railways and bridges had also been destroyed, and such basic services as electricity, mains water and sewage disposal were not available to a major part of the population in some countries.

Rebuilding the infrastructure was obviously essential. The USA had become the wealthiest large country, and it helped its western European allies to embark on an ambitious programme of rebuilding, providing much of the necessary financial assistance.

On the political scene many changes occurred. The Soviet Union, which had won moral respect for its war effort and the terrible losses it had suffered, developed new economic and political links with its central and eastern European neighbours, and later also with countries elsewhere in the world. Many of the old European colonies in Africa and elsewhere attained their independence, and millions of people emigrated to new countries and continents as a result of the war and other political and economic upheavals.

During the war years, the ingenuity of scientists and engineers had been focused on the problems of war, but in peacetime some of their innovations, such as those in telecommunications (radar), mathematics, computers and materials, found new and exciting applications. Despite many conflicts, the 20 years after 1945 were a period of improving economic conditions, technical progress and optimism. Construction followed this general trend. There was much rebuilding as well as new construction to satisfy the need for housing and other buildings (Seaden, 1994). Besides an increased domestic demand, projects requiring the participation of large contractors promoted the development of the construction industry, and some contractors became genuine multinationals. Even so, leading construction firms remained smaller, on average, than the top firms in manufacturing.

After the accelerated development of the construction industry in the first 25 years or so after the Second World War, the oil crisis of 1973–74 dealt a severe blow. There were far fewer foreign contracts, and domestic demand was also reduced in industrialized countries. Construction did not experience a new revival until the 1990s. The Soviet Union and the eastern bloc reacted with a 10-year delay to the increased energy prices which, in Western countries, virtually imposed a tax on development. This certainly aggravated the Comecon countries' economic problems, which were the consequence of high military costs and inefficient economic management.

The period between 1945 and 1995 brought with it an immense increase in productive capacity in goods and services, and our knowledge in all fields grew substantially. Many families became wealthier, and the standard of living improved for a substantial number of people in most countries. Nevertheless, despite the huge social and economic changes experienced in the second half of the twentieth century, many people remained trapped by chronic unemployment, poverty, and/or ethnic and other conflicts, and were thus deprived to some extent of the benefits of the scientific and economic progress achieved. It also gradually came to be realized that the resources of our planet are limited and that too little attention had previously been paid to protecting nature and the environment.

The construction industry learned to build such advanced structures as tall buildings, long-span bridges and roofs, buildings with sophisticated services and, if the financial resources and appropriate social conditions had existed, could no doubt have constructed decent homes for everyone during the period.

This somewhat sketchy round-up of history from 1945 to 1955 serves only as a background for the construction industry to aid readers in an understanding of its development during this period. Below, discussion is restricted to events in the construction sector during this 50-year period.

HOUSING AND URBAN DEVELOPMENT

HOUSING AS A SUBSECTOR OF THE ECONOMY

Between one- and two-thirds of the total building volume in any particular country is housing. Residential construction is therefore usually the largest subsector, as well as the greatest investment subsector: one-fifth to one-third of gross fixed investments is absorbed by residential construction. In the twentieth century, particularly in its second half, housing and municipal construction, including urban development, have been activities in which private individuals, organizations and public authorities co-operated in many ways, sharing financing by different methods. There have been some countries and periods in which public participation was high.

As the dwelling stock within a country increases, so more and more resources must be spent on maintenance, repair and renewal. Housing tenure defines the rights and duties of the consumer in the housing sector. It is an important component of housing conditions, and traditionally varies in form in different countries. The three basic forms of tenure are: owning, renting, or being a member of a co-operative. Ownership can be public or private; co-operative housing can be based on common or shared ownership, or co-ownership. These basic forms have acquired specific features as a result of historical and social development and the housing policies of various governments, which usually contain measures on tenure.

For most families, buying a house is probably the largest single purchase they will make during their lives. Families spend a substantial part of their income on their home, either in rent or repaying a mortgage. After health, security and employment, housing tends to be families' next greatest concern, and yet poor housing conditions may exist for a significant part of the population: even in the so-called 'wealthy countries', there is invariably a sector of the population that is unable to resolve its housing needs on its own.

NEW RESIDENTIAL CONSTRUCTION, 1945–95

During the Second World War, most of the countries involved had to reduce the volume of new residential construction. Together with the destruction of the war, this gave rise to a severe and universal housing shortage. The immediate post-war years were given over to salvaging or renewing the existing damaged housing stock and preparing major new housing programmes.

A basic index of the housing conditions in a particular country is the number of dwellings available. In order to compare data from countries with different populations, the number of dwellings per 1000 inhabitants can be calculated. The level of new housing construction is shown by the number of dwellings built in a given year per 1000 inhabitants.

After the war, the number of dwellings available per 1000 people was highest in industrialized countries such as the USA and Sweden, where there were more than 300 dwellings per 1000 people. At the other end of the scale were the less developed, more war-ravaged countries, such as Turkey, Poland, Yugoslavia and the Soviet Union, where fewer than 240 dwellings were available per 1000 population. The housing conditions in most other countries fell between these two extremes. During the immediate post-war years, most countries built fewer than three dwellings per 1000 inhabitants per year. By the late 1960s and early 1970s, this had been raised to an average of about 6–11 dwellings per 1000 per year. Following these peak construction levels, the volume of new housing was considerably reduced again in Western countries after 1974, but housing conditions had nevertheless greatly improved by the 1980s and 1990s.

These figures reveal a specific feature of housing as a commodity: the gross amount of housing available can be increased by a rate of only 2–3% per year; the net increase (i.e. new housing minus demolitions) is even smaller. This means that it takes many years, perhaps as long as 10 to 20 years, to effect substantial improvements, and during that time a high level of residential construction must be maintained. For this reason, after the Second World War many countries embarked on long-term housing programmes rather than 'quick-fix' solutions. Several governments (such as the French, British and German) supported new public housing. The guaranteed long-term demand favoured the introduction of prefabricated industrialized systems, the development of which is described later in this chapter. Such systems were aimed at putting up dwellings fast at low cost, without particular heed to durability. The standards of later dwellings generally improved.

In eastern Europe, new residential construction grew in parallel with that in western Europe, but production continued into the 1980s. In the Soviet Union and other countries with central economic planning, large state-owned design and contracting organizations were established in order to achieve a rapid improvement in housing conditions. Large new residential districts were constructed, and there was considerable investment in mechanization and prefabrication. Most of the new housing in cities was effected with direct or indirect state participation. Housing in the villages was left to individuals, who may have received some financial assistance but who frequently encountered great difficulty in purchasing materials that were primarily allocated to government-sponsored construction. Quality was sometimes inadequate and often no sound social structure could be sustained in the concentrated, hastily built large new residential areas which, with their vast, uniform blocks of flats, were frequently rather drab in appearance.

In the countries with central economic planning, the housing shortage was aggravated by low rents that failed to cover the costs of even regular maintenance and repair, and because under this system almost every family could afford a newer and more expensive flat, demand was thus increased well beyond the possibility of supply. It would be unfair, however, not to recognize that despite these deficiencies, housing conditions were improved in these countries for millions of families.

The most recent statistical data (Annual Bulletin, 1995) confirm that as a consequence of massive post-war residential construction in most countries, housing conditions have much improved in Europe and North America. At the end of 1993, Denmark, France, Sweden and Switzerland had more than 470 dwellings per 1000 inhabitants, i.e. one dwelling per 2.1 people. This was attained partly as a result of the reduced size of families and households. Only a few countries, such as Kazakhstan, Turkey and Yugoslavia, had fewer than 300 dwellings per 1000 inhabitants at the end of 1993. Of course, the general improvement in the levels of housing did not eliminate the differences in housing conditions in various countries, including differences in the size and equipment of dwellings.

The published data (Annual Report, 1995) also confirm that the number of new dwellings built annually has fallen below the earlier peak levels in most countries over the past 20 years. The current level of three or fewer new dwellings per 1000 inhabitants per year will lead to a deterioration in housing conditions if it is sustained. Data for countries with a well organized statistical service are readily available. These contain information on the age, height, and services of the dwelling stock and new dwellings (size and equipment), the proportions of urban to rural and public to private housing, and data on the building industry and materials. Unfortunately, the definitions used are not always identical, which causes difficulties in making international comparisons (Sebestyén, 1994).

THE CHANGING CITIES

Following the Second World War, the global structure of cities, as well as their internal structures, changed in several ways. The process of urbanization continued, the population of cities grew in absolute terms and also as a proportion of the total population, although with variations among individual cities. In the less developed countries, the population in general, and that in cities in particular, grew faster than the populations in industrialized countries. Some cities acquired an important new status, such as Berlin, which affected their composition, and there were several regions where some cities grew faster than others, such as the west coast of the USA.

In the industrialized countries, much of the housing stock that had been created during the previous 200 years had become degraded, and the dwellings no longer suited contemporary requirements with regard to their cost, size and services. This often resulted in the abandonment of buildings, despite the housing shortage. Some of those who considered their housing problem to be hopeless, illegally occupied vacant dwellings. The total number of these so-called 'squatters' was probably negligible, but their subsequent behaviour did give rise to many problems. A much larger number of families simply had no choice but to accept substandard living conditions. Areas in which such dwellings predominated were known as 'slums'. Governments, municipalities and landlords attempted to evacuate and rebuild such buildings, but while this provided a solution to some of the problems, such as ensuring a reasonable income for the landlord, it did not solve the housing problem of most of the slum-tenants as they were unable to afford the higher cost (rent or purchase price) of the upgraded dwellings. Consequently, more recently there has been a policy of attempting to improve such slums at an affordable cost level. Middle- and upper-class families continued to move out from city centres, and the consequent process of suburbanization followed the pre-war trend.

The idea of traffic-free shopping precincts in the centre of existing cities was conceived in war-ravaged Rotterdam. The shopping centre constructed there, Lijnbaan (designed by Van den Broek and Bakema), served as a model for shopping precincts in other European cities, such as Kalverstraat in Amsterdam, Hohe Strasse in Cologne, Kärnterstrasse in Vienna and Váci Street in Budapest. A new development in urban planning resulted from the competition engendered by the various new forms of commercial retailing. Small shops in city centres, whether independents or members of a chain, had to compete with large department stores, supermarkets and, as car ownership increased, with out-of-town hypermarkets and superstores. City-centre shops are faced with high rents, and new inner-city shopping centres are therefore often built in combination with other facilities such as hotels and railway and underground terminals so as to attract the greatest number of people (e.g. Montreal and Osaka). A good indoor environment (air quality, lighting and security) is important in department stores, particularly in underground premises.

NEW TOWNS

Urban experts had already realized by the end of the nineteenth century that housing and urban problems could not be solved by simply renewing the existing cities. The Garden City and the New Town concepts were attempts at alternative solutions. In his book *Tomorrow: A Peaceful Path to Social Reform*, published in 1898, Englishman Sir Ebenezer Howard proposed Garden Cities as an alternative to large congested towns, ensuring decent housing at affordable prices with an abundance of green. Letchworth Garden City was established in 1903, and Welwyn Garden City followed 16 years later. Several Acts of Parliament and reports dealt with the problems of town planning and housing in the UK from 1909, but the Garden Cities provided only a very limited relief to major cities before 1945.

The idea of New Towns was revived after 1945. While the original objective of the New Towns was retained, it was decided that, in addition the use of cars should not have an adverse impact on residents, and this was attained by the separation of cars from pedestrians and by the provision of car-free shopping precincts.

A number of New Towns were established in several countries during the first half of the twentieth century, but the concept acquired a new meaning after 1945 in the UK, where Acts of Parliament on the subject of New Towns made special arrangements for their establishment, status and management. Between 1946 and 1950, 14 New Towns were approved in the UK, with a further 14 to follow. Their total population was envisaged to be 3 million by the year 2000. New Towns such as Basildon, Bracknell, Crawley, Harlow, Hatfield, Stevenage, Corby, Peterlee and Cumbernauld were initially planned to have a population not exceeding 40 000–80 000, but these targets soon had to be revised upwards.

The idea and construction of New Towns was copied in many countries, albeit in different ways. In Sweden, Satellite Towns were built to relieve Stockholm (e.g. Farsta, Vallingby), while in France, New Towns were based on existing villages and rather larger areas were delineated for restructuring (e.g. Cergy-Pontoise, Evry, Trappes, Vallée de la Marne, Melun-Senart and, more recently, Lille-Est, Le Vaudreuil, Isle d'Abeau and one near Marseilles). In the USA, attention was given to planning New Towns with pleasing landscaping such as lakes, wooded areas and undulating ground (e.g. Reston and Elk Grove Village). In the countries with strong central planning and ambitious industrialization plans, New Towns were built for the families of the employees of new industrial complexes, such as Eisenhüttenstadt and Hoyerswerda in the former German Democratic Republic, Nowa Huta in Poland and Dunaújváros in Hungary.

There is some justification for claiming that the New Towns were generally successful, even if they only partly achieved their original objectives, not least because they usually ended up by growing beyond their planned size, contrary to one of their fundamental principles. But when one considers that only a small percentage of the population of any single country actually lives in New Towns, their limited impact becomes obvious.

HOUSING AND URBAN PLANNING POLICIES

Industrial development and urbanization increased housing problems enormously, leading governments to formulate policies for improvement.

The word 'dwelling' may seem a simple one to define, but in fact it is not: its functional requirements and technical characteristics differ from country to country and depend on tradition, to say nothing of the changes associated with time. Technical features are becoming more complex, and living patterns are also changing. Furthermore, dwellings are built with a great variety of architectural design solutions. They can have one, two or more levels and even in blocks of flats two-level dwellings (maisonettes) have become common. Large glazed surfaces, balconies and storage rooms are more frequent. Blocks of flats can be medium-rise or high-rise, and many studies have looked at the advantages and disadvantages of high buildings. Multistorey buildings may contain access to two or more dwellings on each floor from each staircase and, again, numerous studies have examined the consequences of these and other design characteristics. Town-planning codes were introduced to protect the public interest (fire regulations, etc.) and in some zones there were more regulations (destination and height of buildings, etc.) that had to be respected.

Dwellings are also mass products and it is therefore possible to study their optimal characteristics and the best policies. This is particularly necessary when public money is involved. In the second half of the twentieth century, various design, technical and cost guidelines, norms and standards were devised and implemented for such purposes. The participation of the future occupants in the design process has also been found to be useful, and various interactive computer-assisted design programs have been developed for that purpose (Allen *et al.*, 1995).

Improvements in housing, even in the most affluent countries, did not embrace all families and individuals. As before, various sectors of the population experienced difficulties in obtaining decent shelter. The main groups that fell into this category were low-income families, the elderly, young people and recent immigrants from poor countries. Obviously, the best way to solve the affordability problem is to increase the income available to these groups, but there are various short-term strategies that can be applied:

- tax strategies (e.g. reduce the tax on land used for residential purposes);
- incentives (e.g. public land can be sold at a discount if it is to be used for residential purposes with a certain proportion of low-cost housing);
- regulations (e.g. a density bonus, i.e. permitting higher density if more small low-cost units are built);
- financing measures (subsidies, low-interest loans);
- design measures (starter homes, shell housing, 'grow housing');
- assistance with home ownership (Brink, 1992).

Since 1945, the pattern of home ownership has undergone a transformation in many countries. Governments have offered inducements to home ownership, such as tax relief, and the proportion of those who own their house or dwelling has increased accordingly. At the same time, rented housing continued to be an unfavourable area for capital investment, and this has resulted in a reduced amount of rented accommodation available, which has been particularly detrimental to low-income families. In recent years there have been various attempts to reverse this trend and to stimulate investment in dwellings to be offered for rent by making such investments more lucrative.

In view of the immense problems in cities, various new schemes for so-called 'utopias' were devised. Unlike naturally evolving cities, those that are artificially planned and created, such as Brasilia, need time to prove their viability. Le Corbusier's dream ('*la ville radieuse*') never really came anywhere near being realized (Le Corbusier and Jeanneret, 1933). '*Ekistics*', devised by the Greek Doxiades as a discipline of human settlements, has been useful as a forum to enhance knowledge on housing and human settlements, but the problems of practical life have remained as enormous as before.

Urban planning had the task of creating better conditions for city-living. Sir Colin Buchanan, an acknowledged expert in urban matters, summarized the effectiveness of urban planning thus:

> In spite of the great efforts made since 1950, when planning seemed poised to make a major contribution to social and economic welfare in much of the world, the verdict after 25 years would probably amount to no more than an affirmation that things would have been worse had no planning been invoked. Despite the huge effort, urban and regional problems continue to be a major preoccupation of government in most countries.
>
> Buchanan, 1978

It is a personal matter whether this result is seen as satisfactory or not, and it is debatable whether a more positive verdict could be delivered today.

THE CONSTRUCTION INDUSTRY

THE GLOBAL SCENE

In industrialized countries, the construction industry threw off its medieval shackles prior to the Second World War. After 1945 and the years of revival and a return to economic development, the industry went on modernizing, stimulated by the favourable climate engendered by high demand. Just over 10% of the world's gross domestic product

(GDP) was invested annually in the construction of dwellings, buildings, civil engineering works and utilities.

Clearly, the structure of an industrial sector such as the construction industry has an impact on its operations. In metallurgy, electric power generation and the petrochemical industry, a high degree of concentration was, and still is, the dominant feature. By contrast, in construction, tradition dictates that there are many small firms. Even today, a great number of small firms characterizes the industry, although medium-size and large contractors have recently consolidated their position, some even becoming multinationals. Similar trends have prevailed in the architectural and engineering design fields.

After 1945, the building construction sectors in the developed countries quickly grew to dominate their home markets again, while large firms continued to grow and work on an international scale. Bechtel, Morrison-Knudsen, Stone & Webster, Parsons and other US contractors became the world's leading international contractors. There was a time when Morrison-Knudsen had as many as 400 000 employees on its payroll (Linder, 1994). Some British firms developed along a different route to internationalization. Wimpey, Costain, Taylor Woodrow, and Laing have specialized in housing, combined with civil engineering, construction engineering and contracting abroad.

During the 1950s some European and, later, Japanese and Korean firms appeared as competitors on the global market. Soviet and eastern bloc state-owned companies also acquired projects. The largest of these was the Aswan High Dam in Egypt, on which a workforce of more than 33 000 laboured. The eastern bloc companies often worked at a loss, occupying only a marginal and temporary share of the world market.

By the 1970s, the enormous increase in the revenue of the petroleum exporting (OPEC) countries created the financial basis for monumental construction schemes, primarily in the Middle East. These huge projects spurred on the internationalization of the construction industry, and much of the revenue from these projects was repatriated. Large workforces had to be mobilized for the execution of these massive construction schemes, and although the supervising staff were usually drawn from the firm's home country, the mass of workers tended to be hired on low wages from third world countries. Firms from low-wage economies had a competitive advantage over contractors from high-wage countries, but this advantage was lost as soon as the wage levels increased in the former, such as occurred in South Korea.

During the 1980s, the oil revenues of the OPEC countries diminished, and the volume of international contracts consequently declined. In some cases, overdevelopment in airports, harbours and other facilities also constrained demand. On the other hand, the market in South East Asia has grown considerably.

Theoretically, the end of wars should result in good opportunities for reconstruction. In practice, however, the smouldering aftermath of wars such as those in Vietnam, Iran, Iraq, Afghanistan and Lebanon, often delayed reconstruction.

In developing countries, the benefits of large projects can be dubious. Nature, environment and the domestic economy may suffer as a result of them. An increased awareness of these detrimental effects has resulted in a reassessment of investment and assistance policies.

A construction industry with a different structure emerged in countries with centrally planned economies, such as the former Soviet Union, where drastic and forced centralization created large design and contracting firms. This centralization was reversed in the countries that returned to a market economy at the beginning of the 1990s and most large firms were broken up into smaller units.

Specialist firms, such as those involved in roofing, insulation, piling, painting, HVAC and electrical works, tend to be smaller than those in general contracting.

THE NATIONAL SITUATION

A comprehensive overview of the construction industry in the leading countries, with special attention to the large companies, is given below.

In 1992, the estimated total construction output of the major European countries was: Germany ECU 176 billion, Italy ECU 102 billion, France ECU 97 billion, the UK ECU 65 billion, Russia ECU 59 billion, Spain ECU 57 billion and The Netherlands ECU 27 billion. In western Europe in the early 1990s, the 30 largest firms together employed about 800 000 people. Although together with large American and Japanese contractors they actually employ only about 3% of the total construction industry workforce, they carry out most of the large projects in the world. In 1993 there were 18 construction companies in western Europe that had a staff of more than 20 000 people. Of these, 10 employed more than 30 000 people: Bouygues, SGE, Eiffage, GTM-Entrepose, Bilfinger & Berger, Philipp Holzmann, BICC, Trafalgar House, Hochtief and FCC (French, German, British and Spanish firms).

In the UK, the 11 largest groups had a combined turnover totalling 35% of the gross value of construction. Most large firms are diversified, with several having branched out into property development, financing and the manufacture of building materials. At the beginning of the 1990s, the largest contractors in the UK were: Trafalgar House, BICC, Tarmac, AMEC, Wimpey, P&O, Laing, Mowlem and Costain.

In France in 1989, the turnover of the 11 largest firms amounted to 24% of gross construction output there. It has been found that productivity per person in the largest firms was 30% higher than that in the medium-sized firms. The largest contractors were Bouygues, Eiffage, GTM-Entrepose, Spie Batignolles, Dumez, Cegelec, Colas and SAE.

It is a peculiar characteristic of the construction trade that most of the business is conducted between industrialized and developing countries, with very little taking place between developed countries (NRC, 1988; Lee and Walters, 1989).

In Japan, the big five general contractors (Kajima, Obayashi, Taisei, Takenaka and Shimizu) play an important role. They each employ a staff of about 10 000 people, and each has its own research institute to work on pioneering projects such as super-tall buildings, and offshore, underground and outer-space structures. Prefabricated houses have never provided more than 12–15% of the total new housing market in Japan. Despite this, some firms, such as Sekisui, Misawa and Daiwa, have managed to attain a capacity of 10 000 – 15 000 units per year. Prefabricated houses are usually lightweight, earthquake-resistant and have a steel or timber frame (Bennett, 1993).

THE BUILDING MATERIALS INDUSTRIES

The building materials industry throughout the world increased production after 1945. In 1948, West German factories produced 5.6 million tons of cement; by 1957 this had increased to 19.3 million tons. In the USSR, production volumes for the same years were 6.5 million and 28.8 million tons, respectively. Italy produced 3.3 million tons of cement in 1948, and this had increased to 11.9 million tons by 1957. France produced 5.8 million and 13.9 million tons of cement for these two years, respectively, while in the UK, cement production grew from 8.5 million to 12.0 million tons between 1948 and 1957. More recently, the reduced volume of construction has placed pressure on cement production. The annual cement consumption per capita in almost all European countries was lower in 1991 than it was in 1980; taking France as an example, only 370 kg were produced in 1991, compared with 524 kg in 1980. Naturally, the same adverse effect has been felt in gravel, sand, concrete and mortar production, along with that of most other building materials.

World steel production amounted to 150 million tons in 1950, 600 million tons in 1970, and 770 million tons in 1990. It is estimated to reach 800 million tons in 2000 (Schulz, 1993). The spectacular post-war growth of steel production slowed down during the 1970s and 1980s. However, the investment made in the period before this, created a production capacity that is greater than the estimated production (or consumption) for 2000. In 1989, the four largest steel producing countries were the USSR (160 million tons per year), Japan (108 million tons), the USA (88 million tons) and West Germany (41 million tons). Steel production methods have undergone substantial modernization. According to recent information, about 90% of the steel being produced in Japan and Germany is by the modern continuous steel casting method. In the USA, about 65% is by this method, but in the former USSR only 17% is.

Other structural materials are produced in smaller quantities, but the growth potential for some is superior to that of steel. In 1990, the world's aluminium production was 18 million tons, that of other metals was 38 million tons, and of plastics, 98 million tons. Polymer production has overtaken steel production by volume for some years now. Although the strength of ordinary plastics is only about one-tenth that of steel, fibre reinforcement can increase this to the level of steel. Reinforcement with ceramic fibre gives a strength well in excess of that of steel.

In Western Europe in 1993, there were seven building material manufacturing companies that employed more than 20 000 people: Saint-Gobain, Pilkington, Holderbank, Lafarge Coppée, RMC, Redland, and Blue Circle (British, French and Swiss firms).

The share of total production taken by recycling differs among structural materials. In 1990, the shares were: 55% for steel, 45% for glass, 35% for paper, and 27% for aluminium, but only 10% for plastics. Information from Germany indicates that 85% of the aluminium waste in the building industry there is recycled.

According to data collected by the European Association of Insulation Materials (EURIMA), the annual production in the main groups of 15 Western countries was: 55.5 million m^3 of mineral wool, 19.3 million m^3 of polystyrene, 3.6 million m^3 of polyurethane, and 3.0 million m^3 of others. Germany had the highest production in each of these groups (about 30% of the total), followed by the UK, France, Italy and the Benelux countries.

INDUSTRIALIZATION, PREFABRICATION AND MECHANIZATION

INDUSTRIALIZATION

After the Second World War, the high demand for new housing, schools and other buildings in most European countries provided favourable conditions for the development and use of more up-to-date technologies. The leap from the traditional labour-intensive methods to modern ones has been called the industrialization of construction (Sebestyén, Platzer and Braun, 1989). The production of building materials and components, as well as of many building processes, were industrialized.

The leading French experts Bonnome and Léonard (1959) and Blachère (1988) defined industrialization as being mechanization in essence. They added that industrialization is characterized by the technology of construction and not by the product. While basically in agreement, I consider that the industrialization of construction comprises more than this. It usually also means the introduction of new technologies, such as prefabrication, or of modern *in situ* processes, such as the up-to-date *in situ* French concreting method *béton banché* or the various uses of slip-forms for chimneys, bunkers and silos, and the use of modern form-work ('tunnel' shutters, etc.) and pre-stressing methods (e.g. for tanks for fluids). Industrialization is also characterized by modern design methods that use scientific knowledge about structures, building physics, fire and computer technologies.

In order to promote industrialization, experimental projects have been carried out in several countries. One large-scale programme in the USA was entitled 'Operation Breakthrough'. Various new techniques were tried out under its auspices in the 1970s, e.g:

- pre-cast concrete load-bearing panels (Atlanta, Georgia; Yonkers, New York; Montreal, Canada; Columbia, Maryland);
- wood-framed modules (Wilmington, Delaware; Battle Creek, Michigan);
- fibre-reinforced resin with fillers moulded into panels (Valley Center, California);
- steel-framed modules (Lafayette, Indiana; Avon, New York);

Fig. 2.1 Maison Alfort, Paris, France: large panel building, System Camus. *Source:* Gy. Sebestyén (1965) *Large Panel Buildings*, Akadémiai Kiadó, Budapest.

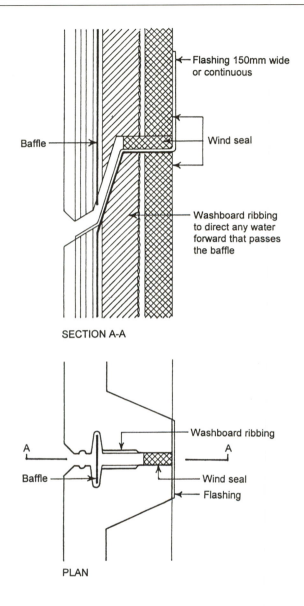

Flashing 150mm wide or continuous

Baffle

Wind seal

Washboard ribbing to direct any water forward that passes the baffle

SECTION A-A

Washboard ribbing

A   A

Baffle

Wind seal

Flashing

PLAN

Fig. 2.2 Open-drained joint for pre-cast concrete panel. *Source:* J. Strike (1991) *Construction into Design*, Butterworth.

- glass-fibre reinforced plastic and paper honeycomb modules (Redondo Beach, California);
- closed modules (Philadelphia, Pennsylvania).

Although the project contributed to the industrialization of construction, it did not yield the real 'breakthrough' that was expected.

PREFABRICATION

Prefabrication is one form of industrialization. It is based on the industrial manufacture of building components off-site or near the site. Prefabrication can be traced back to the distant past, but it gained greater use with industrial development. Timber was (and still is) a basic material, but the pre-cutting of stones has been also practised, and nowadays prefabrication can take place with all structural materials: timber, steel, aluminium, concrete and polymers.

Prefabrication has always been a technique used on sites with difficult local characteristics. As long ago as the late eighteenth century, the British were sending prefabricated housing to Australia and Africa, and in the 1830s, the Manning 'Portable Colonial Cottage for Emigrants', which could be assembled in a few hours, was being produced and shipped to sites around the world. At the beginning of the twentieth century, British and American bridge-building firms were despatching thousands of tons of pre-assembled bridge sections to Africa (Linder, 1994).

Prefabrication for dwellings comprises two distinctly different subsectors: houses, and multistorey residential buildings. A prefabrication industry evolved for single-family houses that was separate from most of the controversies of the multistorey market. Experiences have been mixed, however, especially for those who thought of building large factories modelled on the car manufacturing or ship-building sectors.

In Britain the first new systems after 1945 were the Portal House (with pressed steel and plywood), the Aluminium Bungalow (with aluminium trays produced in an aircraft factory), Arcon and Uni-Seco. Tens of thousands of each were built, but in the 1950s these systems were abandoned in favour of more advanced ones.

In the USA, a ship-building company made an unsuccessful attempt to prefabricate houses. More successful, at least for a period, was the initiative of the New York developer William Levitt, whose firm, Levitt & Sons, built 17 000 cheap and nearly identical houses between 1947 and 1951, turning them out like cars on an assembly line. Thus Levittown was built, which became the subject of much criticism because of its monotonous appearance. The firm did not survive the death of its founder.

The manufacture of timber houses has been realized in various forms, such as pre-cut construction, frame and infill, panelized, volume elements (volumetric big boxes) and mobile homes. The use of structural sandwich elements (stressed skin panels) is one of the more recent developments in panelized construction.

The idea of mobile homes (also called 'manufactured housing') was conceived in the early 1920s. In 1992, approximately 15 million Americans lived in more than 7 million manufactured homes. The cost of a unit is below the cost of a typical newly constructed site-built home. The number of new manufactured homes installed each year in the USA is about 20% of the number of total single-family completions. A single-wide or single-section mobile home is usually 14 ft (4.20 m) wide and up to 70 ft or 85 ft (21.0 m to 25.50 m) long, built on a permanent chassis, with or without a permanent foundation, and connected to the utilities. A double-wide (or triple-wide) mobile home consists of two or more sections combined on site (Bernhardt, 1980). The basic type is the standard coach design; a variant is the expandable type (Dietz, 1946–1980).

Factories for houses became successfully established in North America, and this sector became the manufactured building industry of the USA. Capacity reached 10 000 houses per annum in some cases, but was generally lower (Skyline, Guerdon, Champion Home, Fleetwood, Lear, Hussey, Kennedy, Logan, Scarponi, Taylor). In Japan, a similar industry emerged (Misawa, Daiwa, Sekisui, National House). The capacity of some Japanese home-builders currently exceeds 10 000 units per year, and highly automated manufacturing methods are applied. In several European countries (e.g. Sweden, Finland, Germany and Austria), a number of different sized factories produce prefabricated timber houses, or houses using other technologies (such as steel-framed).

Prefabrication received a new impetus from the appearance of concrete. Pre-cast beams and columns were the first to be produced, and the range was later broadened to include wall blocks, wall panels, floor and roof panels and many other components. For a time, 'system building' was a buzz-word in industrialized building. It usually encompassed comprehensive systems of construction, of which by far the most notable were large-panel housing and light-frame schools. In industrialized systems building, subsystems and components are integrated into an overall process, utilizing industrialized production, transportation and assembly techniques (Dietz and Cutler, 1971).

After 1945, a great number of new housing units had to be built in Europe within a short period. In the multistorey market, the reinforced concrete large-panel buildings seemed to provide the best solution (Sebestyén, 1965). Pioneers of this were France and Denmark, the USSR, and other eastern European countries. It was assumed that the large-panel processes would provide greater productivity at no higher cost than traditional construction. Several systems were developed, and factories were established for the manufacture of large-size reinforced panels. In the West, the French companies Camus, Coignet, Pascal, Balency, and Costamagna, the Danish firm Larsen-Nielsen, and the British groups Bison, Wates and Reema were the most notable. In eastern Europe, systems indigenous to each country were developed. The use of the large-panel systems contributed substantially to the improvement of European housing conditions within a short period. On the other hand, prefabrication in new housing never came to exceed a minority of the total, even if heavy large-panel and lightweight prefabrication are considered together (Die Fertighaus-Bauindustrie, 1984). Large-panel systems had the highest share of new (urban) residential construction in eastern Europe.

It was some 10 to 20 years before it became obvious that while these systems did produce dwellings in large numbers, the inherent restrictions of most systems required too many compromises. The dwellings proved to be no cheaper than the customary technologies, and their flexibility in use was limited. On the other hand, technical defects such as driving rain penetration (among many) were soon eliminated. The solution developed was the open-drained vertical joint with a baffle between large pre-cast concrete panels; the French call it a 'joint of decompression'. In the horizontal joint, a sill prevents the penetration of driving rain.

Industrialized system building is based on prefabricated large-size components. This restricts the freedom of the designer and the introduction of subsequent changes during use. The requirements for flexibility, variability and adaptability have been much debated and, while those promoting a system always tried to prove that their system does not restrict the design or use, it is undeniable that systems with large components are encumbered by such constraints. Increasing the number of components and allowing additional, non-standard components can reduce these constraints, but not eliminate them entirely. Systems with a given list of large-size pre-cast components have been defined as 'closed', and cannot satisfy the wish for 'open', i.e. unlimited, freedom in design. Publications promoting individual systems often claim to illustrate the great variety of design solutions possible, but to some extent these publications actually demonstrate the opposite, that there is in fact only a limited range of alternatives.

At the same time as the large-panel and *béton banché* systems were developed, primarily for housing, various industrialized systems for schools were created, e.g. CLASP (Consortium of Local Authorities Special Programme) and SCOLA in the UK, and Fillod in France. The greatest number of schools and other buildings were built with the CLASP system, using standardized steel trusses, aluminium windows and door units. As with the large-panel systems in housing, the CLASP and other lightweight systems in school buildings satisfied much of the peak demand, but when the demand slumped, most of these systems were abandoned. Systems for industrial halls and other multipurpose buildings were also developed in these years.

One of the most detailed analyses of system and industrialized building in general was summed up by Russell (1981). Most of his critical comments can be accepted as valid, but it would be wrong to condemn the industrialization of construction in its totality. Russell wrote: 'Seen only as a panacea, whether by architect, administrator or politician, the building systems idea is of little value.' Following this and other similar comments, the term 'system building' practically vanished, despite the fact that at the same time the system theory continued to flourish, although it also came in for some scathing criticism for having unrealistic ambitions (Gall, 1978).

When the programmes for new housing finally declined in the late 1970s and 1980s, the application of these systems (and of system building in general) was substantially cut back. The idea of 'industrialization' itself fell into disrepute in the UK, although this was not the case in many other countries, such as the USA, France or in Scandinavia.

Although some claim that the terms 'open' and 'system' are mutually exclusive, the search for such 'open' systems generated an alternative philosophy of industrialized building. This consists not of a set of components, but a set of design rules that determine the system by dimensional co-ordination only, leaving free the choice of materials and structures. One of the most elaborate of such systems is the Dutch 'Open Building' approach initiated by Habraken and developed further by van Randen, Carp and others. It distinguishes the support (the columns of the building's frame) from the 'infills' (partitions and services), and ensures their dimensional compatibility (Lukez, 1986).

Manufacturers of concrete components are inclined to be in favour of systems that have a set of components, whereas designers (architects) tend to favour truly 'open' approaches, but the whole debate about the open or closed approach has now become slightly dated anyway (Kendall, 1987).

Despite the doubts about systems building, the advantages of prefabrication remain undeniable. The prefabrication of concrete and reinforced concrete components have developed into a major industrial branch. During the post Second World War boom in industrialized housing, factories were established exclusively to manufacture the components for such residential buildings. Each factory of Camus, Coignet and others in the West and in the so-called 'Dwelling Building Corporations' (*domostroytelnye kombinaty*) in the Eastern bloc produced panels for between 1000 and 10 000 dwellings per year. Most of these have had to reduce their production during the past decade, or to enhance their range by also manufacturing components for other purposes, such as industrial buildings.

The factories of pre-cast concrete components make use of various technologies, partly depending on the products. For the beams of industrial buildings, long pre-stressing beds are often used. Wall panels may be produced horizontally or vertically. In the latter case, they are manufactured in pairs or in 'battery' forms, in which six to 12 panels are cast simultaneously. To accelerate the production, thermal curing is frequently used.

Large-scale production (prefabrication) was also developed for doors and windows (from wood, steel, aluminium or plastics), kitchen and bathroom units and appliances, partitions and façade wall elements. Industrialization and prefabrication have the two basically different approaches of 'heavy' and 'lightweight' technologies. The first is based on concrete (Sarja, 1991), the second on timber, steel, aluminium, glass and polymers (Sebestyén, 1977). While 'pure' solutions exist in both categories, they are often used in combination, enabling the designer to

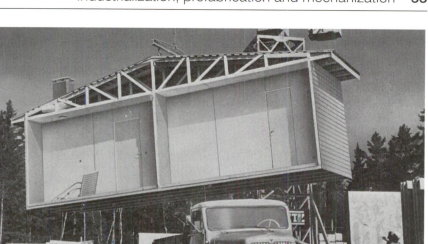

Fig. 2.3   Lightweight timber module, Finland. *Source:* Gy. Sebestyén (1977) *Lightweight Building*, Akadémiai Kiadó, Budapest.

exploit the advantages of both. Prefabrication has increased productivity in building, improved working conditions by transferring part of the process from open-air building sites to closed factories, and brought construction nearer to the conditions of modern industry.

MECHANIZATION

As we have already seen, mechanization is an important factor in the technical advancement of construction. The steam engine could find only a restricted application in building. The invention of the internal combustion engine (both petrol and oil) and the electric motor changed this (Peurifoy, 1956). The working parts of machines can be controlled by mechanical, hydraulic, pneumatic or electronic means, as well as a combination of these. Hydraulic and other modern systems have replaced rope drives in, for example, excavators, scrapers, graders and bulldozers.

Fig. 2.4 Insertion of lightweight module into multistorey reinforced concrete frame, Japan. *Source:* Gy. Sebestyén (1977) *Lightweight Building*, Akadémiai Kiadó, Budapest.

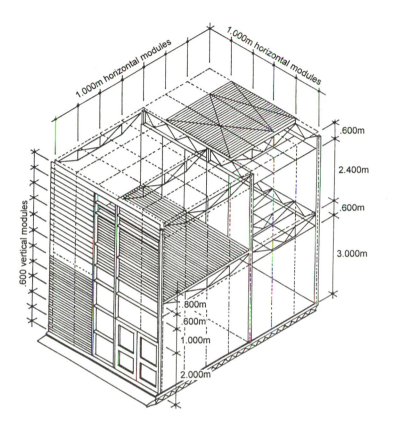

Fig. 2.5   CLASP school construction system, lightweight steel frame, England. *Source:* J. Strike (1991) *Construction into Design*, Butterworth.

Although some types of building machinery such as mobile concrete mixers and tower cranes were available before the Second World War, they have been used widely only since the 1950s. Tubular steel scaffolding has completely replaced rope-lashed timber scaffolds (McNeil, 1990).

Building machinery of different sizes and capacities has been developed for different jobs. For several categories of very large construction, or in work such as open mining, machines of a unique size or capacity have been designed. The largest bucket wheel excavators, such as the one manufactured by Orenstein & Koppel of Lübeck, can shift 200 000 m³ of soil a day. The largest tractor shovel, such as the Clark 675, has a bucket of 18 m³. The largest dump truck, the Terrex Titan, can carry 350 short tons (324

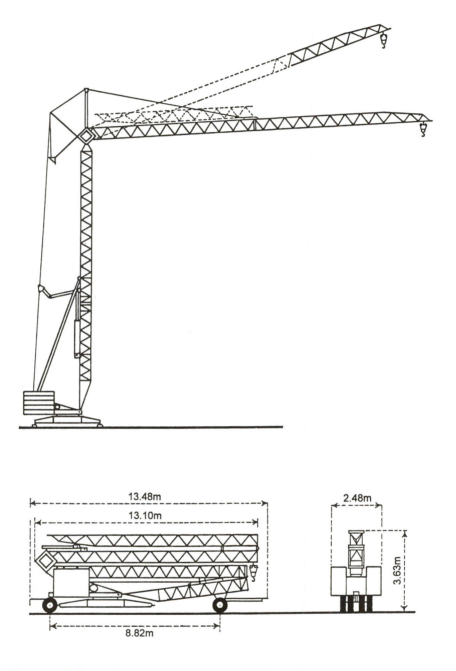

Fig. 2.6   Self-propelled tower crane, Potain GMH 825, France; maximum load: 800 kg at 18.40 m hoist height and 25 m radius. *Source:* Courtesy of Company Potain.

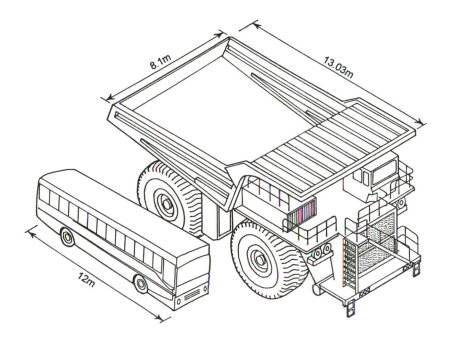

Fig. 2.7   The world's largest truck, Komatsu 930 E, Japan; maximum useful load: 315 tons. *Source:* Newspaper publication.

tons). The largest bulldozers have engines that can develop over 1000 hp (745.7 kW). Concrete pumps had previously a maximum transport range of 30 m vertically and 120 m horizontally; nowadays limits are 400 m and 1600 m, respectively. Likewise, rams used to have a falling weight of perhaps 15 tons, now, in offshore work, falling ram weights of 180 tons are applied. These are obviously only approximate figures, and do not include machinery from the former USSR, where machines for extremely large constructions were also manufactured. Nevertheless, they serve to indicate the upper end of the range of building machines.

For certain civil engineering projects (such as harbours and dams, and the Delta storm-barrier works in The Netherlands) machinery has been specially designed and produced. All the major industrialized countries have an industrial sector producing building machines. Heavy machinery for the construction industry, such as excavators and tower cranes, are manufactured by large companies like Caterpillar, Deere, Komatsu, Manitowoc, Liebherr, Schwing, Richier, Kato, Ruston-Bucyrus, Potain and Poclain. Some of these firms also produce large machines for agriculture and mining. Smaller electric tools, such as power drills, are manufactured by firms that also produce general purpose tools, e.g. Black & Decker and Bosch.

The annual production value of building machines in the USA is about US$14 billion. It is a highly concentrated industrial sector, and out of the total of 700 manufacturing firms, just a few account for the majority of the production and export. The largest is Caterpillar, and other major producers are Case, Indresco, Clark, V.M.E., Deere, Terex and Manitowoc. In Germany, the annual production value of the industry manufacturing building and building materials machinery is approximately DM 12 billion, of which one-third is attributable to building machinery, and two-thirds to building materials manufacturing machinery. More than half of the production is exported, and the sector employs about 50 000 people.

Building machines use a number of fluids. A hydraulic bagger weighing 60 tons, may contain 2500 l of fluids, of which only 1000 is diesel oil; it also needs 1300 l of hydraulic oil and a smaller quantity of various other lubricants (Fortkord, 1992).

Some of the basic trends in the development of building machinery are: the extension of subtypes, making both larger and smaller machines; adding special new tools to machines; attaining higher performance, longer life, less maintenance and repair, and better transportability (for large machines without dismantling); reducing exhaust fumes and noise, both for the driver and the environment; shock-free functioning and less vibration; reducing fuel consumption; improving safety measures/protection; and developing new types of oil (Fortkord, 1992). Electronic controls, microprocessors, microcomputers and loading sensors are all increasingly being used in building machines. The move towards automation and robotization is discussed in Chapter 5.

The progress made in mechanization may be illustrated by the following data. In 1960, in the West German building industry, 31 people had a collective output of DM 1 million. In 1990, the same output was produced by only 10 people. In 1960, in the German building industry, the weight of machines and instruments per worker was 1 ton; by 1990 this had increased to 5 tons. Germany has been a leader in building mechanization in Europe for some time and this is reflected in the activities and publications of eminent German engineers such as Professors G. Garbotz, W.E. Fauner, G. Kuhn, F. Gehbauer, W. Poppy and T. Bock. Germany is the largest exporter of building machines, exceeding the output of even the USA and Japan. Industrialization, prefabrication and mechanization have become powerful contributors to the progress of construction.

THE PERFORMANCE CONCEPT

USERS' REQUIREMENTS: PERFORMANCE

Over the course of many hundreds or thousands of years of construction practice, a very large body of knowledge on building has been accumulated, and stored in technical books on architecture, materials, structures and tools, and passed on from one generation of craftsmen to another. A designer or builder was expected to be conversant with this body of knowledge, and had a duty to follow the rules or recommendations of the experts. This was reasonable when the choice of materials and the method of using them was restricted, but things are different nowadays. A good designer with innovative instincts may come up with ideas for which no precedent exists. What then ensures that his or her professional conduct is responsible? The answer to this question might lie in the new idea of the performance concept, in which the technical characteristics of the building's components, their materials and production methods are not prescribed, but their performance, based on the requirements of the users, is defined. How to achieve the required performance is left to the designer: he or she must ascertain by calculations or tests that his or her solution will satisfy the brief.

The objective of defining the performance can be realized only after the users' requirements have been identified and quantified. This has proved to be a major challenge for researchers and, although the basic requirements have been defined, there are still questions open for research, such as odour control and, more generally, air purity requirements.

In earlier periods, the requirements of buildings were primarily ones of space and appearance, and the system of human requirements was conceived only recently, partly as a consequence of the proliferation of new materials and structures. It was recognized that fulfilment of the users' requirements could not be adequately ensured simply by formulating quality levels of building materials and structures, and that defining the required performance of a particular building and its components might be a more effective solution. This led to the birth of the performance concept, which initiated a revolution in the drafting of codes, standards and specifications. The new thinking restricts these documents to the required performance – satisfying the users' requirements – without specifying the process that would yield the desired result.

The performance concept enables the designer and the contractor to achieve a certain standard of performance by the use of very different materials and designs, to evaluate alternatives and to consider innovative solutions. At the same time, the performance system protects the client, the future occupants and society from undesirable surprises, because the responsibility of the designer and the contractor lies in guaranteeing the building's performance. In this regard, the basic internationally agreed norms have been summed up in the International Organization for Standardization (ISO) standards 6240, 6241, 9699 and several others, which detail the application of the concept. The performance concept has become accepted practice for formulating and checking the requirements that buildings must satisfy.

THE *'AGRÉMENT'* SYSTEM

As a means of objectively evaluating new materials and processes, the so-called *'agrément'* system was introduced. It was first launched in France and was soon adopted in many other countries. The system requires that manufacturers wishing to introduce a new product, component or system must have these examined and evaluated by a nationally recognized institute that specializes in such work. An *'Agrément* Certificate' is issued if the product complies with the requirements.

The *agrément* system is useful in those fields where national and international standards do not yet exist. It ensures careful examination prior to practical general use and thereby protects the public interest, clients and users. On the international level, the UEAtc (the European Union of *Agrément*) was established to ensure the mutual recognition of *agrément* documents. At the time of writing, 15 European countries are participating in the UEAtc, each having one member institute in the organization. At meetings in Brazil in 1994 and Paris in 1995, it was decided to expand the *agrément* system to cover other continents and to set up a new international organization for that purpose.

The UEAtc has published technical guides in the following fields: claddings, windows and glazing, wall and floor coverings, insulation, roofings, structural fasteners, equipment and miscellaneous. UEAtc reference documents have been published on lightweight houses, heavy prefabricated panels, light claddings, roller shutters, lightweight partitions, plastic renderings, building sealants, above ground drainage systems, and glass reinforced polyester for use in building.

Quite recently a new organization, the European Organization for Technical Approvals (EOTA), was established within the European Union for the purpose of supervising at intergovernmental level the European technical approvals to be issued for areas not standardized by ISO or the European standardization institution CEN.

MODULAR AND DIMENSIONAL CO-ORDINATION

THE SYSTEM AND ITS APPLICATIONS

Dimensional co-ordination has been practised for a long time. Examples are stonemasonry or, in Japan, room dimensions, which have been defined as multiples of the *'tatami'* floor mats. In modern times, industrial development has necessitated co-ordination of the dimensions of various building elements, such as wall and floor components, and appliances such as ovens and refrigerators. The idea of having a basic dimension and defining all other items as multiples or fractions of this resulted in the search for what became known as the *'module'*.

The principal objective of modular co-ordination is to assist the building industry and its associates by ensuring that all components fit with each other, that their assembly is possible without cutting, and that they are readily interchangeable. Dimensional co-ordination is a convention on related sizes for the co-ordinating dimensions of building components and the buildings incorporating them, for their design, manufacture and assembly. Modular co-ordination is dimensional co-ordination employing the basic module or a multimodule, which is a selected multiple of the basic module. The modular grid is a rectangular reference system in which the distance between consecutive lines is equal to the basic module or multimodule. It may be two- or three-dimensional. The term 'reference system' defines a system of points, lines and planes to which sizes and positions of components relate, both in design and in measurements. The grid may be simply a modular one, or, preferably, a multimodular one.

For some time, two competing dimensions were proposed: 10 cm and 12.5 cm. As an international module, 10 cm was accepted after the Second World War, although this does not exclude another dimension being used as a design module if there is sufficient justification. There was also some disagreement about multiples. For housing and commercial buildings two dimensions were proposed: $3 \times 10 = 30$ cm and $4 \times 10 = 40$ cm. The first leads to design dimensions of 90, 120, 150, 180, 240, 360, 480 cm and so on; the second to dimensions of 80, 120, 160, 240, 360, 480 cm, etc. There is some preference for multiples of 30 cm. For long-span industrial buildings, multiples of 120 cm or 300 cm are often used, giving 12, 18 and 24 m. Whichever dimensions are chosen, the most important thing is to ensure compatibility between the various products from different manufacturers. Dimensional co-ordination, as well as conventions on joints, junctions and tolerances, is needed for this.

All 'systems' of industrialized construction have selected some kind of modular and dimensional co-ordination (Sarja and Hannus, 1995). The international agreements on modular co-ordination are contained in the following (and some other) ISO standards: 1006, 1040, 1789, 1790, 1791, and 2848.

JOINTS, TOLERANCES AND MEASUREMENTS

Adjacent building components must have enough space to be fitted together or locked into each other, but the space between them must not exceed a predetermined size. The characteristics of the joint or junction must therefore be known.

Joints have a great number of functions. ISO 3447 defines them as:

- to control the passage of fire, smoke, heat, sound and odours;

- capacity to withstand compression, tension, bending, shear, torsion, vibration, impact, abrasion, creep;
- to support joined components and resist differential deformations of joined components;
- to have a specified minimum life and permit dismantling, reassembly and replacement.

The maximum and minimum component and joint size must be determined. The joints may be open or filled with a sealant, and the components may be fastened to each other or the frame; all of these variables have repercussions on the dimensions of the components and joints. Tolerances permit variations of size (ISO 1803/1 and 1803/2), and the design, manufacture and assembly processes must adhere to the established rules of tolerance. The numbers of the most important ISO standards on joints, tolerances and measurements in building are: 1803, 3443, 3447, 6284, 6927, 7078, 7727 and 7976.

Setting out the place of the designed building on site is an ancient craft. In modern times it has been assisted by various instruments and, quite recently, by satellites. The practice of on-site measurements must be harmonized with the systems of modular and dimensional co-ordination, joints, junctions and tolerances. Modular and dimensional co-ordination simplify site operations by rationalizing the process of setting out, positioning and assembling the building components, and both are now common practice in modern industry.

QUALITY AND STANDARDS

CODES AND STANDARDS

Construction affects important areas of public concern such as health and safety. Public authorities of all types have issued codes regulating various aspects of construction. In previous centuries these were primarily local, but with the emergence of national authorities they gradually became transformed into national codes. In large countries where individual and local communities have a high level of autonomy, such as the USA, local or regional codes have been replaced by federal codes.

Other regulatory tools, known as standards, have the advantage of being voluntary agreements by different parties: producers, consumers and authorities. Legislation can define to what extent standards are mandatory. For products, standards are appropriate tools of regulation; for construction, codes have been the basic instruments in many countries for defining the rules to be followed by different participants in the process. In modern times, standards seem to be gaining the upper hand over codes, or at least are now being applied in some fields that previously came under the aegis of codes.

Standardization on a national level is usually followed by international standardization. In the nineteenth century, travellers on Great Britain's early railways were compelled to change trains during their journeys, as different railway companies used different track gauges until a national standard of 4 ft 8½ in was agreed on. And those who travel to different countries nowadays are only too well aware of the inconvenience caused by the lack of a single international standard for electrical plugs and sockets.

Worldwide, there are more than 200 organizations drafting international standards, but 96% of all published standards originate from three Geneva-based institutions: ISO, the International Electrotechnical Commission (IEC), and the International Telecommunications Union (ITU). In recent years, the Brussels-based European standardization institutions CEN and CENELEC have also become important originators of international standards. While ISO standards are voluntary, European (CEN) standards, once approved, are mandatory for European Union (EU) member countries.

In addition to traditional fields of international standardization, such as steel, cement, screws and nails, new areas have emerged, such as quality management, hygiene, environment, services and new technologies. The Construction Products Directive 89/106 EEC (CPD 89/106) is a basic EU document that harmonizes terminology and technical concepts, indicates classes or levels for essential requirements, and serves as a reference for harmonized standards and technical approvals. The essential requirements are defined as:

- mechanical resistance and stability;
- safety in case of fire;
- hygiene, health and the environment;
- safety in use;
- protection against use;
- energy economy and heat retention.

Interpretative documents have been published for these six essential requirements.

Standards ensure that products and services conform to the same technical requirements and quality level. Within ISO, some 200 international technical committees are engaged in various fields. Approximately 40 have direct relevance to construction, although several others are also of some importance. Some of those relevant to the construction industry are listed below:

- TC 43   Acoustics
- TC 59   Buildings
- TC 71   Concrete

- TC 98   Structural design
- TC 162   Windows and doors
- TC 163   Heat insulation.

Some of the most important CEN technical committees are:

- TC 53   Scaffolds and formwork
- TC 89   Heat insulation of buildings
- TC 94   Ready mixed concrete
- TC 124   Timber structures
- TC 125   Masonry
- TC 135   Steel structures
- TC 163   Sanitary equipment
- TC 189   Geotextiles.

Agreements between ISO and CEN ensure the necessary co-ordination and co-operation.

QUALITY AND ITS CERTIFICATION

In order to verify whether the quality of construction achieved is at least as good as that specified, quality must be controlled. This includes taking samples, making visual inspections, measuring, destructive and non-destructive testing, and laboratory experiments. For an entire building, quality control is more complex. As products, buildings are unique and consist of many components, which makes it far from easy to come up with a concise definition of their quality.

Quality can be controlled by the producer itself ('first party'), or by the client ('second party), or even by a 'third party', usually a quality control organization specializing in this task. In France and other countries that follow French practice, insurance companies are contracted for quality control, a procedure that can include on-site laboratory tests. Recently in quality control, it has become general practice not to wait until the prod-uct is completed but to take the necessary steps during the production process to ensure that the final quality conforms to requirements. This is the concept behind the term 'quality management', which dictates that a producer should have a quality policy and a quality system. The quality policy expresses the overall intentions and direction of an organization with regard to quality. The quality system comprises the organisational structure, responsibilities, procedures, processes and resources for imple-menting effective quality management. Design and contracting compa-nies also have to establish a quality management system. Small firms do not require full-time staff for this, but large organizations need a full-time quality management unit. Naturally, good quality can be achieved by careful work and without a separate quality management function, but the use of a quality system provides greater surety that this goal will actually be attained.

Internal quality assurance engenders confidence about quality in the managers of an organization. External quality assurance provides such confidence to the purchaser (client). A systematic survey on quality management is carried out by certification bodies. These issue certificates that provide purchasers with an assurance of quality. In the UK, the National Accreditation Council for Certification Bodies (NACCB) oversees this function. Quality certification in the UK is currently carried out by 36 general or specialized accredited certification bodies, the largest and best known of which is the British Standards Institution (BSI).

Four categories of certification are recognized by the NACCB in the UK. In Category 1, the quality system of the suppliers is certified. The conformity with product standards is certified in Category 2, while in Category 3 the fitness of a product for its intended purpose is given in cases where no agreed standards are available. The British Board of *Agrément* is one of the certification bodies for Category 3. In Category 4, the competence of the personnel engaged in quality verification is certified.

Quality management and quality systems have been standardized by ISO in the standards ISO 8402, 9000, 9001, 9002, 9003, 9004–1, 9004–2, 9004–3 and 9004–4. These are in extensive use and have their equivalents in CEN, and in national (BSI etc.) standards. The ISO 14000 standards on the management of environmental obligations can be considered to be a continuation of the ISO 9000 standards (Cascio, Woodside and Mitchell, 1996).

BUILDING RESEARCH AND INNOVATION

THE DEVELOPMENT OF BUILDING RESEARCH ORGANIZATIONS

Up to the twentieth century, eminent scientists and engineers developed new knowledge for construction, but there were no independent building research institutes. By the beginning of the First World War, a good deal was known about construction, but more information was needed, and so, after preparatory work during the war, the first important building research organization, the Building Research Station (now the Building Research Establishment, BRE) was established in the UK in 1921. Since then, every industrialized country has established a national building research institute. The role of these public or semi-public institutes is to protect the public interest (safety of buildings, requirements of public hygiene, etc.), while at the same time enabling the fragmented building industry to conduct industrial research in the same way that other industries do.

Public building research institutes were originally financed fully or mainly by governments. There were some cases (e.g. Belgium) where a (royal) decree provided for industrial financing to come from a mandatory levy on turnover or salaries, but otherwise authorized the institute to function as a public organization. The number of staff working in building research institutes increased steadily from 1945 until it peaked at the end of the 1970s, after which most institutes were compelled to cut back on staffing levels. From the 1980s onwards, governments began to reduce the budget for building research. This was motivated by more than a need to reduce spending: it was felt that having carried out useful work in preparing codes and standards, building research institutes should now be more concerned with the problems of industry. In most cases the institutes were successful in switching their focus, and now work for the industry, deriving some of their income from industry commissions. In the 1980s, some governments even went so far as to consider closing their national building research institute. The result of these deliberations was usually some sort of change in the size and status of the institute, such as the introduction of a type of privatization and a reduction of public financing, but with the institutes continuing to operate.

The research institutes built up their testing and research facilities between 1945 and 1975. Although far from comparable with the expensive facilities of nuclear physics, for example, building research institutes did acquire new laboratories for research on large-scale structures, heat, moisture, air quality, fire, acoustic properties and human comfort. After 1974, however, most building research institutes were forced to abandon further expansion plans. A brief overview of the more important types of laboratories and testing facilities in building research institutes is given below.

- **Facilities to test real-size structures affected by static or dynamic loads and/or by fire.** Such testing facilities have been built in all major institutes, including the governmental and industry institutes in Japan (Kajima, Takenaka, etc.), and the BRE in the UK at the Cardington Large Building Test Facility (LBTF).
- **Large testing facilities for fire**. Several institutes have these, including: TNO-Bouw in The Netherlands; CTICM in Maizières-les-Metz, France; Ghent University in Belgium; and NIST-BFRL in Gaithersburg in the USA.
- **Boundary layer wind tunnels**, which simulate the effects of wind on buildings at scale factors of between 1:500 and 1:100 are available at CSTB in Nantes (France) and BRE in the UK among many.
- **Heat, moisture and driving rain testing facilities**, usually for full-size façade sections, rooms or houses that are exposed to heat, moisture and driving rain.
- **Human comfort laboratories** in which either real people or models can be observed and measured under various indoor conditions of air temperature, draught, humidity, light and noise.

- **Human reactions (subjective and medical) to air pollution and odours**: in 1995, the French CSTB announced its intention to build a new laboratory called ARIA to study this field (ARIA, 1995).
- **Acoustic laboratories** of which the two basic types are: rooms with hard reverberating walls and rooms with sound-absorbing walls.
- **Sky simulators** (also called 'artificial skies'), are available at, for instance, the Fraunhofer-Institut für Bauphysik in Stuttgart, Germany; the Lawrence Berkeley Laboratory in Berkeley, USA; and the former Institute for Building Physics in Moscow, Russia.
- **HVAC laboratories** to measure the performance of HVAC equipment, including boilers, radiators, thermostats and whole systems, e.g. at the Gaz de France Laboratory at St Denis, France and the Institut für Bauphysik in Stuttgart.
- **Large size sand boxes** to test foundations, retaining walls, pipes and other structures buried in the ground, e.g. at CEBTP in St-Rémy-les Chevreuses, near Paris, France and in Moscow at the Research Institute for Structures.
- **Modelling dams and flood barriers**, e.g. at LNEC in Lisbon, Portugal.

Building research institutes have consolidated their work over the past few decades and are now confronted with the usual problems of research management: selection of research projects from among competing alternatives; research planning, interim, continuous and final control of research; career development and personnel motivation schemes, contacts with industry, implementation of research results and publications policies. The complexity of the management of building research institutes is illustrated by the 1995 programme of the French CSTB, a world leader in the field, which contains 134 individual research programmes and 50 different topics running as doctoral work. Very high-level planning and evaluation work is needed to run such a complex operation, keep track of progress, and implement the results (CSTB, 1995).

THE INSTITUTIONAL STRUCTURE OF BUILDING RESEARCH

Building research has developed a network of building research institutes, both public and private, plus other institutions such as universities. Some of the leading national building research institutes are:

- Building Research Establishment (BRE);
- Building & Fire Research Laboratory within the National Institute of Standards & Technology (NIST-BFRL), USA;
- Institute for Research in Construction within the National Research Council Canada (NRCC-IRC), Canada;
- Centre Scientifique et Technique du Bâtiment (CSTB), France;
- TNO-Bouw, The Netherlands;

- Centre Scientifique et Technique de la Construction (CSTC), Belgium;
- Building Research Institute within the Ministry of Construction (BRI-MoC), Japan.

There are about 50 such institutes in the world, the largest employing a staff of 500–1000, and most having a staff of at least 100–250.

Large contractors have recently begun to develop their own research bases, with Japanese companies leading the field. The larger Japanese industrial building research institutes are:

- Kajima Institute of Construction Technology;
- Kumagai Gumi Research and Development;
- Obayashi Corporation Technical Research Centre;
- Shimizu Research and Development Division;
- Taisei Corporation Technology Research Centre;
- Mitsui Research;
- Toda Institute of Technology.

The Kajima Institute was established in 1949. It has a staff of about 250 and is equipped with laboratories for large structures, hydraulic works and environmental problems. The Kumagai Institute also has a laboratory for large structures, and a floating dock for studying marine structures, caissons, mooring posts and sea berths. The institutes in Japan usually incorporate projects of great importance for the future such as robotics, earthquake-damping and cleanrooms in their programmes.

Some of the large contractors in other countries also have their own research institutes, e.g. the Laing Laboratories and Taylor Woodrow, both in the UK. In collaboration with Mitsui of Japan, Taylor Woodrow has also established a laboratory for testing marine structures such as floating platforms. In some countries the construction industry has its own institute serving several companies. Research institutes of this kind include the Construction Research Institute in Austin, Texas (USA) and the European Research Institute in the UK. These are financed by large contractors.

Much of the research in construction is being carried out by manufacturers' research organizations, such as Pilkington, Saint Gobain, Alcoa, Reynolds and Danfoss, and by institutes in other fields, such as the environment, climate, biology and design (Perry, 1995). An increasing volume of building research is now being undertaken at universities.

An international network of contacts has become an important element in research. Building researchers participate in a great number of international organizations, thus enhancing their knowledge and contributing to a more efficient dissemination of research results.

Several specialized international professional organizations are active in certain fields of construction research:

- BIBM   International Bureau of Precast Concrete;

- CEB   Euro-International Committee for Concrete;
- CIB   International Council for Building Research, Studies and
           Documentation;
- FIP   International Federation for Prestressing;
- IABSE   International Association for Bridge and Structural
           Engineering;
- IAEE   International Association for Earthquake Engineering;
- IASS   International Association for Shell and Spatial Structures;
- ISIAQ   International Society of Indoor Air Quality and Climate;
- ISSMFE   International Society for Soil Mechanics and Foundation
           Engineering;
- RILEM   International Union of Testing and Research Laboratories for
           Materials and Structures.

The International Council for Building Research, Studies and Documentation (CIB) is the international forum where building research institutes can exchange and develop their experiences on the overall problems of building research.

Some organizations have been established under the umbrella of the EU:

- ECCREDI   European Council for Construction Research,
            Development and Innovation;
- ENBRI   European Network of Building Research Institutes;
- ENCORD   European Network of Construction Companies for
            Research and Development.

The development of building research bodies has been a major factor in the transformation of construction from a practical, experience-based craft into an up-to-date industry that uses scientific results and is keen to develop further through research.

TECHNICAL PROGRESS: INVENTIONS AND INNOVATIONS

Technical progress is composed of scientific discovery and advance, invention, innovation and improvement. Not all inventions can be developed into applications, and much technical progress is the consequence of small improvements in science and technology. Technical progress enables greater production and productivity, improved quality, a reduction in the use of resources and the introduction of new products (Rosenberg, 1976, 1982). Particularly during the past 500 years, society has tended to be governed by welfare economics that aimed to maximize the utility obtained from individuals (utilitarianism). Technical and technological progress contributed to greater welfare and affluence, and this can usually be measured by economic indicators such as better cost-benefit ratios, higher productivity, lower costs, and – on the macroeconomic level – a higher per capita gross national product. While reducing the direct demand for labour, technical progress has also improved the competitive position of firms, industries and countries and has resulted in more work opportunities (Katsoulacos, 1986). The objectives of technical progress have been reconsidered recently (see Chapter 9).

Applying the technical developments of its various disciplines and branches, the progress of the construction industry is often self-generating. Moving away from its tradition-bound character, construction is increasingly open to progress, and its segmented structure is evolving towards integration, which is favourable for advancement. The technical progress in construction has been very much the result of innovative engineers, architects, contractors and manufacturers. While construction undoubtedly places great reliance on tradition and empirical experiences, it has been much transformed by innovation, and this is even more likely to be the case in the future as construction becomes more science-based and science-oriented (Bernstein and Lemer, 1996). Much industrial research is concentrated in large research organizations. Although these have come up with inventions, 'lone' inventors have also played a large part (Jewkes, Sawers and Stillerman, 1958). In construction, most inventions and innovations are generally the vision of designers and building materials manufacturers rather than the work of building research institutes or contractors. The research institutes do, however, have an important role in testing, validating and defining the performance of inventions and innovations submitted to them. To create an environment that is conducive to innovation and invention should be the aim, indeed the duty, of all progressive firms and organizations.

SUMMARY

The destruction of the Second World War was followed by optimism and high expectations for the future. Ambitious programmes were launched to eliminate the housing shortage and satisfy the demand for other types of new buildings. During a period of two decades much was achieved globally, and millions of families moved into new dwellings. In Europe, industry, infrastructure and cities were rebuilt and modernized. Urban services such as electricity, water and gas, public transport, road, rail and telephone networks were all expanded. The construction industry began to industrialize, introducing mechanization, prefabrication and system building. Small and medium-sized contractors remained numerous but large companies, including those producing building materials, machines and equipment for buildings, engineering/architectural practices, consulting firms and contracting companies gained strength.

The intellectual tools of modern construction, such as codes, standards, the performance concept-based brief and specifications, modular and dimensional co-ordination, quality management and building research began to evolve after 1945. Technical progress includes invention, innovation and improvement. Following classic and neoclassic welfare economic theory, these aimed to provide the maximum satisfaction and utility to the public. Methodologies to measure economic effectiveness in technical progress, such as the use of the discount technique for cost-benefit analysis, have been devised.

This overview of the past 50 years reveals that the construction industry has achieved much over the period. In the following chapters we will examine the components that led to this development.

BIBLIOGRAPHY

Allen, J., Ambrose, I., Brink, S. (eds) (1995) *Making Them Meet: Proceedings of CIB W69 Meeting*, Copenhagen, 4–8 October 1994.

Annual Bulletin of Housing and Building Statistics for Europe and North America, 1980, 1990, 1991, 1992, 1993 (1995), United Nations, New York and Geneva.

ARIA (1995) in *CSTB Magazine*, 84, May, 35.

Badger, W.W. and Mulligan, D.E. (1995) Rationale and benefits associated with international alliances, *Journal of Construction Engineering and Management*, 121(1), March, 100–11.

Bennett, J. (1993) Japan's building industry: the new model, *Construction Management and Economics*, **11**, 3–17.

Bernhardt, A.D. (1980) *Building Tomorrow: The Mobile/Manufactured Housing Industry*, Massachusetts Institute of Technology (MIT).

Bernstein, H.M. and Lemer, A.C. (1996) *Solving the Innovation Puzzle: Challenges Facing the U.S. Design & Construction Industry*, ASCE Press, New York.

Blachère, G. (1988) *Building Principles*, Report EUR, 11320 EN, Luxembourg.

Bonnome, C. and Léonard, L. (1959) L'industrialisation du batiment, *L'encyclopèdie pratique de la construction et du batiment*, Aristide Quillet, Paris.

Brink, S. (1992) Policy strategies for affordable housing in cities. In *Proceedings of CIB W69 Symposium*, Lisbon, Portugal, CIB Publication 158, 58–74.

Buchanan, C. (1978) Town planning. In Williams (ed), *The History of Technology*, Vol. VII, Oxford Clarendon Press, 958–82.

Cascio, F., Woodside, G., Mitchell, Ph. (1996) *ISO 14000 Guide*, McGraw-Hill.

CSTB (1995) Programme de recherche 1995 du CSTB, *Cahiers du CSTB*, Cahier 2793, May 1995.

Die Fertighaus-Bauindustrie in der Bundesrepublik Deutschland als Modell für Rationalisierung durch Industrialisierung im Bauen (1984) Heft Nr. 04.100 des Bundesministers für Raumordnung, Bauwesen und Städtebau.

Dietz, A.G.H. (1946–80, revised edns) *Dwelling House Construction*, The MIT Press, Cambridge, Massachussetts and London.

Dietz, A.G.H. and Cutler, L.S. (eds), (1971) *Industrialized Systems for Housing*, MIT.

Fortkord, C.D. (1992) Bau- und Baustoffmaschinen: Trends und Perspektiven. *Baumaschine+Bautechnik*, BMT, June, 156–61.

Gall, J. (1978) *Systemantics*, Pocket Books, New York.

Goldfield, D.R. and Brownell, B.A. (1990) *Urban America: A History*, Houghton Mifflin Company, Boston.

Ito, M. *et al.* (1991) *Construction R&D in Western Europe*, University of Reading, Reading.

Jewkes, J., Sawers, D. and Stillerman, R. (1958) *The Sources of Invention*, Macmillan & Co.

Katsoulacos, Y.S. (1986) *The Employment Effect of Technical Change*, Wheatsheaf Books/Harvester Press.

Kendall, S. (1987) Notes on 'Open Systems' in building technology. *Building and Environment*, **22**(2), 93–100.

Le Corbusier and Jeanneret, C.E. (1933) *La Ville Radieuse*, Boulogne.

Lee, J.R. and Walters, D. (1989) *International Trade in Construction, Design, and Engineering Services*, Ballinger Publication.

Linder, M. (1994) *Projecting Capitalism: A History of the Internationalization of the Construction Industry*, Greenwood Press.

Lukez, P. (1986) *New Concepts in Housing Supports in The Netherlands*, MIT, Cambridge, MA.

Masterman, Ch. F.G. (ed). (1973) *The Heart of the Empire: Discussions of Modern City Life in England*, Harper & Row, London.

McNeil, I. (1990) *An Encyclopedia of the History of Technology*, Routledge, London and New York.

NRC (1988) *Building for Tomorrow: Global Enterprise and the U.S. Construction Industry*, National Research Council, USA.

Perry, A.H. (1995) Trends and perspectives in structural systems for buildings and infrastructure. In *Proceedings of CIB Congress*, Amsterdam, 8–9 May, 115–34

Peurifoy, R.L. (1956) *Construction Planning, Equipment, and Methods*, McGraw-Hill Book Company.

Rosenberg, N. (1976) *Perspectives of Technology*, Cambridge University Press.

Rosenberg, N. (1982) *Inside the Black Box: Technology and Economics*, Cambridge University Press.

Russell, B. (1981) *Building Systems: Industrialisation and Architecture*, John Wiley & Sons.

Sarja, A. (1991) Industrialized building technology as a tool for the international building market, *Betonwerk + Fertigteil-Technik*, **11**, 35–43.

Sarja, A. and Hannus, M. (1995) *Modular Systematics for the Industrialized Building*, VTT, Technical Research Centre of Finland.

Schulz, E. (1993) Die Zukunft des Stahls im Spannungsfeld zwischen Ökonomie und Ökologie, *Stahl und Eisen*, **2**.

Schweizer, G. (1994) *Zeitbombe Stadt*, Greif Bücher.

Seaden, G. (1994) Macro-economic framework of construction research, *CIB Bulletin*, **4**, 18–19.

Sebestyén, G., Platzer, M. and Braun, C. (eds) (1989) *Trends in Building Construction Techniques Worldwide*, CSTB-CIB, Paris.

Sebestyén, G. (1965) *Large Panel Buildings*, Akademiai Kiado.

Sebestyén, G. (1977) *Lightweight Building Construction*, George Godwin/John Wiley & Sons.

Sebestyén, G. (1994) A bulletin of statistics: some considerations, *Construction Management and Economics*, **12**, 373–5.

Strike, J. (1991) *Construction into Design*, Butterworth Architecture.

Teaford, J.C. (1993) *The Twentieth-Century American City*, Johns Hopkins University Press, Baltimore.

The evolution of knowledge

3

INTRODUCTION

Mathematics grew in importance during the seventeenth century, becoming a very different science from the mathematics of earlier epochs (Whitehead, 1926). Modern mathematics and physics are based on discoveries made in the seventeenth century by scientists such as Sir Isaac Newton, Gottfried Leibniz and Robert Hooke, among others. This was the 'century of the genius'. In the footsteps of these natural scientists came, in later centuries, such innovators of technology as James Watt, George and Robert Stephenson, Nikolaus Otto, Rudolph Diesel and Thomas Edison (Singer *et al.*, 1957 to 1978).

The craft of construction was traditionally based on empirical experience, learning by trial and error, success or failure. Its transformation into a modern industry required the application of science, as well as the inspiration of ingenious architects and engineers who were also great inventors or innovators, such as Isambard Kingdom Brunel, Gustave Eiffel, Marie Eugène Freyssinet, Eduardo Torroja and Pier Luigi Nervi. Branches of applied physics such as mechanics, heat and moisture analysis and acoustics emerged. Some mathematical methods were developed specifically for the needs of building and engineering. Much of this knowledge has recently become known as 'building physics', a term that embraces parts of chemistry (corrosion), biology (mould and decay), and medical science, but usually not encompassing mechanics.

Without research, we would never have been able to construct skyscrapers or long-span bridges, develop plant for heating and air-conditioning, or introduce new materials. The results of that research and technology are increasingly transformed into codes, regulations and standards, and are finding their way into educational curricula. This chapter tells the story of how construction has managed to close the gap of knowledge with other industries.

THE BIRTH OF MODERN SCIENCE

STRUCTURAL MECHANICS IN THE SEVENTEENTH AND EIGHTEENTH CENTURIES

Our knowledge about structures has been acquired gradually since the seventeenth century. Initially, this field did not even have a name, and yet it has now become an established group of disciplines. The name index in the *History of Strength of Materials* (Timoshenko, 1953) contains 673 entries!

In 1638, Galileo published *Two New Sciences*, one of which was the mechanics of materials. Galileo erred in his analysis of the flexed beam (Dorn, 1970), but was corrected by the French physicist Edme Marriott in 1680. Newton shares with Leibniz the merit of inventing the differential and integral calculus. Hooke discovered that for elastic materials the distortion or deformation is proportional to the acting forces or stresses (Hooke's law). The Swiss mathematicians from the family Bernoulli applied their calculus to problems in the mechanics of solid bodies. Jacques (or Jakob) Bernoulli was the first to state that at each point, the curvature in a beam's deflection is proportional to the bending moment at that point. Leonhard Euler, who studied for a while under Jean (or Johann) Bernoulli, continued the work on the geometrical forms of elastic curves. This took him to the study of beams as well as columns, more particularly buckling columns, a problem that has kept scientists busy right up to the present day. Joseph Lagrange discovered the possibility of an infinite number of buckling curves (beginning with one half-wave). Charles Augustin de Coulomb combined theoretical and experimental work. His publications demonstrate that he had clear ideas about the distribution of internal forces over the cross-section of a beam, and his theories on friction and torsion are still in use today.

Formal education on structures along with the creation of applied mechanics as a discipline began in France around 1720. The propagators of these studies were the new military schools for artillery and fortification personnel. The professor of mathematics at the School of La Fére was Bernard Forest de Belidor. In *La science des ingénieurs*, (1729) he dealt, among other things, with the statics of retaining walls and the theory of arches and flexure (Dorn, 1970). Following the French example, the English instituted the Woolwich Military Academy in 1741.

Progress in the discipline was marked by controversies, such as that in which John Muller and Thomas Simpson clashed over the design of the Blackfriars Bridge (Chapter 1). Charles Hutton, a professor at Woolwich, published *The Principles of Bridges* in 1772, which contributed to scientific advances and to the establishment of new university chairs (e.g. at Cambridge) in applied mechanics, then termed 'experimental philosophy'.

In many countries, the education of civil engineers was organized after the French model, with the emphasis placed firmly on military matters, bridges and roads (*ponts et chaussées*), such as at the Zurich and Vienna polytechnical institutes, and the Military Academy at West Point in the USA (Timoshenko, 1953). During this period, scientists all over Europe established some kind of national academy for science in their respective countries. The first was in Naples in 1560, followed by Rome in 1603, England in 1662 (the Royal Society), France in 1666 and, somewhat later, Russia in 1725 and Berlin in 1770.

THE STRENGTH OF MATERIALS AND THE ANALYSIS OF STRUCTURES IN THE NINETEENTH CENTURY

The superior mathematical background of scientists in France proved a catalyst in the development of the mathematical basis of the theory of elasticity. Coulomb's work was further developed by the Frenchman Claude Navier, who in 1826 provided the theory of the beam, its behaviour and deflection under load, that is still in contemporary use.

In the theory of the strength of materials it is assumed that the cross-section of the beam remains plane during deformation, and that the material follows Hooke's law (Timoshenko, 1953). It was mainly French scientists (Augustin Cauchy, Siméon Poisson, Bénoit Clapeyron, Barrédes Saint-Venant) who introduced the basic ideas about elasticity. Cauchy made the distinction between strain and stress, and William Rankine was doing similar work in Scotland. The work of Saint-Venant on bending and torsion initiated the combining of the theories on the strength and elasticity of materials. Clapeyron devised equations for the calculation of moments in continuous (multispan) beams. Thomas Young continued Hooke's work by discovering the specific relationship in every material between the tension stress and relative elongation (Young's modulus).

In the UK, industrial development and the needs of the railways served as a backdrop to the development of the science of the strength of materials. Rankine's books (*Applied Mechanics* (1858) and the *Manual of Civil Engineering* (1862)), appeared in more than 40 editions and were used to instruct engineers well into the twentieth century (Dorn, 1970). The Scottish physicist James Clerk Maxwell was one of the most productive scientists of the nineteenth century, and laid down the basis of photoelastic stress analysis.

The first structural materials testing machine was built by the Frenchman Emiland Marie Gauthey. The elastic limit and the fatigue of materials were areas that were exercising scientists such as Friedrich Wöhler, Bauschinger and Kirkaldy. Testing made a significant contribution to the improvement of structural design, and instrumentation was later enhanced, in the twentieth century, by the strain gauge, the tensometer, the deformeter and the computer. In the 1870s Alberto Castigliano devised the first general solution for the design of indeterminate structures by introducing the principles of the strain energy and the least work.

During the last quarter of the nineteenth century several German scientists gained prominence. Especially worthy of mention are Mohr, Bauschinger, Föppl and Engesser. The theory of arches, vaults and trusses led to important and perceptible advances.

Graphostatics (or graphical statics) was introduced by Karl Culmann, a professor in Zurich, and developed by his successor Wilhelm Ritter. Further progress was made by Cremona in his *Graphic Statics* (1872) and Mohr.

THE ORIGINS OF BUILDING PHYSICS

Aristotle believed that heat was a quality, like colour or smell, and that it could therefore not be measured. By the late medieval period, however, heat was recognized to be a quantity, and therefore measurable. Galileo constructed the first thermometer in 1591, and Anders Celsius created the centigrade or Celsius scale for measuring heat in 1742.

What is now called physics was termed 'mixed mathematics' in the eighteenth century, and included, among other subjects, astronomy, optics, statics, hydraulics, geography, navigation, surveying and fortification (Hankins, 1985). At that time the military schools offered the best education in mathematics, most notably the French École Royale de Génie at Mezière.

Robert Boyle, Joseph Louis Gay-Lussac and John Dalton established the basic laws on the volume and pressure of pure and mixed gases. These laws, named after their inventors, form the basis of contemporary building physics. The discovery of the laws of heat and energy (such as the first and second laws of thermodynamics) are associated with a number of scientists, including Nicholas Carnot, James Joule, Rankine, Silvanus Thompson and Hermann von Helmholtz.

The founding fathers of the science of light and optics were Newton and Christian Huygens. Newton and Huygens established the corpuscular and wave concepts, respectively. Both theories survived the unscientific and amateur treatises of the German poet Johann von Goethe, and in the twentieth century the two seemingly conflicting theories were synthesized (Westfall, 1971).

A number of physicists contributed to the theories on electricity (e.g. Luigi Galvani and Alessandro Volta), magnetism and electromagnetism. Among the most notable is Michael Faraday who, together with Peter Barlow, is considered to be the inventor of the electromotor. Important contributions were also made by André Marie Ampère, whose name is immortalized as the unit of current intensity in the same way that Volta and Georg Ohm later gave their names to the units of electric tension and resistance, respectively. Maxwell contributed to science in the fields of heat, electricity, magnetism and the theoretical and mathematical formulation of phenomena of physics. The Maxwell – Boltzmann distribution is named after him and Ludwig Boltzmann, who 'founded' statistical mechanics.

The eighteenth century was both the period of the Enlightenment and the Industrial Revolution. In that period James Watt was one of the creators of the steam engine (1765), a decisive factor in subsequent industrial development. George Stephenson constructed the first steam locomotive in 1814 and built the first railway line in 1821. Otto is considered to be the inventor of the internal combustion engine, building the first in 1876. This initiated the development of the car and the use of motors in industry and oil extraction, leading to the creation of the petrochemical industry.

This condensed history of science and technology (prior to the twentieth century) demonstrates the solid and scientific basis on which the construction of buildings and structures has been founded over the past 300 years.

MATHEMATICS

There have been a great many important and innovative mathematicians over the past 300 years (e.g. Newton, Leibniz, Euler, Gauss, Lagrange and Poisson). As a consequence of their work, there is now a significant body of knowledge available to the engineer. For example, probability theory, a classical branch of mathematics, has, during the past 50 years, found an important application in the solution of technical problems such as structural analysis, by replacing deterministic models with probability-based ones, the introduction of which required the use of mathematical statistics and quality control, both relying extensively on methods of probability.

MATRIX ALGEBRA AND THE THEORY OF GRAPHS

The nineteenth and the twentieth centuries saw the discovery of new branches of mathematics such as the matrix calculus, the theory of graphs and various numerical methods of solving complex problems. The English mathematician Arthur Cayley was the first to publish on matrix algebra (1858), which has since acquired an important place in mathematics. A square or rectangular array of numbers is called a matrix, and the algebra, based upon matrices, finds applications in various engineering fields such as the structural design of tall buildings, long-span roofing membranes and shells. Another field of application is the optimization of engineering or operational research alternatives by using linear and non-linear programming.

The graph theory is another new branch of mathematics. It approaches problems by geometric methods. Although graphs were used much earlier, as in the problem of the bridges at Konigsberg, their theory has been greatly developed following the publication of the monograph by the Hungarian mathematician Denes König in 1936. A graph consists of a set of elements (nodes, vertices, points) and a set of members (edges or arcs) with a relation of incidence that associates each member with a pair of nodes. The best known applications of graph theory are to be found in the network analysis or chart flows, now commonly called the 'critical path method', in the optimization of pipe or conduit networks, in the minimization of travel paths and costs, and in decision trees for decision-making. Problems visualized by graphs can also be transformed into matrices and solved by algebraic methods.

THE FINITE ELEMENTS METHOD

For the numerical solution of engineering problems that cannot be handled with the usual analytical methods, the finite elements method was developed. In finite difference calculus, functions make discrete changes to the argument, whereas in differential and integral calculus, the argument changes continuously. Such calculus began to appear as early as in the works of Pierre de Fermat, Isaac Barrow and Leibniz, but as an independent method it is only some 50 years old. The term 'finite element' was first used only in 1960, however, as structural engineers adopted it. Later the method was also used to solve systems of (partial) differential equations in heat transfer, acoustics, fluid and solid mechanics for which exact solutions were not possible. The differential equations were transformed into forms amenable to numerical approximation (Lewis and Ward, 1991; Reddy, 1993). In the numerical solution of partial differential equations by the finite element method, a system of algebraic equations defining the approximate solutions is introduced. The finite difference approximation provides values of the solution at discrete mesh points of the domain. The problems are usually searched within a certain region of interest within a boundary, and are called boundary value problems (Crouch and Starfield, 1990). (When, as a young researcher, I first applied my own numerical approximation methods to heat transmission problems, I did not realise that I was using a similar method. I based my work on my familiarity with the moment distribution of structural analysis, and even 'enhanced' the solution by applying an alternative, the relaxation method, borrowed from the analysis of rigid-joint frames.)

SOME OTHER TRENDS IN MATHEMATICS

Modern mathematics has many branches and it is impossible to review all the recent trends that find an application in construction. Calculus, algebra, probability, topology, group theory and others are all applied, frequently in combination. For example, the fractal concept, originally developed by the French mathematician Benoit Mandelbrot (1982), may be applied where deterministic models are inadequate and chaos seems to rule. One such application is the study of cracks in concrete, as in fracture or damage mechanics, by fractal considerations (Stroeven, 1994).

According to the romanticized legend, the 20-year-old French mathematician Évariste Galois discovered the group theory in 1832 on the night before he died in a duel. The property or rule by which two members in a group are combined is called the group property or closure. The theory has since become an important component in modern mathematics (Cracknell, 1968).

The chaos theory, devised in the early 1960s by Edward Lorentz in continuation of some earlier work by Jules Henri Poincare, states that minute inaccuracies or uncertainties of initial conditions make it impossible to predict the future precisely.

Large-scale engineering problems may require solutions to hundreds or thousands of linear and/or non-linear equations, which can only be undertaken by modern digital computers. The popularity of numerical methods has therefore progressed hand in hand with the increasing use of computers. Specific engineering problems have led to the elaboration of some specialized mathematical methods. For the purposes of space structures, formex algebra was devised. This consists of two main groups of entities, namely a set of abstract objects called 'formices' and a set of rules through which these objects can be manipulated and related (Nooshin, 1984). Formex algebra (and the interactive programming language Formian based on it) is used for geometric shape modelling (originally for designing geodesic forms and shells), graphics and data generation for finite element analysis programmes. In the generation of geodesic forms, to which we will return later, a polyhedron is transformed to obtain a projection on a surface (sphere, ellipsoid and paraboloid).

COMPUTERS

THE BIRTH AND DEVELOPMENT OF THE COMPUTER

Various early attempts at creating a computer preceded those we have today. Charles Babbage worked on a general purpose mechanical computer at the beginning of the nineteenth century. It was never completed. The principles of his 'analytical engine' were different from those of the modern electronic computer (Wilkie, 1995), based on the binary system, the advantages of which were recognized by John von Neumann (von Neumann, 1959), but in its use of punched cards to store both numbers and the sequence of operations to be performed in many different computations can be seen the germ of the principle behind the modern machines.

In 1937, Alan Turing published a theory of a hypothetical machine and also defined a test that would serve to verify if a computer had 'artificial intelligence': the machine posing as a human being and defying an interrogator to detect the deception. During the 1940s, many worked towards producing an electronic computer, including von Neumann, Presper Eckert, John Mauchley and others (Wilkie, 1995). In 1944, Howard Aiken and a team from IBM built Mark I. In 1946, the 100 ft (30.48 m) long ENIAC (Electronic Numerical Integrator and Calculator), was made, using 18 000 (!) vacuum tubes. UNIVAC I was built in 1951. These first computers using vacuum tubes (valves) as switches were later defined as first-generation machines.

(I myself belong to that dwindling generation who worked on vacuum tube computers. In the heat of summer I had to visit the computer at night because during the daytime its vacuum tubes would overheat. It was like paying clandestine visits to a secret love, which in a way it was at that time.)

The second generation of computers was based on the solid-state transistor, invented in 1948, which replaced the vacuum tube. The increasing use of integrated fabrication techniques resulted in the third generation in about 1964 and the fourth in about 1970, the latter computers characterized by the use of 'chip' technology. This is the popular name for a small integrated circuit package containing many logic elements. It is the product of the semiconductor industry and can store information. Personal computers (PCs) appeared in the 1970s, and by the end of the decade these could be used as workstations, suitable for applications that had previously been restricted to large computers (mainframes).

Fifth-generation computers have large store areas and fast processing capability, and are able to interact with people and share the resources of a network (see later). The capabilities of computers (including personal computers) are continuously being enhanced, and interaction with them, i.e. active communication between the user and the computer, has become more general (Newman and Lamming, 1995).

> Today, a few thousand dollars will purchase a personal computer that has more performance, more main memory, and more disk storage than a computer bought in 1965 for a million dollars.

> *Patterson and Hennessy, 1990*

The production of mainframes catapulted IBM into the league of industrial giants. Subsequently, it was the manufacturers of personal computers (in descending order of PCs sold, Compaq, IBM, Apple, Packard Bell and NEC) and their component parts (e.g. chip-producers Intel, NEC, Toshiba, Hitachi and Motorola) that experienced spectacular growth. More recently, the software developers (Microsoft, Oracle, Computer Ass. Int., Novell, SAPAG and Sybase) have taken the lead. Today there are some 200 million computers in the world, with 40% of all homes in North America, and 20% of all households in Western Europe now having one or more PCs. Some 60 million computers are sold annually worldwide at present.

TELEPROCESSING, NETWORKS, PROGRAMMING LANGUAGES AND OPERATIVE SYSTEMS

In parallel with the development of the computer itself (the 'hardware'), great advances have also been made in the programming and actual use of the machines (the 'software'). In the 1950s, computers were typically placed in a central area and users had to visit the computers to use them. Teleprocessing was introduced in the 1960s, giving access to computers via the telephone line. Later, time-sharing was introduced, whereby remotely located users could communicate through the telephone line with the computer, using teletype or a typewriter terminal. Databases, which are computerized record-keeping systems like a kind of electronic filing cabinet, have also been established for machines of all sizes from minicomputers to the largest mainframes. Initially independent, personal computers may now be connected to central processing units and may thus make use of common resources such as printers and data files.

Area networks have been established on a local basis (local area networks, LANs) or for a wider area (metropolitan, regional, national, international and global). Networking is growing, and many PC users subscribe to commercial on-line network systems such as America Online, Compuserve (both with over 3 million users) and Prodigy in the USA. Europe lags somewhat behind North America in this respect. LANs offer advantages such as data sharing, service sharing, better security and electronic mail over stand-alone machines (Flowers, 1996). The Internet network was originally established for military researchers in the USA. The appearance of the World Wide Web, linking multimedia documents over the Internet, contributed to its spread around the world. It now connects some 60 million users worldwide, and the number of subscribers continues to grow rapidly: there could be 500 million by the year 2000. The Internet service available varies widely, starting with the basic level accessed through a modem telephone connection, up to levels that include electronic mail (e-mail), bulletin boards and so on. For large users, speed may be a restriction and new ways have been introduced to overcome this, e.g. Concert Internetplus (Summers and Dunetz, 1996).

The original languages (Fortran, Cobol, Algol, etc.) that were used to instruct the computer (Wexelblat, 1981) have increasingly been replaced by operating systems, which allocate resources in the hardware for the execution of processes or programs without the need for operator intervention (Barrett and Wagner, 1996). The most commonly used operating systems are those of Microsoft (Windows), IBM (OS/2) and Apple, all of which can be supplied with additional hardware and software packages that enhance the capacity and functions. The main types of network operating systems are Netware, LAN Manager, IBM LAN Server, UNIX and OS/2 (Hunter, 1995).

There is currently a trend away from large centralized host computers towards distributed systems of different sizes that communicate and interact across a network. These can be accessed by network computers (NCs), which can be cheaper than PCs (Hunter, 1995), (Chapter 8).

COMPUTER GRAPHICS, COMPUTER-AIDED DESIGN AND 'VIRTUAL REALITY'

The basic documentation of construction consists of the drawings that define the plans and the details of the building or structure. The drawings are prepared during the design process, which encompasses many disciplines: architecture, structure, mechanical and electrical engineering, and quantity surveying. Since the 1960s, computers have been able to assist in the design process with the development of computer graphics and, subsequently visualization has reached a high level (Gallagher, 1995).

Architectural computer-aided design (CAD) is used for the modelling of buildings, most of which are complex products. A building consists of spaces, enclosing structures, surfaces, joints, internal structures and services. A large number of modelling methods has been developed for architectural use. There are also programs that produce optimal floor plans of dwellings or commercial buildings. Each branch of engineering design has its own specific requirements when designing and preparing its drawings. CAD can develop methods for each branch, and, more efficient still, can devise methods that can be used by every design branch. Design time can be reduced with CAD, although still more 'user-friendly' methods are needed (Carrara and Kalay, 1994). Modern drawing management systems are more effective when used as part of a network and when files are stored on a server (see below).

Various images (stereo, axonometric or in perspective) and animation can be generated by computer programs. A design model can be demonstrated from a moving perspective, and computer-generated holograms can further enhance the design model. Such solutions are now being termed 'virtual reality' models, and research is ongoing to make virtual reality systems applicable to practical purposes (Smeltzer, 1994). Sensors, head-mounted displays, joysticks, control systems and transputers, are all used to produce virtual reality images, and when these are in stereo, special glasses are also required. Virtual reality images can serve both the lay public and the specialist.

PARALLEL PROCESSING AND OTHER TRENDS

The speed and capacity of computers is increasing as a result of the development of new chips, among other reasons. Multiprocessors employ a number of processors working from the same memory. An increase in the number of multiprocessor systems enables multiple activities or operations to be executed simultaneously by different processors. This parallelism provides 'scale-up' and 'speed-up' in the use of the computer, both of which are favourable for customers. One of the fastest networks at the moment is SuperJanet (Super Joint Academic Network by the UK Education and Research Networking Association, UKERNA) in the UK, which links about 60 universities and research centres. Its top speed is 155 million bits a second. At this speed, the London telephone directory could be transmitted in less than one-tenth of a second. Fastethernet is another fast network (100 million bits per second), supported by various network equipment manufacturers (Johnson, 1996).

Although most advanced computers have reached considerable computing speeds, very large computations require even faster output. However, there seem to be practical limitations to this evolution, and only the massive parallel computer is generally considered capable of breaking through current limits (Kato *et al.*, 1993). Such computers may have several hundred microprocessors, and their calculation speed is much greater than that of the largest mainframes. By combining, for example, 100 microprocessors each with a performance of 100 million instructions per second, it is now possible to gain supercomputer performance at a fraction of the cost of a supercomputer (Adeli and Kamal, 1993).

The 1990s saw the dawn of a new period: the combination of computers and telecommunications, often called 'interactive multimedia'. The trend towards smaller, faster and cheaper computers may be attained in the future by new breakthroughs such as single electron devices, molecular computing, nanomechanical logic gates and reversible gates. To complement these, wide geographical areas can be covered by the use of fibreoptic cables (Wilkie, 1995).

Configurable computing is being developed to increase computing speed. This is achieved by using hardware circuits that can be modified at almost any point during use with very low configuration time in response to changes in the input data or processing environment.

STRUCTURAL ANALYSIS IN THE TWENTIETH CENTURY

Structural design is the engineering application of structural analysis, which is itself an application of structural mechanics, a derivative branch of mechanics, and a sector of physics.

A GENERAL SURVEY

(When I started my engineering studies in the late 1930s, I remember being shown the graphostatics drawings made by my father as part of his civil engineering studies in the 1900s (he graduated in 1907). Besides graphostatics, my studies included the classic calculations. We learned with enthusiasm the then brand-new method of analysing rigid-joint frames by successive approximations developed by Hardy Cross, the 'moment distribution method'. We also experimented with its alternatives, such as the relaxation method (Southwell, 1936)).

The development of the analysis and construction of structures in the twentieth century was marked by the publication of several excellent books, including those by Mörsch (1902–1922), Lorenz (1913), Flügge (1934) and Girkmann (1956). A new revolution in structural analysis started in the late 1930s and 1940s with the study of behaviour when nearing collapse or at the ultimate strength. This led to 'plastic' or 'limit' state design.

In the USA, Galambos and colleagues (1982) have listed the following major structural engineering advances since the Second World War (the engineer who has achieved much in that particular field is shown in brackets):

- theory of plasticity (W. Prager)
- reliability theory (A. Freudenthal)
- finite element analysis (R. Clough)
- stability theory (F.R. Shanley)
- dynamic analysis (N. Newmark)
- expert systems (S. Fenves).

Galambos has himself made several important contributions to the field.

Structural analysis has been supported by developments in instrumentation, particularly that for measuring strains from which internal stresses could be calculated. The electrical resistance strain gauge appeared in the USA during the late 1930s and has gradually become a universal tool in building research.

The theory of structures has progressed considerably during the past 50 years. New models have been developed and validated through control calculations, experiments and practice. The most important progress in structural analysis has been the advent of electronic computation. The creative designs of shells, bridges, space trusses and skyscrapers have all contributed to new developments in structural design.

THE NEW PRINCIPLES OF STRUCTURAL DESIGN

Structural design is based on structural analysis, which comprises the calculation of stress, strain and deflection. In this design, certain assumptions have to be made about the behaviour of the structure and its materials.

The most important progress made in structural design during the past few decades has been the change from the purely deterministic models and design with permissible stresses, towards probability-based models and design for ultimate or limit states. This process has occurred in parallel with the abandoning of the strictly elastic and linear models in favour of other models that offer varying degrees of plasticity and non-linearity. Previously, structural design was based on empirical knowledge and experiments. Nowadays, computational mechanics, i.e. the modelling of reality, reduce the need for experimentation, although this still remains important for the validation of models (Kersken-Bradley *et al.*, 1991; Ladevèze and Zienkewicz, 1992). Under the former method of structural design, the stresses caused by the design load were not to exceed a certain allowable stress, which was then deemed to be the failure stress after the reduction by a safety factor. The method did not ensure consistent levels of safety and performance in all members of the structure, and there were differences in design strategy for different materials. A major innovation in design, reflected in the current codes, has been the introduction of limit state design, together with the partial factor format. The designer has to prove that all the structures and components would resist, with reasonable safety, the worst expected loads and deformations that could occur, and that they have adequate durability for their intended lifetime. The structure is supposed to fail when it can no longer meet the following two limit states:

- the ultimate limit states causing failure, including instability
- the serviceability limit states comprising deformations.

The adverse combinations of random effects also have to be considered by the designer. In this, partial safety factors reflect certain contingencies and the probability that any particular limit state will be reached must be below certain values. Ultimate limit states correspond to the following adverse states:

- loss of equilibrum of the structure or a part thereof
- attainment of the maximum resistance capacity of sections, members, or connections by rupture, fatigue, corrosion, or excessive deformation
- transformation of the structure or part of it into a mechanism
- instability of the structure or part of it
- sudden change of the assumed structural system into a new system
- unacceptable or excessive deformation.

For each specific limit state, the relevant basic variables should be identified. These variables are characterized by actions and environmental influences, the properties of materials and soils, and by geometric parameters. The choice of the various levels of reliability should take account of the possible consequences of failure in terms of risk to life or injury, the potential economic losses, and the degree of social inconvenience. Such a choice should also take account of the amount of expense and effort required to reduce the risk of failure.

When designing a structure, it must be decided whether a simple or more complicated model should be selected. Simple models make calculations easy, but their exactitude may be limited. Complicated models reflect behaviour better, but calculations are more complex and errors overlooking failure modes can occur. Structural design makes use of computer science as well as numerical analysis, the latter forming the basis of continually evolving computer software programs.

Actions on structures can be random or dynamic, following some regular function. The analysis of structure, responding to random dynamic actions such as wind and earthquakes, can be extremely complex. Therefore, whenever possible without endangering safety, dynamic response is simplified by static analysis. The parameters in structural analysis (such as the modulus of elasticity, yield limit, ultimate strength, etc.) are generally considered to be random variables, and eventually also to be time-dependent. Design frequently assumes elastic behaviour under low-action effects, and plastic behaviour under high-action effects.

FRACTURE MECHANICS

Most research in structural analysis is aimed at obtaining better knowledge of the behaviour of structures and their materials under actions and loads. This is then combined with progress in theoretical modelling of the physical reality and better calculation models. In structural computation, the extent of damage is evaluated and compared with one or more ultimate states. The possibility of the occurrence of defects and cracks is taken into account and fracture mechanics, which studies the conditions around cracks, is therefore widely used.

Fracture mechanics is a part of the branch of science that is concerned with the strength of materials. Extreme or prolonged loading of a solid body causes large deformation or fracture, a separation of parts of the body. Fracture mechanics studies these conditions. Fracture mechanics is faced with different phenomena for individual materials. Cracks in concrete are common and have various characteristics; the significance of cracks in reinforced concrete can vary (Elfgren, 1989; Elfgren and Shah, 1991). In timber structures, cracks may frequently develop at points with high concentrated stress, such as in notched beams or around holes in glulam or timber beams. In steel, cracks due to fatigue are typical (Carpinteri, 1994). Currently, there is progress towards damage mechanics, which allows the forecasting of conditions prior to the appearance of macroscopic cracks.

STRUCTURAL DESIGN CODES

As knowledge about structural design grew, it gradually found its way from scientific publications into practical recommendations, and later formed the basis of national and international codes. While it may seem unusual to demonstrate development through the growing details of codes, an example of this type may be appropriate. The total number of pages of the US AISC Specification was 15 in 1923. In 1986 the same document consisted of 219 pages (Galambos, 1990).

The limit state design method was introduced soon after 1945 in the structural codes of eastern European countries. In the USA, this method was first introduced as an alternative for both steel and reinforced concrete structures in 1959, but progressed slowly. Limit state design was only officially approved for bridges in the USA in 1976. The US ANSI A.58.1 Load Code, based on load and resistance factor and probability-based design principles, was published in 1982.

The international standard ISO 2394 *General Principles for the Verification of the Safety of Structures* has been the basis for harmonizing structural design rules on an international level. In 1974, several international organizations, including IABSE, CIB, CEB, FIP, RILEM and ECCS, agreed to set up the Joint Committee for Structural Safety (JCSS) in order to prepare internationally harmonized codes for structural design. At the end of the 1970s, the Commission of the (then) European Economic Community (EEC) began work on the Eurocodes, making use of the JCSS' results. This activity was transferred to the European Committee for Standardization (CEN) at the end of 1989. The basic EEC guidelines on the Eurocodes was formulated in the interpretative document *Mechanical Resistance and Stability*. This defined the general requirements relating to the safety of construction work (Eurocode No. 1, 1995).

In 1990 CEN created the Technical Committee TC 250 to continue work on the following Eurocodes (CEN numbers ENV 1991 to ENV 1999):

- Basis of Design and Actions; Part I: Basis of Design (Background Documentation, 1995).
- Concrete, reinforced concrete and pre-stressed concrete structures.
- Steel structures.
- Composite steel and concrete structures.
- Timber structures.
- Masonry structures.
- Foundations and geotechnical engineering.
- Structures in seismic zones.
- Aluminium structures.

Some of the special codes are discussed in Chapter 5 in the sections on concrete, reinforced concrete, steel, aluminium and timber structures.

The codes and standards of our time reflect the most up-to-date knowledge on structural analysis, but research is continuing for further perfection (Ellingwood *et al.*, 1982; Beedle, 1990).

Some of the best designers in the past were also great innovators of construction, and this was part of their creative work. Although innovative structural design makes use of existing standards and codes, it also prepares the ground for their improvements. While modern structural design remains a creative art, it is also a process that should be based on a knowledge of the most recent scientific achievements. Structural analysis has played a significant part in transforming the construction craft into a modern industry.

SOME FASCINATING EXTERNAL LINKS

While building research and structural engineering are matters of intellectual interest, they have only an indirect relevance to the practice of construction, so this is just a brief look at the use made of research in these areas by sectors other than construction. (e.g. manufacturing). The testing equipment developed for structural analysis is used to test cars, buses, aircraft, cables, safe boxes, etc. For example, the Swiss Federal Testing Institute (Eidgenössische Material – und Prüfungsanstalt, EMPA) was specifically established to serve various economic sectors, and wind tunnels are widely used for testing outside the construction industry (Potthoff *et al.*, 1994). The following fascinating cases prove that distant fields obey similar or identical laws of nature.

> In 1834, Scott Russell was watching a barge being drawn along the Edinburgh to Glasgow canal by a pair of horses. Suddenly the barge was stopped. The water was thrown into some agitation. After a short time a solitary wave of simple form emerged and began to move steadily along the canal.
>
> *Wilkie, 1995*

Russell observed the wave on horseback for some time. When a large solitary wave started behind a small one, it could pass through the small one almost without interference. This phenomenon was described in mathematical terms only in 1967 by the Kortweg-de Vries equation, the analytical solution found for the behaviour and propagation of isolated waves called solitons travelling without a change of form (Drazin, 1983). Naturally, this phenomenon is important in designing and building embankments, dikes, dams and sluices. In the twentieth century, however, it has been found that solitons also occur in a quite different field,

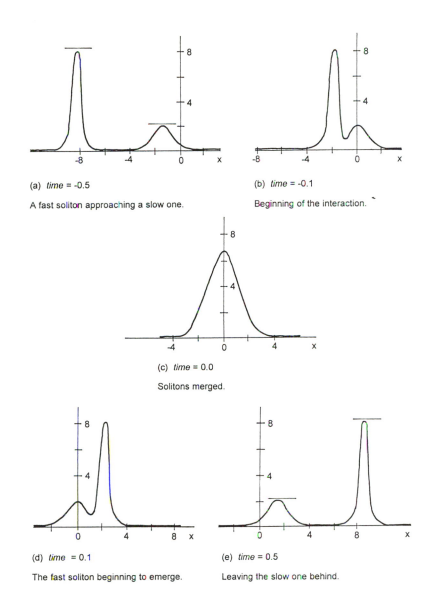

(a) *time* = -0.5

A fast soliton approaching a slow one.

(b) *time* = -0.1

Beginning of the interaction.

(c) *time* = 0.0

Solitons merged.

(d) *time* = 0.1

The fast soliton beginning to emerge.

(e) *time* = 0.5

Leaving the slow one behind.

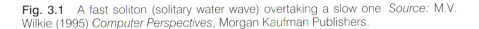

Fig. 3.1   A fast soliton (solitary water wave) overtaking a slow one. *Source:* M.V. Wilkie (1995) *Computer Perspectives*, Morgan Kaufman Publishers.

namely in optical fibres. The use of fibreoptic cables as a transmission medium allows wide geographical areas to be covered. The transmission of messages is not only fast but, more importantly, free of interference.

Construction engineers have sometimes initiated research in fields quite different from their own in order to obtain answers to their problems. For example, to improve lightweight cable structures, research was carried out on the spider's web (*Araneus diadematus*) (Perry, 1995).

Chemical researchers working on interstellar dust and graphite vaporization discovered in 1985 ('serendipitously', as they put it) that a pure carbon cluster of 60 atoms forms a molecule that has the same shape as that of a geodesic dome patented earlier for the purpose of dome structures. The inventor, the American Richard Buckminster Fuller called a dome geodesic if the lines (bars) of a three-way grid on the surface of a sphere are geodesics, i.e. great circles of the sphere. This can be obtained most easily if equal regular triangulation is made on all faces of an icosahedron, and the resulting network is projected from the centre of the icosahedron on to the surface of its circumsphere (Kroto and Walton, 1993). Buckminster Fuller coined the word 'Tensegrity', a contraction of tensional integrity. In tensegrity structures, a continuous network of tensile elements interacts with a discontinuous set of compression elements

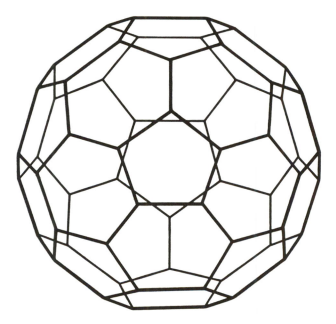

Fig. 3.2 C60 buckminsterfullerene: a carbon molecule discovered in interstellar dust with the same form as geodesic domes. *Source:* H. W. Kroto and D. R. M. Walton (eds) (1993) *The Fullerenes*, Cambridge University Press.

(Pugh, 1976; see also Chapter 6). Chemical researchers gave the new molecule the name 'Buckminsterfullerene' (also known as a buckyball or fullerene), and it seems to have potential in the fields of semiconductors, microscopic engineering, pharmaceuticals and polymers (Billups and Ciufolini, 1993). Later it was found that certain viruses also have the structure of fullerenes (Tarnai *et al.*, 1995), and this explains why structural engineering researchers (Nooshin, Huybers, Happold, Berger, Geiger, Bini, Tarnai, Levy) found themselves in the company of chemical researchers (Kroto, Smalley) in 1996 at the event marking the 100th anniversary of the birth of Buckminster Fuller (1895).

The link between such widely different disciplines was preceded and accompanied by research in pure mathematics and geometry on placing figures on planes, spheres and in space (Fejes Toth, 1964; Tarnai and Gaspar, 1987). Moreover, crystallography also has an interest in these problems.

These examples should be sufficient to illustrate the point: building research has gone a long way from pure empiricism and is now gradually becoming a valued partner in modern science.

STRUCTURES IN SEISMIC ZONES

This and the following section consider structural analysis for seismic actions and wind. These are actions that require fundamental considerations and in which much progress has been attained. Other actions such as impact, explosion, etc. are not specifically discussed here, although adequate analysis methods are also available for these.

EARTHQUAKES: MAGNITUDE AND INTENSITY

According to the theory of plate tectonics, the Earth's crust consists of 12–15 plates that move over the viscous mantle in relation to each other. Stresses build up between plates as a consequence, and these cause earthquakes (Levy and Salvadori, 1995). The shape of some plates is relatively well known, such as the dividing line between the Eurasian and North American plates in the Atlantic Ocean. The same applies to the dividing line in the eastern Pacific Ocean, but not to that in the region around Japan and Siberia. It is difficult to foresee earthquakes. The earthquake at Kobe in 1995 occurred along a tectonic fault of secondary importance that until then had been more or less ignored.

Fractures or faulting of the earth's crust can cause earthquakes. During an earthquake two types of waves are produced: pressure or primary waves, and shear or secondary waves. The different velocity of the two types makes it possible to calculate the distance between an observation point and the source of the earthquake. The centre of an earthquake inside the earth is called the focus or hypocentre, and the point on the earth's surface directly above it is called the epicentre. Earthquakes induce ground tremors that may be described as a series of multidirectional random acceleration pulses. The duration of the ground oscillations in an earthquake is usually less than 1 second near the epicentre, but increases with distance. The amplitude of an earthquake may vary from 1 mm (in a mild shock) to 70 mm and even 220 mm in a destructive or devastating quake, respectively.

Earthquakes and their destruction have been recorded since ancient times, and considerable efforts have been concentrated on research into understanding the causes, predicting quakes and designing buildings to withstand them (Green, 1987; Fajfar and Krawinkler, 1992). Over the centuries, earthquakes around both sides of the Pacific Ocean, around the Mediterranean Sea and in the Middle East have caused catastrophies, claiming the lives of millions of people: 50 000 people perished in the Lisbon earthquake in 1755; the Tokyo earthquake in 1923 left 142 000 people dead; the one in Tangshan, China, in 1976 claimed 240 000 victims.

Earthquake engineering is a relatively new discipline. For example, in Japan it can be traced back only as far as 1892, one year after the Nohbi earthquake. The first 147 m high building in Japan, the Kasumigaseki building, was built as recently as 1968, using an earthquake-resistant design.

The disturbance caused by an earthquake is measured by its magnitude. Charles Richter, a seismologist at the California Institute of Technology in Pasadena, devised the scale that bears his name to measure the magnitude of earthquakes in 1935. According to this, an earthquake that causes a 0.001 mm movement of a certain instrument at a distance of 100 km from the epicentre has a magnitude of 1, while movement of 0.01 mm has a magnitude of 2. The scale thus grows by powers of ten from 0 to 8.9, the largest earthquake measured to date. Advances have been made since in seismology and a more refined scale is used nowadays, although it is still called the 'Richter scale'. This new scale is based on the measurement of the strength of very long period waves.

The effect of an earthquake at a particular location is defined by its intensity, commonly measured on the modified Mercalli scale, a standard used since 1931. It is not a precise scale, however, as the damage to buildings and the human perception of the earthquake influence it. The scale grades earthquakes from 1 (very weak, felt by few people, if any) to 12 (total destruction).

THE IMPACT OF EARTHQUAKES ON STRUCTURES

An earthquake at a particular site is defined by the maximum level of ground motion or, more recently, by the spectral acceleration, ground velocity and displacement, peak horizontal and vertical accelerations and duration of strong tremors. A number of ground motion models has been devised, and these can serve as the basis for a probabilistic design as well as for the reliability analysis of existing structures (Ellingwood, 1994).

The response of a building to the ground motion depends on the stiffness or flexibility of the structure, its natural frequency, its damping capacity and ductility, the behaviour of the soil and foundations, and the character and duration of the earthquake. All this can now be modelled and computed adequately, although interaction between the foundations and soils and the behaviour of soils must be investigated further.

Buildings and structures vibrate in response to an earthquake. The level of vibration depends on the building's natural period of vibration frequency, which is shorter for stiff structures. Tall buildings tend to be more more flexible than low ones. Resonance occurs when the natural period of vibration is equal to the ground's earthquake period, and this increases the risk of collapse. One important property is ductility, which is the ability of the material or structure to bend, stretch and twist beyond its elastic limit without breaking or suffering significant loss of load-bearing capacity. It has been recognized that constructing buildings with greater ductility is of increasing importance.

Previously, structural design aimed to achieve earthquake-resistant structures. The new thinking retains this idea for small or moderate earthquakes, but combines resistance with controlling and damping the structure's response to the earthquake. Buildings should thus remain structurally undamaged during moderate earthquakes, and be able to dissipate sufficient energy to avoid structural collapse during severe earthquakes by, for example, incorporating failure points that break to prevent total collapse. Similar principles apply to designing against the impact of wind.

STRUCTURAL DAMPING: PASSIVE AND ACTIVE

Structural damping is the ability of the structural system to dissipate the energy from vibration due to an earthquake or wind. As a result of damping, the structure's own vibration, and therefore the damaging impact of the earthquake, is reduced. Damping can be increased by passive and/or active systems.

Passive systems do not require external energy, which means that they are effective without the need for any electrical devices. The two basic passive systems are base isolation (elastomeric) and mechanical damping (sliding). The base-isolation systems have a relatively low horizontal rigidity, i.e. their fundamental period is longer than that of a building without base isolation. Laminated rubber bearings that separate the structure from its base foundation have a damping effect and reduce the vibration of a building's superstructure. Passive mechanical damping can be achieved with various devices, such as diagonal cross-shaped bracing with sliding cylinders. The braking function of the cylinders absorbs energy, thus reducing the vibration of the structure. Friction-based frame and magnetic damping devices are alternative solutions. A new idea for passive damping is a system based on a rigid container with a liquid, such as silicon oil, inside. This absorbs and dissipates the vibration energy.

An active system uses a mechanical device, usually installed on the top floor of the building. This acts on the response of the building to the ground motion of an earthquake or on wind loading, and reduces the building's vibration amplitude.

Active and passive systems can be combined in the same building. In such hybrid arrangements the active device protects against weak and moderate earthquakes, while the passive system operates during severe earthquakes.

LESSONS FROM EARTHQUAKES

Earthquake monitoring over the past 20 years has provided an increasing amount of data on ground motion and the reaction of structures. Monitoring includes an increasing number of systematic post-earthquake studies, the installation of instruments in seismic regions, and structural monitoring. The studies carried out have also provided principles and data on zoning and microzoning (Rosenblueth and Garcia-Perez, 1994). Ground motions have been observed in the USA and Japan since about 1932 to 1933, and more pertinent statistical data are still to be collected. The recently introduced model codes can now cope adequately with problems of seismic design. Nevertheless, further research is needed because site effects in some recent earthquakes, for instance, were different from those anticipated in design. In addition, realistic models have to be developed for shear, flexure, eventual progressive collapse and soil liquefaction (which is the change of sandy or silty soils into a mixture with a soupy consistency following saturation with water).

The Mexico City earthquake in 1985 had a magnitude of 8.1 and a maximum intensity on the modified Mercalli scale of 9 and 10. Many medium- and high-rise buildings were damaged, most in the lake zone where the poor subsoil characteristics amplified movements. Many damaged structures had vibration periods near or equal to 2 seconds, i.e. the same as ground motions of long duration. Some of the most common damage included diagonal cracking and buckling of reinforcement in concrete structures, pounding of adjacent buildings, column failures due to bending, axial compression and shear failure.

The 1989 Loma Prieta earthquake in California had a surface-wave magnitude of 7.1, but strong shakings lasted only about 10–15 seconds.

The peak horizontal ground acceleration was 0.64 g (64% of gravity); the vertical acceleration was 0.47 and both had nearly equal amplitudes. While unreinforced masonry buildings were damaged, the Bay Bridge remained intact. Structures sited on deep loose soil were particularly vulnerable (Lew *et al.*, 1990).

The earthquake in Northridge, USA, in 1994 had a surface magnitude of 6.8. Strong shakings lasted about 15 seconds. The peak horizontal acceleration was 0.25–1.00 g, and the peak vertical acceleration was 0.48 g. In terms of its magnitude, it was not a large earthquake, but severe damage was nevertheless caused because the epicentre happened to be in a populated urban area. Fires drew particular attention to the importance of this risk (Todd *et al.*, 1994).

In Kobe, Japan, the 1995 earthquake reached a magnitude of 7.2. Maximum accelerations were 0.5–1.0 g, maximum velocities were 50 cm/s. The lateral shaking was considerably more violent than expected because local faults and soft ground amplified it. In total, 74 000 houses were destroyed and the cost of the damage caused exceeded US$100 billion. This earthquake was another warning that, despite progress, perseverance with research was needed (Sato, 1995; Somerville, 1995). The Akashi-Kaikyo Suspension Bridge, with a center span of 2022 m and not too far from Kobe, was under construction at the the time of Kobe earthquake. Investigations have shown that the foundations of the towers (about 300 m high) suffered a small displacement. This was then able to be taken into consideration during the process of the construction (Tada, 1995).

Recent earthquakes have demonstrated the superior performance of structures that have been designed according to the most recent codes and knowledge compared with those designed and built previously or without consideration to seismic hazards. Obviously, knowledge and experience continue to accrue from the most recent earthquakes, and codes and structural design have consequently to be improved still further (*NEHRP Handbook*, 1992; *Preliminary Reconnaissance Report*, 1995). Indeed, codes and standards are constantly under review. On the international scene, the International Association for Earthquake Engineering published its seismic code in 1982. At the instigation of the European Union (EU), CEN published its Eurocode 8 on structures in seismic zones in 1993. Eurocode 8 differentiates between countries with low seismic activity and those with a strong likelihood of earthquakes, and envisages the subdivision of national territories into seismic zones. For design purposes, the peak ground acceleration is defined and represented by an elastic response spectrum described by three translational and three rotational components. The rotational components are considered for tall buildings and bridge piers only. Three profiles of soil are defined: rock and stiff soil; medium soil; and loose granular soil and clay with reduced stiffness. Lifelines (bridges, pipelines and railways) are very important, and automatic supply-shut off and stop systems should be installed to restrict the consequential damage of earthquakes (*Wind and Seismic Effects*, 1994).

Despite our progress in earthquake-resistant construction, we need to enhance our knowledge of construction in seismic areas still further since movements in the crust of our planet will continue to cause earthquakes. It is clearly not possible to make buildings completely safe from damage, but improvements are both possible and necessary. The best that can be hoped for is damage limitation and the avoidance or minimization of casualties. In any case, the progress already made in seismic design has allowed tall buildings and long-span structures to be built in seismic regions such as California and Japan.

WIND

THE WIND LOAD

Wind is the result of a number of factors such as atmospheric pressure differences, differential radiation of the sun, and the rotation, curvature and surface characteristics of the earth. It consists of two components: a steady flow; and a turbulent fluctuating system. The first has a mean wind speed; the second, a fluctuating velocity due to turbulence or gusting. The dynamic component causes vibration and flutter of structures (CIB 193, 1996).

Strong winds such as hurricanes and typhoons have destroyed many buildings, bridges and other structures. It has been estimated that an average of 250 000 buildings are damaged during windstorms in the UK each year. The annual repair cost amounts to £60 million and this does not include secondary costs and consequential damage. In single severe storms, such as in those in 1976, 1987 and 1990, in Japan, more than 1 million buildings can be damaged (Blackmore, 1995). Climatic models and actual weather reports suggest that the increase in greenhouse gases in atmospheric air is changing the world's climate, which will lead to stronger winds in some regions and weaker winds in others. This, in turn, could have an impact on current codes and structural design principles (Collier *et al.*, 1994). The increase in the number of buildings and structures that are vulnerable to wind requires a thorough study of wind action and structural response.

The Saffir/Simpson scale defines five hurricane strengths with wind speed in the strongest category (5) exceeding 249 km/h. Recent hurricanes in the USA destroyed tens of thousands of homes (hurricanes Camille, 1969; Hugo, Cat. 5, 1989; Andrew, Cat. 4, 1992). Hurricanes, typhoons, earthquakes, landslides, vulcanic eruptions can be followed by tsunamis which are impulsively generated ocean waves. Wave heights

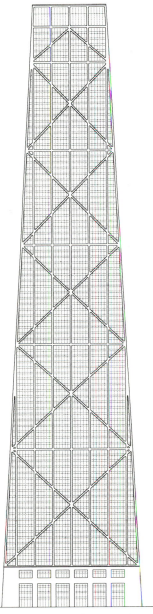

Fig. 3.3 Hancock Building, Chicago, USA: exterior diagonal bracing. *Source: Courtesy of Messrs F. Sebestény and P. Rabb, Technical University of Budapest, Faculty of Architecture.*

can reach up to 10 m, even 30 m in exceptional cases, and can cause major destruction. Appropriate design and construction can reduce damage even in family houses, for example by using adequate soil anchoring (Marshall, 1993, 1994).

STRUCTURAL RESPONSE TO WIND

Large stiff structures follow fluctuating wind without appreciable amplification or attenuation. Such structures may be analysed under the action of static equivalent wind force. The response of large flexible structures depends on the frequency range of the impacting fluctuating wind force. The dynamic response of the structure will be amplified at frequencies at or near its natural frequency. Such structures are classified as 'dynamic', and the dynamic stresses to be expected should be determined. An excessively flexible structure may produce instability, which may necessitate a change in the design.

Wind induces along-wind and cross-wind motions on the façades of tall buildings. Along-wind motions, primarily caused by the buffeting effects of turbulence, are calculated by using the gust factor, which depends on the properties of the structure and the characteristics of the wind. Cross-wind motions, which cause movements of the building and its internal spaces, adversely affect the comfort of the occupants.

A.G. Davenport, a world-renowned wind analysis researcher, has listed the following imperatives in the wind-related structural design of major buildings:

- the mapping of pressure coefficients over the surface of a building
- the estimation of internal pressures, which are dependent on the leakage characteristics of the building
- the determination of the resultant forces and moments that must be resisted by the building's structural system
- motions such as displacements and accelerations
- the measurement of wind in the streets nearby
- the measurement of the aeroelastic derivatives
- the forces due to the motion of the structure
- the dispersion of pollutants.

HEAT, MOISTURE AND INDOOR AIR

The thermal environment has become an important component of human comfort and satisfaction. The first requirement is to ensure good temperature conditions in buildings, and this is closely connected with appropriate humidity content and other parameters (draught etc.) of the indoor air. Thermal problems are a subset of thermodynamics and the science of the properties of moist air (i.e. of air mixed with water vapour), is called psychrometrics. The purity or pollution of indoor air and its impact on the occupants of buildings are discussed later.

HEAT TRANSFER

We would expect that temperature (or in more general terms thermal conditions) in buildings should satisfy the majority of occupants. To be able to assess thermal conditions, the thermal process (termed heat transfer) has to be considered. Heat transfer is the transmission of energy by thermal conduction, convection, or radiation, or a combination of the three. Heat is transferred under steady state or under non-steady conditions. Completely steady conditions scarcely exist in real life, but if conditions change only slightly they are approximated and assumed to be steady-state (ISO 9251). Non-steady conditions can be periodic, transient or random. Much of our knowledge about heat transfer was created during past centuries and applied to buildings in the twentieth century. By the 1930s, our basic knowledge about heat transfer was available and published (Fishenden and Saunders, 1932; Dufton, 1933; Beckett, 1936).

The most important element in heat-flow calculations is the determination of the quantity of heat through building components and elements. The quantity of heat passing through a wall or other component is proportional to the thermal transmittance of the construction. This has been annotated in some countries by the symbol 'k', but the symbol 'U' has now been accepted internationally. A building component that has constant thickness and thermal properties that are uniform or can be regarded as being uniform, is considered to be thermally homogeneous. A solid brick or concrete wall is accepted to be thermally homogeneous (ISO 6946/1).

The inverse of thermal transmittance is thermal resistance, for which the symbol 'R' is used. The thermal resistance is directly proportional to the thickness of the component and inversely proportional to the thermal conductivity (transmissivity) of the material used. The Greek letter λ (lambda) is used as the symbol of thermal conductivity (transmissivity) which depends on the properties of the material and its moisture content (ISO 10051). There are accepted methods of calculating the thermal resistance in more complicated cases, such as multilayer components, for air layers (unventilated, slightly ventilated, or well ventilated), for windows and other glazed surfaces, and for thermal bridges. The heat flow is also affected by its direction, which may be upwards, downwards, or horizontal, and by the boundary conditions, i.e. whether the structure is surrounded by external air, unheated internal space (such as a roof or cellar space), or by the ground. The international standards set by ISO TC163 and CEN TC 89 contain the necessary information: ISO 6946–1 and 2, ISO 9251, ISO 9288, ISO DIS 10456, ISO DIS 13786, and others.

The heterogeneity of the external envelope means that the heat insulation levels vary through the envelope's surface. Calculation methods have been developed to determine the heat-flow conditions, the temperature and the resulting thermal resistance of heterogeneous walls or floors (Pratt, 1981). Ideally, the precise solution for this is provided by differential equations, although the finite elements method provides practical numerical solutions. Finally, simplified calculation methods, including tables for common cases and computer programs, have been devised for different heat flow problems, including the calculation of thermal resistance.

It has been assumed that if the various components of the external envelope have at least the prescribed thermal resistance, then the internal premises of the building would function satisfactorily from the point of view of heat insulation. It will be seen, however, that this assumption may lose its validity under certain conditions, such as in the case of inadequate ventilation.

Substantial research efforts have been concentrated on heat-transfer problems, and these have led recently to the publication of further standards, e.g. the ISO DIS 13791, which provides the procedure for calculating the internal temperatures of a space without mechanical cooling in summer.

MOISTURE AND AIR TRANSFER: SURFACE AND INTERSTITIAL
CONDENSATION

Air invariably contains a certain quantity of moisture, and heat transfer is always accompanied by moisture transport, which is a form of mass transfer. Mass transfer includes the transmission of moisture and/or air within and between premises, in the latter case through openings or separating structures (walls, floors, roofs) (ISO 9346). The indoor air is felt to be pleasant or acceptable if it contains moisture between certain limits. Below those limits it is experienced as being too dry, above them as too humid. In most non-tropical countries, it is more common for air to be too humid and to cause more problems than dry air.

Excessive amounts of moisture were traditionally removed by ventilation through windows and doors, but this has changed recently. As a result of energy conservation measures, heat insulation levels have been increased, rooms and windows have been made more airtight, and ventilation rates have been reduced (Fisk, 1981). Although indoor air humidity was not yet the focus of attention before the Second World War, the introduction of hollow bricks and cavity and multilayer walls had already presented cases of condensation, leading to the first research on vapour transfer and ventilation (Rowley and Algren, 1929; Sheard, 1937; Rowley et al., 1938; Rowley, 1939; Rowley et al., 1939; Warner, 1939, 1940). Warm air can carry more moisture than cold air, so that an amount of vapour that causes no problems in warm air, can cause condensation in cooler air. As moisture is transported as part of the air, the problems it poses have to be studied together with those of heat flow (Künzel, 1994).

There are basically two forms of condensation in buildings: surface condensation and condensation within the enclosing structures (interstitial condensation). Both types occur when the moisture content of the air reaches saturation point. An indirect, simplified method for analysing interstitial condensation is to calculate the annual moisture balance and the maximum amount of accumulated moisture (kg/m^2) due to interstitial condensation. More advanced computer models have also been developed, the so-called 'Glaser methods'. There has been a great number of studies into humidity problems (Burch, 1993; Burch and TenWolde, 1993; Burch and Thomas, 1994; Kumaran, undated; Sanders, undated) and computer programs have been written that predict conditions.

Condensation occurred 'on a disaster scale' in the UK and other countries between 1967 and 1970, with more than 200 000 dwellings seriously affected (Allen, 1995). Other types of moisture problems have occurred since, and the causes are vividly described by Allen (1995) with deep professional insight. Overcrowding or lack of ventilation at night at reduced room temperatures increases the relative humidity to saturation level, thereby contributing to the occurrence of condensation. Thermal bridges can be the source of local condensation. The desire to conserve energy has also resulted in lower indoor temperatures, equally increasing the probability of condensation. Wet wall and floor surfaces lead to the growth of mould, which, apart from being unsightly, may have an adverse effect on the health of a building's occupants. Wet surfaces or humid cavities within constructions can cause the degradation of building materials and a reduction in heat insulation levels with aggravating effects. A reduced ventilation rate also results in the accumulation of pollutants in the indoor air, again a source of complaints and an adverse influence on health. (See Chapter 4 for a further discussion on this).

Complaints and consequential damage have kept many experts, researchers and the courts busy during the past 30 years. The causes, remedies and measures of prevention are now well understood, however, and the principles of good practice have been established in textbooks, codes and standards, although the heat, air and moisture codes of different countries contain differences that need to be reconciled in future (Hens and Janssens, undated).

INDOOR AIR PURITY

AIR QUALITY REQUIREMENTS

In addition to thermal requirements (including air temperature, movement and humidity), increasing attention is now being paid to air purity. This is fully justified considering the growing number of complaints and health problems that are caused by air contamination.

According to ISO 6242–2, the users' objectives concerning air purity are:

- to limit the ingress and/or accumulation in indoor air of contaminants (gases, particles, microbes, aerosols) detrimental to the comfort, injurious to the health of the occupant, or degrading to the building or its contents
- to provide an adequate supply of oxygen for the occupants and the combustible appliances
- to control nuisance due to odours
- to control relative humidity (this last requirement is currently being discussed along with the thermal requirements).

The parameters of these requirements may be interpreted in terms of the air supply rate, such as air changes per hour, air supply per person, air supply per square metre of floor space, and air supply per combustible appliance.

Throughout the world, air contains a nearly constant amount of nitrogen (78% by volume), oxygen (21%) and argon (0.9%), but varying amounts of carbon dioxide (on average around 0.03%) and water vapour (up to 3.5%). Trace quantities of inert gases (neon, xenon, krypton, helium, etc.) are also invariably present. Other gases are usually considered contaminants or pollutants. It is generally considered desirable to remove these gaseous pollutants from buildings as they may have an adverse effect on the occupants, even if they are present in only small concentrations. Recently, increasing attention has also been focused on ions in the air, electric and electromagnetic fields and various forms of radiation (Matériaux, 1993). (See later in this section). As the quality of air can now be characterized adequately, performance requirements can now replace ventilation requirements in codes on air quality (Buttenwieser and Kirchner, 1994).

AIR POLLUTANTS

The main sources of indoor air contamination are:

- emission from surface materials
- radon and soil gases
- smoking
- solid particles
- biological particles and micro-organisms
- odour influences.

In cities, air is polluted with sulphur dioxide, lead, carbon monoxide, nitrogen dioxide and ozone. Polluted air is unhealthy because the particulate matter it contains can penetrate deep into the lungs. Disabled, elderly, ill, allergic and hypersensitive people all have a greater need for good air quality.

Emissions from surface materials can be at:

- constant rates, such as from particleboards after some time
- slow decay rate, such as from furniture, floor and wall coverings
- rapid decay rate, such as from paints and polishes.

The objective (measurable) and the subjective (perceived) air pollution depends on the age of materials in the room, the ventilation, the temperature and the humidity.

Formaldehyde gas is one of the more common emissions from surface materials and is associated with furniture, some varnishes, lacquers and floor carpets. A high airborne concentration of it causes irritation to the mucous membrane. Radon is a radioactive gas that can constitute a health hazard at higher concentrations (Millet and Bienfait, 1991). The soil is the commonest source of radon in the air, but radon can also come from radiation from building materials such as slags and fly ash. Contaminated ground can also be the source of methane gas. Methods of protection against radon and methane are:

- building radon sumps
- underfloor extraction
- creating higher internal pressures than those outside to lessen gas ingress
- making the envelope of the building impervious to radon and landfill gases
- permanent ventilation
- replacing the soil around the building.

A radon sump consists of a small pit linked to the underlying permeable layer of aggregate or fill. Plastic underground pipes run from the sump and vent outside the building. Radon is drawn into the sump by a low-powered fan fitted near the end of the pipework, and then discharged harmlessly into the outside air. The sump can be placed outside if the floor area of the building is not too large. Increased ventilation of the crawl space under the ground floor is another method of keeping radon away from living quarters. Regulations in many countries now limit the concentrations of both formaldehyde and radon.

Some indoor air pollutants (e.g. radon, asbestos and benzene) are also carcinogenic and should not be present. Others are acceptable up to certain limits but are a matter of concern over that level, such as: respirable suspended particulates (including tobacco smoke), nitrogen dioxide, carbon monoxide, carbon dioxide, formaldehyde and some others. Benzene and formaldehyde are volatile organic compounds, of which more than 900 have been identified in indoor air, and several of which may affect health (Banhidi et al., 1994).

As already mentioned, a great variety of solid particles and micro-organisms such as mould and fungi can also contaminate the air.

Common indoor micro-organisms and biological particles include mites and their faeces, skin scales from humans and pets, fungi, mould and bacteria. Tobacco smoke is another common indoor pollutant. The effect of tobacco fumes on active smokers is already well known, and their effect on the health of passive smokers has also been the subject of much research recently. As a consequence, restrictions on smoking have tended to become more widespread.

A number of indoor air quality factors have been the subject of research, including turbulence of air and draught (Fanger *et al.*, 1988). Some research uses artificial people, so-called 'manikins'. These are actually complex measuring and control instruments placed in an appropriately prepared puppet (Wyon, 1988). Research has also been carried out using real people, either measuring their body characteristics or interviewing them about their comfort and satisfaction levels. The requirements of spaces that demand an extremely high standard of air cleanliness are discussed in Chapter 6.

INDOOR ODOURS

The human olfactory sense organ, the nose, is sensitive to several hundred thousand odorants in the air. Two new units of odours, the olf and the pol, were introduced by Professor Fanger of Denmark in 1988 to answer the need for a method of measuring perceived indoor odours. They are based on the acceptability of odour and sensory irritation (Fanger *et al.*, 1988). The olf is a quantitative unit of pollutant strength, 1 olf being the emission rate of air pollutants from a standard person. The pol is a measure of perceived air quality, and 1 decipol, one-tenth of a pol, is the pollution caused by one standard person (1 olf) ventilated by 10 l/s of unpolluted air. The ventilation rate required for comfort can be calculated from the determined air pollution level.

Another method for assessing odours, based on documents VDI 3881 and 3882, has been developed in Germany. It would seem to be less applicable for indoor air assessments, but in some respects it could complement the Fanger method (Mayer and Schwab, 1995). The measurement of odours in the air requires skills that are not yet universally available. Further studies are needed into measuring methods and classifying building products for emissions relevant to odour thresholds.

SOME RELATED ASPECTS

Air quality can readily be improved by the reduction of pollution and by more heating and ventilation, but at a cost as all of these measures lead to higher energy consumption. The optimum cost equilibrum between these factors should be sought within the parameters of comfort in the design of buildings.

The impact of ions in the air (aeroions) and electric fields have received much attention of late (Jokl, 1989). At present, it is generally accepted that extreme ion and power field conditions can affect human well-being and health, although in most cases the impact on health is usually considered insignificant. Various risks, such as living near electricity power lines and using or being exposed to various types of electric/electronic devices ('electromagnetic smog'), require more research. Television (TV) sets and computer screens emit electromagnetic radiation, and this low-frequency magnetic field is thought to be harmful, although the evidence is as yet inconclusive. Even if the precise causes cannot yet be identified, complaints are keeping scientists busy. Considering that exposure to TV and computer screens will be almost universal in the not too distant future, causes of even minor health effects should be considered carefully. For this reason, manufacturers have begun to introduce computer screens with reduced emissions.

A further problem with electromagnetic radiation is that it may disrupt the functioning of electronic equipment. This can have serious consequences, and so spaces that contain items such as electronic medical instruments must be protected from such radiation. Protection can be achieved by the installation of steel sheet or steel wire cages, free-standing independent protection screens, or screens incorporated into partitions. The reverse situation exists in military buildings that house delicate electronic equipment which must have an envelope that is transparent to electromagnetic radiation. Domes called radomes have been developed for this purpose. Glass reinforced plastics meet the requirements.

THE SONIC ENVIRONMENT

SOUND AND NOISE

Sound and noise were subjects studied by people such as Aristotle, Vitruvius, Newton and Euler, and Greek and Roman theatres were built with good acoustics. Modern acoustics has its origin in the end of last century with the publications by Lord Raleigh (1877) and Sabine (1900).

With the return of peace in 1945, more and more urban dwellers felt noise to be a nuisance: noise generated by neighbours; noise within the dwelling or workplace; and noise from traffic and industry. More recent noise sources are amplifiers and television, aeroplanes, cars, trains, machines, lifts and building services. Excessive noise damages hearing and there is now more noise then ever (Lord and Templeton, 1986; Eargle, 1990; Chew, 1995; Heutschi, 1995). Noise control has become a universal requirement, and its goal is to reduce the level of sound reaching the listener's ear (Gösele and Schüle, 1972; Harris, 1994).

The terms 'noise' and 'sound' are often used interchangeably, but sound is generally descriptive of useful communication or pleasant things such as music, whereas noise is mainly used to describe dissonance or unwanted sounds (Prout and Bienvenue, 1990). Loudness is a listener's impression of the amplitude of a sound. Its unit is the phon. Sound intensity (noise level) is the average rate at which sound energy is transmitted through a unit area normal to the direction of sound propagation. Its unit is the decibel. The acoustic equivalent level is defined by ISO 1996.

ACOUSTIC REQUIREMENTS

A user's acoustic requirements are defined in ISO 6242–3 and elsewhere (Blachère, 1987). The objectives to be achieved are:

- to provide freedom from annoyance from intrusive noises
- speech privacy between rooms or spaces
- a suitable acoustic quality within rooms or spaces.

The acoustic comfort, quality and privacy depend on the airborne sound insulation, the impact sound insulation, the acceptable sound pressure levels and the reverberation time of rooms or spaces. The basic method of checking compliance with specifications is made through curves of reference values (both for airborne and impact sounds). The reference curve is shifted towards the measured curve, and the unfavourable deviations at various frequencies (expressed in hertz) are compared with prescribed limit values. There are also limit values on installation noise and vibration. The noise of building equipment must be reduced right at its source. For ventilation systems this may mean using extra silencers and sound attenuators.

The resistance to sound transmission increases as the mass of the floor or wall increases. This is why older buildings, with their heavy walls and floors, provide good sound insulation. Modern walls and floors are much lighter and the transmission of airborne sounds has consequently increased. Although noise reduction may seem to be adequate through a particular wall or floor, it can still be inadequate if noise is able to 'leak' through windows, doors, ducts or pipes. Stopping flanking sound is therefore important.

A special branch of acoustics deals with concert halls, theatres, auditoriums and assembly halls. In such premises, the main objective is to ensure that both the audience and the performers can enjoy clear and undistorted sound.

Airborne sound power flow can be measured by standardized methods. It is more difficult to measure structural sound power, i.e. structureborne sound flow. Several methods are based on accelerometers (usually a pair) mounted on the structure, both in the laboratory and on real building structures. Techniques for the measurement of sound intensity have progressed much in the past 20 years. This has led to a better understanding of the sound field radiated from walls and floors, resulting in new techniques for the determination of the sound transmission loss of structures and the characteristics of acoustic materials. These new measurement techniques provide information not only on the entire structure, but also on the differential sound transmission of complex structures.

The reduction of the transmission of structureborne noise is necessary for lightweight structures, particularly for low frequency noise. Ordinary plasterboard walls may not be sufficient for noise control; three sheets of plasterboard on double stud structures with mineral wool between them provide better noise reduction at not too high an additional cost. Joining the structures with viscoelastic dampers eliminates resonance. High transmission loss for lightweight double-panel partitions, especially at low frequencies, has been achieved by means of small acoustic secondary sources placed in the air gap between the panels. This technique is called active acoustic control.

Numerical modelling has clarified the sound insulation of sandwich walls and the phenomenon of flanking sound. For the purpose of complex acoustic problems, such new numerical methods as statistical energy analysis, the finite element method, and the boundary element method have been applied. These methods are the result of increased computer power. A more accurate knowledge of the properties of buildings and sound absorptive materials and structures should improve noise control in buildings (Cops and Vermeir, 1995).

FIRE

FIRES IN THE PAST

Ever since buildings have existed, fire has been a potentially destructive force. In other ages, timber and other organic materials were most at risk; in our time, plastics are the main combustible material, with the additional danger that burning plastics emit toxic gases and smoke.

Throughout history, disastrous fires have been the catalyst for the introduction of various codes in various countries, at first concerning fireplaces, chimneys, materials and safety distances. For example, a fourteenth century ordinance in London forbade the building of chimneys from wood (Schultz, 1985), and the London Building Act was introduced as a consequence of the Great Fire of London in 1666 (Harmathy, 1993). Nevertheless, fire continued to be a serious threat. Fire destroyed 13 acres (5.3 hectares) of New York in 1835, despite a fire code issued in 1647, and a fire in Chicago in 1871 killed some 250 people and destroyed more than 17 000 buildings. Great fires broke out in Boston in 1872 and 1889, and in San Francisco in 1851 and 1906. In China, more than 300 schoolchildren died in a theatre fire in 1994. Despite the heavy toll of fires, serious research into fires in buildings is a product of only the past 60 years, with J. Snell from the USA, K. Kawagoe from Japan, H. L. Malhotra and P. H. Thomas from the UK, T. A. Harmathy from Canada, W. Becker from Germany, and O. Pettersson from Sweden being among the most prominent researchers.

Direct and indirect losses resulting from fires have been estimated to cost 0.1–0.5% of a country's gross domestic product (GDP) (data collected by the World Fire Statistics Centre, London). Fires kill 6000–7000 people each year in the USA, some 2000 in Japan and more than 1000 in the UK. Data compiled from various sources show that in 1989 the number of fires per 10 000 people was 85 in the USA, 80 in the UK, and 5 in Japan. In the same year, deaths from fire amounted to 22 per million people in the USA, 16 in the UK, and 14 in Japan.

Most fires occur in residential buildings. Among the commonest causes identified are cooking, smoking, electric heaters, matches, play and arson. In commercial buildings, hotels and assembly halls, the absence of adequate escape routes and exits still causes many casualties.

FIRES AND FIRE TESTS

It was possible to take efficient measures against fires only once an understanding of fires, their origin, their course and consequences had been gained. Fires destroy or damage buildings and property, kill people or impair health. Fires develop as a consequence of the ignitability of building materials, furnishings and building contents. Ignitability is the capacity of a material for being ignited, and is something that should be known when assessing materials for their potential contribution to the development of fires (ISO 5657). Other properties that are important are the combustibility performance of materials in fire (ISO 1182) and the smoke (fumes) that arise during burning or smouldering.

The development of a fire is significantly affected by the reaction to the fire of various products in it, i.e. the rate that heat is released as measured by the calorific energy released per unit time, by a specific material during combustion. For this and other characteristics, standardized test methods had to be defined in order to obtain comparable results. This has proved difficult, and there is still controversy about some test methods (ISO 5660–1). The first tests were carried out some 100 years ago in order to verify the performance of structures in fire. Early tests used gas, oil and wood or a combination of these as fuel (ISO 834–3). With such a wide variety of test conditions, it was difficult to compare and evaluate the findings. The first attempts towards a more uniform test method were made in 1918 in the USA when an ASTM Committee introduced a time – temperature curve close to the current ISO standards. Tests cannot fully reflect the conditions of an actual fire, but the aim has been to devise fire tests that make it possible to prescribe certain limit values that will provide sufficient safety (Harmathy, 1981). ISO 834 defines the parameters governing standard fire tests. The objective is to determine fire resistance, and test results give a fire resistance classification or rating expressed as a period of time for which certain criteria are satisfied. This can then be compared with the fire resistance rating required. Full-scale room tests for surface products are standardized in ISO 9705.

Flash-overs, which are defined as a sudden transition to a state of total surface involvement in a fire of combustible materials in a confined area, and pieces of burning material can dramatically increase the spread of a fire and must be assessed in some way. Differences in the test methods used in various countries are gradually being eliminated.

MODELLING AND QUANTIFYING FIRES

In order to describe fire as an accidental action for the purposes of engineering analysis, information on the occurrence rate and intensity of fires must be obtained (*Actions on Structures: Fire,* 1993). Modelling and quantifying fire spread, and our knowledge of the behaviour of materials in fire have progressed and led to the new branch of knowledge called 'fire safety engineering' (Quintière, 1990; Thomas, 1993; Uesugi *et al.*, 1993). Fire resistance tests are useful but inadequate to describe conditions in fire. For that purpose, models are needed. Engineering research uses various types, including mathematical and physical (analogous) models, and both find application in fire research (Kanury, 1987; Spalding, undated). Apart from some early model experiments (such as the one in Vienna early this century, see Anon, 1906), systematic work on fire models did not begin until the Second World War (Thomas, 1992). 'Zone' modelling, where the space is subdivided into 'zones', thereby simplifying the processes to be described, was developed in the USA.

Modelling may use computational fluid dynamics in the study of fire growth and smoke movement. The data requirements are complex: initial and boundary conditions are needed, ignition, flame spread and heat release must be determined, and data on furniture have to be known. Despite significant results, further research is required on modelling conditions.

SMOKE

Experience has shown that loss of life and injury are often caused by the smoke and fumes created during a fire rather than by the fire itself. The fight against fires must therefore include the detection of smoke, a reduction in the likelihood of noxious fumes, and the removal of smoke.

Mortality from fires can be reduced by controlling the spread of smoke (*Smoke Control in Buildings*, 1994).

Smoke can move either upwards or downwards in stairwells, lift shafts and chutes. Upward smoke movement is usually referred to as normal stack effect. This exists when outside temperatures are low. Downward smoke flow is referred to as reverse stack effect, and this exists when the outside air is warmer than the indoor air. The movement of smoke is also affected by wind and the expansion of the smoke. Smoke spread can be controlled by dividing a building into compartments, by sufficiently strong airflow, by air pressure differences across barriers, and by gaps and cracks in and around the barriers. Pressurization and compartmentation of stairwells and fire and smoke dampers are means of fire check and smoke control. Where air conditioning and ventilation ductwork intersects a fire resistant compartment, fire dampers should be installed (Loyd, 1994). Mobile fire dampers within ducts are operated automatically or manually and are designed to prevent the passage of both fire and smoke. New types of heat resistant glass are available to stop the spread of fire by stopping the passage of flame, (radiant) heat and smoke for a specific period of time.

PREVENTING, DETECTING AND FIGHTING FIRES

Protection against fire includes appropriate design, early detection, fighting fire outbreaks and measures after fires have been extinguished (Paulitz, 1994). Fire detectors (flame, heat and smoke detectors) and fire extinguishing equipment have been developed and improved. One commonly used method is sprinklers, which are automatic systems of water pipes with sprinkler heads at suitable intervals and heights designed to detect, control and extinguish the fire by the discharge of water. Sprinklers are permanently situated and self-activated by sensors. The first sprinkler system was installed in the USA, probably in 1852. There are two basic types of sprinklers: wet and dry systems. Pipes are continuously full of water in the first, whereas there is no permanent water supply in the second. The addition of a non-corrosive antifreeze may prevent the freezing of the water in the system. Regular maintenance must ensure that the system functions in fire.

Practical methods are also needed to reduce the likelihood of upholstered furniture fires, which can result in flash-overs and thus higher fatalities. Prevention of fire initiation should eliminate the source of ignition and keep fuel away from that source. The management of fire impact consists of risk management and equiping the building with sprinklers, fire walls, dampers, fire doors, escape routes and smoke control. Tall buildings, sometimes comprising a high atrium, are now an additional challenge for fire safety; smoke can be partly controlled by adequate natural venting (CIB W14/93/3(J)).

The past few decades have seen considerable progress in investigating (Pettersson, 1994):

- the reaction of materials to fire
- fire growth in a compartment
- the fully developed fire compartment
- fire spread between buildings
- the behaviour in fire of load-bearing and separating building structures
- smoke filling in enclosures and smoke movement in escape routes and multistorey buildings
- the interaction of sprinklers and fire
- the process of escape
- the systems approach to the overall fire safety of a building, including human response models.

Fire researchers have gradually extended their activities to fires in industrial plants, underground spaces and other premises (Uehara, 1993).

Fire research has been able to provide fire safety professionals with the means to quantify fire risks and hazard, and computer-based models can now simulate these risks in various types of buildings. HAZARD is a computer-based fire hazard assessment method developed in the USA, and FIREDOC is a US computer-based card catalogue of fire research literature. Fire research has given us a better insight into the causes of the loss of human life and material damage in fires, and has thereby enabled us to reduce these losses in the future.

SUMMARY

Modern buildings and structures are increasingly being designed and constructed using scientific methods. This trend has its origins in the scientific revolution of the seventeenth century. The new ideas in mathematics, physics, and, later, in engineering, also had a fundamental impact on construction. Various mathematical fields such as analysis, probability theory, matrix algebra, graph theory, group theory, finite elements methods and mathematical statistics were developed for structural analysis and other engineering problems. Some examples, such as fullerenes and solitons, demonstrate the growing co-operation between building research and other scientific disciplines. As a result, we now live in an age where science is recognized as a means of life or death (Bernal, 1953).

The invention of computers during the 1940s and 1950s opened up new possibilities for the construction industry. At first the so-called mainframes were developed, followed by the personal computer, and these have since been combined by teleprocessing and networking. Computer graphics has been applied to design work. Modern mathematics and computers have enabled designers to solve difficult computational problems. This, and our growing knowledge about the properties of materials and the behaviour of structures has resulted in modern design methods, codes and standards, and allowed the construction of skyscrapers, towers and long-span structures (buildings and bridges) that can withstand dynamic actions such as earthquakes and wind.

Research has clarified the problems of heat and moisture transfer in buildings, surface and interstitial condensation, has improved heat insulation and ventilation together with energy conservation. The conditions for ideal indoor ambience, air quality, health and human comfort have been defined. Indoor air pollutants have been researched, along with electromagnetic radiation, radon and ions. The knowledge acquired about fire and smoke have created the new discipline of fire engineering. Research on noise has enabled the design of premises with good acoustic characteristics despite increasingly lightweight building envelopes.

The result of the processes described in this chapter have been the introduction of a solid scientific basis for construction. Building research has itself become a partner to other scientific disciplines, contributing to the overall evolution of knowledge.

BIBLIOGRAPHY

Actions on Structures: Impact (1992) CIB Report No. 167, Rotterdam.
Actions on Structures: *Fire* (1993) CIB Report No. 166, Rotterdam.
Adeli, H. and Kamal, O. (1993) *Parallel Processing in Structural Engineering*, Elsevier Applied Science.
Allen, W. (1995) The pathology of modern building, *Building Research and Information*, May/June, 139–46.
Anon. (1906) Denkschrift Über die Brandversuche in Wiener Modelltheater, R. Spiesa Co., Vienna.
Banhidi, L. *et al.* (eds) (1994) *Healthy Buildings '94*, Proceedings of Conference, Budapest, 22–5 August 1994, 2 vols.
Barrett, M. L. and Wagner, C. H. (1996) *C and UNIX*, John Wiley & Sons.
Beckett, H. E. (1936) The effect of moisture content on the thermal resistance of insulating wallboards, *Inst. Heat. Vent. Eng. Journal*, 4(38), 87–90.
Beedle, L. S. (1990) Why are specifications different? *ASCE J. Construct. Steel Research*, **17**, (1 and 2), 3–32.
Bernal, F. D. (1953) *Science and Industry in the Nineteenth Century*, Routledge & Kegan Paul.
Billups, W. E. and Ciufolini, M. A. (eds) (1993) *Buckminsterfullerenes*, VCH Publishers.
Blachère, G. (1987) *Building Principles CEC*, Brussels, EUR 11 320 EN.
Blackmore, P. A. (1995) Wind damage in urban areas: a UK perspective. In L. S. Beedle (ed.-in-chief) and D. Rice (ed.), *Habitat and the High-Rise Tradition and Innovation*, Proceedings of the 5th World Congress, Amsterdam, pp 1129–49.
Breitschaft, G. *et al.* (1992) The structural Eurocodes – conceptual approach. In *Proceedings of the IABSE Conference, Davos*, IABSE, Zurich.

Burch, D. M. (1993) An analysis of moisture accumulation in walls subjected to hot and humid climates, *ASHRAE Transactions 1993*, **99**(2), 1013–22.

Burch, D. M. and TenWolde, A. (1993) A computer analysis of moisture accumulation in the walls of manufactured housing, *ASHRAE Transactions*, **99**(2), 977–90.

Burch, D. M. and Thomas, W. C. (1994) *MOIST. A PC Program for Predicting Heat and Moisture Transfer in Building Envelopes*, NIST Special Publication 853.

Buttenwieser I. and Kirchner, S. (1994) Label danois de qualité de l'air intérieur, *CSTB Magazine*, **74**, May, 42–5.

Carpinteri, A. (1994) *Handbook of Fatigue Crack Propagation in Metallic Structures*, North-Holland/Elsevier Science, 2 vol.

Carrara, G. and Kalay, Y. E. (1994) Editorial, *Automation and Construction*, 2–3, July, 103–4, and articles in the issue.

Chew, C. H. (1995) The influence of inclined buildings on road traffic noise, *Applied Acoustics*, **1**, 29–46.

CIB/W14/93/3(J) (1992) *Proceedings of 12th Joint Panel Meeting of the UJNR Panel on Fire Research and Safety*, BRI, Tsukuba, Japan.

CIB 193: Actions on Structures. Wind Loads (1996), CIB Publication 193.

Collier, C. G. *et al.* (1994) Extreme surface winds in mid-latitude storms: forecasting and changes in climatology, *Journal of Wind Engineering and Industrial Aerodynamics*, **52**, 1–27.

Cops, A. and Vermeir, G. (1995) Progress in building acoustics. *Noise/News International*, March, 10–25.

Cracknell, A. P. (1968) *Applied Group Theory*, Pergamon Press.

Crouch, S. L. and Starfield, A. M. (1990) *Boundary Element Methods in Solid Mechanics*, Unwin Hyman.

Davenport, A. G. (1967) The treatment of wind loading on tall buildings. In A. Coull and B. Stafford Smith (eds), *Tall Buildings*, Pergamon Press, 3–44.

Dorn, H. (1970) Applied mechanics and the origins of engineering education. In D. P. Billington and P. Mark (eds), *Civil Engineering: History, Heritage and the Humanities*, Princeton University.

Drazin, P. G. (1983) *Solitons*, Cambridge University Press.

Dufton, A. E. (1933) Heat requirements of a house, *Inst. Heat. Vent. Eng. Journal*, **1**(2), 99–104; **1**(3), 156–63; **1**(4), 209–16.

Eargle, J. M. (1990) *Music, Sound and Technology*, Van Nostrand Reinhold.

Elfgren, L. (ed.) (1989) *Fracture Mechanics of Concrete Structures from Theory to Applications*, Chapman & Hall.

Elfgren, L. and Shah, S. P. (eds) (1991) *Analysis of Concrete Structures by Fracture Mechanics*, Chapman & Hall.

Ellingwood, B. *et al.* (1982) Probability-based load criteria: load factors and load combinations, *ASCE J. of Structural Division*, **108**(ST5), May 978–97.

Ellingwood, B. R. (1994) Probability-based codified design for earthquakes, *Engineering Structures*, **7**, 498–506.

Eurocode No. 1, Basis of Design and Actions, Part 1 – Basis of Design, Background Documentation, 1st Draft, January 1995, Eurocode 1.1 Project Team.

Fajfar, P. and Krawinkler, H. (eds) (1992) *Nonlinear Seismic Analysis and Design of Reinforced Concrete Buildings*, Elsevier Computational Structural Mechanics, Elsevier.

Fanger, P. O. *et al.* (1988) Air turbulence and sensation of draught, *Energy and Buildings*, **12**, 21–39.

Fejes Toth, L. (1964) *Regular Figures*, Pergamon-Macmillan, N. Y.

Fishenden, M. and Saunders, O. (1932) *Calculation of Heat Transmission*, HMSO.

Fisk, D. J. (1981) *Thermal Control of Buildings*, Applied Science Publishers.

Flowers, R. (1996) *Computing for Site Managers*, Blackwell Science.

Flügge, W. (1934) *Statik und Dynamik der Schalen*, Springer-Verlag, Berlin.

Galambos, T. V. *et al.* (1982) Probability-based load criteria: assessment of current practice, *ASCE J. of Structural Division*, **108** (ST5), May, 959–77.

Galambos, T. V. (1990) Developments in modern steel design standards, *J. of Construct. Steel Research* **17**, (1 and 2), 141–62.

Gallagher, R. S. (1995) *Computer Visualization*, Solomon Press.

Girkmann, K. (1946, 1956) *Flächentragwerke*, Springer-Verlag, Berlin.

Gösele, K. and Schüle, W. (1972) *Schall. Wärme*, Feuchtigkeit, Bauverlag GmbH.

Green, N. B. (1987) *Earthquake Resistant Building Design and Construction*, Elsevier.

Hankins, Th. L. (1985) *Science and the Enlightenment*, Cambridge University Press.

Harmathy, T. Z. (1981) The fire resistance test and its relation to real-world fires, *Fire and Materials* **5**(3).

Harmathy, T. Z. (1993) *Fire Safety Design and Concrete*, Longman Scientific Technical.

Harris, C. M. (1994) *Noise Control in Buildings*, McGraw-Hill.

Hens, H. and Janssens, A. (undated) *Enquiry on HAMCaT Codes*, IEA Annex 24, Task 1-Modelling Publication.

Heutschi, K. (1995) A simple method to evaluate the increase of traffic noise emission level due to buildings, for a long straight street, *Applied Acoustics*, **3**, 259–74.

Hunter, P. (1995) *Network Operating Systems*, Addison-Wesley.

IAEE, International Association for Earthquake Engineering (1982) *Basic Concepts for Seismic Codes*.

Johnson, H. W. (1996) *Fastethernet Dawn of a New Network*, Prentice Hall.

Jokl, M. V. (1989) *Microenvironment*, Charles Thomas Publisher, Springfield, Illinois.

Journal of Wind Engineering and Industrial Aerodynamics (1993) August, 899.

Kanury, A. M. (1987) On the craft of modelling in engineering and science, *Fire Safety Journal*, **12**, 65–74.

Kato S. *et al.* (1993) Application of massive parallel computer to computational wind engineering, *Journal of Wind Engineering and Industrial Aerodynamics*, **46** and **47**, 393–400.

Kersken-Bradley, M. *et al.* (1991) *Estimation of Structural Properties by Testing for Use in Limit State Design*, JCSS Working Document, May 1991.

Kessler, G. C. and Train, D. A. (1991) *Metropolitain Area Networks*, McGraw-Hill.

Kroto, H. W. and Walton, D. R. M. (eds) (1993) *The Fullerenes*, Cambridge University Press.

Kumaran, M. K. (undated) *Heat, Air and Moisture Transport through Building Materials and Components: Symbols and Terminology*, IEA Annex 24, Task 3.

Künzel, H. M. (1994) *Verfahren zur ein-und zweidimensionalen Berechnung des gekoppelten Wärme- und Feuchtetransports in Bauteilen mit einfachen Kennwerten*, Doctoral Thesis, Stuttgart, University of Stuttgart.

Ladevèze P. and Zienkewicz, O. C. (1992) *New Advances in Computational, Structural Mechanics*. Elsevier.

Levy, M. and Salvadori, M. (1995) *Why The Earth Quakes*, W. W. Norton & Co.

Lew, H. S. (ed.) *et al.* (1990) *Performance of Structures during the Loma Prieta Earthquake of October 17, 1989*, NIST Special Publication 778, Gaithersburg, MD.

Lewis, P. E. and Ward, J. P. (1991) *The Finite Element Method: Principles and Applications*, Addison-Wesley.

Lord, P. and Templeton, D. (1986) *The Architecture of Sound*, The Architectural Press, London.

Lorenz, H. (1913) *Elastizitätslehre*, R. Oldenburg-Verlag, Munich.

Loyd, S. (1994) *Fire Dampers*, BSRIA Technical Note TN 6/94.

Mandelbrot, B. B. (1982) *The Fractal Geometry of Nature*, Freeman San Francisco.

Marshall, R. D. (1993) *Wind Load Provisions of the Manufactured Home Construction and Safety Standards*, NISTIR 5189, Gaithersburg, MD.

Marshall, R. D. (1994) *Manufactured Homes – Probability of Failure and the Need for Better Windstorm Protection through Improved Anchoring Systems*, NISTIR 5370, Gaithersburg, MD.

Matériaux: les polluants sous haute surveillance, *CSTB Magazine*, **68**, October 1993, 48–9.

Mayer, E. and Schwab R. (1995) *Geruchsbewertung in Gebäuden nach unterschiedlichen Methoden*, Fraunhofer-Institut für Bauphysik, IBP-Mitteilung 276.

Millet, J-R. and Bienfait D. (1991) Bâtiment et santé: les risques liés au radon, *Cahiers du CSTB*, Cahier 2530.

Mörsch, E. (1902, 5th ed.: 1922) Der Eisenbetonbau-Seine Theorie und Anuendung, Konrad Witwer.

NEHRP Handbook for the Seismic Evaluation of Existing Buildings (1992) FEMA-178; NIBS-BSSC (= Building Seismic Safety Council), Washington D. C.

Neumann, J. von (1959) *The Computer and the Brain*, Yale University Press/Maple Press Company, New York.

Newman, W. M. and Lamming, M. G. (1995) *Interactive System Design*, Addison-Wesley.

Nooshin, H. (1984) *Formex Configuration in Structural Engineering*, Elsevier Applied Science.

Patterson, D. A. and Hennessy, J. L. (1990) *Computer Architecture: A Quantitative Approach*, Morgan Kaufman Publishers, Inc.

Paulitz, U. (1994) *Historische Feuerwehren*, Franckh-Kosmos, Stuttgart.

Perry, A. H. (1995) Trends and perspectives in structural systems for buildings and infrastructure in research and industry. In *Proceedings of CIB Congress*, Amsterdam, 8–9 May, 115–34.

Pettersson, O. (1994) Rational structural fire engineering design, based on simulated real fire exposure. In *Fire Safety Science: Proceedings of the Fourth International Symposium*, International Association for Fire Safety Science, 3–26.

Potthoff, J. *et al.* (1994) Der neue Aeroakustik-Fahrzeugwindkanal der Universität Stuttgart, *ATZ Automobiltechnische Zeitschrift 96* (1994) Heft 7/8, 438–47.

Pratt, A. W. (1981) *Heat Transmission in Buildings*, John Wiley & Sons.

Preliminary Reconnaissance Report of the 1995 Hyogoken-Nanbu Earthquake (1995) English edn, Architectural Institute of Japan, Tokyo.

Prout, J. H. and Bienvenue, G. R. (1990) *Acoustics for You*, R. E. Krieger Publishing Company, Malabar, Florida, USA.

Pugh, A. (1976) *An Introduction. Tensegrity*, University of California Press.

Quintière, J. G. (1990) *Fourth CIB Workshop on Fire Modelling*, CIB Publication 129.

Reddy, J. N. (1993) *An Introduction to the Finite Element Method*, McGraw-Hill.

Roller, D. H. D. (1971) *Perspectives in the History of Science and Technology*, University of Oklahoma Press.

Rosenblueth, E. and Garcia-Perez, J. (1994) Optimal zoning, *Engineering Structures*, **7**, 460–9.

Rowley, F. B. (1939) A theory covering the transfer of vapour through materials, *ASHVE Trans*, **45**, 545.

Rowley, F. B. and Algren, A. B. (1929) Thermal resistance of air spaces, *ASHVE Trans*. **35**, 165.

Rowley, F. B., Algren, A. B. and Lund, C. E. (1938) Condensation within walls, *Heating Piping*, **10** (1), 49–60.

Rowley, F. B., Algren, A. B. and Lund, C. E. (1939) Condensation of moisture and its relation to building construction and operation, *Heating Piping*, **11** (1), 41–9.

Ruley, J. D. *et al.* (1995) *Networking Windows NT 3.51*, John Wiley & Sons.

Sanders, C. H. (undated) *Design Parameters Used to Avoid Interstitial Condensation for a Range of Climates*, IEA Annex 24, Task 2.

Sato, T. (1995) The devastating earthquake in Kobe, *Current Science*, 25 June, 1199–1205.

Schultz, N. (1985) *Fire and Flammability*, Van Nostrand Reinhold Company, New York.

Sheard, H. (1937) Heat transmission through walls 11, *Inst. Heat. Vent. Eng. Journal*, **5** (56), 588–90.

Singer, Ch., Williams, T. E. *et al.* (eds) (1957–78), *A History of Technology*, 7 vols, Clarendon Press, Oxford.

Singer, Ch. (ed.) (1955a) *Studies on the History and Method of Science*, William Dawson & Sons.

Singer, Ch. (1955b) *A Short History of Scientific Ideas to 1900*, Clarendon Press, Oxford.

Smeltzer, G. T. A. (1994) *Information Technology in the Building Industry*, CIB W 82 Working Paper.

Smoke Control in Buildings (1994) *BRE Digest*, No.396, August.

Somerville, P. (1995) Kobe earthquake: an urban disaster, *Current Science*, 25 June, 1205–8.

Southwell, R. V. (1936) *An Introduction to the Theory of Elasticity for Engineers and Physicists*, Oxford University Press, London.

Spalding, D. B. (undated) The art of partial modelling. In *Proceedings of the 9th Symposium (Int.) on Combustion*, The Combustion Institute, Pittsburgh, PA, 833–43.

Spencer, K. L. (1996) *NT Server: Management and Control*, Prentice Hall.

Stroeven, P. (1994) Fractal concept and damage in concrete, *CEB Bulletin d'Information*, **221**, 125–39.

Summers, Ch. and Dunetz, B. (1996) *ISDN: How to Get a High-Speed Connection to the Internet*, John Wiley & Sons.

Tada, K. (1995) Effect of the Southern Hyogo Earthquake on the Akashi-Kaikyo Bridge, *Structural Engineering International*, August, 179–81.

Tarnai, T. *et al.* (1995) Pentagon packing models for 'all-Pentamer' virus structures, *Biophysical Journal*, August, 612–18.

Tarnai, T. and Gaspar, Zs. (1987) Multi-symmetric close packings of equal spheres on the spherical surface, *Acta Cryst.*, A43, 612–16.

Thielen, G. (1994) From micro-structure to structural performance, *CEB Bulletin*, **221**, 79–106.

Thomas, P. H. (1991) Internationalisation of fire research, *Fire Research Safety Journal*, **17** 179–83.

Thomas, P. H. (1992) Fire modelling: a mature technology?, *Fire Safety Journal*, **19** 125–140.

Thomas, P. H. (1993) W14 and Fire Safety Engineering, *CIB Information*, **1**, 1.

Timoshenko, S. P. (1953) *History of Strength of Materials*, McGraw-Hill Book Company.

Timoshenko, S. P. (1959) *Engineering Education in Russia*, McGraw-Hill Book Company.

Todd, D. *et al.* (1994) *1994 Northridge Earthquake*, NIST Special Publication 862, Gaithersburg, MD.

Uehara, Y. (1993) Fire protection and loss prevention in petrochemical plants. In *'93 Asian Fire Seminar*, CIB W14/95(J) paper, Science University of Tokyo.

Uesugi, H. *et al.* (1993) Modelling of fire engineering design in high-rise steel structure. In *'93 Asian Fire Seminar*, CIB W14/95(J) paper, Science University of Tokyo.

Walraven, J (1994) High performance concrete, *CEB Bulletin d'Information*, **221**, 107–24.

Warner (1939) A study of the ventilation of a warmed room, *Inst. Heat. Vent. Eng. Journal*, **7**, (79).

Warner (1940) Ventilation of dwellings, *Journal of Hygiene*, **40** (2), 26.

Webb, W. A. (1990) Bank of China: fire safety. *Tall Buildings: 2000 and Beyond*, 489–95.

Westfall, R. (1971) *The Construction of Modern Science: Mechanisms and Mechanics*, John Wiley & Sons.

Wexelblat, R. L. (1981) *History of Programming Languages*, Academic Press.

Whitehead, A. N. (1926) *Science and the Modern World*, Cambridge at the University Press.

Wilkie, M. V. (1995) *Computer Perspectives*, Morgan Kaufman Publishers.

Wind and seismic effects (1994) *Proceedings of the 26th Joint Meeting*; NIST SP 871.

Wyon, D. P. (1988) The use of thermal manikins in environmental ergonomics, *3rd International Environmental Ergonomics Conference*, Helsinki.

Climate and energy: technical services of buildings

4

INTRODUCTION

Prior to 1800, technical equipment had a mainly subordinate role in buildings. During the past 200 years, however, this has gradually changed chiefly as a result of an alteration in our perception of the purpose of buildings. In early times buildings were seen simply as shelter, affording occupants protection from cold and rain. Nowadays, we also require a pleasant ambience, an acceptable temperature, and lighting and other conditions that provide for human comfort. These requirements have been met by increasingly sophisticated equipment for heating, water supply, lighting and telecommunications as technology has progressed.

Several recent events have had a particular impact on the provision of services in buildings. One was the escalation of energy prices in 1973 and 1974, another was the realization that energy resources are limited and will not last forever, and a third was the threat of climate change caused primarily by the burning of fossil fuel. Together they spurred people on to find ways of energy conservation, including the creation of buildings and building services that were capable of conserving energy.

When energy prices fell a little during the second half of the 1980s the other two factors still remained strong enough to maintain a focus on energy conservation. All over the world, research and development resources were concentrated on this objective, and efforts were especially intense in the field of building because of the amount of energy consumed by construction and the use of buildings. Very soon, action followed and governments changed regulations, making much higher levels of heat insulation compulsory. As a consequence, industry increased the production of insulation materials, and developed equipment and appliances that consume less energy.

Those buildings that were designed or adapted to conserve energy had unforeseen effects on their occupants. As buildings were made more airtight, ventilation rates were reduced, and this was one factor that led to higher humidity, pollution and condensation levels, especially when air temperatures were kept low. The new term 'sick buildings' was coined following complaints about discomfort and poor health in such buildings. Building and medical research began intensive co-operative research on temperature, humidity, air flow, and the influence of micro-organisms and other pollutants in the air in buildings as these were shown to have a major effect on human health, apart from causing degradation of the buildings themselves. For the building industry, all this meant another step towards the world of modern science and technology.

THE CLIMATE AND ITS IMPACT ON CONSTRUCTION

CLIMATE CHANGES

Climate means more than just average weather. It includes the variations (range, extremes, distribution, frequencies) and characteristics of weather components: temperature, wind, precipitation, sunshine and cloud. Life as we know it has been made possible by the earth's climate, although the atmospheric temperature has changed several times since the world began. The 'wobbling' of the earth around the sun creates very slow climate cycles of about 100 000 years duration. The last Ice Age was some 20 000–40 000 years ago. Within these long cycles, other factors, not all precisely identified, also cause climate change. Between the thirteenth and eighteenth centuries, the average temperature in Europe was probably 1° Celsius colder than today. At present, however, it is neither nature nor the cosmos that is the principal cause of change. Rather it is mankind itself, and the projected climate warming over the coming century will be greater and more abrupt than any natural climate variation since the dawn of civilization.

Atmospheric air is a mixture of many gases plus water vapour and pollutants. Certain gases (called 'greenhouse gases') play a crucial role in determining the earth's climate. The main greenhouse gases are water vapour, carbon dioxide, methane and chlorofluorocarbons (CFCs). The quantity of water vapour in the air is determined by a natural process, but the other three are largely a consequence of some human activities that cause a rapid rise in their concentration, contributing to climate change. During the last Ice Age, the level of carbon dioxide in the atmosphere is established to have been around 0.018%, or 180 parts per million (ppm). Around 1800, the atmospheric level of carbon dioxide was 280 ppm. It has now increased to 360 ppm, and can reach 800 ppm in large cities.

A recent study of the history of the Middle East illustrates the impact of climate changes. Reasons were sought for the instability and sudden collapse of the large Mesopotamian civilizations within just a few centuries around 2000 BC. The most probable cause was found to be the climate, which abruptly became extremely dry. The desertion of the Negev desert in the eighth century was generally attributed to the Arab invasion around 700. It now seems, however, that the upheaval was caused by a massive invasion of sand dunes, which incidentally also occurred 15 000 years ago at the end of the last Ice Age (Issar, 1995).

Although most scientists agree that global warming is a fact, there are some who express doubts. The European Science and Environment Forum pointed out that most observation thermometers have been on land, and that measurements over the sea, which began by satellite only recently, do not show a change in the status quo. Nevertheless, the evidence seemed convincing enough to persuade the Intergovernmental Panel on Climate Change (IPCC), governments and others to agree some measures to counteract climate warming, and attempts have been made to underpin these measures with economic analysis. However, even thorough high-level research provides only partial data (Nordhaus, 1994). The problems of economic analysis are discussed further in Chapter 9 with regard to sustainability.

MEASURES TO COUNTERACT CLIMATE WARMING

Average global temperatures have increased by about 0.5°C over the past 135 years. While this lies within the range of possible random variations in theory, it is much more plausible that the increase is due to the rise in the atmospheric concentration of carbon dioxide. It is difficult, perhaps impossible, to make predictions, but it is quite probable that the increasing concentration of greenhouse gases in the air will enhance the heat trapping hothouse effect, leading to average surface temperatures rising by 2–4° across the globe over the next 100 years, which justifies the need for countermeasures (WMO Statement, 1995). Such a change in the climate would not directly threaten life, but it would lead to higher sea levels and therefore to flooding of certain densely populated low-lying areas. More damage would be caused by storms and cyclones, there would be shifts of fertile and arid land, and water resources would become more vulnerable than at present. Furthermore, the direct impact on health, such as more heat stress and an increased incidence of respiratory, allergic and communicable diseases, could increase mortality rates.

Carbon dioxide, which is the main cause of global warming, is produced when fossil fuel is burnt. This is therefore a good reason to reduce the use of fossil fuels and to replace them, as far as possible, with renewable energy such as wind and solar power. Another reason for economizing on fossil fuels is that they are a finite and irreplaceable resource. Energy conservation, particularly the more efficient use of oil and gas, has become a fairly common policy in most countries. The fact that it is

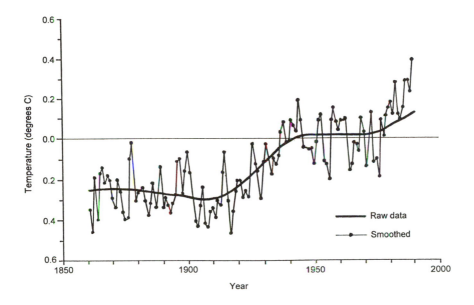

Fig. 4.1 Global average temperatures from 1861 to 1990 (relative to the average between 1951 and 1980). *Source:* IPCC (Intergovernmental Panel on Climate Change).

not carried out more vigorously can be explained in at least two ways. Firstly, while certain measures can be implemented by quite rational and economically viable actions, drastic energy conservation is extremely expensive. Secondly, the scale and speed of global warming is still very much debated, to the extent that there is even one theory that microscopic particles from smokestack emissions slow down global warming, and that the cooling effect could be strongest where aerosol pollution is heaviest, i.e. in the industrialized regions of the world! Historic experience shows that in northern Europe, periods of colder or warmer winters, lasting for a thousand years or more, can suddenly come to an end within a single decade. We must therefore be concerned with both global annual and regional seasonal climate changes.

A significant reduction in net greenhouse emissions would require the diversion of resources away from other areas. While this would be beneficial in the long term, governments tend to be reluctant to make short-term sacrifices for long-term gain, which is why measures such as carbon taxes or tradable emissions permits (see also in Chapter 9) have met with so much opposition, and proposals for vigorous national and international action in order to accelerate energy conservation have had only limited success. Nevertheless, at a major international meeting in Berlin in 1995, participants adopted the 'Berlin Mandate', which concluded that current commitments to maintain emissions of greenhouse gases at the 1990 level until 2000 were not adequate, and established a process that would enable the world to take appropriate action in future years.

Some of the ideas for counteracting the warming of the climate are still in the realms of science fiction, such as mirrors in space to block out some sunlight, spreading iron deep in the ocean to multiply carbon dioxide-absorbing plankton, or pumping carbon dioxide from power stations into the oceans for the same purpose. These might prove to be feasible later on, but more realistic measures are needed in the immediate future in order to combat further temperature increases. Climate change scenarios foresee great social implications: the poor, who have fewest opportunities to respond to climate change, would suffer the most. In the future, the building industry will have a permanent obligation to contribute to the fight against climate change.

OZONE AND ITS IMPACT ON HEALTH

There is a layer of ozone (a molecule containing three oxygen atoms) in the upper stratosphere, primarily above the arctic poles, which shields the surface of the earth against much of the sun's ultraviolet radiation. The area and thickness of this layer have been reduced in recent years, increasing the risk of skin cancer as a consequence. The basic cause of this phenomenon has been found to be the increasing use of chlorofluorocarbons (CFCs) and hydrochlorofluorocarbons (HCFCs) in the production of rigid urethane foams, refrigeration, air conditioning and some furnishing equipment (CFCs and Buildings, 1991).

The seriousness of this growing risk compelled governments to study how any further depletion of the ozone layer could be retarded, later stopped altogether, and finally reversed. International agreements such as the Montreal Protocol call for the phasing out of CFC production by 2000. A European Union (EU) regulation adopted in December 1994 forbids the supply of new HCFCs from 2015 (Butler, 1995a, 1995b, 1995c). The regulation has made the recovery and recycling of used CFCs and HCFCs from commercial and industrial refrigeration and air conditioning systems mandatory. The manufacture and importation of new CFCs has already ceased in some industrialized countries, and the consumption of new HCFCs is expected to be phased out by them in the near future. This has become possible because of the replacement of CFCs and HCFCs by hydrofluorocarbons (HFCs) or mixtures of HFCs that do not harm the ozone layer. The conversion to new refrigerants requires the creation of new equipment or the adaptation of existing stock (Butler, 1994; Butler and Fannin, 1994). The polyurethane (PUR) produced with the replacements for CFCs has a density that is only slightly higher than that of standard PUR.

Although some existing CFC and HCFC refrigerants may have less of an overall effect on global warming than was first thought, most of the HFCs used to replace earlier refrigerants do have a lower direct effect on global warming. In order to diminish the impact of refrigerants on the environment still further, research into and improvement in the handling of services and appliances is necessary, e.g. to avoid unnecessary use of air conditioning. Refrigeration also consumes electricity, and this makes it indirectly responsible for the emission of large quantities of carbon dioxide, the main cause of global warming. This justifies attempts to keep refrigeration, including air conditioning, under tighter control (Calder and Grigg, 1993). Research is also underway to tackle the problem from another direction by the (re-)introduction of absorption chillers as an alternative to vapour compression refrigeration equipment. Absorption chillers were widely used until roughly the 1960s, since when their use declined and virtually disappeared. The objective of the work in this field is to improve the efficiency of absorption chillers to a level where they could compete with compression equipment (Smith, Webb and Wiech, 1992; Smith and Webb, 1993).

The International Energy Agency (IEA) has launched an international collaborative research project on low-energy cooling (IEA Annexe 28). Some of the approaches considered for examination in the project are:

- ground coupling, taking advantage of low soil temperatures
- evaporative cooling
- desiccant dehumidification with evaporative cooling
- night cooling through ventilation and thermal mass utilizing the lower night-time temperatures (Jaunzens and Wylds, 1994).

Ozone is deleterious to human health when it is present in excessive amounts in the outdoor air, as may occur in smog (smoke plus fog). Smog first appeared in the large cities of industrialized countries when the fumes from coal fires caused retention in the atmosphere of emission gases (sulphur dioxide and carbon dioxide). Earlier London smog claimed the lives of many people. As a consequence, the UK parliament approved legislation against air pollution. Since then, coal has been replaced in most countries by oil or gas, but the increased use of cars is a new cause of smog, and thus more ozone, in the air. Smog also causes irritation of the eyes, nose and throat, headaches and nausea. The concentration of ozone can reach 180 $\mu g/m^3$ of air or more, and this has been defined as the level above which health would be impaired. The prevention of smog and high ozone concentration can be assisted by adequate town planning measures.

CLIMATE DATA FOR DESIGN

Studying climate changes has the practical purpose of enabling us to design and construct buildings that adequately and economically protect against the weather and make efficient use of such beneficial climatic phenomena as sunshine.

There now exist national and international lists of climatic data important to construction. These primarily contain information for designers, but also cater for the construction industry, giving, for instance, data that enables the forecasting of frost. ISO DIS 6243 is a draft international standard containing agreements on the climatic design data necessary for building design. It lists the following areas in which data are or may be needed:

- air temperature
- solar radiation (thermal and light)
- long wave and total radiation
- atmospheric humidity
- wind, rain and snow.

Within each area, a number of data are identified and standards on these regulate the form in which they should be measured and expressed. For example, for air temperature, annual, monthly and daily mean, minimum and maximum temperatures, summer and winter temperatures, the number of frost days (when there is frost) and the number of zero transitions (when the temperature passes through zero downwards) are defined. Similar agreements exist on other data, adapted to specific aspects of the climatic phenomenon. For example, the data on strong winds are of great interest; for rain, in addition to mean and maximum values, the maximum rainfall (in millimetres) during shorter periods (one hour, 24 hours, five days) is also of interest.

One set of climatic data that is frequently used in the design of heating services is what is known as 'heating degree hours' or 'heating degree days'. This is termed in the ISO 6397 Standard as 'accumulated time – temperature difference' (ATTD), and the methodology for its computation and presentation are defined. ATTDs are the measure of climatic severity as it affects the energy used for the space heating of buildings. They may be used for predicting, comparing and monitoring the energy used by the heating, and for formulating energy policies. Modern designers use computer programs that draw on databases of climatic data.

ENERGY: RESOURCES, CONSUMPTION AND CONSERVATION

A GLOBAL SURVEY ON ENERGY

Wood was the main fossil fuel in use until the late eighteenth century, when the large-scale mining of coal began. The extraction of oil and natural gas started towards the end of the nineteenth century, but coal continued to dominate the energy supply in developed countries through to the early twentieth century, during the course of which oil and natural gas have increased in importance as fuels. Around 1950, coal accounted for 60% of global energy used; by 1985, its share had fallen to about 30%, with oil and gas taking up most of the shortfall. Other energy sources (nuclear, water and wind) failed to increase their total share over 10% until recently. Nevertheless, fossil fuels such as coal, oil, natural gas and wood still account for 78% of the world's primary energy supply, with hydropower, nuclear power, biomass, solar energy and wind energy making up the remaining 22% (Davis, 1990). The picture is still worse if transport is considered separately, because oil accounts for 97% of the energy used in this sector. In the generation of electricity, the share of oil is down to 10%; nuclear power provides 17% and hydroelectric power 18%; solar and wind energy have a modest 1% share (the remaining share taken by coal, gas etc.). At present consumption rates, oil could last for more than 40 years, gas for more than 60 years and coal for more than 230 years. Demand will naturally rise, but then so will known reserves.

The burning of each of the main fossil fuels produces a different amount of carbon dioxide, the prime cause of global climate change. The burning of wood contributes least to climate change if tree stocks are replaced, otherwise it has a similar impact on the climate as the burning of oil or gas. Despite great efforts to save energy and to increase the share of total energy production that comes from renewable resources, fossil fuels will continue to dominate for some time. Nevertheless, the future of renewable energy resources looks increasingly bright. The cost of generating electricity from the sun and the wind is decreasing, and these energy sources are therefore becoming more viable. For example, the cost of energy generated by photovoltaic cells is higher than that of mains electricity, but in regions without a mains electric supply, it can be the most economical solution.

Along with industry and transport, building is among the most important energy consumers. The production of building materials such as cement, steel, aluminium, glass and plastics, and their various components (e.g. steam-curing of concrete) requires a considerable amount of energy. Cement-making also produces a large volume of carbon dioxide because that gas is released when calcium carbonate (limestone) is transformed into calcium oxide. The approximate primary energy content of some building materials is shown in Table 4.1.

The various construction processes, such as the transport and lifting of building materials and the use of earth-excavating and moving machines, have their own energy requirements. Several studies have compared the energy requirements of buildings constructed from different materials, and it has now been recognized that the energy consumption of a building during its whole life is much more than the energy used during the manufacturing of its building materials and construction. For this reason,

Table 4.1 Approximate primary energy content of selected building materials

Material	kWh/kg	kWh/m3
Sawn timber	0.7	350
Concrete	0.3	700
Bricks	0.8	1400
Steel	6.0	46 000
PVC	18.0	25 000
Aluminium	52.0	140 000

research has concentrated on designs that minimize final total energy requirements.

ENERGY CONSERVATION POLICIES

The following factors can assist in reducing energy consumption in buildings (Zackrison Jr, 1984; Bevington and Rosenfeld, 1990):

- better heat insulation of the external envelope, i.e. reducing the heat loss of the building
- the development/use of services that consume less energy
- the recovery of energy that would otherwise be lost (e.g. from fumes, exhaust air, and external sources such as soil or water)
- the usage of renewable energy forms such as solar power
- the control and measurement of energy consumption
- the introduction of appropriate pricing and tax incentives to reduce consumption and penalties on continued higher energy consumption
- the reduction of indoor temperature requirements
- more efficient energy auditing and management.

Equipment with a potential for energy conservation includes:

- building services such as HVAC, lighting, lifts (elevators)
- household appliances such as ovens, refrigerators, freezers, washing machines, dishwashers, vacuum cleaners and others
- machinery used in buildings such as computers, other office machinery, medical equipment.

Industry is doing its best to develop and manufacture more energy-efficient appliances and machinery (Rabl, 1992; BRE, 1994a). Energy conservation is most successful where it yields benefits to both the owners and the users of buildings (BRE, 1994b, 1994c). The energy consumption cost of a personal computer during its lifetime is modest in relation to its purchase price at 0.2–20%, whereas the energy cost of the lifetime consumption of a refrigerator is approximately equal to its purchase price.

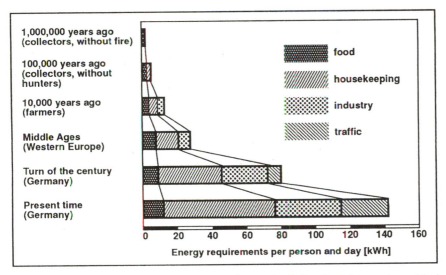

Fig. 4.2   Development of total energy requirements during the history of mankind. *Source:* K. Gertis (1995) Low-energy or low-entropy houses? In *Proceedings of the Building Physics Symposium*, Budapest, 4–6 October 1995, 3–8.

However, the sharp increase that is anticipated in the number of office machines will transform the relatively small amount of energy consumption that office equipment currently accounts for into an amount to be reckoned with. For the purpose of energy conservation, models have been devised that simulate future energy consumption and the performance of particular equipment. Such models enable the client or designer to evaluate alternatives, but these models themselves must be validated and calibrated, and it must be ascertained whether they are accurate. It is also necessary to take verifying measurements in buildings so that the models can be corrected and adjusted (Chapman, 1994).

In several countries, some form of methodology has been devised to measure compliance with an agreed energy efficiency level. Those who qualify are entitled to display a logo indicating this. Some architects and engineers have been successful at designing buildings with innovative energy-saving solutions. One such example is Ove Arup, whose rain-screen cladding system for the University of Northumbria's computer department building consists of glazing panels coated in a layer of photovoltaic material. The panels are connected electrically, and the electricity generated is then fed back into the building's own power circuit. Despite the fact that the character of energy conservation varies in different countries, international efforts have already yielded results. One German study found that the annual consumption of heating oil in one- or two-family houses was reduced from 40 l/m² (400 kWh/m²) in 1973, to 26 l/m² in 1986, and in blocks of flats from 35 l/m² to 21 l/m². The new objective is to reduce this consumption to 18 l/m² and 14 l/m², respectively. A recent study in Belgium found similar data for annual heating energy consumption: 233 kWh/m² in average houses, 121 kWh/m² in recently built houses, and 44.5 kWh/m² in low-energy houses.

There are many measures that have the potential to contribute to energy conservation, but just one, increasing the heat insulation of the external envelope, is explored below.

INCREASING THE HEAT INSULATION

Improving the efficiency of heat insulation means more than simply increasing the thickness of the insulation. It is a complex process that affects the design of the building and all its construction details. It also affects the manner in which buildings are used.

Increasing heat insulation reduces heat loss and therefore heating requirements and energy consumption. The reduction of heat loss through energy-conserving ventilation is discussed later in this chapter. Here we focus on the improved thermal resistance (R) of the external envelope. For homogeneous structures, the thermal resistance is increased by thickening the material layer of the wall, floor or roof, or their relevant heat insulating layers, and by reducing the thermal conductivity of the material. It was traditionally thought to be generally undesirable to increase the thickness of the construction, so for homogeneous structures the only possibility was a reduction in the thermal conductivity of the material. This could be attained by replacing solid bricks with hollow ones, hollow concrete blocks or lightweight concrete. These measures are still in use, but it is now more common to substitute multilayered structures for homogeneous ones. One of the layers in the former is load-bearing, the others are heat-insulating. From the technological point of view, it would be better to place the hard layer (e.g. masonry) on the outside, because this would then provide protection against impact and driving rain, but this arrangement is disadvantageous from the point of view of vapour transport, because the discharge of vapour is prevented by the hard layer, at precisely the point where air already has a low temperature in winter. In theory, it is preferable to have material with high vapour permeability on the exterior, and the hard layer, which is usually the least permeable, on the inside. As this is not a natural arrangement for walls, other solutions have been introduced, either in the form of an air cavity ventilated to the outside, or by installing a vapour-impermeable layer as near as possible to the inside. In principle, the same problems exist for roofs and, accordingly, the solutions are roughly similar. One interesting system is the 'inverse roof', in which the heat insulation is placed on top of the water-proofing layer, which is favourable for avoiding condensation (see Chapter 5).

Transparent (or rather, translucent) insulation technology in the building envelope is the most recent energy conserving idea. Transparent insulation materials have high transmissivity for solar radiation with relatively low thermal conductivity. These materials can be applied to walls, window systems and solar collectors. There are two types of transparent insulation systems:

- absorber perpendicular structures (honeycomb and capillary structures)
- quasi-homogeneous structures (silica aerogel).

At present, the prospects for developing the first category are the more realistic. The materials used in this category are polycarbonate, polymethylmetacrylate and glass. While the development of aerogels is also promising, some of their properties have to be improved as they are currently prone to discoloration and destruction by water. In wall systems, the solar radiation would be transmitted through the transparent insulation material and absorbed by the blackened surface of the opaque brick or concrete wall and by pipes in the wall. The absorbed heat would then find its way through the wall to the inside of the building. The transparent insulation material would also work in a conventional manner to reduce transmission losses. The impact of transparent insulation on indoor lighting would also have to be evaluated in advance. The use of transparent insulation materials is not yet widespread.

Heat insulation should be increased in existing as well as new buildings. Windows have a greater heat loss than walls, and so there is therefore more scope for their improvement. Heat loss through windows can be reduced by improving glazing (double or triple or by using special glass) and by making them and their junctions with the wall more airtight. Heat insulation requirements have been tightened up during the past 20 years in most industrialized countries. Experimental buildings have been constructed to demonstrate extremely low heat loss features, and the lessons drawn can be put into practice in the future.

RENEWABLE ENERGY FORMS: SOLAR ENERGY UTILIZATION

When examining the potential for increased conservation of natural resources, the greater use of renewable energy is of particular importance. Renewable energy comes from nature and effectively, is, inexhaustible. Its main forms are sunshine, wind, water (hydropower) and the earth's internal heat (geothermal), although green plants and organic waste can also be considered. At present, the most promising among these is solar energy, with wind coming a distant second.

Only about 50% of the sun's light actually reaches the earth's surface as 30% is reflected back by clouds and the atmosphere, and 20% is absorbed by the atmosphere. The amount of solar energy actually reaching land areas is only about 15% of the total, and yet this exceeds mankind's present annual consumption of energy by a factor of 2800. However, increasing the actual use of this energy economically from its present low level is no easy task (Nitsch, 1994). The first patent on a method of collecting the energy of the sun was obtained by a A.B. Mouchot in France in 1861. It is only recently, however, that the actual use of solar energy is increasing. There are two basic ways to utilize solar energy: passively, when it is used to heat fluid that is to be stored and used later; and actively, when solar energy is used to generate electricity. Solar heating systems in buildings have three essential components:

- collection of solar energy using collectors located on the external envelope of the building (roof or wall)
- storage of the collected thermal energy in a heat store
- return of the collected or stored energy to the building and its user.

Flat-plate collectors are used most often for solar heat collection. The shortwave solar irradiation transmitted through the glazing heats up fluid or air behind the glazing. This is then stored or used for heating or hot water production. In most cases, collectors are placed on high-pitch roofs parallel to the roof's plane, although they are occasionally placed on the façade walls. An attempt has been made to use transparent heat insulation for this purpose. Heat storage completes the solar system to make its continuous operation possible.

Another application of solar energy is to establish independent energy-producing plants. Various systems have been developed for locations with different sunshine characteristics. Although considerable land is required for active energy-producing plants, research has proved that this need not be a fundamental barrier to the wider use of solar energy. Solar thermal electricity can be generated by:

- parabolic trough collectors
- central receivers placed on top of a tower, and heliostats arranged on the ground around the tower
- solar chimneys in which air is heated under a large transparent collector roof producing an upwind that is converted into mechanical energy by turbines
- solar concentrator mirrors
- photoelectric or photovoltaic cells
- solar ponds with highly saline water near the bottom trapping heat.

The independent generation of solar electricity is not directly a task for the construction industry, but solar collectors and photovoltaic cells are of the highest relevance to buildings. The direct conversion of light to electricity was first observed in 1839 by the French physicist (Alexandre) Edmond Becquerel. Photovoltaic cells with pure crystalline silicon were developed in the 1940s. Advances since then have succeeded in reducing costs, but photovoltaic cells are still not economically competitive. It is to be hoped that costs can be reduced further within the next decade.

Wind energy can be used in various new configurations of wind turbines. There are plans in The Netherlands to produce sufficient energy from this source for 1 000 000 people by 2000 (Lainey and Malcolm, 1994).

The industrial use of geothermal energy has mainly been developed in Iceland, although several other countries (including the USA, Russia and the UK) are also experimenting into the use of the heat from deep underground (Kristjansson *et al.*, 1994).

Despite major efforts, the conversion of wave power into electricity is still in its infancy. A few full-sized wave energy converters have been built to date, and different principles have been studied for the purpose of converting wave-activated motion into the unidirectional rotation of a generator shaft, including the problem of moderating the power fluctuations and ensuring short-term energy storage (Funakoshi *et al.*, 1994; Nielsen, 1994; von Scholten, 1994). Experimental equipment has been built for electricity generators making use of tidal power. Experimental plants also exist for ocean thermal energy conversion. These use the warm water at the surface and the cold water in the depths of the ocean to alternate evaporation and condensation of a working fluid, usually ammonia, to produce energy (Chow, 1994).

Different forms of vegetation can also be sources of energy production. Fast-growing trees such as willows can be cut each year and used as fuel, and biomass is another promising source of energy.

The expectations of nuclear power have been dashed by its adverse environmental effects. Nevertheless, a small, but not negligible, fraction of total energy is produced by nuclear power in most industrialized countries. France is the only country in which a large share of total energy is generated by nuclear means.

During the next decade the use of alternative energy sources will reduce the demand for fossil fuels only marginally, but developmental work will continue.

THERMAL DESIGN OF BUILDINGS

Once all the relevant climatic, energy and comfort requirement data are to hand, the thermal design of the building can begin. This is a complex process in which various alternatives have to be devised and compared. Higher levels of heat insulation cost more but result in greater economies in energy. Similarly, the heating, ventilation and air-conditioning equipment can also be designed to various technical levels, and running costs can be reduced with a greater initial investment.

It is a long time since engineers first established methodologies for the design of heating plants. This process has recently become more complex as more factors than ever before have to be evaluated, which is why so many international standards have been drafted in this area (e.g. ISO 9164, ISO NP 13790, 13791 and 13792). ISO NP 13790 and a related CEN paper define the energy balance of buildings to include the following:

- heat loss due to transmission and ventilation from the internal to the external environment or to unheated spaces
- heat loss or gain due to transmission and ventilation to and from adjacent zones
- internal heat gains
- solar gains
- utilization factor for the gains
- generation, distribution, emission and efficiency control of the heating system
- the energy input of the heating system.

Following calculations, the annual heat and energy requirements for the whole building should be assessed together with an estimate of the contingency resulting from inaccuracy of the input data. The objective of ISO NP 13791 is to provide the methodology with which to define the characteristics of a room in order to avoid overheating in summer and to determine if the installation of a cooling system is necessary. The calculation of energy consumption and heat, moisture and air transport requires knowledge about certain properties of materials. Both in ISO and CEN the work is continuing on further development of international standards in this field.

HEALTH IN BUILDINGS: 'SICK BUILDINGS'

Health is more than simply a lack of illness. It comprises various components of the interrelationship between a person and the ambient surroundings. Most people spend more than half their lives indoors, and their health is therefore greatly affected by the characteristics of closed spaces.

One of the most important factors influencing human health is the feeling of comfort in relation to heat, air quality, light and noise conditions in buildings. The following six factors of heat-related conditions are considered important:

- the temperature of the air, the distribution and changes of air temperature
- the heat radiation characteristics of surrounding surfaces
- the moisture conditions of the indoor air
- the velocity and other characteristics (e.g. turbulence) of moving air

- the thermal properties of the human body (e.g. body and skin temperature, the thermal consequences of human activities)
- the impact of clothing.

A fundamental function of any building designed for human occupation is to ensure the feeling of comfort and warmth of the occupants. Energy conservation has made our buildings more airtight and has reduced ventilation rates, and a consequence of this can be an increase in the moisture content of the indoor air, resulting in condensation and the growth of mould.

People have different reactions to temperature, with some preferring warmer temperatures than others. These differences also depend on habit, age, health and clothing. Other indoor factors such as light, draughts and noise also affect the feeling of comfort or discomfort. In order to be able to quantify thermal sensation, it has been agreed internationally to express this by the 'predicted mean vote' (PMV) index, a function of thermal parameters, clothing and the occupant's activity. The 1994 edition of the international standard ISO 7730, deals with the conditions for thermal comfort in moderate thermal environments. The stated purpose of this standard is to present a method for predicting the thermal sensation and the degree of discomfort or thermal dissatisfaction of people exposed to moderate thermal environments, and to specify the relevant acceptable thermal conditions for comfort.

Polluted, humid or too dry indoor air can all be deleterious to the health of the occupants, causing tiredness, headaches, nausea and even more serious illnesses. The causes are not always easy to identify, but indoor conditions are undoubtedly implicated and are summed up in the popular expressions 'healthy buildings' (giving occupants a feeling of satisfaction with the indoor space) and 'sick buildings' (causing discomfort to occupants). The problem has even acquired a certain notoriety and been labelled 'sick building syndrome'. A combination of various adverse factors such as indoor air temperature, draughts, moisture, condensation, odour, noise and disturbing lighting, not to mention water ingress, are invariably present in sick buildings. If 20% or more of a building's occupants express symptoms without a known causal agent, it is classified as a sick building. Objective measurements often do not immediately reveal the root of the problem as a personal rating of satisfaction may point to anomalies that cannot be expressed by measurements.

During the past 20 or so years, a good deal of building and medical research has been carried out in order to determine the effects of various conditions individually and in combination. The difficulties of such research are compounded by the fact that certain adverse causes may have only a marginal effect on health in the short-term, while their long-term impact may be very serious, especially if the effect of air pollutants

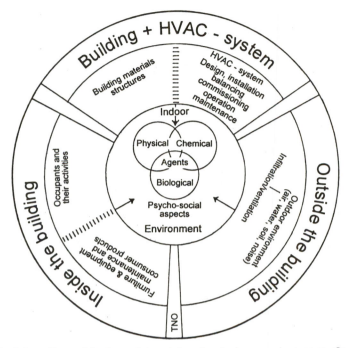

Fig. 4.3 Interaction of factors determining the indoor environment. *Source:* M. Rolloos (1988) Holistic view on indoor environment. In *Healthy Buildings '88 Stockholm and Workshop Proceedings on IAQ-Management*, Lausanne, Switzerland, 1991.

is considered (Bischof *et al.*, 1993). Good indoor conditions can be ensured when the various parameters of the indoor space (air temperature, pollution, etc.) are kept within or below certain limits. Based on research, such values have been established and incorporated into codes and regulations. In several cases, these values are still under debate and are the subject of further research.

The appearance of microbes and allergens in a building is often connected with damage to and malfunction of the building or its ventilation or air-conditioning systems. Mites and fungi also contribute to an increase in asthma, allergies and skin diseases. The incidence of asthma has increased recently and house dust, which is a complex mixture of inorganic dust, mites, skin particles, animal hairs, pollen, and vegetal and animal debris, can be a cause. Most types of vacuum cleaner release a large number of particles into the air, increasing the risks of respiratory problems (Léopold, Cochet and Derangère, 1996). The occurrence of facial skin symptoms has increased with the amount of video display terminal work. The immunological status of people in industrialized countries seems to have changed.

Structural design must ensure that no disturbing deformations and motions are generated in the structure. Vibration can cause discomfort in tall or lightweight buildings. Until this century, people expected buildings to provide virtually stationary accommodation, even under storm conditions, and occupants were usually prepared to accept only extremely low levels of motion in buildings. Modern buildings tend to be more responsive to dynamic forces than their predecessors, however. The criterion for allowable motion is the alarm it engenders in the occupants, and there are certain limit values that are considered acceptable (ISO 6897).

Some 'biotechnologists' claim that modern construction materials and technologies *per se* constitute a risk to human health. While this is true in a few cases, most of these arguments are untenable (Gertis, 1988). One such false theory is the idea that walls need to 'breathe'. The amount of air ventilated through traditional closed or open windows is much more than can pass through traditional brick masonry walls by means of diffusion. The breathing of walls therefore being of negligible magnitude, a requirement for it seems unnecessary and hence misleading. Only ventilation can ensure control of air quality.

BIOLOGICAL AGENTS IN BUILDINGS

The consequences of physical and chemical effects were recognized long ago. Corrosion is one, and recently attention has also been attracted to biological phenomena. While research data have not yet been consolidated into a comprehensive body of knowledge, there are many individual reports on biological influences. Biological agents cause various forms of degradation to buildings, and some are also harmful to health. This is a large subject in itself that cannot be discussed here in detail.

A study by the UK Building Research Establishment (BRE, 1992) identified the following groups of biological growths on exterior building materials: algae, lichens, mosses, liverworts, moulds, and bacteria. Some of these also grow on internal surfaces. Algae, lichen and moss are commonly found growing on the external surfaces of buildings that are subjected to frequent wetting. Liverworts are typically leafy, close-growing, green-coloured plants that are usually found on the surfaces of stone walls where soil and dirt have accumulated. Certain bacteria cause the deterioration of stone, bricks, concrete and metals. Moulds develop on damp and dirty external or internal surfaces. Mould growth has increased in recent years, partly because of energy conservation measures. Growth can begin at a relative humidity of 80% in indoor air, and so the requirement that the partial vapour pressure in the air should remain under saturation point is not enough. A more stringent requirement aimed at maintaining a lower level of humidity in indoor air should be introduced (Erhorn and Reiss, 1992).

The American Hotel and Motel Association has estimated that problems caused by mould and mildew cost the industry about US$68 million in lost revenues and repairs every year. As well as in-room mould, problems can also include mould behind low-permeability wallpaper, for example. Mould behind wallpaper can occur in hot and humid climates during the summer when outdoor moisture is transferred into prefabricated wall construction by way of diffusion and air infiltration. If the wallpaper has a high water vapour-resistance, moisture accumulates behind it, providing an environment conducive to mould and mildew growth (Burch, 1993; Burch and TenWolde, 1993). Surface biocides and fungicidal paints can provide short-term protection against mould, but only an improvement in conditions through better ventilation and heating, appropriate arrangement of wall layers and correct indoor-air pressure can permanently prevent mould growth.

As early as 1900, corrosion of concrete was described in the sewer network of Los Angeles. At the time it was considered to be a purely chemical process and became known as 'hydrogen sulphide corrosion' (Milde et al., 1983; Sand and Bock, 1984), but recent research by chemists, civil engineers and microbiologists in collaboration, has demonstrated the active part played by bacilli (Thiobacilli) in this form of corrosion, which is now termed 'biogenic sulphuric acid corrosion'. Sulphate-reducing bacteria can corrode steel machinery as well as steel pipes for water and gas. A host of such sulphate-reducing bacteria genes been identified (Postgate, 1988).

A quite different cause of stone and concrete decay has been described by German scientists (Bock and Sand, 1986; Kirstein et al., 1986). At the Cologne and Regensburg cathedrals, among others, they found that bacteria that produced nitric and sulphuric acid, together with fungi and algae, are deleterious to stone. Degradation of asbestos cement slabs has also been found to be caused by bacteria that produce nitrates and nitrites (Schiffers et al., 1976). Air conditioning can cause fungal, viral and bacterial infections, bronchial allergies and asthma. Humidifier fever and Legionnaire's disease can both be caused by bacteria in air conditioning and hot water systems. They are rare, but precautions are necessary. It is safest if the temperature of warm water is kept above a certain level (Pickering and Jones, 1986). The disinfection of cooling water by ultraviolet light and the biocide treatment of evaporative condensers are two methods of controlling microbial growth in wet cooling systems.

TECHNICAL SERVICES OF BUILDINGS

INTRODUCTION AND SURVEY

It is possible to construct the envelope of a house just as it was done a thousand years ago but one would not now be satisfied with the technical equipment of an earlier age because our expectations have changed radically with the passage of time. Previously, buildings were built to protect from heat and cold and the elements, and their services were confined to stoves and kitchen equipment. The technical progress of construction is very much characterized by the development of costly technical services in buildings. In German these go under the comprehensive name of 'Haustechnik'; in English we can use the expression 'technical services'. Progress has been achieved in three directions. Firstly, technical services cover new areas, and the list of them is becoming longer all the time. Secondly, those services are continually being made more efficient. Heating used to mean simply a fire burning in a stove; today we can control temperature and its distribution. Thirdly, technical progress in materials (polymers etc.), components, design and production of technical services has stimulated progress. One such development is the prefabrication of service units, sometimes called 'heart units'. These are complete bathroom/shower/kitchen assemblies, containing all the pipes, fittings and other components necessary for installation (Wise and Swaffield, 1995).

All equipment in buildings consumes some energy, and there have been successful attempts to modernize the 'hardware' and 'software' of technical services so as to achieve lower energy consumption and to consume less water.

The following section gives a brief survey of a few selected areas of technical equipment and services, mainly those in which much progress has been achieved. Some services such as telecommunications are discussed elsewhere.

VENTILATION, HEATING AND AIR CONDITIONING

Ventilation

The purpose of ventilation is to ensure the quality of the indoor air without causing a feeling of cold or draught. This was traditionally achieved by openings in the external envelope: windows, doors and ventilation stacks. A demand for better air quality led to the introduction of artificial (mechanical) ventilation. In most cases, however, a combination of natural and artificial ventilation was retained, providing the advantages of both. In buildings with air-conditioning and windows that could not be opened, however, natural ventilation was often completely dispensed with, which led to the complaints discussed earlier. The new demand for energy conservation has also resulted in research into providing natural ventilation wherever this would be sufficient or possible. Whatever ventilation system is used, the best (and costliest) arrangement is demand-controlled ventilation, with which each occupant can individually control ventilation flow rates based on the air quality as that person perceives it, or on some objective measure. Research in several countries, including the UK, has shown that in most offices and schools, natural ventilation could provide appropriate indoor conditions, although mixed-mode ventilation and possibilities for individual control of the indoor conditions could yield the perfect solution (Walker and White, 1992; Bordass, Entwisle and Willis, 1994; Walker *et al.*, 1994; White and Walker, 1994).

In houses and blocks of flats up to four storeys high, unwanted moisture can be removed through passive stack ventilation via ducts from the ceiling of kitchens, utility rooms, bathrooms and WCs (Stephen *et al.*, 1994). Passive stack ventilation systems function as a result of the difference in indoor and outside temperature and the effect of wind passing over the roof. Should this not be sufficient, active support of ventilation by artificially increasing the temperature difference and/or the draught may be used. Contaminated air must be removed from buildings and fresh air supplied. The heat of the exhaust air can be used to warm or cool the supply of fresh air, thereby reducing energy consumption.

In traditional dilution ventilation, air and pollutants are mixed throughout the room. A new system called displacement ventilation, with many advantages over dilution ventilation (Skistad, 1994) has been pioneered in Scandinavia. In the most common form of this system, fresh air enters the room at its lower part, flows along the floor, rises up to the ceiling in the convection currents caused by the occupants and office equipment, and is then extracted by outlets in the ceiling. The air should move at a low velocity in order to avoid draughts, and the air supplied should be at least 0.5° C cooler than that in the room so that it does not immediately rise towards the ceiling. Displacement ventilation has become more popular during the past 15 years as in certain cases it may provide better air quality than dilution ventilation while still using the same amount of ventilating air.

A partly or totally cooled ceiling is an effective way to transfer a large heat load away from the room. Its advantages are an absence of draught, a smaller air flow, and economical operation. Cooled ceilings can also be used in combination with displacement ventilation. Under-floor air distribution has similar advantages to displacement ventilation. Optimum and minimum ventilation rates for different buildings have been established and serve as a guide for design.

Heating systems

Throughout history, premises have, with few exceptions, been heated individually. Central heating only became possible when iron or steel pipes, boilers and radiators were introduced, so that in effect central heating can point to a past of only 200 years.

Central heating systems supply heat to spaces in buildings through pipes (steam or hot water), ducts (air), or electric conduits. Steam and hot water systems, or so-called hydronic systems, are commonly used in mainland Europe, although steam systems have recently been losing popularity to hot water systems. Air systems are far more common in North America, where air conditioning (requiring air with a controlled temperature and moisture) is widespread (McQuiston and Parker, 1994).

Hot water systems can be operated either by gravity or by force. A gravity system uses the difference in density between the supply and return water; a pump maintains the flow. Gravity hot water systems are being used less and less. Tall buildings have forced systems because the usual pressure in pipes is not sufficient to raise water to the required height; pressure conditions in hot and cold water pipes have to be designed with consideration of the height of the building.

Thermal storage in HVAC systems is the temporary storage of high- or low-temperature energy for later use, e.g. storage of solar energy for night heating, summer heat for winter use, and winter ice for space cooling in the summer (*1991 ASHRAE Handbook*). The storage media are usually water, soil, rocks and other solid materials.

Components of heating systems

The basic equipment for producing heat in a building is a furnace for an air system or a boiler for a hydronic system. Furnaces provide heated air through a system of ductwork into the space being heated. Boilers are pressure vessels designed to transfer heat produced by combustion to a fluid, which usually is water. Boilers, which are essentially heat exchangers, are made of cast-iron, steel or copper, and are connected to a pipe system that delivers the heated water to the points of use, returning the cooled water to the boiler.

To exploit the energy content of fuel more fully, a new type of heat exchanger, the condensing boiler, has been developed. This cools the hot waste gases from combustion to condense the water vapour, which then gives up its latent heat in evaporation. The condensate is slightly acidic due to the presence of sulphuric and nitric acids. For this reason, corrosion-resistant materials such as some aluminium alloys or stainless steel are used. Chimneys must have smooth internal surfaces in order to improve draught, which is less because the lower temperature of the fumes reduces the temperature difference between the flue gas and the outside air (Morin and Chandelier, 1994; Morin *et al.*, 1995). Not only do condensing boilers have lower energy consumption, they also have lower emission levels. Their compactness is a further advantage. They can be wall-hung, floor-standing or frame-mounted, and so may eliminate the need for a boiler room. Condensing boilers can be used in conjunction with conventional boilers; their combined operational use depends on external temperatures and heat loads (Lillywhite, 1988).

In hydronic systems, the output of the so-called terminal units (radiators, convectors, finned tube units) that distribute the heat through a combination of radiation and convection, has been much improved. The heat pump principle can be used for heat recovery so that heat that is normally rejected is saved and used. Heat recovery can also be combined with heat storage. The term 'heat pump' is applied to units in which heat is moved from one place to another with the primary purpose of heating. (In principle, the same happens in refrigeration plants, but in that case for cooling.) Most heat pumps are air-to-air units using air both as a heat source and as the heat sink. Other types of heat pumps use earth and stones or water as the heat source and/or as the heat sink.

Appliances have been developed that produce in a single unit the heat for central heating, the supply of warm/hot water, recuperate heat and control ventilation. Most of the future developments in heating will be the consequence of work currently being undertaken. For example, the heating appliances of dwellings were developed for earlier, higher heat loads; for smaller performances, more economic ones could be developed. Other probable changes could be: a wider application of condensing boilers for oil heating, wider use of heat pumps, and improved controls and systems combining supply functions.

Air conditioning

Present-day air conditioning, which is the environmental control of the interior of a building, is the result of many years of research and development. The most common system contains an air-handling unit (chiller, heater, humidifier, dehumidifier), fans, ductwork, coils and filters. In the single-path system, heated or cooled air is supplied to spaces at a required temperature. In dual-path systems, heated and cooled air is sent in separate ducts to spaces and mixed just before entry. In air-conditioning systems, heated or cooled air has to be supplied in a humidified or dehumidified condition. The terminal units are unit ventilators, fan-coil units, variable air volume boxes and others. Air-handling units are normally supplied factory-assembled. Most units for large buildings used to be made for roof-top installation and thus did not require any useable space within the building. Their reduction in size has led to the manufacture of packaged units.

The refrigeration used in air conditioning consumes electricity and produces carbon dioxide. This is one reason for using air conditioning sparingly (Calder and Grigg, 1993). At first, absorption chillers were used in parallel with vapour compression units, but they were later abandoned. Very recently, interest in them has been revived, and research is currently underway to verify whether they could be improved and reintroduced to the market (Smith, Webb and Wiech, 1992; Smith and Webb, 1993).

HVAC systems controls

HVAC systems can be either simple or sophisticated. Large HVAC systems have automatic controls (ASHRAE, 1991; Levenhagen *et al.*, 1993), and are sometimes referred to as supervisory control systems, building automation systems, energy management systems, energy monitoring and control systems or facility management systems. Most of these control the temperature of hot water or air, the humidity of the air, the air pressure and the flow rate. Other functions can be alarm reporting and energy reporting. For control purposes they can have pneumatic, mechanical, electrical or electronic control. Sensors measure controlled variables and convey values to the controllers, such as thermostats and humidistats, which seek to maintain the desired values of the controlled variables. Sensors that convert thermal or other energy to electricity are known as transducers. The sensor and the controller can be combined in a single instrument such as a room thermostat.

Residential heating is commonly controlled by a wall thermostat. As the control processes become ever more sophisticated, simple wall thermostats with bimetallic strips are being replaced by microelectronic models containing microprocessors that can control equipment to follow set programs. Modern residential electronic controls are vastly superior to the old thermostats. They can have several programs a day with a different schedule for each day of the week. They also provide enhanced energy efficiency.

In modern HVAC automatic control systems, direct digital control, where the controller function calculations are made by a computer or microprocessor, is available (McQuiston and Parker, 1994). In well-designed and well-managed buildings, comfort and energy efficiency go together (Bromley, Bordass and Leaman, 1993a; Sterling, Bieva and Collett, 1993; Bordass, Bromley and Leaman, 1995). An effective control-system operation and maintenance programme can add years to the life of the system components and yield substantial energy savings while providing a comfortable and healthy environment for the building's occupants (Gupton Jr, 1988; Willis, 1993; Willis and Perera, 1995). The systematic monitoring of energy consumption in buildings provides empirical information that gives us a better understanding of energy performance (*1991 ASHRAE Handbook*, 1991).

LIGHTING

The luminous environment

Scant attention has traditionally been paid to optimal natural and artificial lighting in housing, although candles and torches were well known from ancient times. Sunshine had a mystical function in some ancient Egyptian and Mexican buildings. Abbot Suger commented thus on the monastery of Saint Denis (see also Chapter 1):

> The entire sanctuary is flooded by a wonderful and uninterrupted light entering through the veritably holy windows.

> *Quoted in Foster, 1993*

It was not until the twentieth century, however, that people came to realize that adequately lit living and working environments are indispensable for their physical and psychological well-being. Lighting conditions are a major factor in human comfort. Lighting has grown into an important field of building research, and has acquired great importance in architectural design, as can be seen from this statement from Le Corbusier:

> Architecture is the learned, correct and magnificent play of masses under light.

> *Quoted in Foster, 1993*

Electric lighting is barely 100 years old, and much research has been carried out during the past 50 years to perfect natural and artificial lighting. Scale models, artificial sky laboratories, computer programs and measurements are the tools of such research. The design of buildings and light fittings draws on the knowledge thus acquired.

The luminous environment is the interplay between a room, its natural light and electric light. Lighting is often poor in rooms even though it could be improved at little cost. Lighting can be accentuated or unaccentuated, monotonous or varied. Glare and colour factors contribute to overall satisfaction or dissatisfaction with lighting (Flynn *et al.*, 1992). In modern offices, commercial establishments and some other buildings, electric lighting may be the largest single consumer of electricity and it can amount to about half or even more of the total energy consumption. In the USA, domestic electric lighting directly accounts for one-fifth of the total electrical energy used nationally; the commercial sector accounts for one-third. (Ander, 1995).

The heat generated by electric fixtures can lead to an increase in cooling requirements, which creates an additional (indirect) energy impact. It is therefore sensible to save energy wherever possible by a more rational use of daylight and artificial lighting. New types of lamps and control of unnecessary illumination could be the source of some savings, and more can be achieved by recovering the heat produced by light fittings, particularly in offices, department stores and other buildings with large internal spaces and high illumination levels (Cuttle and Slater, 1975). As a general guideline, the introduction of the maximum possible daylight into the interior of buildings can be recommended, but lighting should ensure not only sufficient luminance but also prevent glare or excessive brightness.

Lighting sources

Electric lighting began at the end of the nineteenth century with the carbon filament lamp. The metal filament lamp, using osmium, was introduced in 1898, and 10 years later the tungsten filament became widespread (Pritchard, 1995). As carbon is not used in lamps any more, incandescent lamps can be defined as light sources in which a metallic solid is heated to a temperature high enough to produce visible radiation.

A newer type of light source is the electric discharge lamp, in which a gas is subjected to an electric discharge. The two types, low and high pressure, were introduced between and subsequent to the two world wars. Low-pressure lamps, often termed fluorescent lamps, tend to be used in buildings. In common parlance these are sometimes referred to as neon lights, but this term reflects only the first type of gas used. The first fluorescent lamps had a diameter of 38 mm. Since then, their size has been reduced in both diameter and length. They are now increasingly replacing incandescent lamps, making use of their superior efficacity (de Groot *et al.*, 1995). Replacing an incandescent bulb with a compact fluorescent one can cut lighting costs by up to 80%.

Electric discharge lamps are filled with gas and vapour. High pressure lamps (also known as high intensity discharge (HID) lamps) are mainly used in public spaces (shops, hotels, offices, decorative outdoor). The most recent product from Philips is the Mastercolour CDM (ceramic discharge metal halide) lamps, which have a stable colour over their lifetime (an average 6000–8000 hours). High pressure sodium (HPS) lamps have been developed for accent lighting applications (Carlton, 1991). The lifetime of a filament lamp is about 1000–2000 hours. Low-pressure lamps last 9000–16 000 working hours, and high-pressure lamps 12 000–24 000 hours. Modern incandescent lamps are 100 times more efficient than the first carbon-filament lamps. The halogen lamp gives a light yield of 30–35 lumen/watt whereas a normal incandescent lamp gives only around 14 lumen/watt.

Tubular lamps were introduced before the Second World War. As well as the original cool colour, claimed to be like daylight, they are now available in various shades. Even so, their application is normally restricted to offices, kitchens, bathrooms and subsidiary spaces. The halogen light, on the other hand, has been much favoured by interior designers for its intense concentrated light. Certain types of halogen lamps (e.g. the electrodeless compact fluorescent lamp and decorative reflectors) have been specifically developed for shoplighting (de Bijl *et al.*, 1992). Some of the latest inventions are the new metal halide lamps, the induction lamp and the two-photon phosphorous lamp. Their durability is longer with better light-yield, but they are not yet in general use. Research is particularly focused on the colour rendering of lamps (van Kemenade and van der Burgt, 1988; van Kemenade *et al.*, 1990; van der Burgt *et al.*, 1995; van Kemenade and van der Burgt, 1995). It is almost certain that the incandescent lamps in present use will gradually give way to new types. At present these are more expensive but, as mentioned, their durability is up to eight times longer, which also contributes to their energy conservation advantages.

Lighting controls

In offices, depending on the external lighting, controlled levels of artificial lighting can be ensured automatically with appropriate switching control systems that turn the electric lights off when there is ample daylight. Dimming controls continuously adjust electric lighting to predetermined requirements (Szerman, 1994). The performance of the currently dominant commercial light source, the fluorescent lamp, is strongly dependent upon thermal conditions. Proper control of room temperature can ensure that the fittings are operating at their most efficient level. As discussed, heat dissipated from the light system adds to the building cooling load in summer, and decreases the heating requirements in winter. Energy can be conserved by designing adequate airflow and heat storage conditions, favourable configurations of lamps and cooling load profiles (Treado and Bean, 1988).

Innovative daylighting

Improved planning and new arrangements of spaces can improve daylighting by:

- the use of mirrored louvres and light shelves reflecting illuminance on to white ceilings as secondary diffusers
- prismatic glazing
- nearly horizontal baffles mounted on windows
- light pipes with back-up lamps.

Light piping can collect sunlight on the roof and distribute it in the building using fibreoptic technology (Flynn *et al.*, 1992). There are many examples of its realization (Littlefair, 1989), such as the Albany County Airport in Colonie, New York, where the skylit solar court provides 40% of the lighting and 20% of the heating. A microcomputer, programmed with the solar altitude and azimuth angles until 2000, continuously gauges the indoor and outdoor environment and selects the most energy-efficient position for the louvres. On a bright winter day, sunlight-heated warm air is circulated throughout the building. At night, the louvres are shut to trap heat. In summer, the louvres reflect direct sunlight but admit diffuse light.

Innovative daylighting devices such as mirrored louvres increase daylight levels towards the rear of rooms, improve daylight uniformity within a space, control direct sunlight and reduce glare and discomfort for occupants (Littlefair, Aizlewood and Birtles, 1993). Translucent plastic or plastic-coated fabrics are much used over stadiums, sport halls, shopping centres and railway stations. Fabric covers transmit about 15% of the light reaching them. While innovative daylighting devices and design features are not yet universal, there are already a great number of buildings that are making better use of daylighting and achieving substantial energy savings (Ander, 1995).

Light control for buildings has inspired architects to use new materials and systems. Renzo Piano required diffuse lighting to avoid damaging the paintings in the De Menil collection in Houston, Texas. Baffles hanging from ductile-iron trusses provide such light at the same time as helping to control the interior temperature. The ferrocement baffles are made from concrete reinforced with steel mesh and moulded into thin delicate shapes. The special material used was particularly suitable for precision castings (for museum lighting in general see Chapter 6). The south façade of the Arab World Institute building in Paris (architect; Jean Nouvel) has nearly 250 3 m × 3 m metal panels, which incorporate 30 000 shutters activated by photoelectric cells, thereby keeping natural lighting levels constant; an expensive but ingenious solution to a problem. In the Hongkong and Shanghai Building in Hong Kong, a periscopic arrangement of mirrors brings sunshine into the building's central atrium.

Research into the luminous environment and its results are contributing to the transformation of construction into a modern industry.

ELEVATORS

Hydraulic and, later, electric elevators were introduced in buildings during the nineteenth century. Since then they have developed to an astonishing degree. Elevators that serve tall buildings have sophisticated computer controls for receiving, storing, sorting and executing various requests for use. Problems have emerged in very tall buildings in which express elevators, with speeds of 9–15 m/s have been installed. The acceleration and high speed cause rapid ear pressure change leading to discomfort and pain. In some tall buildings, such as the Chicago Sears

Tower, speed has been reduced, particularly in descent. With very high buildings under design, the problem is even more acute. In such buildings, very high speed shuttle elevators would operate between the ground floor and sky lobbies, and local elevators stacked on top of one another would serve local zones. The high speed elevators would require arrangements to prevent discomfort, such as prepressurization at the sky lobby and/or depressurization at ground level. An adequate solution to the elevator problem is a pre-condition for the construction of super-high buildings.

SUMMARY

The energy crisis during the 1970s shook the economy of the whole world. High energy prices and the recognition that fossil fuel resources were finite had a major impact on the building industry, where massive research began to save energy in the construction and use of buildings. More recently, it has been recognized that a reduction in fossil fuel consumption is also necessary for other reasons: the burning of coal, oil and gas is accompanied by emissions of various gases that cause air pollution and climate warming. While the causes of climate change are still under debate, and the change itself is doubted by some scientists, recent meteorological data have been sufficiently convincing to prompt the acceptance of certain initial measures approved on an international level to counteract the trend of climate change and the accumulation of so-called 'greenhouse gases' in the atmosphere.

Refrigerants (CFCs) have been identified as another wrongdoer: they are destroying the ozone layer in the atmosphere, thereby increasing harmful radiation on the ground. CFCs are gradually being substituted by other materials that do not affect the ozone layer.

Smog is a form of outdoor air pollution. Its principal source, the burning of coal in households, has been reduced, but it is still sometimes prevalent in certain cities because of a high concentration of vehicle exhaust fumes. Smog is harmful to health and should be kept under control.

Improved heat insulation, better heating, ventilation, air conditioning, lighting and other measures have succeeded in reducing energy consumption in buildings. Simultaneously, the share of renewable energy sources (passive and active use of solar energy, wind and others) has increased. The thermal design of buildings has been adapted to the better understanding of the climate, the changing pattern of energy consumption and its consequences on the building envelope and technical services. In buildings of modern thermal construction occupants sometimes complain of and suffer from health problems. Consequently, the 'sick building syndrome' expression was coined and measures to create a healthy indoor ambience have been explored.

Corrosion is deleterious to buildings and among the various causes biological agents (mould, mites, etc.) are of increasing concern. They often also affect the occupants.

During the past 100 years, the technical services of buildings such as lighting, heating, ventilation and air conditioning (HVAC) systems, their components (e.g. condensing boilers and controls) and elevators have become more sophisticated. New ways of using daylight, plus artificial illumination sources with elaborate controls have been introduced. In very tall buildings, the problem of the acceleration of high-speed lifts and the sudden pressure changes caused continue to pose difficulties because of their affect on human health.

All in all, the technical services of buildings are becoming 'high-tech' products.

BIBLIOGRAPHY

Ander, G. D. (1995) *Daylighting Performance and Design*, Van Nostrand Reinhold.

1991 ASHRAE Handbook (1991) SI Edition.

Bevington, R. and Rosenfeld, A. H. (1990) Energy for buildings and homes, *Scientific American*, September, 39–45.

de Bijl, A. *et al.* (1992) A new effective high quality lighting system: QL the electrodeless compact fluorescent lamp. In *CIBSE National Lighting Conference Proceedings*, 257–66.

Bischof, W. *et al.* (eds), (1993) *Sick Building Syndrome, Documentation*, C. F. Müller, Karlsruhe, Germany.

Bock, E. and Sand, W. (1986) Applied electron microscopy on the biogenic destruction of concrete and blocks. In *Proceedings of the Eighth International Conference on Cement Microscope*, Orlando, Florida, 285–302.

Bordass, W. T., Bromley, A. K. R., Leaman, A. J. (1995) *Comfort, Control and Energy Efficiency in Offices*, BRE IP 3/95.

Bordass, W. T., Entwisle, M. J., Willis, S. T. P. (1994) Naturally-ventilated and mixed-mode office buildings: opportunities and pitfalls. In *CIBSE National Conference Proceedings*, 26–30.

BRE (1992) *Control of Lichens, Moulds and Similar Growths* BRE Digest 370.

BRE (1994a) *Future Energy Use and Carbon Dioxide Emissions for UK Housing: a Scenario*, BRE, IP 9/94.

BRE (1994b) *Energy use by Office Equipment: Reducing Long-term Running Costs*, BRE IP 10/94.

BRE (1994c) *Financial Benefits of Energy Efficiency to Housing Landlords*, BRE IP/11/94.

Bromley, A. K. R., Bordass, W. T. and Leaman A. (1993a) *User and Occupant Controls in Office Buildings*, BRE/169/17/5, PD 43/93.

Bromley, A. K. R., Bordass, W. T. and Leaman, A. (1993b) *Improved Utilisation of Building Management and Control Systems*, BRE/169/17/5, PD 10/93.

Burch, D. M. (1993) An analysis of moisture accumulation in walls subjected to hot and humid climates, *ASHRAE Transactions*, **99** (2).

Burch, D. M. and TenWolde, A. (1993) Computer analysis of moisture accumulation in the walls of manufactured housing, *ASHRAE Transactions*, 99 (2).

van der Burgt, P. J. M. *et al.* (1994) Application aspects of new PL-T compact fluorescent lamps. In *CIBSE National Lighting Conference 1994*.

van der Burgt, P. J. M. *et al.* (1995) A new generation of metal halide lamps in polycristaline alumins: In *CIE 119–1995 23rd Session Proceedings*, 486–7.

Butler, D. J. G. (1995a) *Alternative Refrigerants: Environmental and Safety Issues*, BRE, PD10/95.

Butler, D. J. G. (1995b) *New EC Regulations on CFCs and HCFCs: Implications for Building Services*, BRE, PD21/95.

Butler, D. J. G. (1995c) *New Refrigerants: Environmental and Safety Issues*, BRE, PD76/95.

Butler, D. J. G. (1994) *Drop-in Replacement of HCFC22 (R22)*, BRE, PD132/94.

Butler, D. J. G. and Fannin, T. (1994) *Trials with New HFC-based Refrigerants*, BRE, PD24/94.

Calder, K. and Grigg, P. (1993) *The CO_2 Impact of Refrigeration Used for Air Conditioning*, BRE 169/17/16, PD 6/93.

Carlton, S. *et al.* (1991) White HPS lamps with a color temperature of 2700 K, *Journal of the Illuminating Engineering Society*, Winter, 134–9.

CFCs and buildings (1991) *BRE Digest*, **358**, based on D. J. G. Butler (1989) CFCs and the Building Industry, BRE Information paper, IP 23/89.

Chapman, P. F. (1994) A geometrical model of dwellings for use in simple energy calculations, *Energy and Buildings*, **2**; see also other articles in the same issue.

Chow, P. Y. (1994) Ocean thermal energy conversion structures, *Structural Engineering International*, **2**, 85–8.

Cuttle, C. and Slater, A. J. (1975) A low energy approach to office lighting, *Light and Lighting*, January/February.

Davis, G. R. (1990) Energy for Planet Earth, *Scientific American*, **3**, 21–7.

Erhorn, H. and Reiss, J. (1992) *Schützt der Mindestwärmeschutz in der Praxis vor Schimmelpilzschaden?* Fraunhofer-Institut für Bauphysik, IBP Mitteilung 224, Stuttgart.

Fargus, R. and Hepworth, S. (1994a) *Application of Neural Network Control to Building Services*, BRE, PD117/94.

Fargus, R. and Hepworth, S. (1994b) Taking control with neural networks, *Building Services*, June, 51–2.

Flynn, J. E. *et al.* (1992) *Architectural Interior Systems. Lighting. Acoustics. Air Conditioning*, Van Nostrand Reinhold.

Foster, N. (ed.) (1993). *Solar Energy in Architecture and Urban Planning*, Conference Proceedings, Florence, Italy, 17–21 May 1993, CEE/H. S. Stephens & Ass.

Funakoshi, H. *et al.* (1994) A prototype wave power converter, *Structural Engineering International*, **2**, 94–6.

Gertis, K. (1988) Bauen und Gesundheit. In *IABSE Proceedings P-126/88*, 45–60.

de Groot, J. J. *et al.* (1995) Miniaturisation of fluorescent lamps (an overview of innovations). In *CIE 119 1995–23rd Session Proceedings*, 456–9.

Gupton, G. W. Jr (1988) *HVAC Controls: Operation and Maintenance*, Van Nostrand Reinhold, New York.

Haustechnik Heute (1987) *Bundesamt fur Konjunkturfragen*, Bern.

Heating and Cooling Systems in Buildings, NISTI R88–3860, Gaithersburg, Maryland

IEA Annex 28 (background publication) (1989) Energy conservation in buildings and community systems programme, International Energy Agency.

Issar, A. S. (1995) Climatic change and the history of the Middle East, *American Scientist*, July-August, 350–5

Jaunzens, D. and Wylds, S. (1994) Low energy cooling: a research perspective, *Building Sevices*, November, 53.

Jones, B. I. (1994) Tidal power plants – experience in the UK, *Structural Engineering International*, **2**, 96–8.

van Kemanade, J. T. C. and van der Burgt, P. J. M. (1988) Light Sources and Colour rendering: additional information to the Ra Index, *National Lighting Conference*, CIBSE.

van Kemenade, J. T. C. *et al.* (1990) Display lighting: a system approach using HID lamps, *CIBSE National Lighting Conference 1990 Proceedings*, 323–34.

van Kemenade, J. T. C. and van der Burgt (1995) *Towards a User Oriented Description of Colour Rendition of Light Sources*, CIE 119, New Delhi.

Kirstein, K.-O. *et al.* (1986) Mikrobiologische Einflüsse auf Betonkonstruktionen, *Beton-und Stahlbetonbau*, **8**, 202–5.

Kristjansson, R. *et al.* (1994) Geothermal energy, *Structural Engineering International*, **2**, 105–8.

Lainey, L. and Malcolm, D. (1994) Large vertical axis wind turbine generator, *Structural Engineering International*, **2**, 82–4.

Léopold, A., Cochet, C. and Derangère, D. (1996) Performance des aspirateurs ménagers vis-à-vis de la rétention des poussières et des allergènes, *Cahiers du CSTB*, Cahier 2878, March 1996.

Levenhagen, J. J. and Spethmann, D. H. (1993) *HVAC Controls and Systems*, McGraw-Hill.

Lillywhite, M. (1988) Exploding condensing boiler myths, *Building Services, CIBSE Journal*, **10**(6), 59–60.

Littlefair, P. J. (1989) *Innovative Daylighting Systems*, BRE Information Paper, IP 22/89.

Littlefair, P. J., Aizlewood, M. E. and Birtles, A. B. (1993) *The performance of Innovative Daylighting Systems*, BRE 114/6/3, PD354/93.

McQuiston, F. C. and Parker, J. D. (1994) *Heating, Ventilating and Air Conditioning. Analysis and Design*, John Wiley & Sons.

Milde, K. *et al.* (1983) Thiobacilli of the corroded concrete walls of the Hamburg sewer system, *Journal of General Microbiology*, 1327–33.

Morin, P. and Chandelier, J. (1994) Conduits de fumée métalliques. Vingt ans d'études sur la corrosion, *CSTB Magazine* **73**, 20–3.

Morin, P. *et al.* (1995) Durabilité des conduits de fumée raccordés à des chaudières fioul à haut rendement, *Cahiers du CSTB*, Cahier 2795, April 1995.

Nielsen, K. (1994) Wave power converters, *Structural Engineering International*, **2**, 88–91.

Nitsch, J. (1994) The global potential of renewable energy sources, *Structural Engineering International*, **2**, 72–5.

Nordhaus, W. D. (1994) *Managing the Global Commons. The Economics of Climate Change*, The MIT Press.

Pickering, C. A. C. and Jones, W. P. (1986) *Health and Hygienic Humidification*, BSRIA Technical Note 13/86.

Postgate, J. (1988) Bacterial world built on sulphur, *Scientist*, 14 July 1988, 58–62.

Postgate, J. (1978) *The Sulphate Reducing Bacteria*, Cambridge University Press.

Pritchard, D. C. (1995), *Lighting*, 5th edn., Longman Scientific and Technical, Harlow.

Rabl, A. (1992) Aspects énergetiques de la bureautique, *CSTB Magazine*, **55**, June, 56–8.

Sand, W. and Bock, E. (1984) Concrete corrosion in the Hamburg sewer system, *Environmental Technology Letters*, **5**, 517–28.

Schiffers, A. *et al.* (1976) Untersuchungen der Zerstörung von Asbestzementplatten und Beton im Naturzugkühlturm des Kraftwerkes Ensdorf, *Energie*, **9**, 252–4.

von Scholten, C. (1994) Wave power test plants, *Structural Engineering International*, **2**, 91–4.

Skistad, H. (1994) *Displacement ventilation*, Research Studies Press and John Wiley & Sons.

Smith, B. *et al.* (1988) Elusive solution to monumental decay, *New Scientist*, 27 June, 91–4.

Smith, J. T. and Webb, B. C. (1993) *Absorption Chiller Efficiency*, BRE, PD 185/93.

Smith, J. T., Webb, B. C., Wiech, C. (1992) *Large Scale Absorption Chillers: A Review of Operating Experience*, BRE 169/17/16, PD168/92.

Stephen, R. K. *et al.* (1994) *Passive Stack Ventilation Systems: Design and Installation*, BRE Information Paper 13/94.

Sterling, E., Bieva, C., Collett, C. (eds) (1993) Building design, technology, and occupant well-being in temperate climates. In *ASHRAE Proceedings*, 17–19 February.

Szerman, M. (1994) *Auswirkung der Tageslichtnutzung auf das energetische Verhalten von Bürogebäuden*, University of Stuttgart, Doctoral Thesis.

Treado, S. J. and Bean, J. W. (1988) *The Interaction of Lighting, Heating and Cooling Systems in Buildings – Interim Report*, NISTI R88–3860 Publication, Gaithersburg, MD.

Walker, R. R. and White, M. K. (1992) Single-sided natural ventilation – how deep an office? *Building Serv. Eng. Rev. Technol.*, **13** (4), 231–6.

Walker, R. R. *et al.* (1994) *Efficiency of Ventilation in Office Buildings*, BRE/112/1/4, PD228/94.

White, B. S. (1990) Adding the biological ingredient, *Chartered Quantity Surveyor*, October, 47.

White, M. K. and Walker R. R. (1994) *The Effectiveness of Natural Ventilation in Offices*, BRE/112/1/4, PD 326/94.

Willis, S. (1993) The application of artificial intelligence to building management, *Building Serv. Eng. Rev. Technol.*, **14** (4), B14–B15.

Willis, S. and Perera, E. (1995) Keeping control of comfort, *Building Services*, February, 43.

Wise, A. F. E. and Swaffield, J. A. (1995) *Water, Sanitary and Waste Services for Buildings*, Longman Scientific & Technical.

WMO Statement (1995) *WMO Statement on the Status of the Global Climate in 1994*, WMO Publication, No. 826, Geneva

Zackrison Jr, H. B. (1984) *Energy Conservation Techniques for Engineers*, Van Nostrand Reinhold.

The changing technology

5

THE PROCESS OF TECHNOLOGICAL PROGRESS

Technology is the application of science to production, which also includes construction. It embraces techniques, processes, materials, machines, tools, information, the buildings themselves during the course of production and, ultimately, their subsequent use (Ofori, 1994). Technology develops in different ways in individual countries but international trends also exist and, with the current forms of globalization, these trends have become more pronounced. The development of technology can be characterized by increasing productivity of labour and capital, new products to satisfy demand, better conditions in construction, improved quality, usability, durability, and, recently, by increased protection of the environment, and conservation of resources to ensure sustainable growth. The conservation of resources generally requires there to be a smaller energy consumption and a reduction in the amount of materials such as steel, cement and timber used. It is also expressed by reducing the weight or thickness of structures. All such trends ultimately make economic sense if they improve performance: that is if they result in cheaper buildings of better quality with greater durability.

The construction technologies and their development are affected by the industry's pecularities, such as the non-repetitive character and ever-changing place of production. The technologies used changed from the traditional to the modern somewhat later in construction than in other industries, but during the past two centuries a remarkable metamorphosis has occurred. Turner (1986) distinguished six major technological revolutions in construction:

- the traditionally hand-crafted secondary trades were industrialized (1800–1900)
- the use of iron and steel divorced the frame from the envelope (1851–80); later, reinforced concrete was introduced for frames

- new metals and alloys and new industrial processes were applied to the envelope: aluminium, steel and glass (1900–50)
- application of synthetics: sealants, laminates, resilient flooring (1900–80)
- electrical power becomes all-pervasive in buildings (1890–1950)
- heating, ventilation and air conditioning (HVAC) were made feasible by the development of electricity and sheet metals.

But the revolution did not stop there, and since Turner wrote his survey in 1986 there have been many further technological innovations, including:

- the appearance of new or, very recently, modified building materials: fabrics for roofs and for geotechnical purposes, high-performance concrete, plastics with improved properties in fire
- taller buildings and longer spans designed with adequate resistance to earthquake and wind
- more complex indoor services with special consideration to health, hygiene, energy conservation and protection of the environment
- robots for construction processes
- sophisticated structural and architectural design methods
- application of up-to-date mathematics, computers and information technology.

Vandepitte (1993) provided the following (abridged) list of innovations in civil engineering:

> Slurry walls, ground and rock anchors, reinforced earth retaining structures, vertical sand and wick drains, groundfreezing techniques, geotextiles, auger and root piles, segmental concrete bridge construction with segments either precast or cast *in situ*, incremental launching methods for concrete bridges ... prestressed concrete, suspension and cable-stayed bridges, orthrotropic steel bridge decks, suspension bridges with aerodynamically stable suspended floor structures ... tunnels built by immersing large precast sections into a dredged trench, automated tunnel boring machines, trenchless tunnelling for underground utilities, tunnels constructed by jacking precast sections through embankments, jointless concrete and 'whispering' asphalt road pavements, roller-compacted concrete dams, breakwater armour of hydrodynamically stable prefabricated concrete units and steel or concrete offshore structures ...

Innovations and inventions contribute not only to the progress and competitiveness of construction in general, but also to the performance of individual firms in particular.

Construction practice, especially site work, may be regarded as the battlefield of the whole construction process. It is a challenge to succeed against such adversaries as inclement weather, mud, carelessness, and the size and complexity of a particular operation. However, it can all be a source of great satisfaction once the vision is realized. Manufacturing and construction techniques and their constraints have always affected the design of buildings, all the more so today with the wealth of new techniques that have been developed. Designers therefore need to be acquainted with technological aspects, at least as far as these affect design.

The changes made in construction technologies have contributed to transforming construction into a modern industry. This chapter is devoted to selected innovations in construction materials and technologies.

BUILDING MATERIALS AND STRUCTURES

TECHNOLOGY TRENDS

The first building materials were used just as they were found in nature: stone, clay, timber and parts of plants. Eventually they were shaped by some mechanical process. Following the discovery of fire, burnt clay bricks were invented. Later, some 5000 years ago, metallurgy was developed. Copper, lead, bronze and then iron were added to the range of building materials. With the discovery of binding materials, such as natural pozzolana, burnt limestone and gypsum, mortar and concrete could be produced. At the end of the eighteenth century, iron, and in the nineteenth century, cement, concrete and steel enhanced the stock of building materials. Finally, during the past 100 years, a great number of materials has been added to the existing ones: reinforced concrete, special concretes, aluminum, new steel alloys and plastics. The latest development is the appearance of composites and materials engineered according to pre-specified requirements (Charlot-Valdieu and Cope, 1993; Illston, 1994). Among the new composites are:

- special concretes
- wood or waste-wood, resin-bound, glued (Pimienta *et al.*, 1994)
- coated and multilayered glass
- alloys, eventually coated
- polymer sections reinforced with steel, aluminium or timber sections (e.g. for windows)
- sandwich panels (e.g. with hard faces and a foam core, or framed structures with a heat insulating core such as mineral wool).

The following new technologies, all contributing to the industrialization of the building industry, are now being used for manufacturing building components:

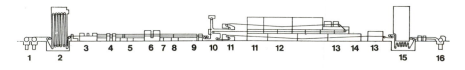

Fig. 5.1 Continuous steel stripcoating, Coloracier, France (1=steel strip; 2= compensating feeder unit; 3=degreasing; 4=brushing; 5=hot rinse; 6=phosphatizing; 7=chromatizing; 8=cold rinse; 9=chromium rinse; 10=upper coating; 11=lower coating; 12=dewatering unit; 13=cooling unit; 14=polymerization; 15=discharge storage; 16=winch). *Source:* Gy. Sebestyén (1977) *Lightweight Building*, Akadémiai Kiadó, Budapest.

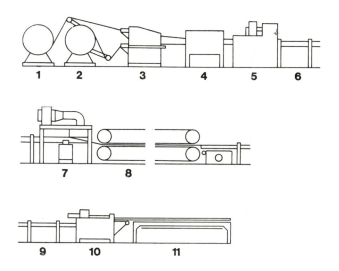

Fig. 5.2   Production of sandwich panels with polyurethane foam core, Kunststoff Verfahrenstechnik Dr Ernst GmbH and Co KG (1=first coil; 2=second coil; 3=rolling machine; 4=heating stage; 5=adhesive application; 6=adhesive consolidation; 7=foaming unit with exhaust equipment; 8=twin strip; 9=hardening stage; 10=cutting unit; 11=lift-off table) *Source*: as Fig. 5.1.

- continuous cold-forming and coil-coating of thin metal sheets
- bending and pressing metal sheets
- casting aluminium façade components with decorative surface relief
- vacuum-forming of thermoplastic components
- reinforcing plastics by fibres
- manufacturing multilayer (sandwich) panels
- gluing timber
- extrusion of aluminium or plastic sections.

The construction of buildings can be divided into three main groups of technologies:

- producing the load-bearing structure (walls, floors, etc.)
- activities producing non-load-bearing structures (partitioning, rendering, painting, cladding, tiling, etc.)
- providing the building with services (heating, water supply, lighting).

Some technological developments for load-bearing structures have been:

- For foundations: caissons, cofferdams, slurry walls, soil reinforced by geotextiles or geomembranes
- For scaffolding: tubular steel scaffolding with different types of couplers, welded steel scaffolding sections
- For masonry: hollow fired clay or concrete blocks, mortars with polymer additives, fibres or reinforcement, incorporation of heat insulation into masonry or masonry blocks
- For the superstructure: cast *in situ* concrete walls, structures for tall buildings and long spans
- For connecting components: welding, riveting (including tension rivets), bolting (including friction types), screwing (including self-tapping types), gluing and sealing.

The list of innovations applied to non-load-bearing parts of the buildings is equally long. It includes the use of new materials such as fast-drying paints, mechanization (e.g. by electric tools), and the introduction of safer and more durable products.

The impact of building materials on the environment has recently been studied and analysed. Open-cast (surface) stone or clay quarries, for example, spoil the environment. This can be remedied, to some extent, by planting new flora, but sometimes the destruction is irreparable and quarries have to be closed. Proper management can avoid deforestation, which is still endangering forest resources. The impregnation of wood also has a questionable environmental impact. Another aspect to be considered is the energy implications of the use of various building materials.

CONCRETE AND REINFORCED CONCRETE

Introduction

Portland cement and reinforced concrete were invented in the nineteenth century. During the twentieth century they became important building materials and were developed into many different types such as lightweight, pre-stressed, high-strength and decorative concretes. A number of additives and chemicals are used to modify and improve their properties, e.g. plastifiers, porosity producers, accelerators, retarders, and frost resistance and form-release agents.

High alumina (bauxite) cement concrete was developed in the First World War. It has the advantage of setting rapidly, but its other properties led to loss of strength and even collapse. This type of concrete is therefore used infrequently or not at all, and attention is now devoted to inspection and regular monitoring of existing high alumina cement structures (BRE Digest 392, 1994).

Concrete and reinforced concrete have a number of special applications for specific performance requirements, such as in the oil industry (fast setting), in the nuclear power industry (heavy concretes for radiation shielding), bridges, tunnels, chimneys, silos, caisson foundations and offshore structures. Concrete protects the steel reinforcement from corrosion if the concrete has a sufficiently high cement content, is sufficiently compacted and if the reinforcement is covered to an adequate thickness by the concrete. Recently, there has been concern about the risks of steel corrosion, which can be caused by inadequate care in design and execution and by certain additives such as calcium chloride, which is used to protect fresh concrete from frost (BRE Digest 389, 1993) and to de-ice motorways and bridges. The production of crack-free concrete and the use of new corrosion-resistant reinforcing bars are new ways to prevent the corrosion of the reinforcement.

Structural codes

The structural design of reinforced concrete was developed around the turn of the twentieth century. The first standards, all based on the principle of permissible stress, were issued during the first few years (INTEMAC, 1994):

- 1903, Switzerland: *Provisorische Normen für Projektierung, Ausführung und Kontrolle von Bauten in armiertem Beton* (EMPA)
- 1904, Prussia: *Bestimmungen für die Ausführung von Konstructionen aus Eisenbeton im Hochbau*
- 1906, France: *Instructions Relatives à l'emploi du Beton Armé*
- 1907, UK: *Report of the Joint Committee on Reinforced Concrete*
- 1908, USA: *Requirements for Reinforced Concrete or Concrete-Steel Constructed Buildings* (Abel and Billington, 1980).
- 1910, USA: *Standard Building Regulations for the Use of Reinforced Concrete.*

Many other codes were published subsequently, e.g. in the USA by the American Concrete Institute (ACI) in 1920, 1928, 1936, 1941 and later (Abel and Billington, 1980). A period of 50 years was necessary for the introduction of the new principle of limit state design, which now is universal, e.g. in Eurocodes 2 and 4, dealing with the design of concrete, reinforced concrete and composite steel-concrete structures.

The new CEB/FIP Model Code for Concrete Structures already contains design rules for concrete with characteristic cylinder strengths up to 80 N/mm² (Walraven, 1994a, 1994b, 1994c). The recommended extensions to the Model Code are contained in the *CEB Bulletin d'Information No. 228* (High Performance Concrete, 1995).

Structural analysis can be based on the theory of elasticity, plasticity or the non-linear approach. Eurocode 2 allows the use of non-linear analysis, and this is being applied in an increasing number of cases. It takes account of the influence of the non-linear deformation properties of elements independent of the non-linearity due to second order effects. At the same time, inconsistencies in the safety concept and methods of structural analysis have been pointed out, and research is being undertaken to improve the methods of structural analysis further (CEB 229, 1995; Levi, Marro and Viara, 1995).

Lightweight concrete

Lightweight concretes are produced either with lightweight aggregates, natural or manufactured, or with additives to produce porosity (cellular concrete). After early hopes for the structural application of lightweight aggregate concretes, recent research on high-performance lightweight concrete once again shows potential for such use. These have densities and 28-day compressive cube strengths in the 1400–1950 kg/m³ and 35–75 mPa range, respectively (Sandvik and Hammer, 1995). Aggregates may be of expanded sintered clay (Leca, Liapor), expanded fly ash (Lytag), expanded shale (Solite, Hydite), or expanded slate (Ikeda, 1995).

One well-known application is the twin cylindrical towers of the Chicago Marina City, where the floor slabs were made of lightweight aggregate concrete (Clarke, 1993).

Pre-stressed concrete

The Frenchman Marie Eugène Freyssinet was one of the leading exponents of pre-stressing, which increases resistance to bending and prevents or reduces the formation of cracks. It introduces compression into the concrete either by stressing the steel reinforcement prior to concreting or after the concrete has reached a certain strength. Freyssinet built a number of remarkable reinforced concrete structures, including the Plougastel Bridge, near Brest, France. Completed in 1930, it had three 180 m span hollow-box reinforced concrete arches, the longest concrete spans in the world at that time. He patented pre-stressing in 1928, and built several pre-stressed structures before, during and after the Second

World War, such as the Luzancy Bridge over the Marne River, France, in 1946, which has a 55 m span.

Research and experiments are underway to introduce external pre-stressing, which could increase durability (Macchi, 1994). New potentials for pre-stressed structures are provided by the introduction of high-strength concrete and some other developments such as composite box girders for bridges, which have concrete slabs for the top and bottom, and corrugated steel webs (König, 1993; König, Duda and Zink, 1994).

High-performance concrete

In the past 25 years, high-strength concrete has been added to the list of structural materials available. Such concretes have a compressive strength from 80 N/mm^2 up to 130 N/mm^2, which is the practical upper limit of any concrete with ordinary aggregates. Recently, the term high-strength concrete seems to be being replaced by the term 'high-performance concrete' (High Performance Concrete, 1995). High strength can be attained by:

- application of silica fume
- reduced water:cement ratio
- extensive use of plasticizer
- application of cement with a high strength potential.

The use of silica fume is the most important condition for producing high-strength concrete. Silica fume, which is a by-product of the melting process used to produce silicon metal and ferrosilicon alloys, has particles 100 times smaller than those of cement, and the use of even a small amount results in very dense concrete, which then has special properties of abrasion and chemical resistance.

Dispersing agents or plasticizers are applied to improve the workability of concrete and to reduce the amount of mixing water required, and hence the water:cement ratio, which for high-strength concrete usually lies in the 0.22–0.40 range. The cement must have the appropriate composition, and a high degree of grinding fineness (High Strength Concrete, 1990). Improved workability may result in avoiding the need to vibrate, so that the concrete flows into the formwork without compaction, thus creating a self-compactable high-performance concrete (Okamura and Ozawa, 1994). Structural high-strength concrete is often densely reinforced. For this reason, and also because of the low water:cement ratio and the surplus of fine particles which makes the mix sticky, good workability is essential. Designing for high-strength concrete must take account of the fact that the tensile strength, relative to compressive strength, is less than for normal concrete. The hydration process must be kept under control because overheating may jeopardize the required quality (van Breugel, 1991). In designing structures with high-performance concrete, certain aspects can acquire special importance, such as ductility or robustness. With high-strength concrete, the cross-section of columns and walls can be reduced. In high-rise office buildings, for instance, this can increase the area for sale or rent. For adequate good load transfer, the end of the columns with reduced cross-section may have to be strengthened, e.g. by steel fibres (short cut wires).

The first tall building constructed with high-strength concrete structural columns was the 70-storey Lake Point Tower in the USA (1965–8), with a design strength of 52 N/mm². Since then, compressive strengths of 60–115 N/mm² have been achieved. The Helgelandsbrua (bridge) in Norway was built in 1990, with a span of 425 m, using concrete with a maximum design strength of 65 N/mm². Other applications are offshore and underwater structures, bank safe-deposits, highways and barriers (Walraven, 1994a, 1994b, 1994c). A new idea is to develop the 'welding' of pre-cast concrete components by using high-performance concrete. Progress in this field can be illustrated by considering that 50 years ago a concrete B 160 meant it had a strength of 160 kg/cm², whereas today it means a strength of 160 N/mm², a concrete 10 times stronger!

A number of research requirements have been identified in relation to high-strength concrete, such as shear behaviour, minimum reinforcement, fire resistance, permeability for liquids and gases, anchorage of bars and strands, crack development, creep and shrinkage, fibre reinforcement, high-strength lightweight concrete, most appropriate profile of steel reinforcement, frost durability, sensitivity to mixing procedure, resistance against alkali-silica reactions, among others (High Performance Concrete, 1995).

Exposed concrete surfaces

Several technologies have been developed to ensure blemish-free surfaces of uniform colour (CIB Report 24) for exposed architectural concrete surfaces. Retarders are applied so that the cement can be brushed off the surface. Decorative aggregates, such as crushed porcelain, glass or stone, are used on the exposed surface. Pre-cast components with sculptured surfaces are produced in formwork made from various materials, usually concrete, steel, plastics or plaster. A thorough knowledge of the blemishes, discoloration and surface irregularities possible enables the manufacturer to opt for the appropriate materials, technology and precautions (CIB Report 5). Coloured concrete surfaces can be produced with either coloured or painted concrete using organic or inorganic pigments (Perez Luzardo, 1992). Care has to be taken about durability and weathering.

Further trends in concrete technology

The ultimate properties of concrete depend on the ingredient materials used and the way it is produced. The technologies involved in the production of concrete, such as preparing the aggregates, mixing, compacting, vibrating and curing, have been mechanized and perfected. Machines and plant are available for the various processes (high-efficiency mixers, vibrators, curing chambers and ready-mixed concrete plants).

Ready-mixed concrete has made a major contribution to the development of concrete technology. The first ready-mixed concrete plants were established in the USA at the beginning of this century. Their development began slowly, and their widespread appearance had to wait until after 1945. Today, ready-mixed concrete is universally applied, producing a great variety of concrete and mortar. The process has been automated with the aid of up-to-date computer systems. In France, 650 companies currently have 1500 ready-mixed concrete plants and a fleet of 6000 special trucks, with an annual production of 36 000 000 m³ of concrete, amounting to a 40% share of total national cement consumption.

Hardened concrete is a two-phase material comprising aggregates and a hydraulically hardened paste. Research is focusing on optimizing the composition of the paste in order to improve its properties.

Research has recently intensified into early-age thermal cracks. This is not only relevant to high-strength concrete but also to other types, particularly pre-cast concrete, which was often cured at high temperatures almost immediately after casting. Such early high-temperature curing resulted in cracking and quality deterioration. As a consequence of this latest research, curing conditions can now be improved (Emborg, 1994). The deficiencies in macroscopic models of concrete for the purposes of explaining cracks prompted researchers to develop models on a theoretical numerical-geometric basis. Such models can simulate fractures in brittle disordered materials such as concrete and rocks. For this purpose, random lattices have been developed in which the successive elimination of the lines that connect the nodes of the lattice simulates the development of cracks (Schlangen and van Mier, 1991, 1995). Research at the US National Institute of Standards and Technology (NIST) aims to predict the properties and performance of concrete, thereby enabling the planning of a more precise mix and technology. Thus concrete could be planned in advance as 'virtual concrete'.

STEEL AND ALUMINIUM

Cast iron, wrought iron and steel

Iron has been known about for a long time, but its use expanded in the seventeenth century. In St Paul's Cathedral, London (built between 1675 and 1710), two iron chains were used to counteract the outward thrust of the dome, and iron columns were used in the old House of Commons (London, built in 1714). Concealed iron cramps, cross-ties and reinforcing bars were commonly used in eighteenth century English masonry. In the first half of the nineteenth century cast and wrought iron was applied in combination: cast iron for compression members and wrought iron for members subjected to tension and bending. After 1840, wrought iron was applied for most structural purposes, but after 1900 steel became dominant.

As a construction material, steel has undergone several changes during the past 100 years. A higher carbon content increases its strength, although this is limited by the requirements for weldability. New alloy steels combine high strength with ease of welding. Hot-rolling of I, L and U steel sections has always required a large investment, but in return has offered the capacity for mass production. The I sections were ideal for beams, but their shape was less suitable for columns as they have reduced stiffness when bent in the plane of the flanges. For the purposes of columns, composite sections were therefore built up. The perfection of hot-rolling machinery, however, made it possible to produce wide-flange sections with improved resistance to buckling. The development of automatic continuous welding machines made another solution possible: namely to design sections individually according to their design load and then to produce welded sections.

Weathered steel was originally developed for railway carriages. It was first applied for architectural and structural purposes in 1961 by architect Eero Saarinen for the exterior of the John Deere office building at Moline in Illinois. The first bridge constructed from weathered steel was built in 1964 in Detroit, Michigan. This type of steel, best known by its proprietary name of Cor-Ten, is still in use for bridges and industrial buildings.

The use of stainless steel in buildings is growing. In Japan, 15% of stainless steel production is used by building. Only about 5% is used in Germany, but this is increasing.

The early means of fastening and jointing were screws, bolts and rivets. These are still in use (with some developments, e.g. shot pins and high friction grip bolts), but welding has taken over as the most important method for jointing and fastening steel members.

In common with all other structures, in earlier years steel structures were also designed using the permissible stress method. About 30 years ago, however, designers adopted the limit state methods. In the USA, for example, specifications for the design of highway bridges have included limit state design provisions for steel beam and girder bridges since 1971. The most recent design code for steel structures is Eurocode 3.

Structural analysis may be based on the first- or second-order theories. The first-order theory uses the initial geometry of the structure; the second-order theory accounts for the change in the shape of the structure under load. The simpler form of plastic analysis is the rigid-plastic method. The more advanced plastic method takes two forms: the elastic-perfectly plastic method and the elasto-plastic method. Composite structures (steel plus concrete) require a reduced amount of steel as they make use of the concrete's compressive strength and the steel's tensile strength. Shear connectors such as headed studs are welded to the hot-rolled steel sections to provide the necessary shear force transmission in composite structures.

Cold-formed steel

The introduction of cold-forming opened up new possibilities. Steel sheet and sections can be cold-formed by means of roll-forming machines or press brakes (Toma *et al.*, 1992). The most frequently used thin sheets have a thickness of 0.4–3.0 mm, although heavier gauges can also be produced. Manufactured from very thin material, slender sections with different shapes (C, U, L, Z, O) are possible. For special purposes such as claddings, roofs and composite floors, specific profiles may be used. Cold-rolling is the most productive method and is therefore mainly used for standardized profiles. Composite floors are made with concrete cast on top of the steel sheet decking with possible additional reinforcement primarily for taking the shear and bending stresses. Buckling of thin steel members was found to be a frequent cause of failure. Three types of buckling (local, distortional and lateral-torsional) have been identified (Davies, 1994).

New means have been developed for jointing and fastening thin cold-formed steel sheets, e.g. blind rivets, self-tapping screws, gluing and seam locking. Thin metal sheets must be well protected against corrosion. Steel sheet is usually galvanized or, for visible applications, additionally plastic-coated. Coil-coating is the most productive plastic-coating of thin steel (or aluminium) sheets. Sections can be manufactured from coated sheet, or be galvanized and coated after forming. Important uses for galvanized cold-formed corrugated steel or aluminium sheets (coated or uncoated) are frames of low-rise or medium-rise buildings, supports for partitions, roof deckings, claddings and floors. Codes for the use of cold-formed steel were created later than those for hot-rolled steel. The 1974 code of the Canadian Standards Association was still based on permissible stress design, although with a limit state option. The 1984 revised code was already based entirely on limit state design principles (referred to as load and resistance factor design). The plastic design approach was introduced simultaneously in Europe and the USA. Eurocode 4 contains the principles for composite structures (Easterling and Kim Roddis, 1992).

Steel structures

Steel and concrete are continuously in competition for use as the basic structural building material. Concrete gained ground in the first half of the twentieth century, but steel has made a comeback in recent years. As already mentioned, their combined use in composite structures is now widespread. Both steel and concrete are used in heavy construction (bridges, tall buildings, long-span structures, etc.), and steel has been increasingly used in lightweight structures (Blanc, McEvoy and Plank, 1993).

The construction of tall buildings and long-span bridges was made possible by the production of large-size hot-rolled steel sections. Bolted connections have been improved with high-strength friction grip bolts. The stability of multistorey steel frames is ensured by good connections and appropriate bracing. Various steel systems have been developed for tall buildings, such as shear frames, shear trusses with or without outrigger trusses, framed tubes, modular tubes, trussed tubes and superframes. Single-storey portal frames (haunched or unhaunched) and also trusses or lattice girders are much used for industrial buildings. Truss and bridge construction witnessed enormous advances during the nineteenth century. Slender iron and later steel beams and bracing rods permitted lightweight solutions and long spans (ECCS, 1988; Ambrose, 1994).

Steel has a number of uses outside the construction industry, but the production of constructional steel has become an industrial sector in its own right. In each of the larger European countries, about 1 000 000 tonnes of constructional steelwork is manufactured and erected annually. There are fabricators, suppliers, and erecting and contracting firms specializing in such structures. These can offer their own systems, which means that construction can be realized quickly without much storage space on site for components. This has led to supply by the so-called 'just-in-time' method.

Aluminium

While steel and reinforced concrete are the most widely used structural building materials, the use of aluminium has also increased in a number of fields recently.

Aluminium was first produced between 1800 and 1830, but its industrial production only started between 1830 and 1870. The first European Recommendations for Aluminium Alloy Structures (ERAAS) were published in 1978. The specific weight of aluminium is only one-third that of steel, and its corrosion resistance is good. Both are cogent reasons for its use, but on the other hand, its strength is inferior to that of steel and its cost is much higher. Structural shapes can be obtained by extrusion, casting and building up by various means into combined sections. The shap-

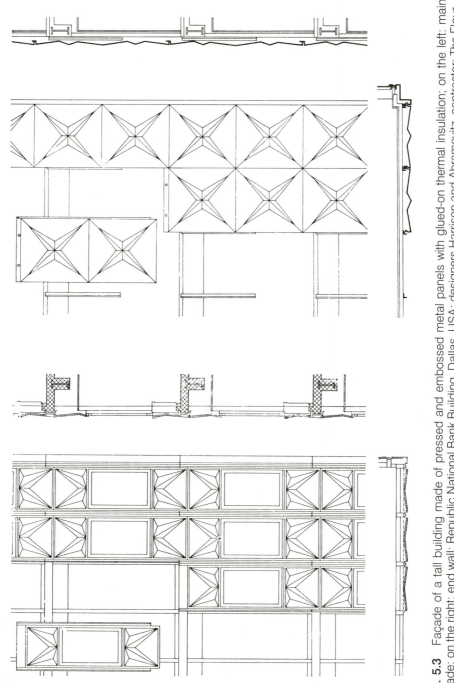

Fig. 5.3 Façade of a tall building made of pressed and embossed metal panels with glued-on thermal insulation; on the left: main façade; on the right: end wall; Republic National Bank Building, Dallas, USA; designers Harrison and Abramovitz, contractor: The Flour City Ornamental Iron Co. *Source:* Gy. Sebestyén (1977) *Lightweight Building*, Akadémiai Kiadó, Budapest.

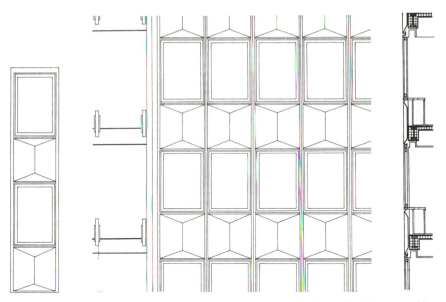

Fig. 5.4   Curtain wall with two-storey pressed metal panels, 99 Park Avenue, New York; designer E. Roth & Sons; contractor General Bronze Corp. *Source:* Gy. Sebestyén (1977) *Lightweight Building*, Akadémiai Kiadó, Budapest.

ing has an impact on the form, which is why aluminium is used in different shapes from steel. Casting of usually silicon or magnesium alloy aluminium façade panels was developed by Kubota in Japan and Alusuisse in Switzerland. Such panels are normally 4–10 mm thick. Among the many examples completed are the façades of the ILO building in Geneva and the BMW Centre in Munich.

Aluminium can be lacquered or coil-coated, and there is also a surface treatment developed specifically for aluminium, anodic oxidation technology. This gives the material a hard and coloured surface, and provides good protection against corrosion. The colour can be produced either in a bath containing a solution of metal salts, or by direct colouring (self-colouring) in a bath containing aromatic sulphonic acid and certain additives. The colours depend on the chemicals used and include gold, bronze, brown, grey and various combinations.

TIMBER

Wood is one of the most ancient building materials. It is still widely favoured, but the way it is used has undergone radical change. Its properties vary considerably and its efficient use therefore requires strength grading. Visual or machine strength grading can be used, and graded timber is marked. Strength classification is now standardized throughout Europe by CEN standards EN 338, EN 384, EN 518 and EN 519.

Timber has a high strength to weight ratio. Its strength and stiffness are dependent on the direction of load in relation to the grain. It is strong and relatively stiff parallel to the grain. However, it is prone to cleavage along the grain if tension stresses are perpendicular to it. It has low shear strength and shear modulus. Higher moisture content reduces both its strength and elasticity, and a part of the original strength will anyway be lost over time. Under load, timber creeps and deforms. Serviceability therefore often governs structural analysis. Structural analysis, detail-design and processes of technology take care of a number of the specific problems of timber structures, such as buckling, behaviour around notches, prevention of interstitial condensation, protection against moisture, insect and fungal attack, and fire. The specific requirements of structural analysis are considered by Eurocode 5, by, for example, defining five load duration classes, prescribing the need for a European Technical Approval in the case of special proprietary connections, and so on. The partial coefficient method is generally recommended for structural design, but the more advanced safety index method is also authorized (Larsen, Kuipers and Ehrentreich, 1989).

Gluing and the introduction of new types of mechanical fastenings have opened up new possibilities in the use of timber. New forms of structural members can be produced with glued laminated timber (glulam). 'Scrimber' is a new structural timber product invented in Australia. It is made from debarked logs of fast growing tree species, crushed, mixed with resin and pressed into large blocks that are sawn to lengths of up to 12 m. Various types of wood-based panels have been developed. The first was plywood, which consists of an uneven number (at least three) of bonded layers (veneers), cross-laminated (i.e. with adjacent layers having the grain at right angles) and glued. Fibreboard and particleboard, which are more recent, can be mineral bonded (with cement or gypsum) or bonded with some form of organic binder. Oriented stranded board was introduced in Germany and further developed in the USA, e.g. wafer-boards and flakeboards. Laminated veneer lumber is similar to plywood; its advantage is that it can be produced with larger dimensions.

A large number of organic adhesives has been developed, each with specific properties. Several adhesives contain formaldehyde (phenol, urea or melamine formaldehyde). Others are epoxy- or polyurethane-based. Some of the adhesives can withstand outdoor exposure and temperatures above 50°C.

Two types of timber fasteners are currently used: those where the load is transferred along the shank, such as dowels, staples, nails, screws and bolts; and those where the load is transmitted over a large bearing area at the surface of members, such as split-rings, shear plates and punched metal plates. Specially shaped connecting hardware is also used for mechanical timber jointing (Breyer, 1988). The disadvantages of traditional fasteners such as bolts and dowels have led to the invention of a new type of fastener, the so-called expanding tube fastener (Leijten, 1994a, 1994b). By local reinforcement, the splitting of the timber can be prevented. Consequently, in conjunction with densified veneer wood reinforcement (an alternative for tropical species), a high-capacity joint has been created.

Densification is a process in which, by the addition of chemicals (polymers etc.) and then heating and compression, the density of softwood is raised to approximately 1400 kg/m^3. The first patent for densified solid wood was issued in 1886, but its application for timber jointing is still at the experimental stage.

The innovations described above have made the design and assembly of new types of timber products and structures possible, e.g. tapered, curved or pitched cambered beams, glued thin-webbed beams, stressed skin panels, sandwich panels, trusses, portal frames and arches.

Stressed skin panels consist of webs in the direction of the span connected with wood-based sheets forming the skins on one or both sides. They can be produced by gluing or with mechanical joints. The webs are usually of solid timber and the sheets are some form of board, e.g. plywood. They are extensively used in prefabricated timber frame construction as walls, roofs and floors. As structural members, their load-bearing capacity and stiffness exceeds that of their individual constituents. Family houses of timber construction may have a timber frame that is made on site or assembled from prefabricated panels, or else have a modular (box-like) structure. To resist wind and other lateral forces, horizontal diaphragms, diagonal bracing, and shearwalls are applied. The stressed skin principle, introduced this century, enables the inclusion of the panels in the structural calculations.

Glulam has been used to construct long-span roofs such as the olympic stadium 'Vikingship' in Hamar, Norway (span 96.4 m) and the Sport Hall in Hakon, Norway (span 85.8 m) (*Glulam Award*, 1994). Some timber structures have been built with spans exceeding 100 m. The transformation of traditional timber construction, often made from axe-dressed hardwood, into modern timber construction, is one more achievement in the technical progress of construction.

GLASS AND LIGHT ENVELOPE STRUCTURES

The oldest known glass dates from 10 000 BC and was made in Egypt. However, glass became a common building material only during the second millenium, and modern glass is only some 200 years old (Sedlacek *et al.*, 1995). The transparency of glass was first truly appreciated in Gothic cathedrals, and their large coloured glass windows have been a source of fascination ever since. Consequently, both craftsmen and architects strove to develop transparency further.

New types of glass

In the twentieth century, the glass industry has been transformed from a traditional manufacturing sector into a powerful and capital-intensive branch of the economy. In addition to the building industry, which required more and more glass, car manufacturers emerged as new and important clients. Sheet glass was produced with different characteristics, such as safety glass (shatterproof or splinterproof), frosted, polished, ornamental and wired glass. For the purposes of plate glass with high optical quality, casting, rolling, grinding and polishing technologies were developed, and automated fabrication lines became common in the 1930s. It was in the 1960s and 1970s that Pilkington introduced the new float-glass process.

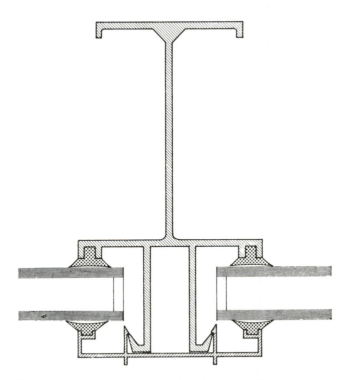

Fig. 5.5 Glass façade with aluminium bracing (Alusuisse), Jovail watchmaker plant, Brügg-Biel, Switzerland. *Source:* Gy. Sebestyén (1977) *Lightweight Building*, Akadémiai Kiadó, Budapest.

To understand the changes that have taken place over the past 25 years, the basic characteristics of glass and glazing are summed up below. The use of glass as a structural material requires that its specific property (brittleness) be taken into account (Sedlacek *et al.*, 1995). This is possible by using tempered glass. The deflections of large glass panes can be calculated by finite element programs. The visible transmittance of a glazing is the fraction of visible light energy transmitted through it. The shading coefficient of a glazing is the ratio of its solar heat gain compared with the gain through a clear, single glass. The thermal transmittance (U) value was defined in Chapter 4. The performance properties of glazing can be affected by tinting, metallic coatings, multilayering, gas fills and combinations thereof.

One of the new types of flat glass is solar control glass, which is transparent enough to permit the penetration of useful solar radiation, but is able to colour itself and reduce solar radiation penetration when this is undesirable. Such glass has a coated surface on either the outside or inside. The coating can be of one layer or, more frequently, a system of several layers. A variable transparency can be attained by various technologies, the most usual being the electrochromic systems (Chevalier and Chevalier, 1991). Another technology developed for variable transparency is the thermochromic process (Munding and Bagheri, 1990). Coated glass that responds in a preplanned way to external influences, thereby improving conditions inside, could be called 'intelligent' glass. Liquid crystal systems are another form of controllable coating (produced by Asahi of Japan and St Roch in Belgium). Low-emissivity glass such as Pilkington's hard-coated K-glass is usually made with a thin layer of indium tin oxide, with silver or copper-indium tin oxide applied to the inner surface to restrict the passage of radiant heat. Fire-resistant glass is a new contribution to fighting the spread of fire and halting the passage of smoke and flame for a predetermined period of time. In certain circumstances, such glass also insulates against the heat produced by fire, by resisting the passage of radiant heat for a specified period.

To assist in energy conservation, there are various types of glazing with improved insulating qualities available:

- double glazing with a low-emissivity coat
- triple glazing with a low-emissivity coat and argon gas cavity
- vacuum or aerogel glazings (the aerogel is a transparent, microporous silicate foam).

If low-emissivity glass is used in double glazing, the coating is usually on the inside of a double-glazed unit. Low-emissivity glass provides better heat insulation due to the substantial reduction of long wavelength radiation. As already mentioned, further improvement can be achieved by filling the cavity between panes with low conductivity inert gases such as argon.

For the Louvre Pyramid in Paris, designed by I.M. Pei & Partners, a water white glass was produced in order to obtain perfect transparency. The application of these new high-tech glazing solutions will expand in the future if they become less expensive.

Structural glazing

Glass has traditionally been inserted into a frame or sash and held there by putty, synthetic rubber section, or some other glass stop. With the introduction of large glass panes and large glass surfaces, new types of glazing had to be developed.

The ambition of creating an all-glass façade is not a new one. The Crystal Palace in London (1851) was the first glass building to amaze the world. The great architects of the first half of the twentieth century, such as Le Corbusier and later Mies van der Rohe, attempted to develop large uninterrupted glass façades, but the technology to allow this was created only during the past 30 years. Considerable research efforts were required from designers, such as Foster, Pei, Ove Arup and RFR (Peter Rice, Martin Francis and Ian Ritchie), and manufacturers such as Pilkington, Asahi and St Gobain, to attain the present technical level (Rice and Dutton, 1995). The latest development in the all-glass façade is the so-called structural glazing. This is a façade system, where the external wall consists of glass only, with thin joints between panes which are rendered watertight with silicone. For the purposes of frame-less glazing, glass with a hard coating and improved resistance to impact is the best type. Glass with a high degree of reflective properties provides a uniform mirror-like façade and hides the structure behind. Structural glazing offers new possibilities for architects in the aesthetic treatment of buildings.

Tempered or toughened glass is required for structural glazing. This is produced by heating the glass panes in a furnace, having first cut them to their final shape, and then chilling them with cold air from a jet system, with the result that the outer surface is placed in compression and the inner part under tension. Tempered glass panes have high bending strength (Sedlacek *et al.*, 1995). The two basic structural solutions that have emerged are hanging or gluing the glass panes on to the structure. Tall, large panes can be clamped at the top and hung, or they can be sus-pended through holes drilled in the panes. The first solution has been used for entrance halls with large external glass panes (e.g. the Radio City Building in Paris), the second for façades with several lines of glass panels above each other. The steel suspending device should not come directly

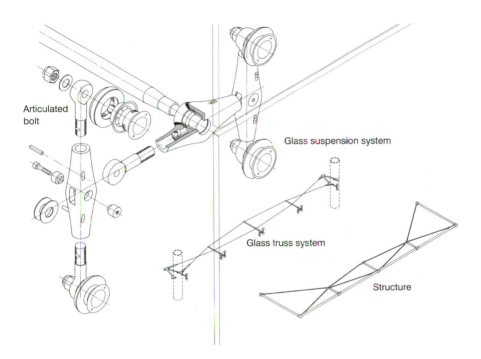

Articulated bolt

Glass suspension system

Glass truss system

Structure

Fig. 5.6   Structural glazing, City of Science, la Villette, Paris, 1986; designer: RFR Partners and A. Fainsilber. *Source:* P. Rice and H. Dutton (1995) *Structural Glass*, E & FN Spon.

into contact with the glass; a thermoplastic spacer is commonly used between steel and glass. One of the earliest buildings to use glass suspended through fixing holes was the Willis Faber & Dumas building in Ipswich (architect Sir Norman Foster). This method was perfected for the Paris La Villette complex (designer RFR).

Glass panes bolted individually on to the structure proved to be an advanced new solution for flush glass envelopes. Pilkington developed the flush countersunk machine screw fitting with a patented sealed spacer. The system is now known under the name 'Planar'. An advanced support and wind bracing system of suspended structural glazing relies on the use of stainless steel cable trusses, adapted originally from sailing yachts (Eekhout, 1992; Rice and Dutton, 1995). In glued glass façades, the glass is held in place with special silicone glue (*vitrage extérieur collé*) and, in principle, no metallic parts are visible on the outside. Nevertheless, mechanical

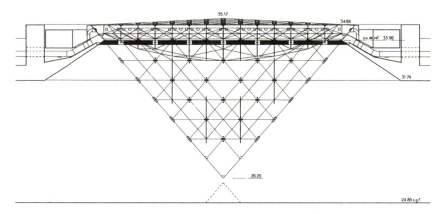

Fig. 5.7 Structural glazing, Grand Louvre, Paris, Inverted Pyramid, 1993; designers: I. M. Pei and RFR, P. Rice. *Source:* P. Rice and H. Dutton (1995) *Structural Glass*, E & FN Spon.

point supports and/or glass stiffeners may be used. Similarly, roof elements can be supported by glass beams. Large halls with glass roofs are another new type of construction. The supporting structure is usually made of a non-corroding alloy in order to avoid difficult maintenance work.

Light claddings and curtain walls

In many present-day buildings, the vertical load-bearing function is separated from the façades. Load is carried by a steel or reinforced concrete frame, instead of masonry walls, and the façade is made of a lightweight structure. The two most common solutions for such façades are lightweight cladding and curtain walls. Lightweight cladding is typically used for medium-height buildings, primarily for industrial or commercial premises without excessively large windows. Thin cold-formed steel or aluminium sheets, with or without some coloured coating, are often used for claddings. The façades of skyscrapers usually have large non-load-bearing surfaces that are fixed to the load-bearing structure (Lane, 1992). Such façades are termed *curtain walls*, and much of their surface is glazed. The introduction of curtain walls called for a solution to several problems: structural integrity, and stability as the curtain wall is affected by various actions such as wind pressure and suction, driving rain, differential thermal movement between the structure of the building and the curtain wall, etc. Most of these have now been solved, in some cases only after costly errors, e.g. the Boston Hancock Building, where shattering glass required replacement with improved detailing.

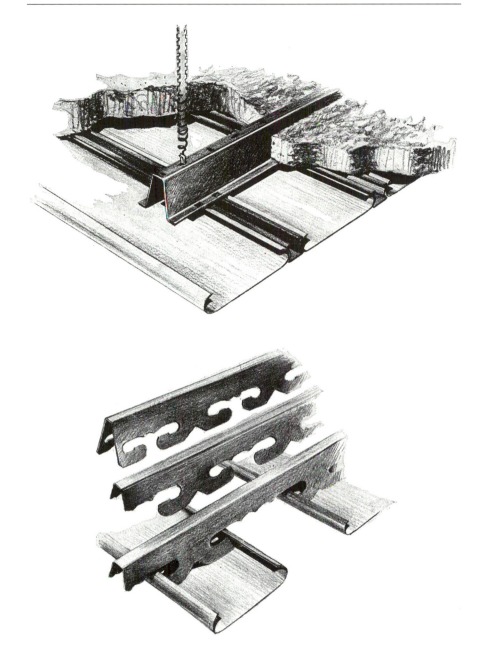

Fig. 5.8 Suspended ceiling, cold-formed aluminium sheet, Luxaflex, Hunter Douglas, The Netherlands. *Source:* Gy. Sebestyén (1977) *Lightweight Building*, Akadémiai Kiadó, Budapest.

The earliest curtain walls in tall buildings had a 'stick' system, i.e. vertical mullions, transoms, frames and insulated panels. From 1950 onwards, panel systems with pressure equalization were applied. Later, steel or aluminium panels were pressed like a car body. For some buildings in Japan, Switzerland and Germany, aluminium panels were cast as one piece. The next stage was the introduction of structural glazing and various advanced systems, such as forced air ventilation. The new technologies of light cladding and curtain walls have enabled designers to shape the façades of buildings in new ways.

POLYMERS AND POLYMER COMPOSITES

Polymers

The modern chemical industry produces a wide range of synthetic materials, many of which are applied in construction. The most important products are the polymers and polymer composites. A polymer is a very large molecule comprising hundreds or thousands of atoms. The polymer concept emerged in the 1920s, and since then the number of polymers has increased spectacularly. There are three large groups: thermoplastics, thermosets and elastomers. Thermoplastics and thermosets together form the plastics group (Hall, 1989). The most widely used thermoplastics are: polyvinyl chloride (PVC), polyethylene (PE), polypropylene (PP) and polystyrene (PS). They melt on heating and may be processed by a variety of techniques such as moulding (e.g. injection moulding), calandering, extrusion, and thermoforming; all these processes usually involve heating. Thermosets, or thermosetting resins, include alkyds, amino and phenolic resins, epoxies and polyurethane (PU).

The beginning of commercial production of some polymers and their two predecessors occurred as follows:

- natural rubber, UK/USA, 1839
- cellulose nitrate, USA, 1870
- polystyrene, Germany, 1930
- polyvinyl chloride, Germany/USA, 1933
- polyurethane, Germany, 1943
- epoxy, USA, 1947.

Polymer composites

As the name implies, polymer composites are made from two or more components. One of these may be an additive or fibre, and foaming agents, which are used to process foamed polymers, are frequently used. Fibres can be made from glass, carbon or a polymer such as aramid (Kevlar). In fibre-reinforced polymer composites, the fibres are embedded in some form of plastic, termed a matrix (Hollaway, 1990). Polymethylmethacrylate and polycarbonate are used to produce organic glass. PU and PS are much used in heat insulating materials or as components thereof. These are just some of the basic examples of the manifold uses of polymers.

Plastics and the composites manufactured from them have low moduli of elasticity. The required rigidity of a structure must therefore be derived from the shape rather than from the material. Shapes with high rigidity are three-dimensional surface structures such as domes, shells or folded plates. To achieve or increase rigidity, fibre-reinforced sheets in appropriate forms are used, e.g. by troughing, ribbing, or supporting the sheet in a sandwich structure. Corrugated sheets are rigid in one direction but not in the other. In sandwich panels, the polymer foam constitutes the core; the two faces may be metal sheets or some form of hardboard. The use of a soft cover layer such as paper is also possible. The most productive technology for making sandwich panels is continuous manufacture. The two cover faces are produced from coated steel or aluminium sheet coils, which are corrugated with rollers. The foam is produced, equally continuously, between the two metal faces of the future sandwich panels. Following heat treatment and a hardening of the foam, the three-layer sandwich is cut to its definitive length. Such sandwich panels are used for both external walls and roofs.

Fabrics made from glass and/or synthetic fibres, saturated and coated, and plastic membranes are relatively new building materials. Their two main uses are in roofing and soil mechanics as a reinforcement. These materials are grouped together under the name of geosynthetics, which comprise geotextiles, geogrids, geomembranes, geolinear elements and geocomposites.

Plastics have developed into a much used and versatile building material. They come nearest to the idea of pre-engineered materials produced with predetermined properties. Structural components were already fabricated during the 1930s but the first real all-plastic house was only exhibited in Paris in 1955 (designed by Schein, Coulon and Magnant). The Monsanto House of the Future (designed by Hamilton and Goody) was assembled in 1957 from glass fibre reinforced plastic shells with multiple honeycomb cores cantilevered from a concrete core. Others followed, e.g. the Futuro house in Finland, the Sekisui house in Japan and the Varedo house in Italy. Such houses were isolated attempts that did not lead to any serial application, however. More lasting success was achieved in constructing all-plastic cabins, kiosks, bathrooms and structural components such as wall units.

WINDOWS

Windows were traditionally made from wood. During the past 100 years steel has captured only a small part of the market, while aluminium has managed a 20–30% share in some countries. During the

Fig. 5.9 Experimental polymer house, Monsanto, USA. *Source:* Gy. Sebestyén (1977) *Lightweight Building*, Akadémiai Kiadó, Budapest.

past 20 years, plastic windows have been used increasingly. Their share exceeds 50% in Germany. In France, wood, aluminium and plastic all take a one-third share.

PVC is the most commonly used polymer for windows. Extruded sections are made with single-chamber or multichamber cross-sections which can be manufactured strong enough, otherwise they may require stiffening with steel or aluminium inserts. The corners are usually welded. The PVC used for windows must be impact-resistant. It is normally grey or white, but can be coloured or lacquered. Other plastics used for windows are polyurethane and glass-fibre reinforced polyester. Wood, steel, aluminium and plastics can all be combined in different ways in windows. Replacement windows is an important market for the plastic type.

DRY-ASSEMBLED PARTITIONS, CEILINGS AND RAISED FLOORS

As already discussed, modern architecture has replaced many of the earlier external masonry walls with dry-assembled claddings, curtain walls and glazings. A similar development has taken place in the interior of buildings, where masonry partitions have been replaced by dry-assembled partitions. Partitions can be assembled from prefabricated panels, or they can be built from vertical supports and boards. The invention of

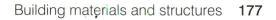

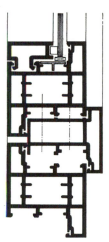

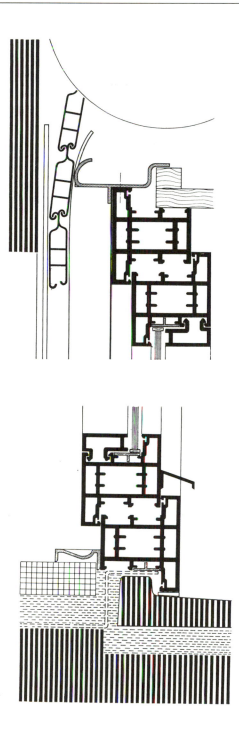

Fig.   5.10 Impact-resistant PVC balcony door, upper vertical cross section, Trocal, Dynamit-Nobel, Germany. *Source:* Gy. Sebestyén (1977) *Lightweight Building*, Akadémiai Kiadó, Budapest.

plasterboard and light steel sections was the primary (but not the only) basis for a multitude of commercially available systems and individually designed solutions.

The massive reinforced concrete or composite steel-concrete floors of yesteryear have been largely retained, however, because of the need for adequate stiffness, fire resistance and sound insulation. But suspended ceilings or raised floors (or both) have been added to provide space for the various services (electrical, air ducts, etc.). Suspended ceiling systems often incorporate the lighting sources with or without heat recuperation. They usually have some decorative or acoustic design. Raised floors usually offer the opportunity of having electric sockets on a grid, thereby satisfying the requirements of modern offices for flexible arrangements, lighting and telecommunications.

ROOFS

Low-pitch and flat roofs

The materials for traditional pitched roofs were selected from nature and shaped for use: wood shingles, stone slabs, slate, fired clay tiles, bark, palm leaves, thatch and straw. Over time, new roofing materials were developed: concrete, metals (copper, lead, zinc, aluminium, steel and stainless steel), asphalt, bituminous felt and plastics. For low-pitch and flat roofs, there are four basical types (*A Decade of Change and Future Trends in Roofing*, 1985):

- asphalt roofs
- built-up roofing
- single membranes and elasto-plastic systems
- inverted roofs.

Asphalt roofs are widely used in the Americas. A sheathing felt is laid over the roof deck and this is then covered by layers of mastic asphalt, which is usually protected by solar paint. Built-up roofing has been much used in Europe, at first with several layers of bituminous felt bonded together with hot bitumen. The roofing is protected from heat and ultraviolet radiation by a layer of gravel. Although they performed well if they were prepared with good workmanship, they were accident prone if basic rules of good design, execution and maintenance were ignored. Built-up roofs have recently been made with new types of materials such as organic resin (phenolformaldehyde) treated glass-fibre mats. Modern built-up roofs can be constructed from prefabricated panels (consisting of an insulating board with a roofing membrane on top) anchored to the underlying structure with fasteners, and with sealing strips ensuring continuous joining and waterproofing.

Single membranes (also called single-ply systems) are non-bituminous membranes such as butyl or PVC sheet. The polymeric or elasto-plastic systems include neoprene (chloroprene), polyisobutylene, butyl, PVC, Hypalon (chlorosulphonated or chlorinated polyethylene or ethylene propylene diene monomer, EPDM). In several systems the membrane is loose-laid, sealed or fastened just at the edges. This allows for differential movement and stretching of the materials. Loose gravel ballast provides protection and anchorage against wind uplift. A loose-laid elastomeric roof membrane can also be placed on top of a heat-insulating expanded polystyrene layer, which would otherwise be vulnerable to hot bitumen. Polymer-modified sheets can be reinforced with fibreglass or polyester mats. The main materials used for single-ply membranes are:

- thermoplastic (PVC)
- elastomer (EPDM)
- plastomer (PIB).

The PIB roofing membrane contains three important components:

- the PIB sheet itself
- the non-woven synthetic fleece backing
- the prefabricated sealing edge.

Single-ply membranes are usually mechanically fastened and often protected by ballast. The fastening systems can be spot- or linear-affixed, penetrating the membrane or not. The fastener must be strong enough to prevent it from being pulled out from the deck. Sprayed *in situ* polyurethane foam roofs also belong to the membrane roof family. They also require protection from sunshine (e.g. by elastomeric coating). Their advantage is that they cope easily with complicated roof contours.

In inverted systems, a lightweight heat insulation is placed on top of the waterproofing membrane. The heat insulation (which must have a high vapour resistance) is then covered by a layer of gravel or paving slabs to provide protection against wind uplift and sun (Künzel, 1995). Liquid-applied membranes (based on bituminous or synthetic formulations) are used mainly in remedial work. For some, a fibrous mat is laid over the roof before applying the resin or bituminous dressing compound (Flat roof design: waterproof membranes, 1992).

Fabrics and membranes for roofs

Long-spanning roofs over large spaces are made increasingly from polymers. In Europe, PVC-coated woven polyester fabrics have been much used for roofs. It is an inexpensive fabric but, due to degradation of the PVC by ultraviolet light, its durability is limited. In the USA, poly-tetrafluoro-ethylene (Teflon) covered glass-textile and polyamide fibre

(Kevlar, Nomex) textile is much used for roofing. It has a non-stick property so the roof remains fairly clean. Although its durability is longer, in fire it releases more toxic fumes than those made from other combustible polymers. The roof of the Munich olympic stadium (designed with the participation of the German architect Frei Otto) was made not from fabrics but of a net of steel cables clad with acrylic sheets.

AUTOMATION AND ROBOTS

ROBOTS IN CONSTRUCTION

Construction is the largest industrial sector and yet it is also the most archaic. Most construction processes are individual and non-repetitive, which does not make them suitable for automation. On the other hand, if broken down to their constituent processes, many of them are of a repetitive character. These processes are also labour-intensive with many safety risks. Productivity is usually not sufficiently high and it is difficult to control quality. These features justify attempts at automation and the use of robots. After substantial progress in the use of machines, the construction industry has begun work on the introduction of robots. Robots are being applied to an increasing number of construction processes in the following fields (Mathonnet and Salagnac, 1986; Proceedings of International Symposia on Robotics in Construction, 1988; Iwamoto *et al.*, 1994; Visconti *et al.*, 1994; Kuntze *et al.*, 1995; Leyh, 1995):

- soil excavation and moving
- technologies for concrete and reinforced concrete
- manufacturing building components
- lifting, transporting and assembling building materials and components, on-site welding
- bricklaying
- slip-form processes
- interior finishing: painting, tile-laying
- tunneling and underwater work
- processes under dangerous or health-impairing conditions (e.g. in nuclear power stations and hazardous waste clean-up)
- inspection and repair of wall surfaces (with climbing robots).

Some countries, such as the USA, Japan, France, Israel and the UK, are making significant efforts in robotization of construction work. Periodic international symposia (International Symposia on Automation and Robotics in Construction, ISARC) review developments in the area (Chamberlain, 1994).

AUTOMATED CONSTRUCTION SYSTEMS

Large Japanese construction companies have begun developing complete automated construction systems, as the following two examples illustrate. The Shimizu Manufacturing System by Advanced Robotics Technology (SMART), claimed to be the world's first all-weather automatic system for building, was used in the construction of the Juroku Bank Nagoya Building. The on site automatic plant is enclosed by roof and walls. It adds floors like building blocks, with the construction proceeding from the ground upwards. Within the plant, work progresses comfortably and safely, unaffected by weather. Having built a prototype building with the Automated Building Construction System (ABCS) in 1993, the Obayashi company is now developing that system for wider use.

ENVIRONMENTAL TECHNOLOGIES

Among the new responsibilities and technologies of the industry, are a number of environmentally related ones, such as the cleaning of conta-minated land, disposal and recycling of construction and other waste

Fig. 5.11 Automated construction, Ohbayashi, Japan. *Source:* Courtesy of Company Ohbayashi.

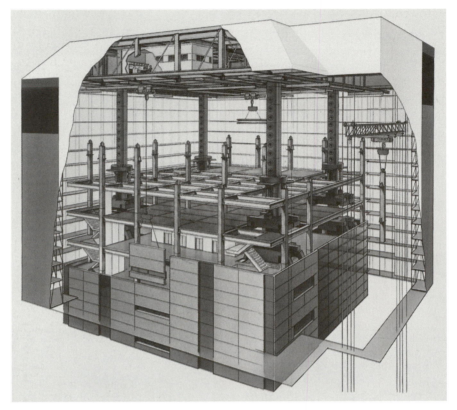

Fig. 5.12 System for automatic high-rise building construction, Shimizu, Japan. *Source:* Courtesy of Company Shimizu.

(solid, hazardous, etc). These areas can yield welcome revenues, and some firms have therefore developed special expertise in the field (Moavenzadeh, 1994).

CLEANING CONTAMINATED LAND

Land and its soil can be contaminated by various human activities: dumping, spilling or simply careless discharging of solid or liquid waste from industrial and other economic activities as well as households. Soil that has been contaminated by gases and leaching liquids can harm the health of those living or working in the area. It can also corrode or otherwise damage buildings and equipment, or poison animals and vegetation. The size of the problem can be seen from the estimated US$150 billion cost of cleaning up and rehabilitating sites and environments in the former West Germany and The Netherlands (van Breugel, 1994). Cleaning contaminated land is therefore an increasing priority.

In the UK, tough new laws require that land for development or redevelopment must be checked for contamination, including land that is already occupied by buildings. The three basic categories of land decontamination are: off site, on site and *in situ*. The off site process involves the removal of contaminated soil, usually to plants specialized in decontamination. In the on site process, soil is removed from its original place but is cleaned nearby. In the *in situ* process, the soil is cleaned without actually moving it. The selection of which process to use depends on the soil, its contamination and quantity, the groundwater flow conditions, and the intended future use of the land.

Soil can be cleaned by hydraulic, pneumatic, thermal, chemical-physical, or biological methods. The least expensive of these is the biological method, by which the contamination is devoured by bacteria. Heavy metal contamination can be cleaned up with water that contains appropriate chemical agents. For contaminated sand-soil, thermal cleaning is favoured. In the first phase, the soil is heated, to eliminate its water. In the second phase, the organic contaminants are cleaned away, at a temperature of 600°C. In the third phase, at an even higher temperature, the sand is transformed into a glass-like substance, and the gases generated by the process are disposed of at a temperature of 1200°C. Military cleanups are often costly affairs. According to a 1990 estimate, there were more than 14 000 suspected toxic sites on 1579 military installations in the USA alone (Ichniowski, 1991).

LANDFILLS

Ugly and foul-smelling dump sites are no longer tolerated in the developed countries. High-tech landfills are created instead to dispose of waste. Naturally, the first objective is to reduce the quantity of waste, which is often taken care of by incineration and recycling. Even so, large quantities of waste remain, for which landfills are needed. As mentioned, these are now high-tech waste disposal facilities which may have as many as 12 layers of soil, clay and synthetic liners below and above the waste. They also have a method of monitoring groundwater, detecting and collecting methane gas and leachate (Rubin and Buckner Powers, 1991). Waste disposal sites must be designed and managed in such a way that harmful substances reach the biosphere and hydrosphere only in limited and acceptable quantities. The layers in a landfill over the subsoil and under the waste can be (from the bottom upwards):

- composite clay liner
- geomembrane
- double layer geonet
- geotextile
- composite clay liner

- geomembrane
- geocomposite drain
- geotextile.

The contractors and managers of landfill sites often experiment with various cover materials, together with plans to increase degradation-enhancing moisture by pumping in air and spreading leachate over the top of the site. Plastic geomembrane sheets are used to reduce the permeability and increase the chemical resistance and durability of the landfill cut-off barriers (German Geotechnical Society, 1991). In Europe, landfills are usually lined with a smaller number of layers than in the USA.

Cut-off walls consisting of self-hardening cement-bentonite are used to contain leachate and/or gases both at landfill and former industrial sites. Single-phase, self-hardening slurry trench cut-off walls are constructed by excavating a trench under cement-bentonite slurry. This remains fluid during excavation, but hardens within about 24 hours to form the barrier. Geomembranes, which are flexible and made from a variety of polymer resins (butyl rubber, polypropylene, polyvinyl chloride, chlorinated polyethylene, ethylene propylene rubber) are frequently incorporated into the slurry to act as the main element of the barrier. At the international level, ISO Technical Committee TC 190-Soil Quality is working on soil quality, classification, definition of terms, sampling of soils, measurement and reporting of soil characteristics (Hortensius and Nortcliff, 1991). Soil fills may be needed for reasons other than waste disposal. In all fills compaction is to be controlled.

CONSTRUCTION WASTE: RECYCLING

Scant attention used to be paid to the reduction, disposal or recycling of construction waste, but this has now changed. The amount of construction and demolition waste produced each year in western Europe amounts to approximately 0.7–1.0 tonne per inhabitant (Kibert, 1994). This is twice as much as the municipal solid waste generated. In France, the waste from construction and demolition operations amounts to some 24 million tonnes per year, of which 10 million tonnes comes from demolition (Charlot-Valdieu 1996). The EU estimates that the union will generate 175 million tonnes of demolition, and 40 million tonnes of construction, waste in 2000. Directive 91/156/EEC on waste management was adopted in 1991 and its implementation is progressing in EU member states.

The first obligation of construction firms is to reduce the volume of construction waste and, if possible, to avoid dumping it without some useful purpose (Skoyles, 1987). Little construction and demolition waste is being salvaged or recycled, at present, but as its volume is set to increase gradually, more firms are now specializing in reuse and recycling. Some buy waste from industry (e.g. from the wood and paper processors) and manufacture from that and their own waste building components such as fibreboard, particle board and chipboard. Inorganic construction waste from stone, bricks, concrete, and mortar is crushed and used as aggregate etc. (Buttenwieser and Favennec, 1995).

Removal of iron and steel is necessary during recycling, and this steel waste can then be reused by the steel industry. Historical components such as old timber beams, stone carvings and terracotta façade pieces should be rescued for reuse in some form. The recycling of plastics involves sorting out the various types as each requires different recycling technologies. Thermoplastics (PE and PVC) can be recycled by granulating and pressing them into new products, such as windows. No contaminated or otherwise agressive material should be used in recycling without appropriate treatment (e.g. waste containing asbestos fibres or lead-based paint). Water recycling should also be expanded in the future and various products are already available commercially to aid in water recycling (e.g. the 'Pressure Butt').

Recycling should make sense from an economic point of view, but this is not always the case in practice. On the other hand, not all the waste that could be recycled economically is. It has been calculated in Switzerland that up to 40% of plastics could be recycled economically whereas in fact only 10% is recycled (Stumpf, 1994).

DEMOLITION TECHNOLOGIES

Whether they have had a long or short service life, the time generally comes for most buildings to be demolished. Some of the demolition technologies applied are:

- wire rope pulling
- demolition ball
- pneumatic ball
- explosion
- hydraulic jack
- cutting with thermal lance or other heat source
- the Nibbler.

These techniques and machines are well known, with the exception of the 'Nibbler', perhaps, which was developed not long ago by the UK Building Research Establishment. It is used to break concrete slabs and walls by applying large bending moment on them. Magnetic separation of steel is usually carried out by a magnetic pulley, drum or suspended magnet.

Demolition is easier if the structures can be dismantled without destruction, but this is only possible if the structures are designed that way. Such structures are termed 'demountable', and there are many good examples and much experience of them (Reinhardt and Bouvy, 1985). The basic idea is to apply rigid structural connections in such a way that they can be removed without damaging the structural members. Design for demountability (or disassembly) is aiding sustainability because it reduces demolition waste and conserves resources.

SAFETY ON SITES

A report of the British Health and Safety Executive stated that construction is the most dangerous industry in the UK, with more deaths and injuries than in any other sector (Health and Safety Executive, 1988). During one decade, 1500 people were killed and 25–30 000 suffered injuries that necessitated hospitalization. A further 300–400 000 injuries were serious enough to require at least three days off from work. In the USA only 6% of the total industrial workforce is employed in construction, but 20% of all occupational fatalities occurs in this sector. In Japan, the construction industry employs 10% of the total industrial workforce, but accidents in construction account for 40% of all industrial accidents.

Injuries from falling objects, people falling from scaffolding or unfinished buildings, strains, sprains, cuts and burns are the chief types of accident. Not only do these accidents cause pain and suffering to the workforce, they also cost money, hamper production and convey a bad image. Contractors should make every effort to fulfil their legal obligation, and reduce the occurrence of accidents (Health and Safety Executive, 1988).

DURABILITY AND DEGRADATION

Our most important building materials such as stone, timber, brick and mortar, have been with us now for several thousand years. The limited durability of timber (which under favourable conditions may be several hundred years) has always been known, while other materials were considered to last virtually for ever. A long durability was also assumed for some newer materials such as concrete and aluminium, but much of this optimism has recently been shattered. The main reasons have been (Richardson, 1980; Ransom, 1981):

- the increasingly aggressive and polluted or contaminated environment
- poor workmanship
- inadequate quality of the materials used
- the careless use of buildings.

Both aluminium and concrete are liable to corrode under the current more polluted atmospheric conditions (Hillemeier, 1992). New materials and structures can deteriorate in new ways and their repair may cause problems. Knowledge in one single discipline may not be sufficient to identify their causes. Durability is the outcome of stochastic processes of deterioration and degradation. It is the probability of proper behaviour of a structure at any stage during its lifetime. The modelling of durability requires the knowledge of a great number of initial and subsequent properties and environmental data and the rules governing the changes through time of properties and data. A host of deterioration forms has been identified including abrasion, bleeding, blister, collapse, condensation, corrosion, cracking, crazing, creep, decomposition, deformation, delamination, discoloration, efflorescence, exfiltration, exfoliation, fatigue, fissure, fracture, fungus, heave, infiltration, mildew, mould, rot, shrinkage, spalling, split, stain, warp and yield.

As a consequence of multiplying defects and deterioration in buildings, the durability of materials and the interplay of actions must be studied.

SUMMARY

The change in construction technology is represented by a number of trends, such as the use of new materials and materials with new characteristics, the combination of materials, new structures and components, the reduction of the specific weight of structures (lightweight and curtain walls, light roofs), the application of dry assembly methods, mechanization, prefabrication, introduction of low-maintenance components and others.

The introduction of modern steel technology brought new properties: high strength, weldability, weathering, non-corroding (stainless). New hot-rolled steel sections, cold-formed (corrugated and coil-coated) thin steel and aluminium sheet are produced. Concrete is made with various properties: lightweight, pre-stressed, to be exposed, high-performance (high-strength). The use of timber found new forms in glulam. Glass is used for all-glass envelopes (structural glazing) and is produced with favourable characteristics against the effect of sunshine and for energy conservation. New types of jointing with new types of fasteners, welding and gluing are applied. New types of plastics have found structural and window use. Fabrics are produced for roofs and applied in geotechnics.

Robots have been devised for selected construction processes. The first experimental buildings have been built with automatic construction systems.

Environmental considerations have given birth to new technologies for cleaning contaminated ground, landfills, recycling and demolition. The period of durability of structures and buildings is consciously planned. The degradation, maintenance and repair processes are studied with the objective of achieving optimal economic performance.

The changing technology transforms traditional construction into a modern industry using up-to-date materials, machines and production processes.

BIBLIOGRAPHY

A Decade of Change and Future Trends in Roofing (1985) Proceedings of the Second International Symposium on Roofing Technology, Chicago, Illinois.

Abel, J. F. and Billington, D. P. (1980) *Perspectives on the History of Reinforced Concrete in the United States 1904–1941*, Princeton University.

Ambrose, J. (1994) *Design of Building Trusses*, John Wiley & Sons.

Assessment of existing high alumina cement concrete construction in the UK (March 1994) *BRE Digest*, **392**.

Baker, J. M. (ed.) (1990) *Durability of Building Materials and Components*, Proceedings of CIB-RILEM-etc. Symposium, Brighton, UK.

Blanc, A., McEvoy, M. and Plank, R. (eds) (1993) *Architecture and Construction in Steel*, E & FN Spon.

Blass, H. J. *et al.* (eds) (1995) *Timber Engineering*; STEP, Centrum Hout, The Netherlands.

van Breugel, K. (1991) Computer-based simulation model for hydration and structural formation of cement-based materials. In *Progress in Concrete Research*, Vol.2, Delft, 17–29.

van Breugel K. (1994) New strategies for environmental problems – the role of concrete structures, *FIP '94 Congress*, 29 May–27 June 1994, Vol.2, K12–K17.

Breyer, D. E. (1988) *Design of Wood Structures*, McGraw-Hill.

BRE Digest 389 (1993); see under: Concrete...

BRE Digest 392 (1994); see under: Assessment...

Buttenwieser, I. and Favennec, M. (1995) Le recyclage-concassage des matériaux issus de la démolition au Danemark et aux Pays Bas, *Cahiers du CSTB*, Cahier 2794, April 1994.

CEB 229 (1995) New developments in non-linear analysis methods, *Bulletin d'Information*.

Chamberlain, D. A. (1994) Automation and robotics in construction XI, *Proceedings of the 11th ISARC Symposium*, Brighton, England, 24–26 May 1994.

Charlot-Valdieu, C. and Cope, R. (1993) Des matériaux, des produits des bâtiments pour demain, *Cahiers du CSTB*, Cahier 2670.

Charlot-Valdieu, C. (1996) État des lieux et prospective de la démolition en France, *Cahiers du CSTB* Cahier 2876.

Chevalier and Chevalier (1991) Pour maîitriser la transparence des vitrages: les systèmes electrochromes. *Cahiers du CSTB*, Cahier 2512.

CIB Report no. 5 (1966) The production of concrete of uniform colour and free from surface blemishes, CIB W29 (also in French); see also under: The Production...

CIB Report no. 24 (1973) Tolerances on blemishes of concrete, CIBW29 (also in French); see also under: Tolerances...

Clarke, J. L. (ed.) (1993) *Structural Lightweight Aggregate Concrete*, Blackie Academic & Professional.

Concrete cracking and corrosion of reinforcement (1993) *BRE Digest*, **389**.

Davies, J. M. (1994) The interaction of light gauge steel with other materials, *New Steel Construction*, **2**(2), April, 18–19.

Easterling, W. S. and Kim Roddis, W. M. (eds) (1992) *Composite Construction in Steel and Concrete II*, ASCE Publication, New York.

ECCS (1988) *International Symposium on Steel Bridges*, 25–26 February 1988, London.

Eekhout, M. (ed.) (1992) *The Glass Envelope*; TU Delft.

Emborg, M. (1994) Development of mechanical behaviour at early ages including mathematical models and methods for computation of thermal stresses and cracking risks *RILEM TC-119TCE Report* (draft), 1–30.

Flat roof design: waterproof membranes. (1992) *BRE Digest*, 372.

German Geotechnical Society (ed.) (1991) Geotechnics of Landfills and Contaminated Land, International Society of Soil Mechanics and Foundation Engineering (ISSMFE) Ernst & Bower, Berlin.

Glulam Award 94 (1994) Kannike Tryk A/S, Denmark.

Hall, C. (1989) *Polymer Materials*, Macmillan Education.

Health and Safety Executive (1988) *Build Safety – A Report by H. M. Inspector of Factories and the Construction National Interest Group*, HMSO, London.

High performance concrete (1995) *CEB Bulletin d'Information*, 228.

High strength concrete (1990) *FIP/CEB Bulletin d'Information*, No. 197, FIP.

Hillemeier, B. (1992) Durability in design, detailing and construction. In *Post-Congress Report of IABSE*, 1–6 March 1992.

Hollaway, L. C. (1990) *Polymers and Polymer Composites in Construction*, Thomas Telford, London.

Hortensius, D. and Nortcliff, S. (1991) International standardization of soil quality measurement procedures for the purpose of soil protection, *Soil Use and Management*, **3**, 163–6.

Hurst, M. K. (1988) *Prestressed Concrete Design*, Chapman & Hall.

Ichniowski, T. (1991) Military cleanups are a slow affair, *Engineering News Record*, April, 26.

Ikeda, S. (1995) Development of lightweight aggregate concrete in Japan, *Proceedings of Symposium on Structural Lightweight Aggregate Concrete*, 20–24 June, Sandefjord, Norway, 42–51.

Illston, J. M. (1994) *Construction Materials*, E & FN Spon.

INTEMAC (1994) *Normas para la utilizacion del hormigon armado*, INTEMAC, Spain.

Iwamoto, M. *et al.* (1994) A system of vertically sliding and installing exterior curtain walls of a building, *Automation in Construction*, **3**, 21–43.

Kibert, C. J. (1994) Sustainable construction, *Proceedings of CIB TG 16 Conference*, 6–9 November 1994, Tampa, Florida, USA.

König, G., Duda, H. and Zink M. (1994) Novel and advanced applications of pre-stressed concrete in bridges. In *Spannbetonbau in der Bundesrepublik Deutschland 1990–1994*, DBV-FIP, 71–76.

König, G. (1993) Robuste Spannbetonwerke. In *Festschrift. Prof. Dr Manfred Wicke zum 60*, Geburtstag, 185–207.

Kuntze, H-B. *et al.* (1995) On the dynamic control of a hydraulic large range robot for construction applications. *Automation in Construction*, **4**, 61–73.

Künzel, H. (1995) Zum heutigen Stand der Kentnisse über das UK-Dach, *Bauphysik* **17**(1), 1–7.

Lane, J. (1992) *Aluminium in Building*, Ashgate.

Larsen, H. J., Kuipers, J. and Ehrentreich, J. (eds) (1989) *Timber Structures*, EUR 12136 EN-DE-FR.

Leijten J. M. (1994a) *Physical and Mechanical Properties of Densified Veneer Wood (dvw) for Structural Applications*, Technical University of Delft.

Leijten, A. J. M. (1994b) New developments in reinforced timber joints. In F. K. Garas *et al.* (eds), *Building the Future*, E & FN Spon.

Levi, F., Marro, P. and Viara, G. (1995) Non-linear analysis of beams and frames, *Bulletin d'Information*, CEB, 227.

Leyh, W. (1995) Experiences with the construction of a building assembly robot. *Automation in Construction*, **4**, 45–60.

Macchi, G. (1994) *Unbonded and External Prestressing – Role of CEB and FIP*, Working Paper, Oostende, 12 September 1994.

Mathonnet, S. and Salagnac, J-L. (1986) La stratégie japonaise en matière d'automatisation et de robotisation dans la construction, *Cahiers du CSTB*, Cahier 2109.

Moavenzadeh, F. (1994) *Global Construction and the Environment*, John Wiley & Sons.

Munding, M. and Bagheri (1990) *Strahlungsdurchgang von Gläsern mit thermotropem Sonnenschutz*, Fraunhofer-Institut für Bauphysik, IBP Mitteilung 194.

Ofori, G. (1994) Construction industry development: role of technology transfer, *Construction Management and Economics*, **12**, 379–92.

Okamura, H. and Ozawa, K. (1994) Self-compactable high performance concrete in Japan. In *International Workshop on High Performance Concrete*, November 1994, Bangkok, Thailand, 2–1–2–16.

Perez Luzardo, J. M. (1992) *Colour and Texture of Structural Concrete*, INTEMAC, Madrid.

Pimienta, P. *et al.* (1994) Etude de faisabilité des procédés de construction à base de béton de bois, *Cahiers du CSTB*, Cahier 2703.

Proceedings of International Symposia on Robotics in Construction (1988) Bristol, England; Haifa, Israel; Tokyo, Japan.

The Production of Concrete of Uniform Colour and Free from Surface Blemishes (1966) CIB Report No.5.

Ransom, W. H. (1981) *Building Failures*, E & FN Spon.

Reinhardt, H. W. and Bouvy, J. J. B. J. J. (1985) *Demountable Concrete Structures*, Delft University Press.

Rice, P. and Dutton, H. (1995) *Structural Glass*, E & FN Spon.

Richardson, B. A. (1980) *Remedial Treatment of Buildings*, The Construction Press.

Rubin, D. K. and Buckner Powers, M. (1991) Down in the dumps gains new meaning, *Engineering News Record*, 3 June 1991, 26–9.

Sandvik, M. and Hammer, T. A. (1995) The development and use of high performance lightweight aggregate concrete in Norway. *Proceedings of the International Symposium on Structural Lightweight Aggregate Concrete*, 20–24 June 1995, 617–27.

Schlangen, E. and van Mier, J. G. M. (1991) Experimental and numerical analysis of micromechanisms of fracture of cementbased composites, *Progress in Concrete Research*, Vol. 2, TU Delft, 45–70.

Schlangen, E. and van Mier, J. G. M. (1995) Fracture simulations in concrete and rock using a random lattice. In *Progress in Concrete Research*, Vol.4, TU Delft, 29–39.

Sedlacek, G. *et al.* (1995) Glass in structural engineering, *The Structural Engineer*, January, 17–21.

Skoyles, E. R. (1987) *Waste Prevention on Site*, Mitchell, London.

Slurry trench cut-off walls to contain contamination (1994), *BRE Digest* 395.

Stumpf, K. (1994) *Kunststoffrecycling in der Schweiz- eine naturwissenschaftliche, technologische und ökonomische Betrachtung*, EMPA Bericht Nr.231, Dubendorf, Switzerland.

Tolerances on Blemishes of Concrete, (1973) CIB Report No. 24.

Toma, T. (ed.) *et al.* (1992) *Cold-Formed Steel in Tall Buildings*, McGraw-Hill Inc.

Turner, R. G. (1986) *Construction Economics and Building Design: A Historical Approach*, Van Nostrand Reinhold, New York.

Vandepitte, D. (1993) Is civil engineering really conservative?, *Structural Engineering International*, **3**, 261.

Visconti, B. V. *et al.* (1994) Automated construction in the ATLSS building system, *Automation in Construction*, **3**, 35–43.

Walraven, J. C. (1994a) Hochfester Beton: Möglichkeiten und Chancen, *BFT*, **11**, 109–17.

Walraven J. C. (1994b) High performance concrete, *CEB Bulletin d'Information*, **221**, 107–24.

Walraven, J. (1994c) High performance concrete: exploring a new material, *Structural Engineering International*, August, 182–7.

Buildings and structures

6

INTRODUCTION

Over the past 100–200 years, there has been an increasing need for buildings that have very specific functions and services. Designers have had to assimilate the accumulated knowledge on building functions, and this has become the topic for textbooks, curricula and databases containing information on the space requirements for various functions such as the circulation of people, bathing, cooking, furniture arrangement and functional requirements (e.g. the interrelationship between the different elements of a restaurant kitchen) (Neufert, 1980; Mills, 1985).

The building market itself has changed in that it now consists of several submarkets, particularly in large economies (and large cities) where subsectors have emerged specializing in housing, schools, hospitals, offices and hotels. Some developers, designers and contractors who specialize in one particular subsector seldom venture into the field of another. Others have remained generalized, their strength being in serving a restricted geographic area: a city, region or country. Some large specialist organizations are active in all or, at least, in several subsectors. Many contractors now frequently claim that they are specialized in certain fields, that they have a local (domestic) character, or both. Some developers, designers and contractors have extended their activities internationally, some as generalists, others as specialists.

The development described in the building business has progressed in parallel with the differentiation of the products, the buildings. One of the peculiarities of the building profession lies in its great variety and it would therefore be impossible to attempt to cover the changes in most building types. We are born in maternity wards in hospitals, attend nurseries, kindergartens, schools, colleges or universities; we live in houses, flats, youth hostels, barracks or sheltered homes (and sometimes in prisons or gaols!); we enjoy performances in theatres, cinemas, museums, circuses, stadiums and libraries; we work in or make use of offices, banks, shops, department stores, factories, commercial units and farms; we drive our cars to petrol stations and car parks; we visit air, bus and rail terminals; we attend services in churches, mosques, temples or synagogues; we stay in hotels, guest houses and holiday villages; we eat and drink in restaurants, coffee-shops and pubs; when bidding farewell to deceased friends and relatives, and when we ourselves have gone, we visit mortuaries, cemetries and crematoria. The specialization of building functions continues as structures, services, and the control of buildings has become more sophisticated. For obvious reasons, just a few of the building types and civil engineering structures are selected below to illustrate aspects of the transformation of construction into a modern industry. While dwelling products such as houses and flats are among the most important building types, we do not cover them here because they are fully discussed in other chapters.

BUILDINGS WITH VARIOUS FUNCTIONS

OFFICES

The impact of the proliferation of office working was succinctly expressed by Duffy (1980):

> Office buildings have changed our cities: office work has revolutionized our society.

Office buildings of various sizes and cost are important products of contemporary construction. Most of them must satisfy strict economic criteria, although their prestige-promotion value may be more important than economic considerations in some cases (Bailey, 1990). The traditional arrangement of offices, two banks of rooms to a depth of 5.40 m with a 1.80 m wide corridor inbetween, is being replaced by the use of deeper spaces so that new buildings are 20–25 m deep instead of the traditional 13–15 m. In developed countries with a high level of car use, the preferred location for new office complexes are the growth corridors, technopoles and accessible peripheral locations away from congested areas with traffic and parking difficulties.

Economic efficiency finds a comprehensive expression in the term 'floor area ratio' (FAR), which is the usable floor area of a building expressed as a multiple of the site area. The greater the FAR, the larger is the lettable (or saleable) space and, usually, the taller the building is. In the USA, cities set the limit for the FAR in particular districts, and the FAR governs the amount of floor space a developer can build without going through special procedures.

Many technical innovations are applied in the design and construction of modern office buildings (Turner *et al.* 1984), some of which are described in this book. Information technology equipment and conference and meeting rooms require more and more space (Brotchie *et al.*, 1995). To accommodate the information technology support services, office buildings are constructed with raised floors and suspended ceilings and appropriate power supplies. Cellular arrangements in which offices are served by corridors require more space than open-plan arrangements, and the latter is therefore becoming more common. Middle management nowadays get smaller offices than before, and not always high up in the building but rather on the shop floor alongside their team. As personal office space is decreasing, interesting areas with good air quality are more appreciated. Buzz words such as 'cocon office' (*communication and concentration*), 'desk-sharing', 'touchdown desk', 'docking stations', 'multizones' and 'hotel offices' mark certain new ideas in office planning. The increasingly accepted idea of working from home and working flexible hours raised the idea of sharing desks, an arrangement that has not yet found favour, however.

'Shell and core' is a recent concept that requires the internal office areas to be left as a shell on completion of the building so that the tenants may finish them in accordance with their own specific requirements. These changes reduce the cost of the shell within the total cost of the building, while the cost of services and equipment in buildings has been growing steadily in recent years. In order to reduce construction time, the 'fast track' method, often using metal frames and metal deck floors, has been adopted.

Modern office buildings have often given rise to complaints from the occupants, and so satisfaction with the indoor environment is now an important requirement. The clients of prestigious office buildings, such as the headquarters for large international banks, usually not only invest in more luxurious design, expensive materials and fittings, but also apply the most up-to-date technology in order to ensure a good indoor environment and to demonstrate their policy of supporting progress (Riewoldt, 1994). (The problems of 'sick buildings' were described in Chapter 4.)

Evaluation methods for offices have been devised from the viewpoint of facility management (Strategies and Technologies, 1994), including users' perceptions and post-occupancy evaluations, which measure the impact of design factors such as lighting on the productivity of office workers (Lippiatt and Weber, 1992). The most recent prestigious office buildings have become objects of demonstration for modern high-technology construction: some such remarkable office buildings are described elsewhere in this book.

SCHOOLS

Schools built by traditional technologies tended to have uniform-sized classrooms, but they are now designed with more flexible classrooms and provide more space for workshops, libraries, gymnasiums, auditoriums, etc. (Reuterswärd, 1988; Vickery, 1988). Since 1945, classes have become smaller. A change in facilities was required, partly to suit the various activities better, and partly to provide more freedom. The introduction of computers and multimedia equipment also had an impact on the facilities required. In Europe and the USA, the sudden post-war demand for school-building helped the introduction of prefabrication, mostly with light steel frames (e.g. the Fillod system in France). In the UK, school-building consortia were established (Russell, 1981):

- SCOLA Second Consortium of Local Authorities
- CLASP Consortium of Local Authorities Special Programme
- MACE Metropolitain Architectural Consortium for Education
- METHOD Consortium for Method Building.

In the USA, the Californian SCSD (School Construction Systems Development) and the work of architect Ezra Ehrenkrantz (and others) represented the most advanced solutions. The 'systems' contributed to the construction of many post-war schools but disappeared when the school-building boom flattened out.

Indoor climate can present a problem in schools, mainly as a result of carbon dioxide concentration. Opening windows for a sufficient period during breaks can improve matters, or more expensive technical solutions can be incorporated to ensure good indoor air quality.

HOTELS

The hotel business is an important client of the building industry. European countries have always been tourist destinations, but East Asia and the Pacific area (Singapore, Hong Kong, Thailand, Japan, China, Indonesia, Australia and Malaysia) have also become popular with tourists recently.

In 1989–90, the major European countries had the following number of hotel bedrooms: Italy 1.7 million, France 1.3 million, Germany, Spain and the UK each around 1.0 million. These data are not completely comparable because the term 'hotel' has different meanings in different countries and may include or exclude guest houses, boarding and lodging houses, bed and breakfast establishments, inns, clubs, posadas, albergos and motels.

Some national chains have hotels in many cities, and some have become international. The largest hotel chains in Europe currently are:

- Accor (France): a total of 2200 hotels worldwide, hotels named (in descending order of classification) Sofitel, Pullmann, Mercure, Ibis, Etap, Motel 6, Formule 1

- Forte (UK): hotels Exclusive, Meridien, PostHouse, TraveLodge (the chain was bought recently by the media and amusement concern Granada)
- Société du Louvre (France): Concorde, Campanile, and others
- Queens Moat House (UK).

Some American hotel chains are even larger than the European ones. Holiday Inns, for example, has over 300 000 hotel rooms worldwide. Several other chains, such as Marriott and Sheraton have 100 000–200 000 rooms each.

As a result of the excessive building that took place during the 1980s, and the recent unfavourable economic conditions, some 1 million hotel rooms were unoccupied each night in the USA in 1994. Some chains specialize in certain types of business, such as holiday travel, and certain aspects of that, such as time-share facilities.

In designing a hotel, the first task is to decide on the size, shape and internal arrangement of the guest rooms. A second decision is on the system of access to the guest rooms, both horizontally and vertically. In high-rise and high-class hotels, central corridors are much used and single-sided corridors less so. Recently, however, a new type of single-sided corridor arrangement has found favour: the atrium-like central space. The front of a hotel comprises the entrance, reception, lobby, cloakrooms and toilets. The public spaces are the restaurant, bar, lounge, recreation (fitness), meeting and function rooms. Some hotels also have large convention halls. The service areas comprise the kitchen, food stores, laundry and administration. Restaurants vary in character: traditional, speciality, carvery, self-service, snack bars, coffee-shops or pubs.

The hotel trade adapts its services in various ways. One of the trends is to enable guests themselves to control their indoor ambience accurately, for instance by a microprocessor-controlled thermostat termed 'comfort-stat' (Fountain *et al.*, 1994). Another novelty is the provision of telecommunications in rooms. At the other extreme are Japanese hotels that provide no more than tiny cubicles for an overnight stay. No doubt this 'progress' may not find universal favour.

HOSPITALS

From medieval times through to the eighteenth and nineteenth centuries, hospitals were places of mercy that to a great extent, were devoted to care of the dying (Forty, 1980). In the late twentieth century, health care has become a sophisticated and complex activity. In industrialized countries, practically everyone comes into contact with health care, sporadic or intensive at some time in their lives, and a significant part of the population is employed in health care work. With the ageing of the population and with the increasing complexity of medicine, the size of this sector is set to increase further.

Spending on health depends on overall affluence levels. In 1986, health spending per head was US$1926 in the USA, and between US$700 and US$1400 in other industrialized countries, but only US$310 in Portugal, US$247 in Greece and US$140 in Turkey (Cox and Groves, 1990). Many countries assess whether their health care system is adequate by the number of hospital beds there are per 1000 inhabitants, and yet this has been shown to be unreliable as an indicator, as the countries with the highest level of health care may have relatively fewer beds than countries where health care is poor. For example, according to a recent report, there are 3.7 hospital beds per 1000 inhabitants in the USA. In the former West Germany there were 7.4 hospital beds per 1000 inhabitants in 1980; by 1984 this had been reduced to 7.0, and further reductions are planned. In Hungary in 1994 there were 10.5 beds per 1000 inhabitants with plans to improve health care and simultaneously reduce the number of hospital beds. The reason is that better outpatient treatment and more efficient hospital care mean that more can be attained with a smaller number of hospital beds.

In the EU, the health care sector employs 6 million people, including 1 million doctors, dentists and pharmacists. The health sector is an important customer for up-to-date technologies and high-precision instruments.

These days, health care requires numerous buildings with various functions and equipment: hospitals, outpatient clinics, nursing homes and geriatric homes of different sizes. The large communal spaces for the sick that were common previously, have been replaced by smaller rooms and special wards. Earlier this century, isolated pavilions were introduced to prevent the spread of infection. A more recent arrangement is the high-block hospital in which the reduction in distances was thought to increase efficiency. After 1945, a medical boom transformed hospitals: initially with the development of X-rays and penicillin and other antibiotics, and later with a host of new and expensive equipment. Most hospitals are now high-tech and high-cost buildings equipped with the latest machines and instruments. The wards are frequently sited in tall buildings, with the diagnostic, treatment, administration, polyclinic and ancillary supply in a lower, large-surface ('broad-foot') wing. Hospitals with the 'snake-type' or 'acacia-leaf' arrangement have a main traffic axis from which the ward blocks are accessed.

In designing hospitals, architects must co-operate closely with physicians, technology-designers and other specialists. Standardized functional units, or modules can be designed in advance. The architect may make use of these when designing a hospital. Based on experience with the spatial requirements of hospitals, various dimensional co-ordination systems have been devised. In Germany, for instance, where the module of 12.5 cm has always been favoured, the basic design module is 1.25 m, with a structural grid of 7.50 m partitioned to 3.75 m as required. Computer-aided hospital designing programs have also been developed. Large general hospitals have specialized units for certain illnesses. There can also be further specialization within a specific branch of medical treatment; for example, units can be specialized in cardiac, internal transplant or neurosurgery, limb fitting, burns etc. Some other common special treatment units are maternity, accident and emergency, radiology and intensive care. In addition, teaching hospitals, must cater for their educational function with appropriate demonstration and lecturing facilities.

Changes in medical technology also affect the design of hospitals. The Massachusetts General, one of Boston's largest hospitals, now has 45 different types of operating theatre to accommodate the various modern specialist equipments. Brigham and Women's Hospital, also in Boston, has built a US$50 million operating theatre to house a new imaging system for certain operations.

Co-operation at increasingly great distances has become a possibility for certain surgical interventions. 'Virtual design tools' are now used to prepare a simulated operation where a surgeon is able to work on an experimental basis in a hypothetical operating theatre. Medical equipment technologists are educating doctors, hospital specialists and architects about how to handle the up-to-date equipment.

Hospital chains, like hotels, have appeared in the most developed countries. Columbia HCA Healthcare, the largest in the USA, already had 322 hospitals in 1994 when it bought Health Trust, the second largest hospital network. The company's annual turnover now amounts to US$15 billion. Such network giants not only spend a good deal on medical and information equipment, they also accumulate considerable knowledge about hospital design and management, including keeping a check on the economic factors involved.

The purpose of a hospital is healing, which makes it all the more tragic when a patient actually picks up an infection in hospital. Naturally, hygiene requirements are strict, and some high-risk premises have special hygiene criteria. Among the many potential problems are: the microbial load of surfaces ('biofilm'); insufficient purity of air; disease spreading through the service duct system; and the presence of bacteria in drinking water installations. (See also 'cleanrooms', later in this chapter.)

BUILDINGS FOR CULTURE AND LEISURE

The increasing resources devoted throughout the world to culture has resulted in a great number of new museums, opera houses and theatres. New opera houses have been built in recent years in Paris (Bastille), Tokyo, Lyons, Glyndebourne, Tel Aviv, Cardiff, Bilbao and Helsinki.

There are new or expanded museums in London, Cologne, Stuttgart and elsewhere. Many of the new opera houses, theatres and museums have innovative design features, exploiting new technologies in lighting, indoor air and sound control.

In museums, there are two sometimes conflicting criteria for effective lighting:

- to ensure that lighting allows the works exhibited to be viewed
- to minimize the risk of damage to any light-sensitive materials in the works exhibited.

Invariably, the second criterion takes priority over the first. Lighting should be of an appropriate level and should not distort the colours of paintings. Daylighting and artificial lighting can be combined in various ways. Acoustics, as applied to theatres, opera houses and assembly halls, has developed into a complex scientific discipline.

The increase in the amount of free time and affluence of many people has led to an increasing demand for leisure and sporting facilities. In 1995, tourism provided work for more than 200 million people world-wide. The countries with the highest international revenue from tourism in 1995 were: the USA, France, Italy, Spain and the UK. Tourism provides great opportunities for the construction industry. Some entirely new or rapidly growing places have acquired a worldwide reputation: La Grande Motte in France, Benidorm in Spain, Las Vegas and Miami in the USA, and Acapulco and Cancún in Mexico, to mention only a few. In some regions, whole coastal areas have been developed into holiday resorts, such as the Mediterranean coastline of France, Spain, and Italy, and the Alpine regions of France, Austria and Switzerland. Only recently has it been recognized that while the huge investment in tourism in some areas had a beneficial impact on the construction industry and economy in those places, it also had an adverse effect on the environment, and that this must be redressed and further environmental harm prevented.

Facilities for tourism may be completely separated from business hotels or be combined. Sophisticated new facilities have been developed to create tourist features in locations that do not have adequate natural conditions. Some establishments, such as those of the Centerparcs chain, offer an artificial, pleasantly warm climate under a giant glazed dome, creating in a cold or moderate climate the ambience of the subtropics with swimming pools fringed by tropical trees. The new man-made ski-ing facilities are open-air plastic-surfaced slopes with ski-lifts. Much more expensive are the slopes with 'real' (artificial) snow and cooled indoor air within an enclosed space. Such 'snowdomes' have been built in, for example, Japan and the UK (in the Midlands at Tamworth). The *piste*, i.e. the slope, is permanently covered by a 16–35 cm thick machine-produced snow layer that is maintained at the right consistency and temperature.

Leisure and fun are combined with education in science parks such as those at La Villette and Poitiers in France, and Alphen an de Rijn, in The Netherlands. Less serious, although still with some educational ambitions, are the Walt Disney parks in the USA and France. No less attractive and instructive are the parks that feature models or miniaturization, such as Madurodam in The Hague and Catalunya en Miniatura near Barcelona (Torrelles de Llobregat), and attractions such as the Madame Tussaud waxworks in London, Amsterdam and elsewhere.

Artificial facilities are also used in sports training and competition, e.g. man-made 'rock' walls for climbing and indoor water basins with artificial wind for wind-surfing. As may be expected, it is the really large-scale sports facilities, such as stadiums, swimming pools and racing tracks that are the most expensive. All of these form a growing market for the construction industry, with opportunities for creating spectacular long-span structures, some with retractable roofs and various modern control technologies.

BUILDINGS FOR INDUSTRY

Since the Second World War, production and service technologies have undergone many important changes, including:

- a relative or absolute decline of some traditional sectors (metallurgy)
- emerging new sectors (chemical, telecommunications and information technologies)
- the changing nature of transport tasks (growth of road and air transport, a reduced reliance by industry on rail transport)
- the intertwining of manufacturing and clerical work.

The changes in technology called for flexible buildings to accommodate them. Industrial halls can be light-, medium- or heavy-duty. Lightweight halls often have portal frames; medium-duty halls are frequently built with trussed frames; and heavy-duty halls are generally built with reinforced concrete or steel structures and are equipped with gantry cranes. Traditionally, single-storey halls were the most common. Firms, such as Armco, Butler, Conder, Mannessmann, Republic, Thyssen and many others developed standardized structures for such halls. Most of these systems were based on steel structures, especially in continental Europe, but reinforced concrete systems were also developed and built. Various design concepts for portal frames, sawtooth, umbrella, and butterfly roofs, trusses, claddings, floors, lighting, etc. are abundant, all aimed at a more effective response to requirements and to acquiring a competitive advantage over other solutions. For lighting, for instance, sufficient and uniform lighting, well-screened light sources, evenly balanced brightness, a pleasant colour and low operating costs are required. The designer must aim at appropriate natural and artificial lighting arrangements and light sources (lamps, luminaires, etc.). A more recent innovation is the high-bay warehouse with central computer-controlled automated retrieval and transport equipment.

Contractors building for industry have been either independent construction firms or firms affiliated to steel manufacturers. Links with large steel and aluminium companies have transformed many traditional construction organizations into partners with modern industry.

THE MODERN ATRIUM

The atria built in ancient Greece, Rome and the Middle East were open or partly covered in hot weather by canvas. The modern atrium first appeared with the introduction of iron, steel and glass structures. Early examples were shopping galleries (malls) and exhibition halls. During the 1960s, the concept began to develop in North America, where it was increasingly applied in hotels, offices and other public buildings. From there it was brought to other parts of the world (Saxon, 1993, with a detailed 'gazetteer' of realizations).

The hotels by John Portman popularized this design solution. The first was the Regency Hyatt in Atlanta in 1967, followed by the Hyatt Embarcadero in San Francisco in 1973 and the Bonaventura Hotel in Los Angeles in 1976. After many examples by various architects, Portman's more recent hotels have again been characterized by outstanding designs: the Marriott Marquis hotels in New York (1985) and Atlanta (1986). Both have atria over 50 storeys high, and that of the Atlanta hotel has a geometry resembling a whale skeleton from the inside, with ribs of galleries springing from the central elevator spine. Most hotels with atria contain interior corridors and all the bedrooms are oriented towards the exterior. Some, however, also have rooms looking on to the atrium.

The atrium principle has been the basis for several spectacular designs for offices and shopping malls, such as Bercy 2 in Paris (designed by Renzo Piano and Ove Arup). This is a four-storey shopping envelope with a curved roof that resembles a grounded airship.

The atrium has developed into one of the standard ingredients of prestigious new hotels, offices, department stores and other public buildings. Fire safety and the cleaning of the external and internal glazed surfaces are technical problems with atria the solutions to which require special care.

'ADVANCED' AND 'INTELLIGENT' BUILDINGS

'Advanced buildings' is a more neutral term for what is often defined by the buzz-words 'intelligent buildings' and 'smart homes'. These terms originated in North America around 1980 as a consequence of the growth of information technology and its increased use in buildings. In French the expression *domotique* and *domotique collective* for blocks of flats have been coined (Dard *et al.*, 1996).

In an intelligent building or a smart house, building automation and telecommunication systems are combined into an integrated system to provide the best ambience for the building's occupants and to allow effective management of resources. These buildings are certainly advanced, although some buildings can also be termed advanced, not for their integrated control system but for certain high-technology solutions. In home automation, internal networks are integrated and can be accessed by a numerical code (binary unit system (BUS) or a consumer electronics BUS, CEBUS), a personal computer (e.g. by IBM's Home Director adapted to the PC Aptiva) or some other unit. Compaq, Intel, Microsoft, Novell and others are also active in this field. The carriers of the BUS can be power cables, telephone wires, coaxial (television) cable, fibreoptic and wireless carriers such as infra-red, ultrasound, radiofrequency and hyperfrequency. The constituent subsystems of intelligent buildings are:

- building automation systems: indoor climate control, lighting, security and access, fire and maintenance
- computer-aided facility management: information systems
- internal and external communications: cable networks, TV, telephone, fax, electronic mail, word-processing, desktop publishing, teleconferencing
- internal controls: kitchen functions, organization-specific business applications.

Intelligent buildings may be constructed for dwellings (houses and blocks of flats), offices, hotels, hospitals and others. Dwellings for people with disabilities and elderly people have specific requirements for information and communication technologies that can improve independence, mobility, safety and security, and living conditions, and enable people to work from home. Integrated automatic services may help in interpersonal communications and integration into society.

Advanced buildings that have an integrated system of services should be designed and built by firms equipped for such tasks, or by specialists who form an association for the purpose. Besides the usual participants in the construction process, others such as furniture and interior designers, suppliers of security, control, communications data processing and integrated services systems may be needed. Intelligent or advanced buildings will save operating costs and enhance the efficiency of both office and household work. In future, some firms will specialize in the co-ordination work of creating intelligent buildings, and in time such work will become commonplace. In several countries (the USA, Japan, France) intensive work is progressing on a wider use of intelligent buildings. Various large companies are working on specific solutions (Microsoft: Simply Interactive PC (SIPC), Philips, IBM, Bouygues, Dumez, EDF, GDF, British Telecom, France Telecom, etc.).

Some outstanding high-technology advanced office buildings have received international recognition. One of these is the new Lloyd's headquarters in London (architect: Richard Rogers & Partners; engineer: Ove Arup & Partners). Architect Sir Norman Foster has designed several spectacular advanced buildings. Following the Stansted Airport Terminal and the Willis Faber building in Ipswich, his best known design is the Hongkong and Shanghai Bank in Hong Kong. The project was constructed between 1979 and 1985. Its precision-made components from factories around the world were assembled and fitted together to minute tolerances at high speed on a congested site. Among the technological innovations were the new mullion solutions for holding tall glass panes in place, the recovery of the heat generated by computers for heating, a typhoon warning system, and so on. Foster's design for the rebuilding of the destroyed *Reichstag* in Berlin envisages a dome that would have an inverted conical core on the inside. This cone takes in light at its top end and beams light down at its opposite end to illuminate the chamber. Moreover, energy would be conserved by using partial natural ventilation, tapping underground water supplies and drawing off excess heat from a Berlin power station.

It can be safely predicted that 'intelligent', 'advanced' and 'high-tech' buildings will be a large subsector of the future construction industry.

TALL BUILDINGS AND TOWERS

UPDATING THE HISTORY OF TALL BUILDINGS AND TOWERS

In Chapter 1 we looked at the birth of skyscrapers at the end of the nineteenth century and their subsequent advance during the first half of this century. We shall now review what has happened since 1945.

The architecture of tall buildings changed during the second half of the twentieth century. The New York Seagrams Building, designed by Mies van der Rohe in collaboration with Philip Johnson, was one of the first with a modernist approach. The number of tall buildings has increased hugely, and they are now built all over the world, even in earthquake-prone regions, such as California, Japan and South-East Asia. Their maximum height has increased and their design and construction methods have been modernized: new architectural styles (post-modern, de-constructivist etc.) have emerged.

The ambition to build higher and higher was already demonstrated by the French Gothic cathedrals in Chapter 1. This ambition was later

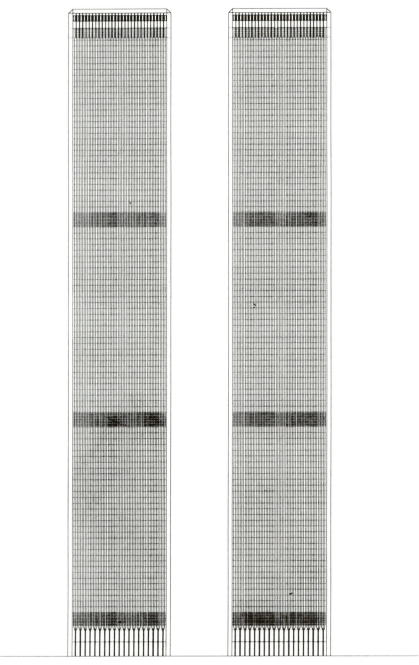

Fig. 6.1 Twin towers of the World Trade Center, New York; height: 417 m, 1972.
Source: Courtesy of Messrs F. Sebestény and P. Rabb, Technical University of
Budapest, Faculty of Architecture.

Table 6.1   Record-breaking tall buildings since 1896 (completion date, height)

1896	St. Paul, New York	95 m
1898	Park Row, New York	118 m
1907	Singer, New York	187 m
1909	Metropolitan Life, New York	213 m
1913	Woolworth, New York	241 m
1929	Bank of Manhattan, New York	282 m
1930	Chrysler, New York	319 m
1931	Empire State Building, New York	381 m
1972	World Trade Center (North Block), New York	417 m
1974	Sears Tower, Chicago	443 m
1997	Petronas Towers, Kuala Lumpur, Malaysia	450 m

revived, and buildings grew taller and taller. The record-breaking tallest buildings (with the year of completion and the height of the buildings in metres) since 1896 are shown in Table 6.1 (see also Figure 1.9). In 1951, the Empire State Building received a 68 m high addition for TV transmission purposes, which made it 449 m high. Table 6.2 lists the 11 tallest buildings in the world in 1986. Since then more tall buildings have been built or are planned. When the twin Petronas Towers in Kuala Lumpur, Malaysia, height 450 m, are completed (1997), it will be the first time that the world's tallest building is outside the USA and, what is more, in a developing country. Several other tall buildings are under construction in the USA, Japan, China and elsewhere (Mierop, 1995).

As in the case of Gothic cathedrals, there came a time when the advancement had to pause because the heights achieved had reached the technical limit. After 1945, many countries needed to build telecommunications towers. At the proposal of Fritz Leonhardt, one of the first concrete transmission towers was built in Stuttgart, then West Germany, in 1954–55. The tower has a viewing platform and a restaurant and became a model around the world for a great number of similar concrete structures. The tallest concrete transmission towers are the 553 m high CN

Table 6.2   World's tallest buildings in 1986

1.	Petronas Towers, Kuala Lumpur, Malaysia	450 m
2.	Sears Tower, Chicago	443 m
3.	World Trade Center, North Block, New York	417 m
4.	World Trade Center, South Block, New York	415 m
5.	Empire State, New York	381 m
6.	Central Plaza, Hong Kong	372 m
7.	Bank of China, Hong Kong	368 m
8.	Amoco Corp., Chicago	346 m
9.	John Hancock, Chicago	344 m
10.	Chrysler, New York	319 m
11.	Library Square Tower, Los Angeles	310 m

Fig. 6.2 CN Tower, Toronto, Canada; height: 553 m. *Source:* E. Heinle and F. Leonhardt (1989) *Towers*, Butterworth Architecture.

Tower in Toronto, built between 1973 and 1976, and the 537 m high Moscow Ostankino Tower, built between 1959 and 1967.

Tall concrete water towers have been built with various imaginative forms, such as the flat conical towers in Riyadh, Saudi Arabia, and those in Kuwait, where the tallest reached 140 m and 180 m. Steel continued to be a structural material used for masts and towers. The tallest steel mast,

Fig. 6.3 Reinforced concrete water towers, Kuwait; height: 180 m and 140 m.
Source: E. Heinle and F. Leonhardt (1989) *Towers*, Butterworth Architecture.

with five rigs and 642.50 m high, was built near Warsaw and completed
around 1970.

STRUCTURAL PROGRESS OF TALL BUILDINGS

Construction to the heights shown in Tables 6.1 and 6.2 has been made
possible by a number of innovations:

Fig. 6.4 Water towers, flat conical reinforced concrete shells, Riyadh, Saudi Arabia, the largest with a volume of 12,350 m³ *Source:* E. Heinle and F. Leonhardt (1989) *Towers*, Butterworth Architecture.

- new materials (new types of steel and high-strength concrete)
- new design concepts (diagonal bracing, vertical reinforced concrete tubular core and perimeter, shear and outrigger trusses, bundled and modular tubes, composite systems)
- the introduction of lightweight curtain wall partitions substantially reducing the weight of tall buildings

- new structures and components (new HVAC equipment, elevators, service controls, passive (and lately active) devices to improve the response of the structures to earthquakes, and new curtain walls)
- the use of computer-based design.

Some of these new techniques are described in various chapters of this book.

The superstructure of most tall buildings and towers is steel, although some have a reinforced concrete core. The Sydney steel tower is sited above an office building that has a reinforced concrete structure. The tallest concrete buildings are the Harbour Plaza, Hong Kong, height 302 m, and 311 South Wacker Drive, Chicago, height 290 m, both built partly with high-strength concrete. The Petronas Towers in Kuala Lumpur, are being built partly from high-strength concrete. The exterior cross-bracing used at the Hancock Tower in Chicago (Fazlur Khan) was subsequently applied to several tall buildings. The Bank of China building in Hong Kong (architect, I.M. Pei & Partners; engineer, L.E. Robertson Associates) has a hybrid structural solution: lightweight steel girders form a three-dimensional frame transferring the loads to the vertical reinforced concrete columns. In the structural and architectural design of tall buildings, certain specific circumstances must be considered:

- the gravitational and lateral forces affecting tall buildings are especially high
- adequate stiffness must prevent excessive lateral drifts, and horizontal top deflections must be kept under certain limits
- the oscillations due to fluctuating wind load must be kept under certain limits
- creep, shrinkage and temperature effects should be limited
- protection against fire should be adequate
- foundations should be able to cope with the load imposed on them including uneven settlements
- the structure should be able to withstand earthquakes.

The two main actions on tall buildings that make their design different from that of other buildings are wind and earthquake loading. Sophisticated calculation methods have been developed for both (see Chapter 3). If necessary, experiments, using shaking tables and boundary layer wind tunnels can prove the design.

In earlier years, various forms of bracing were used: storey-high knees, chevrons and single or double diagonals. Recently, bracings have been made on a large-scale and have appeared on the façades. Another solution for bracing has been the use of concrete shear walls. The objective of attaining increased stiffness has been served by recourse to a different idea: the introduction of the framed tube construction. Tubes provide excellent stiffness for buildings, but they have one drawback: the purpose of the tube is served only if the number and size of the perforations do not reduce its effectiveness. Therefore, if the tube also serves as the envelope, the size of the windows is limited, which may not be ideal from either the aesthetic or practical point of view. A variation of the framed tube is the 'tube-in-tube' or hull-core structure, consisting of an outer framed tube, the hull, and an internal core, which act jointly. Another innovation was the braced-tube structure of Chicago's John Hancock Building. Here the efficiency of the framed tube was increased by diagonal bracing. For the Sears Tower in Chicago, a 'bundled-tube' structure was developed.

The lateral stiffness of a building can also be increased by horizontal cantilever 'outrigger' trusses or girders connecting the core to the outer columns. The 76-storey Hong Kong Bank of China building was designed with a space structure: a three-dimensional triangulated frame.

The design and construction of tall buildings require experienced personnel. Such projects are mostly undertaken by large architectural and engineering firms (Skidmore, Owings & Merrill; SOM, Chicago; Ove Arup, London; OTH, Paris) and major contractors with much experience. An international forum for professional problems with tall buildings is the International Council for Tall Buildings and Urban Habitat.

THE SUPER-HIGH BUILDINGS OF THE FUTURE

The idea of building even higher than hitherto has been raised in the USA and other countries, but it brings with it a number of special technical problems such as the elevators (see Chapter 4) and others. Nevertheless, a new generation of super-high buildings is currently being planned in Japan and some other countries. Takenaka's Sky City 1000 would be 1000 m high. The floor plan of the building would have the form of a ring, with a diameter of 400 m at the base and 160 m at the top. The building would be inhabited by 35 000 people and be the workplace of 1 million. The Millennium Tower planned by Ohbayashi for Tokyo Bay is designed to be 800 m high and have a helical structure. Kajima's Dynamic Intelligent Building (DIB-200) is also designed to be 800 m high. It will consist of 12 vertical cylindrical blocks, interlinked every 50 storeys, each block having a diameter of 50 m. Shimizu's Mega City Pyramid, TRY 2004, is planned to be a 2000 m high pyramid with a braced megatruss structure. It will house 700 000 people and contain numerous facilities. Taisei's X-SEED 4000 is planned to be 4000 m tall, higher even than Mount Fuji, and could house between 500 000 and 700 000 people.

These projects also point to a new functional orientation: the planning of large-scale urban 'megastructures' incorporating various functions of living, working, education and recreation. It would be unwise simply to dismiss these plans as pure science fiction fantasies because some of

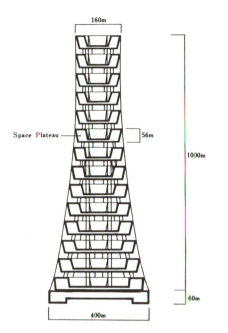

Fig. 6.5 Future super-high skyscraper: Sky City 1000, Takenaka, Japan. *Source: Structural Engneering International*, **4** (1992).

Japan's most highly qualified and experienced contractors stand behind them, although on the other hand, they may never be realized.

The progress made in constructing tall buildings is impressive. These buildings have proved themselves to be capable of withstanding strong winds and some earthquakes. Construction had to become a modern industry to achieve this.

LONG-SPAN STRUCTURES

CLASSIFICATION AND STRUCTURAL ANALYSIS REQUIREMENTS

Although long-span structures amount to little more than a small fraction of the total construction volume, they are nevertheless spectacular modern building products. Their design and execution require up-to-date knowledge and experience, and they are characterized by imaginative design solutions, which are briefly summed up below.

Long-span structures can be longitudinal (bridges) or cover a large space unobstructed by columns, such as in sports stadiums, exhibition and meeting halls, hangars, circuses and theatres. Large spaces have been covered by domes since ancient times, but as we have already seen,

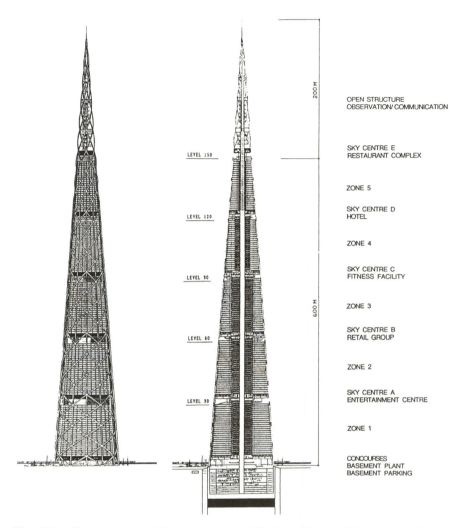

Fig. 6.6 Future super-high skyscraper: Millenium Tower, Ohbayashi, Japan. *Source: Structural Engineering International*, **4** (1992).

their maximum diameter was about 50 m until the very end of the nineteenth century. The spans gradually began to increase to about 100 m during the first half of the twentieth century, and during the past 50 years spans of 200 m and above have been achieved. This was made possible by the work of eminent scientists and engineers such as E. Torroja, P.L. Nervi, E. Saarinen, M. Yamasaki, R. B. Fuller and Z. S. Makowski (Nervi, 1956; Torroja, 1958a, 1958b).

There are two basic solutions to the problem of long-span structures:

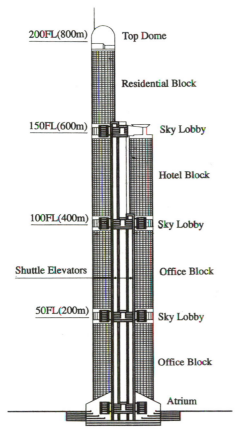

200FL(800m)   Top Dome

Residential Block

150FL(600m)   Sky Lobby

Hotel Block

100FL(400m)   Sky Lobby

Shuttle Elevators   Office Block

50FL(200m)   Sky Lobby

Office Block

Atrium

Fig. 6.7   Future super-high skyscraper: DIB-200, Kajima, Japan. *Source: Structural Engineering International*, **4** (1992).

- supporting structures such as ribs, grids, frames, lattices, trusses, cable networks and a separate roof covering
- roofs that do not require a separate supporting structure, i.e. shells and domes.

Another way of categorizing long-span structures is to differentiate between roofs that are subjected to tension only, and roofs in which there is compression and bending. The use of tensioned members contributes to lightness, but few structures are purely tensioned (air-supported structures). Most are hybrid, i.e. they contain members acting in compression (masts, rings). Tension members have a small cross-section and high strength but are susceptible to fatigue, corrosion and large deformation. Pre-stressing cables can reduce the deformations, otherwise stabilizing is necessary. In suspended roofs there is tension only in the chains, cables or membranes, but an edge ring or anchoring is required (Szabó and Kollár, 1984).

Long-span roofs frequently have a reticulated surface, which means that a set of points (nodes etc.) are uniformly distributed on the surface. Steel (and aluminium) is used for trusses (arching or beams), space lattice structures (single or double layer), cable networks and, in sheet form, for roofs. Reinforced concrete is used for domes, shells and compressed supporting members (columns, compression rings). Vaults are built both from concrete and steel. Shells are thin structures that have to be protected from buckling (Kollár and Dulácska, 1984). Membranes are soft shell structures made of a tensile material. Skeletal domes and vaults are called braced structures. These are lattice structures as they are assembled from triangles composed of axially loaded bars. Timber has been in use since ancient times for domes and trusses. In modern times, new types of timber structure have been invented. The timber lamella system for barrel vaults, for instance, was introduced in the USA by Kievitt in 1925.

During the past 50 years, polymers and technical fabrics have been added to the list of materials used for space structures. With the introduction of fabric and plastic membranes, the use of other new types of roof has become widespread, such as stressed roofs and air-supported roofs. Dual wall air-inflated structures are seldom used.

The structural design of long-span structures may be linear or non-linear. Non-linear analysis is used when the plastic yield and geometric effects (e.g. in the case of large deflections) have to be taken into consideration. Dynamic loading (wind and earthquake) may cause failure as thin structures are particularly vulnerable to such actions. Various mathematical methods are applied for the calculations, such as vector and tensor analysis, matrix algebra, finite element and finite difference methods (Kollár and Hegedüs, 1985). Only large input data sets can describe the geometry of the roof, and the consequent large computational tasks can only be handled by computers. Form-finding (shape-finding) can be assisted by computer simulation or models made of soap film, textiles, rubber, steel wires, ropes, or a heated plastic plate. Gaudi's 'funicular' technique is based on turning a tension structure upside down. Interactive computer graphics may assist exact analysis.

REINFORCED CONCRETE DOMES AND SHELLS

The development of large-span reinforced concrete structures during the first half of the twentieth century (as described in Chapter 1) continued after 1945.

Early reinforced concrete shells were usually built with ribs to a spherical or elliptical vertical cross-section. Shell shapes following the thrust line were introduced, with the advantage that the shape corresponded more to the natural flow of forces (Schlaich and Saradshow, 1994). Examples are the aircraft hangars in Rapid City, South Dakota (1947), with a span of 104 m, and those in Limestone, Maine, (1948). Shells are characterized by their surface: a developable surface (e.g. a vault) can transform into a plane without cutting. This is not possible with an undevelopable surface such as a dome. Vaults have a single curvature, spherical domes and most shells have double curvatures. The (middle) surface of a shell may be created by rotation, translation, or ruling. Domes rotate around an axis. Translational surfaces are generated by sliding a plane curve along another plane curve. Ruled surfaces are generated by sliding a straight line on two curves: conoids and hyperbolic paraboloids ('hypar', HP or saddle-type) are in this group (Farshad, 1992). Felix Candela and Anton Tedesko were among the designers of the first HP shells (in Mexico City and Denver, Colorado). The analysis of thin shells consists of establishing the equilibrum of elements cut from the shell and achieving continuity of adjacent elements after deformation (Billington, 1965). Rigorous mathematical analysis or simplified physical modelling can be used.

The freedom to create new curved shapes led to a great number of forms. According to Torroja, a structure is born by going 'from the pure domain of logic ... into the secret frontiers of inspiration'. Various imaginative symbolic roof shapes have been designed, e.g. the TWA Air Terminal in New York was designed to symbolize wings (Saarinen), the Sydney Opera House symbolizes sails (Utzon) and the Bahai Temple near New Delhi is based on the form of a lotus, a symbol of purity in India (1987, designed by Fariburz Sahba). Candela's synagogue in Guatemala and his restaurant building in Xochimilco are also a reflection of creative imagination.

Prefabrication or repetitive formwork was pioneered by Nervi (hangars, Turin Exhibition Building, warehouse, ballroom roof). The 206 m span reinforced concrete shell of CNIT at La Defense in Paris was assembled from large pre-cast components. The thin Bini shells are constructed on shaped fabrics, such as those supported by shaped landfills; following reinforcement and concreting they are blown to their definitive form. The popularity of concrete shells declined somewhat after the 1960s.

STEEL SPACE GRIDS AND DOUBLE-LAYER GRIDS

Perhaps the first iron structure was the cover of the central part of the Paris Corn Market in 1811, by Belanger and Brunet. Later, steel was introduced for structural purposes. In time, steel plane trusses and later space trusses (grids) were developed. Space grids consist of straight elements interconnected at the nodes. In most systems the straight members are almost exclusively under the action of axial forces. Much depends on the nodes: in practice there are no ideal hinges, so that the structure of the

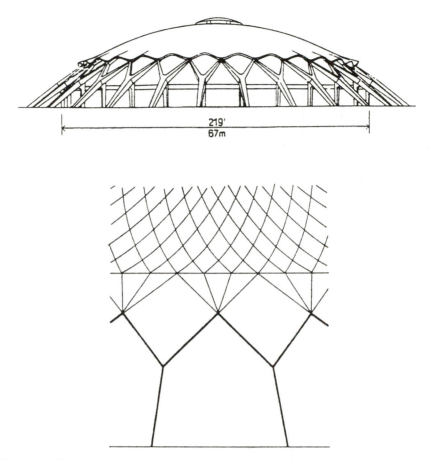

Fig. 6.8 The Small Sport Palace, Rome, Italy; designer: P. L. Nervi. *Source:* P. Csonka (1981) *Héjszerkezetek*, Akadémiai Kiadó, Budapest.

node and the shape of the space grid determines to what extent the moments can be disregarded. The two basic forms of space grids are the double-layer plane grids and the curved (single-layer or double-layer) grids, i.e. domes and vaults (Nooshin, 1984).

Within the group of space trusses, double-layer grids are frequently used (Makowski, 1981). They consist of two plane grids forming the top and bottom layers parallel to each other, interconnected by vertical or inclined diagonal members. The double-layer plane grids have some notable advantages: they are rigid and consequently have relatively small deflections; the buckling of any compression member does not lead to

Fig. 6.9   CNIT Hall, Paris, Défense; span: 206 m, assembled from pre-cast reinforced concrete panels, 1958, designers: Camelot, De Mailly, Zehrfuss, Esquillan. *Source: Knaurs Lexikon der modernen Architektur* (1963) Droemersche VerlagsAnstalt.

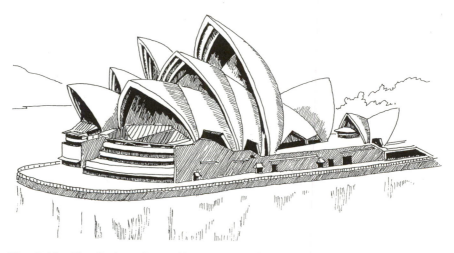

Fig. 6.10   The Sydney Opera House, 1973. *Source:* Oscar Gimesy (1992) *Built from Nothing*, Building Careers Resource Centre of Australia.

collapse; the space between the top and bottom layers can be used for technical services; they can be built from prefabricated components. Lattice grids with a certain regularity are often used as a model for the continuum (Atluri and Amos, 1988). In addition to the normal lattice truss grids, complicated space forms can be built from the members.

A great number of commercial systems have been developed, such as Mero, Oktaplate, Unistrut, Space Deck, Space Grid, Pyramitec, Triodetic, Unibat, Nodus, Vestrut and Ortz. These compete with each other, although some are adapted for specific applications and have different geometries, members and nodes. A few are described briefly below.

One of the first systems was MERO. Introduced in 1942, and still widely used, its inventor was the German Max Mengeringhausen. The MERO system consists of tubular members joined in such a way that their axes pass through the central point of the nodes, which ensures that the joints are subjected to axial forces only. The Space Deck system is built from inverted square-based pyramids consisting of an angle section top tray and four diagonal bracing elements. The diagonals are welded to the corners of the tray and to a centrally disposed boss, which is threaded to receive the main tie bars. The Unistrut system originated in the USA. It has channel-form members, connectors made from pressed-steel plate and identical top and bottom layers. The Canadian Triodetic system consists of aluminium tubes and extruded connecting hubs. It was used for the Toronto Dome, which was completed in 1962. With the British NODUS system, introduced in 1972, it is possible to have grids with various bar arrangements (triangular, square, hexagonal). The NODUS joint

Fig. 6.11   MERO space grid application, Terminal 2 at Frankfurt Airport, Germany.
Source: Courtesy of Company MERO.

is a body split into two half casings clamped together with a high-strength friction grip bolt. The assembly is very easy.

Space frames are also used for the support of various industrial equipment. One such structure is the Vehicle Assembly Building at Cape Canaveral, perhaps the world's largest building. It is 160 m high as well as long-spanned. Its three-dimensional framework consists of steel supports with horizontal steel and lightweight concrete reinforcements, and a total of 100 000 tonnes of steel was used in this construction.

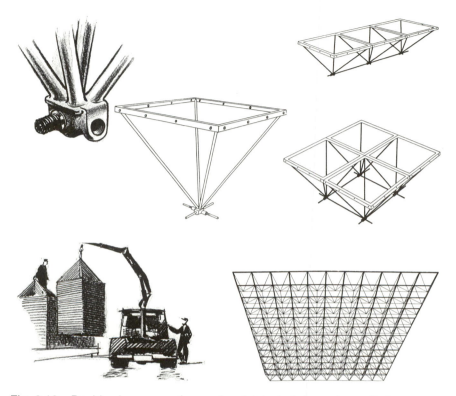

Fig. 6.12 Double plane space frame of prefabricated elements readily transported, Space Deck, UK. *Source:* Gy. Sebestyén (1977) *Lightweight Building*, Akadémiai Kiadó, Budapest.

Metal space grids, domes, vaults and cable structures may all be covered by concrete, thin sheet, membrane or fabric; the roof covering may be with or without heat insulation. New, non-traditional solutions are considered below.

STEEL AND ALUMINIUM DOMES AND BARREL VAULTS

Iron, and later steel, domes and vaults were first built in the nineteenth Century (Makowski, 1985). The barrel vault of the Vienna public baths was completed in 1820. The Crystal Palace in London (Joseph Paxton) was completed in 1851. Later, a great number of forms and geometries were developed, of which the most used are (Makowski, 1984):

- ribbed domes,
- Schwedler domes,
- braced domes,

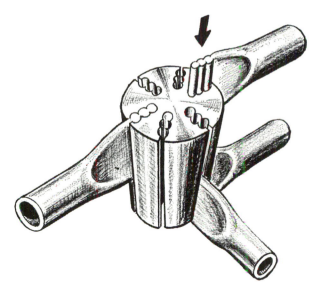

Fig. 6.13 The cylindrical node of the Triodetic (Tentiman) space grid system, Triodetic, Canada. *Source:* Gy. Sebestyén (1977) *Lightweight Building*, Akadémiai Kiadó, Budapest.

- parallel-lamella domes,
- geodesic domes.

The ribbed domes consist of a number of identical radial trussed or solid ribs, interconnected at the crown, usually stiffened by a tension ring at the foundation. Prefabricated, tubular, arched units may facilitate erection. J. W. Schwedler introduced the domes that have since been named after him into the USA in 1863. They consist of meridional ribs connected to horizontal polygonal rings. Their advantage is that the domes may be regarded as statically determinate, although this does not mean that their analysis is simple. Typical braced domes are three-way single-layer grid domes (curved tubular steel domes). In the parallel-lamella domes, a large number of similar units, called lamellas, are arranged in a diamond or rhombus pattern, jointed with bolts and plates. The Astrodome in Houston, with a span of almost 200 m, is a parallel-lamella steel dome. The New Orleans Superdome has the same structure; its diameter is 213 m. These two are thought to be the world's largest.

In 1954, Richard Buckminster Fuller was granted US Patent 2 682 235 (date of application 1951), which became the spring point for the geodesic (also called the 'tensegrity', i.e. tensional integrity) dome. His aim was to build domes from identical elements joined by a simple connector throughout. For this purpose he based his domes on the geometry of one

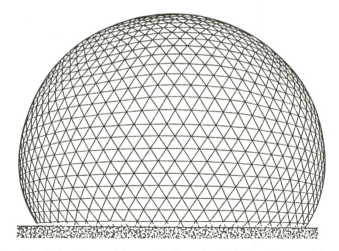

Fig. 6.14 Geodesic dome, Montreal, Canada; height: 50 m, 1967; designer: Buckminster Fuller. *Source*: Abel, J. F. *et al.* (1994).

of the regular polyhedra (tetrahedron, cube, octahedron, dodecahedron, icosahedron). Other solutions were made possible by the use of semiregular polyhedra that comprise more than one type of regular polygon and other forms. One of the first such geodesic dome was constructed at the Detroit Ford plant in 1953 in the form of a hemisphere of 28 m diameter. Bars were first connected to form triangles, and octahedrons were built

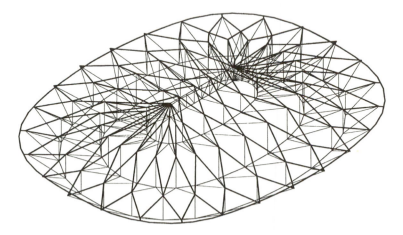

Fig. 6.15 The Hypar-Tensegrity Georgia Dome, Atlanta, Georgia, USA, 1992; designers: M. P. Levy, Weidlinger Associates. *Source:* M. P. Levy and T-F. Jing (1994) Floating saddle connections for the Georgia Dome, USA, *Structural Engineering International*, August 1994. 4 : 3.

Fig. 6.16   Green Dome, Maebashi, Japan, Shimizu. *Source:* Courtesy of Company Shimizu.

up from these. The steel geodesic dome at Baton Rouge was completed in 1959. It has a diameter of 117 m, and an exterior tube framework supports the hexagonal steel panels. Later geodesic domes were built for Expo '67 in Montreal ('Star Tensegrity' dome, US patent 3 354 591), at the EPCOT-Center, Orlando, and in many other places.

A special variant of the geodesic dome is the Kaiser dome. This is a stressed-skin geodesic dome with a single structural element (diamond-shaped aluminium panels) comprising the frame and skin. The first such dome was built in Honolulu in 1957 with a diameter of 44 m.

The Dome of Discovery, completed in 1951, is the largest aluminium dome ever built in the UK; it had a diameter of 104 m.

A recent requirement was to build a dome with a retractable roof. One such is the Toronto Dome, which has a diameter of 180 m, and the

Fukuoka Dome is similar, with a span of 213 m (max.). Its rigid steel roof, which weighs 290 kg/m^2, is covered with 0.3 mm thick titanium sheets.

SUSPENDED, TENSIONED AND AIR-SUPPORTED ROOFS

High-tensile steel cable has made it possible to transmit large axial forces in tension at a relatively low cost. As a result, various forms of cable-suspended roofs were introduced and one of the first important examples was the North Carolina State Fair Arena at Raleigh, USA, completed in 1953. The arena was covered by a roof suspended to a cable net, which was supported by two intersecting and inclined concrete arches (Buchholdt, 1985).

Such roofs can be supported by suspended cables, pretensioned cable beams, nets or grids. The suspension cables are parallel over rectangular spaces, and placed radially over circular, elliptical or trapezoidal spaces. Pretensioned cable beams have a second set of cables with reverse curvature connected to the suspension cables. In pretensioned cable net structures, the suspension and pretension cables lie in one surface and form a net. Pretensioned cable grid structures are double-layer nets or multidirectional systems of intersecting cable beams. The suspending cables can generally be supported by a load-bearing structure such as steel or reinforced concrete columns, ring, arch, frame, cables, etc. An alternative is to support the roof by pressurizing the indoor air. Different materials can be used for the linear tensile components (ropes, cables) (Cook *et al.*, 1994):

- for intermediate performance: polyethylene, polypropylene, polyamide (nylon), polyester, glass fibres and steel
- for high performance: aramid (Kevlar), LCA fibres and steel
- for extremely high performance: high-modulus polyethylene (Spectra, Dyneema), LCA fibres and steel.

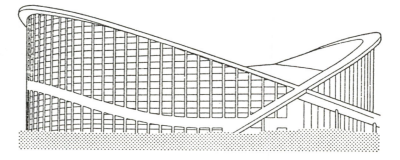

Fig. 6.17 Exposition Hall, Raleigh, North Carolina, USA, two inclined intersecting concrete arches, suspended cable net, 1953. *Source*: Tension Structures and Space Frames, IASS Symposium (1972), Architectural Institute, Japan.

There are early examples of canvas roofs, but the modern air-supported and tensioned fabric era began in Europe with a small structure designed and built by Frei Otto in 1955. The introduction of new fabrics and membranes opened up new possibilities. In the USA in 1946, Walter Bird proposed an air-supported dome (a 'radome') to protect early warning radar antennae. By the mid-1950s, such air-supported roofs had proved themselves in service. However, a hall built in 1970 with an inflated-tube fabric support structure for the Osaka World Exhibition although spectacular, was uneconomic, a disadvantage serious enough to doubt its future. The largest air-supported roof actually to be realized was the Pontiac Silverdome, which has a span of around 200 m. Air-supported (pneumatic) roofs require permanent operational energy and for that reason their use has remained limited.

The new era of fabric roofs was very much the result of the work of a few ingenious designers such as David Geiger, Horst Berger and Frei Otto. They designed and constructed tensile structures for fabric roofs, mostly Teflon-coated fibreglass, in the USA. In Europe, PVC-coated polyester fabric (Trevira) was favoured, however. The latter is cheaper, although its performance does not match that of Teflon-coated fibreglass.

Fig. 6.18 Fabric (Trevira) membrane roof, Germany. *Source:* Gy. Sebestyén (1977) *Lightweight Building*, Akadémiai Kiadó, Budapest.

To date, the world's largest cable-supported fabric roof is the 70 500 seat Georgia Dome in the USA. Completed in 1992 at a cost of US$215 million, it was designed by M. Levy from Weidlinger Associates. It is a 'hypar tensegrity dome' measuring 240 × 192 m. The oval plan cable dome structure, consisting of a triangular network of cables, is supported by a box-shaped concrete compression ring resting on 52 concrete columns. The roof surface is assembled from diamond-shaped hyperbolic paraboloid panels of Teflon-coated fibreglass (Levy, 1994). The total structural weight of such a dome is usually less than that of a rigid steel dome. The Montreal Stadium was completed in 1987 with an unusual 168 m tall giant inclined tower, from which cables suspend a polyurethane and PVC-coated (Kevlar) retractable roof to cover a 200 × 120 m opening (Abel, Leonard and Penalba, 1994).

David Geiger has been the author of several patents for fabric structures. He worked initially in partnership with Horst Berger, and later as an independent consultant. At the same time, the firm Birdair Inc. expanded to construct almost all of the large fabric roofs in the USA. The King Fahd Stadium in Riyadh, Saudi Arabia, was completed in 1985. It has a diameter of 288 m, and its 2 m diameter masts are almost 60 m tall. The stadium has an open centre (structural design, Berger). The largest fabric roof to date is the Haj Terminal at Jeddah, Saudi Arabia, providing shade for the thousands of pilgrims to Mecca (design, SOM and Berger). The terminal was completed in 1981 and covers 47 ha. It has 210 identical cone-shaped canopies that are square in plan, and measure 45 m along each side.

The tensile membrane fabric cover of the New Denver International Airport roof measures approximately 90 × 305 m. It too was designed by Berger and constructed by Birdair Inc. The building consists of a series of tent-like modules supported by two lines of masts of approximately 30 m in length. The roof has two layers of Teflon-coated fibreglass fabric approximately 600 mm apart. The inner liner ensures thermal insulation and acoustic absorption. Its translucency rate is 7%. The peaks and valleys of the roof give it a shape that resembles the Rocky Mountains (Brown, 1994). Several experts and firms specialized in the design, manufacture and installation of tensioned canopies, such as the Buro Happold, Ove Arup & Partners, Canobbio, W. S. Atkins and others.

ECONOMIC DATA

The technical progress attained by modern domes, shells, vaults and membranes can also be measured by their increased economic efficiency. Longer spans have been built with less weight, as can be seen from the data on unit weights of some long-span structures (kg/m²) given in Table

Fig. 6.19 Cable net roof, King Abdul Aziz University Sports Hall, Jeddah, Saudi Arabia; designer: Buro Happold. *Source:* Courtesy of Buro Happold.

Table 6.3   Weight of selected long-span structures (kg/m²)

Pantheon Dome, Rome, 120–124 A.D.	7200
St Peter's Dome, Rome, 1585	2600
Breslau/Wroclaw, Century Hall, 1912, reinforced concrete	1920
Houston Astrodome, 1965, steel parallel-lamella dome	80
Pontiac Silverdome, 1975, air-supported roof	15

6.3. The unit weight of the Houston Astrodome does not include the ring girder. Although comparisons of this kind are always somewhat tentative in nature because of the widely differing durability and other features of the structures, they clearly demonstrate the progress made. Barrel vaults can also be built from various materials, with a unit weight of 12–30 kg/m².

The cost (in US dollars) per ft² of clear span area of some long-span roof structures in 1993 equally reflects the progress made (Table 6.4). Once again, the data are no more than first approximations as they do not take account of lifespan (concrete, steel, fabric) and functional differences.

Table 6.4   Long-span roofs, selected structures, 1993 (US$ cost per ft² clear span area)

Astrodome, Houston, steel skew-trussed dome	74
Superdome, New Orleans, steel trussed lamella dome	81
Kingdome, Seattle, concrete radial rib dome	73
Silverdome, Pontiac, Mich., air-supported fabric	39
Metrodome, Minneapolis, air-supported fabric	40
Skydome, Toronto, steel lattice arch, movable	262
Georgiadome, Atlanta, tensegrity dome, fabric roof	63

BRIDGES

The technical progress of bridges continued after 1945. Steel arch bridges continued to be constructed, but the suspension method was used for the longest spans. The designers of suspension bridges learnt from earlier failures. Their analysis brought to light the inadequate torsional stiffness of most suspension bridge decks, which led to instability. The new bridge designs evolved stable cross-sections to withstand the aerodynamic wind forces. Some of the more remarkable post-war steel suspension bridges are listed in Table 6.5. These suspension bridges are setting world records in span length and pylon height; they also contain a number of technical innovations, such as continuous box girders, hydraulic buffers to restrain longitudinal short-term movements, and tuned mass damping to reduce wind-induced oscillations (Livesey and Larose, 1995).

Table 6.5   Selected steel suspension bridges since 1945 (span length)

Mackinac Straits Bridge, Michigan, USA, 1957	1158 m
Verrazano Narrows Bridge, New York City, USA, 1964	1298 m
Bosporus Bridge, Istanbul, Turkey, 1973	1074 m
Humber Bridge, Hull, England, 1981	1410 m
Great Belt, Denmark, between the Islands of Zeeland and Fünen, 1997	1624 m
Tsing Ma, Hong Kong, leading to the new airport, 1997	1377 m
Akashi Japan, 1998	2022 m

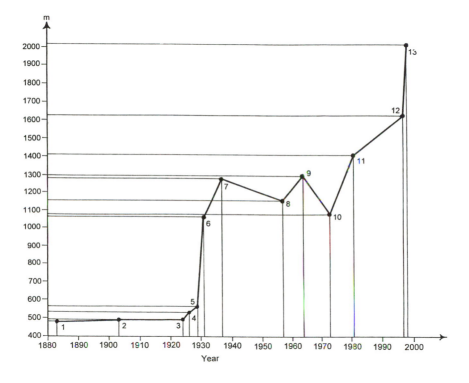

Fig. 6.20   Main span of steel suspension bridges. *Source:* author's diagrams.

Recent studies indicate that suspension bridges with spans of 3000–5000 m could be constructed with today's materials and techniques, and even longer spans would be possible with efficient carbon fibre materials.

For medium-length spans, cable-stayed bridges brought new forms. In suspended bridges, the deck is supported at relatively short intervals by

Fig. 6.21 The Great Belt Link suspension bridge under construction, Denmark; span: 1624 m. *Source:* Courtesy of COWIconsult.

vertical hangers, which are in turn suspended from a chain or a main cable. In cable-stayed bridges, inclined cables support the bridge deck directly in a relatively inflexible way (Podolny Jr and Scalzi, 1986). In suspension bridges, the tension in the hangers is kept in balance by anchorage in the abutments. In cable-stayed bridges the cables transmit the load to the towers and the load is not transmitted to the abutments. The inclined stays, supporting the deck and girders, pass over or are attached to the towers at the main piers. The stay cables can be arranged in harp (parallel), fan or star form; they may be placed in two vertical planes, two inclined planes, or one single (central) plane.

Part suspension, part stayed (hybrid) bridge structures were first built in the first decades of the nineteenth century. A remarkable one was the Dryburgh Abbey Footbridge in Scotland. Completed as early as 1817, with a span of 79.30 m, it collapsed in a violent gust of wind in 1818, which was described by C.L. Navier in 1830. At the end of the nineteenth and the beginning of the twentieth centuries, purely stayed bridges were built (Troitsky, 1977, 1988; Walther *et al.*, 1988). These may be built as cantilever structures, a quite different process from the construction of a suspension bridge. The Severin Bridge across the Rhine in Cologne, with a span of 302 m, was the first to have an asymmetrically placed pylon.

Fig. 6.22   The Akashi Straits suspension bridge under construction, Japan; span: 2022 m.

During the past forty years, the span of cable-stayed bridges has steadily increased. Some examples are given in Table 6.6.

Concrete bridges were first built with arched structures and later with pre-stressing. The Parramatta Bridge in Gladesville, Sydney, Australia, was completed in 1964 with an arched reinforced concrete structure and a span of 350 m. The design of pre-stressed concrete bridges developed, and the maximum spans increased (but remained below the maximum spans of steel suspension bridges). Some examples are given in Table 6.7. The maximum span of pre-stressed concrete beam bridges appears to be around 350 m. Cable-stayed pre-stressed concrete bridge structures have opened up new design possibilities.

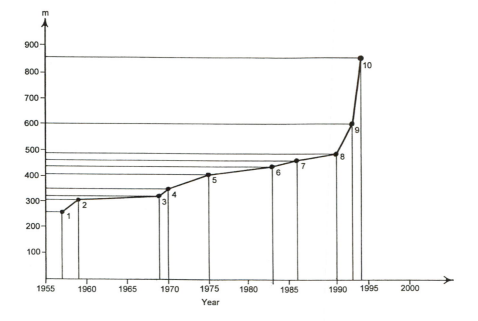

Fig. 6.23 Main span of cable-stayed bridges. 1 = Dusseldorf–North (1957; 260 m); 2 = Cologne–Severin (1959; 302 m); 3 = Dusseldorf–Kniebrücke (1969, 320 m); 4 = Duisburg–Neuenkamp (1970, 350 m); 5 = Saint Nazaire, France (1975, 404 m); 6 = Barrios de Luna, Spain (1983, 440 m); 7 = John Fazer, Canada (1986; 465 m); 8 = Ikuchi, Japan (1991; 490 m); 9 = Yang Pu, China (1993; 602 m); 10 = Le Havre, Normandy, France (1994; 856 m).

Table 6.6 Selected cable-stayed bridges (completion date, span)

1957	Dusseldorf–North	260 m
1959	Cologne–Severin	302 m
1969	Dusseldorf–Kniebrücke	320 m
1970	Duisburg–Neuenkamp	350 m
1975	Saint Nazaire, France	404 m
1983	Barrios de Luna, Spain	440 m
1986	John Fazer, Canada	465 m
1991	Ikuchi, Japan	490 m
1993	Yang Pu, China	602 m
1994	Normandy, Le Havre, France	856 m
...	Tatara, Japan (planned)	890 m

Important contributions to pre-stressed concrete came in France from the firm STUP (Société Technique pour l'Utilisation de la Précontrainte, continuing the work of Freyssinet), from the German Dischinger and

Fig. 6.24   Cable-stayed bridge, Pont de Normandie, France; main span: 856 m.
Source: Freyssinet Photo Service.

Leonhardt, and from the Swiss Christian Menn. Despite some successful examples in lightweight concrete bridges, such as the Second
Cologne-Deutz Bridge across the Rhine with a span of 184 m built at the
end of the 1970s, this material did not find widespread application for
bridges.

Bridges are also employed as elevated streets and railways, road inter-
changes and for pedestrians. Aesthetic considerations are always important (Leonhardt, 1982).

In order to reduce the costs of bridges, construction techniques have
been improved. Prefabrication, travelling formwork and rational centring

Table 6.7   Selected pre-stressed concrete bridges (completion date, span)

1946	Luzancy, Marne	55 m
1949	Sclayn, Maas	63 m
1951	Heilbronn, Neckar	96.5 m
1952	Worms, Rhine	114 m
1959	Bettingen, Main	140 m
1962	Krasnoholmski	148 m
1963	Medway, Thames	152 m
1964	Bendorf, Rhine	208 m

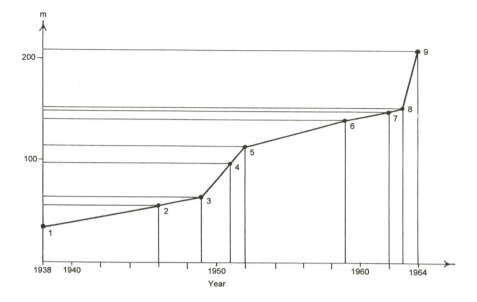

Fig. 6.25 Main span of prestressed concrete beam bridges. 1 = Oelde (1938; 33 m); 2 = Lucancy, Marne (1946;55 m); 3 = Sclayn, Maas (1949; 63 m); 4 = Heilbronn, Neckar (1951; 96.5 m); 5 = Worms, Rhine (1952; 114 m); 6 = Bettingen, Main (1959; 140 m); 7 = Krasnoholmski (1962; 148 m); 8 = Medway, Thames (1963; 152 m); 9 = Bendorf, Rhine (1964; 208 m).

have reduced costs. The cantilever erection method has been introduced for both steel and concrete bridges.

In summary, bridge construction over the past 50 years has had some remarkable successes, resulting in a considerable number of innovative and pleasing structures.

UNDERGROUND, OFF-SHORE AND OUTER SPACE CONSTRUCTIONS

In many cities in industrialized countries, especially in those with cold climates, underground shopping facilities have been developed such as in Montreal, Canada. Japan is investing heavily in underground construction, motivated by the scarcity of urban land. Another attraction of underground life to the Japanese is that the effect of earthquake tremors is much reduced there. On the other hand, fire risks and the problems of evacuation are commensurately greater. The 'Geofrontier Project' has the objective of building a 'cavity for life and work' some 50–80 m below the surface of the ground. Taisei Corporation is planning the Alice City Network, a cylinder of 80 m in diameter and 60 m high, to be built 110 m underground.

New products of construction are the off-shore structures for the oil and gas extraction industry. These can be up to a depth of several hundred metres below sea level and are frequently combined concrete and steel structures. Naturally, structural design has to cope with the special actions to which such structures are submitted. Making full use of its high-tech capabilities, Japan is engaged on a number of off-shore projects, such as deep breakwaters and marine ranches (Ota, 1992).

Orbiting space stations are another entirely new area of construction and, as with most building types, they have their own particular specifications to fulfil. In zero gravity, ceilings, walls and floors become interchangeable. People can move around freely but need to be able to anchor themselves in place in order to perform stationary tasks. Mundane acts such as eating, sleeping or using a toilet can become quite complicated in space and necessitate appropriate design solutions. Construction experts are not immediately equipped to deal with outer space design problems, and to a lesser extent this is also true of the design of the interior spaces of ships, trains and aircraft. Technologists and interior designers with or without a construction background can specialize in interior design tasks for space stations. Countries that have pioneered space exploration have done most of the research in space design. In Japan, 16 construction companies joined the Construction Engineers Group of Aerospace Study (CEGAS) to explore lunar and Martian bases and the production of concrete on the Moon. The Institute for Future Technology of Japan has conducted a five-phase study on future lunar bases, beginning with unmanned missions and ending when more permanent lunar stays for larger groups of people have been made possible. Shimizu of Japan and McDonnell Douglas of the USA are co-operating on various space-related problems.

In the meantime, experience gained from space flights is accumulating. Large permanent space stations will provide a new dimension to the construction industry. The experimental Biosphere II (the Earth is Biosphere I) which was built in Arizona, USA, was aimed at acquiring more knowledge about the behaviour of human communities in an enclosed space during a prolonged period of time. The results of the first experiment were inconclusive.

CLEANROOMS

Modern technology has imposed a new building design and construction task on the industry: cleanrooms, in which the air must be kept completely free of pollution. Contamination can be defined as any condition, material or effect that can degrade the quality or performance of any product or process (Lieberman, 1992). Usually, even small quantities of contaminants can cause degradation. Contamination control to reduce the hazards consists of cleanrooms and clean procedures and devices for ensuring the exclusion of pollution. Although the word 'contamination' is generally used in construction in the context of the ground or soil (Chapter 5), here the term is used exclusively in relation to cleanrooms.

Contaminant particles can be either solid or liquid. Their size can range from approximately 0.001–100 μm in diameter. The smallest object visible to the naked eye is about 30 μm. Clean rural air has 10 μg of total suspended particulate matter per m^3. Concentrations in urban environments are significantly higher.

US Federal Standard 209 D defines cleanliness by the permitted maximum number of particles per ft^3 in various classes from class 1, through 10, 100, 1000, 10 000 and 100 000. The manufacture of precision mechanical devices and pharmaceutical and bioengineering products, and medical and surgical rooms require high levels of air cleanliness. Compared with a standard manufacturing area, a class 10 000 cleanroom costs about four times as much; a class 10 room of the same area may cost 8–10 times more. 'Overkill' in design should therefore be avoided.

The major cost factors lie in the air treatment systems as the air must be filtered with high-efficiency filters and changed several times per minute rather than the few times per hour that is the norm in industrial settings. The HVAC system, the air filters and the airflow control are crucial to good operation. Because of the high output and high quality requirements, their size is much larger, and their cost consequently much higher than for regular spaces. The walls, ceilings, floors, windows and doors of a cleanroom must be constructed from special materials and finishes, all of which inevitably increase costs. Added to this is the extremely expensive fire safety system necessary.

Modular cleanrooms have been developed for a wide range of applications. Customers can select according to their requirements from the range published by the manufacturers. Apart from performance, there is also choice of wall, window and door materials and finishes for each cleanroom module. Individual or modular cleanrooms should be designed as integrated facilities with:

• appropriately selected materials for the wall, floor and ceiling
• sealed lighting fixtures and power lines
• sealed filters.

During the construction of a cleanroom, adjacent rooms must be built in such a way that they do not become sources of contamination. The movement of personnel, tools and materials must follow strict rules and appropriate cleaning and maintenance procedures, all of which must be specified in the design. Some firms have specialized in the design and supply of contamination controlled facilities.

At present, cleanrooms account for only a fraction of total construction volume, although they are already of crucial intrinsic importance, but demand and actual volume is set to increase in the future.

CRIME AND VANDALISM PREVENTION

Many criminal acts are assisted by ease of access and lack of supervising 'eyes' (Jacobs, 1961). Some measures aimed at reducing crime in the domestic context are (Gardner, 1994):

- Stronger front doors with better locks
- Reduced glazing area around doors and more resistant glass
- Window restrictors on all ground floor flats
- Pathways restricted by lockable gates
- Enclosed areas next to ground floor flats
- Lockable drying areas
- Cutting back of overgrown plants
- Visible signs of occupation and surveillance
- Lack of easy access and escape routes and scarcity of cover
- Community oriented environment.

Although these are all laudable measures, overall, planning is a more effective deterrent to criminals than strong locks on windows and doors, which a determined burglar can usually force open eventually.

Vandalism is the wilful damage of property and this is also on the increase (Cheetham, 1994). As a rule, criminals and vandals try to avoid being observed at their task. Crime and vandalism can therefore be reduced by proper design and materials specifications. In addition to 'normal' measures to prevent crime and vandalism, a number of 'high-tech' electronic surveillance devices and systems are now being introduced.

SUMMARY

Following the survey on the technological changes in construction, the trends related to the products of construction are reviewed.

The functions and performance requirements for most types of buildings (such as offices, schools, hotels, hospitals and others) are changing. Specific new design components are the modern atrium, cleanrooms, the integrated electronic systems of buildings and the requirements for underground, off-shore and outer space facilities. Skyscrapers and towers grow ever higher, and bridges are constructed with increasing spans and new design characteristics: suspension bridges, cable-stayed bridges and pre-stressed concrete bridges. Longer spans, new materials (fabrics) and new designs have been introduced for large-surface roofs: domes, shells, space grids and tensioned roofs.

Productivity is usually measured in building by relating the particular product (e.g. a US$1 million building or one hospital bed) to the labour (or capital) input needed to produce such units. This, however, does not reflect the spectacular growth in the performance of buildings and therefore underestimates the increased economic effectiveness of construction.

Modern buildings and structures are ever more sophisticated and can be considered to be 'high-tech' products.

BIBLIOGRAPHY

Abel, J. F., Leonard J. W. and Penalba, C. U. (eds) (1994) Spatial, lattice and tension structures, *Proceedings of Symposium, Atlanta, GA., 24–28 April 1994*, IASS and ASCE.

Atluri, S. N. and Amos, A. K. (eds) (1988) *Large Space Structures: Dynamics and Control*, Springer-Verlag.

Bailey, S. (1990) *Offices*, Butterworth Architecture.

Baird, G. *et al.* (1995) *Building Evaluation Techniques*, McGraw-Hill.

Billington, D. P. (1965) *Thin Shell Structures*, McGraw-Hill Book Company.

Brotchie, J. *et al.* (eds) (1995) *Cities in Competition*, Longman, Australia.

Brown, M. L. (1994) Denver International Airport Tensile Roof Case Study. In *Places of Assembly and Long-Span Building Structures, IABSE Symposium, IABSE Report*, Vol. 71, 121–30.

Buchholdt, H. A. (1985) *An Introduction to Cable Roof Structures*, Cambridge University Press.

Cheetham, D. W. (1994) Management and design for vandalism prevention, *CIB W 96 Symposium Proceedings; Nottingham, 17–18 September 1994*, 38–45.

Christiansen, J. (ed.) (1989) *Hyperbolic Paraboloid Shells: state of the Art*, American Concrete Institute, Detroit, USA.

Cook, M. J. *et al.* (1994) Technical/economic evaluation of cables for long-span structures. In *IABSE Report*, Vol. 71, 25–30.

Cox, A. and Groves, P. (1990) *Hospitals and Health Care Facilities*, Butterworth Architecture.

Dard, Ph. *et al.* (1996) Réseaux de communication et services résidentiels, *Cahiers du CSTB*, Cahier 2869, March 1996.

Duffy, F. (1980) Office buildings and organisational change, In King, A. D. (ed.), *Buildings and Society*, Routledge & Kegan Paul, 255–80.

Farshad, M. (1992) *Design and Analysis of Shell Structures*, Kluwer Academic Publishers.

Forty, A. (1980) The modern hospital in England and France: the social and medical uses of architecture. In A. D. King (ed.), *Buildings and Society*, Routledge & Kegan Paul, 61–93.

Fountain, M. *et al.* (1994) Comfort control for short-term occupancy, *Energy and Buildings*, **1**.

Froger, J. and Crozet, N. (1994) Les propriétés bailleurs privés et le logement des familles à faibles ressources, *Cahiers du CSTB*, Cahier 2731.

Froger, J. and Mallein, Ph. (1995) Concevoir et diffuser une nouvelle technologie d'information, *Cahiers du CSTB*, Cahier 2779.

Gardner, A. (1994) Managing a secure environment: crime prevention as a design generator. *CIB W 96 Symposium Proceedings; Nottingham; 17–18 September 1994*, 46–53.

Heki, K. (ed.) (1986) *Shells, Membranes and Space Frames*, Elsevier, 3 vols, Proceedings of IASS Symposium, Osaka, Japan, 15–19 September 1986.

Jacobs, J. (1961) *The Death and Life of Great American Cities*, Jonathan Cape, London.

Joedicke, J. (1962) *Schalenbau*, Karl Krämer, Stuttgart.

King, A. D. (1980) A time for space and a space for time: the social production of the vacation house, In: A. D. King (ed.), *Buildings and Society*, Routledge & Kegan Paul, 193–227.

Kollár, L. and Hegedüs, I. (1985) *Analysis and Design of Space Frames by the Continuous Method*, Elsevier.

Kollár, L. and Dulácska, E. (1984) *Buckling of Shells for Engineers*, John Wiley & Sons.

Leonhardt, F. (1982) *Brücken/Bridges*, Deutsche Verlags-Anstalt.

Levy, M. (1994) The lightest retractable roof, *IABSE Report*, **71**, 43–7.

Lieberman, A. (1992) *Contamination Control and Cleanrooms*, Van Nostrand Reinhold, New York.

Lippiatt, B. C. and Weber, S. F. (1992) *Productivity Impacts in Building Life-Cycle Cost*, NISTIR 4762, Gaithersburg, MD.

Livesey, F. and Larose, G. L. (1995) Tuned mass dampers for the Great Belt East Bridge, *Structural Engineering International*, November, 223–4.

Makowski, Z. S. (1981) *Analysis, Design and Construction of Double-Layer Grids*, Applied Science Publishers.

Makowski, Z. S. (ed.) (1984) *Analysis, Design and Construction of Braced Domes*, Granada/University Press, Cambridge.

Makowski, Z. S. (ed.) (1985) *Analysis, Design and Construction of Braced Barrel Vaults*, Elsevier Applied Science Publishers.

Mierop, C. (1995) *Skyscrapers Higher and Higher*, Norma Editions.

Mills, E. D. (1985) *Planning: The Architect's Handbook*, Butterworth.

Nervi, P. L. (1956) *Structures*, F. W. Dodge Corporation, New York.

Neufert, E. (1980) *Architects' Data*, BSP Professional Books, Oxford, 2nd international edn.

Nooshin, H. (ed.), (1984) *Studies in Space Structures*, Multi-Science Publishing Company.

Ota, T. (1992) Offshore technologies in Japan to exploit the ocean, *Post-Congress Report of IABSE*, 1–6 March 1992.

Podolny, W. Jr. and Scalzi, J. B. (1986) *Construction and Design of Cable-Stayed Bridges*, John Wiley & Sons.

Reuterswärd, L. (1988) *Handbook for Educational Buildings Planning*, UNESCO, Publication 12.

Riewoldt, O. (1994) *New Office Design*, Laurence King.

Russell, B. (1981) *Building Systems: Industrialisation and Architecture* John Wiley & Sons.

Saxon, R. (1993) *The Atrium Comes of Age*, Longman.

Schlaich, J. and Saradshow, P. (1994) Anton Tedesko and the early history of concrete shells, *Bulletin of the IASS*, **3**, 139–54.

Stafford Smith, B. and Coull, A. (1991) *Tall Building Structures: Analysis and Design*, John Wiley & Sons.

Strategies and Technologies for Maintenance and Modernisation of Building (1994) CIB W 70 Symposium, Tokyo, 2 vols.

Szabó, J. and Kollár, L. (1984) *Structural Design of Cable-Suspended Roofs*, Ellis Horwood and Halsted Press.

Torroja, E. (1958a) *Philosophy of Structures*, University of California Press.

Torroja, E. (1958b) *The Structures of Eduardo Torroja*, F. W. Dodge Corporation.

Troitsky, M. S. (1977, 1988) *Cable-Stayed Bridges*, BSP Professional Books.

Turner, G., Margulis, S. T., Brill, M. and Coburn, C. (1984) *Innovative Office Building Structures and Enclosures: A Survey of Experts*, NBS/CBT and GSA-PBS, Washington, DC.

Vickery, D. S. (1988) *A Facilities Design Guide*, UNESCO, Publication 10.

Walther, R. *et al.* (1988) *Cable Stayed Bridges*, Thomas Telford.

Wittfoht, H. (1984) *Building Bridges*, Beton-Verlag, Düsseldorf.

Management and information

7

INTRODUCTION

The Industrial Revolution was itself based on the Scientific Revolution and technological inventions. Early industrial enterprises were instinctively managed in a similar manner to that used previously in the military and agriculture. Gradually, however, large industrial enterprises began to develop new management methods. By contrast, construction enterprises are to this day still sometimes lagging behind manufacturing when it comes to up-to-date management methods. That is not to say, however, that construction is not as well managed as other industries; to some extent the contrary is true since construction has always required – as far back as the building of the Egyptian pyramids – excellent management skills. Successful builders have always been first-class managers whose skills were rooted in natural talent and experience. In fact, this talent was the very reason for the disdain with which they treated the science of management. Building practitioners, with some reason, considered scientific management to be of use only to academic researchers who cultivated it for their own sake. Researchers could also share the blame for this situation because they frequently sought to avoid confronting theory with practice. No one would deny that human talent and experience will continue to be of critical importance in construction management in the future. On the other hand, one should not readily give up the idea that the science of management can usefully complement empirical skills and instinct.

Management is the act of organizing people and activities, but it is also the term used to describe the top echelon of an organization. Management has both general and specific principles relating to the field it is applied in. This chapter looks at selected recent trends in modern industrial management and information methods, their application and the specific problems of management in the construction industry.

THE MODEL: INDUSTRIAL MANAGEMENT

As already mentioned, industry preceded construction in changing over from medieval methods of management to modern ones, so it is worthwhile examining the path that management in industry was taking before we consider management in construction.

THE BIRTH OF MODERN INDUSTRIAL MANAGEMENT

The father of 'scientific industrial management' was the American Frederick Winslow Taylor who studied methods of working and the means of operating (e.g. shovelling coal) with the purpose of improving them so as to increase productivity, which then could be further improved by linking reward schemes to performance (Taylor, 1911). Taylor also advocated the principle of functional divisions in management.

Time-and-motion studies (methods of time measurement) were introduced in the early 1900s by Frank Bunker Gilbreth and his wife Lillian Molder Gilbreth (Barnes, 1968) and were applied to repetitive processes such as bricklaying.

Early research in the science of industrial management formulated certain basic principles, of which the most generally accepted were that:

- larger companies and larger production units are more efficient than small ones
- large scale production, longer production series, more repetitive processes and standardization of the products yield economies in time and cost
- workers and employees are motivated primarily by their income and, in consequence, optimal systems of salary, bonuses and benefits must be investigated
- there exist optimal methods of technology and management; these have to be explored and applied in order to attain optimal results.

The enthusiasm in the 1930s for a large number of identical products led to studies of repetition in various industrial sectors such as aircraft manufacturing. It is an established fact that the effect of repetition is gradually to reduce the amount of time required to execute identical successive operations or processes. This is due to the increased productivity achieved by training, but also to successive improvements in working methods and the arrangements in the immediate environment of the actual operation. In industry, the accumulated mean value of operational times was found to be reduced to 80% when doubling the number of identical operations (UN ECE, 1963).

The favourable results of studies on repetition strengthened the conviction that industrial organizations can attain the best economic results by being large.

NEW TRENDS IN INDUSTRIAL MANAGEMENT

The new science and its applications developed further during the first half of the twentieth century. The results were summed up, not to say canonized, in several authoritative books by Maynard (1970, 1973). However, new conditions, particularly in the second half of the century, forced researchers to change direction. Trends and publications in management research between 1930 and 1970 reflect the struggle between the old and new ideas.

Strategy policy planning

A number of management researchers analysed the strategy of a company and how it could be of decisive importance in its success or failure. Researchers also investigated the history of successful companies, examining their strategies, policies and methods, and the personalities of successful managers in the hope of finding the secret of perfect management.

Peter Drucker, an Austrian-born American management consultant, studied General Motors and other successful companies. It soon became clear that even successful companies can run into trouble and that therefore they do not provide the ultimate wisdom on success.

Alfred Sloan, president of General Motors from 1924 until 1937, when he became chairman of the board, claimed that top managers have three main tasks:

- to determine the firm's strategy
- to design its structure
- to select its control systems.

But by the 1970s, this philosophy seemed out of date. If a company's success was based on good (long-term) strategic planning, what could explain its subsequently failing? The idea that a company must have a strategic plan now seemed inadequate for success. More flexibility was required.

Gar Hamel and C.K. Prahalad (professors in the UK and USA, respectively) assert that the real function of a company's strategy is to set goals which 'stretch' a company beyond what most of its managers believe possible. Although this already contains a component of dynamic thinking, it still does not seem to provide companies with adequate guidelines.

Is large or small beautiful?

Up to approximately 1945, people believed that large was better than small, an idea that Marxism transformed into dogma, forcing people from small businesses into huge – and, as it turned out, inefficient – Goliaths. Growth was the yardstick of success, multinationals were considered to be the supreme examples of efficient companies, and no nobler goal was known to ambitious youngsters than to gain entry into the top levels of management or establish from scratch their own company and make it grow to giant size, not a new idea in entrepreneurship. Size became a source of debate. On the one hand it was obvious that large companies, even if they experience some difficult periods, will always be important standard-bearers of industrial development. On the other, they may easily become too heavy and cumbersome, whereas smaller companies could be more innovative.

After the Second World War the new battle cry was 'small is beautiful', and this contributed to the emergence of a number of new, ambitious and fast-growing companies. It was realized that real life is too complex to permit the formulation of simple rules for success, and in recent years management science has come forward with the ideas of de-layering, down-sizing and adopting a lean structure.

De-layering and down-sizing

Following the period of building up mammoth corporations with an excessively complicated leadership structure, the reduction in the number of management layers and the idea of a 'flat organization' with 'lean, mean management' have proved useful. The idea of combining large and small found an expression in the new policy of breaking up huge corporations into smaller units with more independence and replacing centralized management with a co-operative system of organizations.

Management 'guru' Tom Peters was one of the first to advocate downsizing. He sensed that information technology would allow firms to eliminate layers of middle managers, bringing top management nearer to production level. His call for lean staffing, a flat organization and fewer levels between top management and production are principles that have long been music to the ears of successful construction managers, who believe in hands-on operational leadership (Peters and Waterman, 1982). Peters recently wrote about the 'demise of size', claiming that cut-throat competition makes companies fitter, as at the beginning of modern industrial development.

Latterly, however, the corporate mood has changed somewhat. Excessive slimming can become anorexia, and too much de-layering can lead to disorganization. Up-sizing and growth are now fashionable again. Various strategies have been defined as growth generating, including the recommendation to concentrate on the core business: focused companies frequently produce better results. In the case of diversified companies, a break-up or de-merger could result in a number of more focused companies.

A new idea: the competitive advantage

New ideas with a strong inclination towards theoretical thinking on practical problems were put forward by Michael Porter from Harvard, including the novel idea of competitive advantage to replace the classical Ricardo idea of comparative advantage, according to which international commerce compels countries to produce the goods for which they have a comparative edge over others. Porter argued that comparative advantage, such as costs of labour and raw materials, have become less important than the ability to innovate, develop products and make technologies more competitive. Porter developed the model of the five forces that are influencing corporate strategy planning (Porter, 1979):

- the threat of new entrants
- the power of suppliers
- the power of buyers
- the threat of substitute products
- jockeying for position among members of industry.

Porter proposed that a company should analyse its product and locate segments of its market in areas where superior performance is more likely because of the favourable position of the five forces. According to Porter, the threat of new entrants can be influenced by factors including:

- economies of scale
- product differentiation
- large capital requirements
- cost disadvantages associated with learning and experience curves.

Porter also suggested that jockeying for position by existing industry members yields the greatest competitive advantage when the following conditions apply:

- many competitors of equal size
- slow industrial growth
- undifferentiated products or services
- high fixed costs in enterprises
- high exit barriers from the industry.

Porter stressed the importance of analysing individual parts of the firm, claiming that competitive advantage could be acquired in each of the following areas:

- firm infrastructure
- human resource management
- procurement
- technology and development.

Porter defined the three generic competitive strategies as being:

- product differentiation
- overall cost leadership
- product focus.

Various economic sectors, including construction, looked into the applicability of Porter's ideas for their field of activity.

Management for change: re-engineering

In the long run, large firms with strategic plans can be successful or still fail. So has strategic planning been of any benefit to business? The alternative would be grabbing opportunities or coping with blows as they arise.

The world is changing, faster now than ever. The main requirement for management is the ability to respond to changes in a creative way. Each firm must be judged on its own merits, and it is claimed that corporate headquarters can create or destroy value in four main ways (Gold, Campbell and Alexander, undated):

- by making vital decisions about appointments or strategy
- by offering a range of high-quality services, from scientific information to useful internal telephone directories
- by establishing connections between business units
- by buying and selling businesses.

The new ideas on 'business process re-engineering', 're-engineering' or 'process redesign' mirror the advice to react quickly to changing conditions. It should create and cultivate innovative strategies and strengths in operating processes.

Firms as systems: the human aspect

Firms and their management can be considered to be complex systems. They usually have a number of subsystems, e.g. for the management of personnel, materials, plant, finances, production, marketing and so on (Newcombe et al., 1990). Any firm in construction has to be an open system because it has to interact with external organizations in order to survive. This explains why systems theory (systems analysis, system techniques) and mathematical methods (operations research, probability theory, programming methods, statistical analysis) are so widely used when dealing with the problems of management (Hall, 1962; Fabrycky and Jorgensen, 1966; Wagner, 1967; Gordon, 1969). However, the systems approach must not fall into the trap of considering the firm to be a mechanism and ignoring the human aspect. To a large extent, time-and-motion studies ignored the sometimes devastating impact they had on workers' health and their attitude to their work. Later production systems tried to redress the balance, however, aiming to achieve high productivity at the same time as keeping the workers satisfied. Henry Ford's notion of mass production with soul-destroying assembly lines and standardized goods was replaced by more human concepts of production.

As a result of the work of behavourial scientists such as Elton Mayo and Abraham Maslow, who systematized human needs and requirements, more attention has recently been devoted to human aspects. Maslow established a hierarchy of human needs beginning with primary ones (air, food, water and housing), continuing with safety and security, and finishing with aspiration for position, rank, image and satisfaction (Maslow, 1943; Herzberg, Mausner and Snyderman, 1959; Herzberg, 1966; Maslow, 1968). The new discipline of ergonomy was developed to deal with the relationship between men and machines, and the safety and efficiency of human work.

The latest management theoreticians – Christopher Bartlett from the Harvard Business School and Sumantra Ghoshal from the London Business School – conclude that attention should be shifted away from designing a single corporate strategy to shaping general organizational purposes, which should be oriented more towards 'human engineering'. This includes generating enthusiasm within the company, coaching executives and establishing closer contacts with workers. Furthermore, management should build competence in order to outperform rivals, encourage entrepreneurship and steer with a lighter touch than before. Knowledge becomes of paramount importance, of which more later.

The increasing concern for human aspects is reflected in the three books of Rosabeth Moss Kanter, who treated a particular corporation not so much as a microeconomy concerned with turning inputs into outputs, but as a mini-society, determined to shape individuals for collective ends (Kanter, 1985). Her second book was a study on contrasts between 'change resisters' and 'change masters' (Kanter, 1990). In her third book, she announced the birth of a new entity, the post-entrepreneurial firm, which creates synergies through restructuring, breaks down corporate barriers to form alliances, and devolves power to innovative units (Kanter, 1992). She recorded an important trend: that managers (bosses) are becoming more powerful in relation to the owners and shareholders of companies, while employees are becoming more insecure, which runs contrary to her proposed 'people-sensitive' strategies. There are, however, attempts to rectify this new form of power-sharing.

In this section we have once again peered over the fence from our own industry into areas of neighbouring activities with the purpose of putting our own problems, to which we now return, into perspective.

MANAGEMENT IN THE CONSTRUCTION INDUSTRY

CONDITIONS FOR THE MANAGEMENT OF THE CONSTRUCTION FIRM

Most of the operations that result in the construction of buildings and public works are carried out by firms (companies, enterprises), an important category of which is the construction firm or contractor. Their management is of special importance because, following the design, the contractor gives real shape to the product. Moreover, the construction process includes features that render its management difficult, such as labour-intensivity, handling and storage of large amounts of bulky materials, difficult site conditions, and tasks of co-ordination of materials and subcontractors.

There are significant differences between construction and manufacturing and so management theories devised for manufacturing are applicable to construction to only a limited extent. It is not even possible to view construction as one homogeneous economic sector. Its constituent enterprises differ in terms of size and professional character, and their managements must also conform to varying characteristics. Large companies experience most of the problems, although it is quite justifiable to consider the management problems of small and medium-size firms.

With regard to the structure of large contractors, they share with their industrial counterparts a linear staff and a functional staff. The co-operation between the two can be organized along the military system of general staff and linear subordination, or by the so-called matrix management method with the dual structure of project managers and functional divisions (Bresnen, 1990). Patricia Hillebrandt (1990) defined large contractors by the following five features:

- they are diversified
- management, not fixed assets, is their main scarce resource
- they have low fixed assets
- they have a positive cash flow
- they subcontract extensively.

It has been found that most large contractors undertake various activities: housing, property development, production of building materials and components, and frequently non-construction activities as well. Experienced managers are inherently important to contractors, a fact that is usually adequately recognized. In certain construction processes, such as large heavy civil engineering work, special machinery also acquires an important function. The low fixed assets required in the construction industry mean that entry to most tasks in the industry is usually easy. It has been said that competition among the numerous small firms within the industry is near perfect, and that the construction industry could not therefore be said to have the structural restraints of capital accumulation that apply to capital-intensive manufacturing industries (Linder, 1994). However, the construction industry, or at least a segment of it, more and more resembles other industries, with respect to imperatives and constraints of capital accumulation and concentration, than has been traditionally recognized. This also means that the various national construction industries are no longer sheltered from external competition and, conversely, that national industries are better able to enter foreign markets. The positive cash flow is a characteristic of contractors in many, but not all, countries, including the UK. It generally results from prepayment by the client, or credit in advance of work to be executed. The large amount of subcontracting, which is practised in all countries in different forms, is a consequence of the basic features of construction.

Lansley (1987) identified three distinct periods requiring different strategic approaches:

- In the stable environment of the 1960s, firms did not need long-term strategies. They had to identify the markets that their skills were most suited to, invest heavily, and improve efficiency by developing their technical and managerial skills.
- During the huge changes in the 1970s, firms had to become flexible, moving within the market while divesting themselves of less profitable businesses. Short-term joint ventures were more appropriate than vertical integration.
- In the 1980s, enterprises were restructured and rationalized in readiness for the next prolonged upswing in economic activity (Betts and Ofori, 1992).

The internal management of construction firms, as indeed of any other type of firm, embraces production, research and development, finance, personnel and materials. Materials management alone, for example, comprises calculating needs, defining performance, quality control, purchase, storage, distribution, transport and recycling. Several studies have found that labour productivity has grown less in the construction industry than in manufacturing; it is exceptional when a study claims that this is not the case (Chan and Lai, 1994). Whatever the truth, productivity is an important measure of technical progress.

Contractors have always paid attention to their personnel, trying to retain good staff permanently and efforts have now redoubled in that direction: in-house training and education is practised; career opportunities are offered; bonus arrangements usually tend to be less complicated than before and more attention is devoted to accident prevention, health care and reduction of absenteeism.

Finally, the management of construction has to work with the defined characteristics of the buildings, which are determined by the designer, who may be the contractor or a totally separate entity. In either case, it is favourable if the design can serve as a basis for the management of the construction. This is why the designer's modelling and presentation of the building need to be studied carefully.

APPLICATION OF INDUSTRIAL MANAGEMENT RESULTS

The specific characteristics of construction have been noted above. Nevertheless, occasionally people have attempted to adapt the results of industrial management to the circumstances of construction. An early example was the Gilbreths' study into improving the productivity of bricklaying, mentioned previously. This area continues to keep building technologists busy. In the former Soviet Union there were masons who achieved high productivity in bricklaying, but to the detriment of quality and architectural freedom. Experiments are still running in some countries (e.g. Germany) to improve the productivity of bricklaying.

The studies on repetition carried out in manufacturing in the 1930s were taken up by the construction industry in the 1960s, in the hope that industrial methods such as large-scale prefabrication of large panels would satisfy the high post-war demand for new dwellings. Studies showed that improvements resulting from repetition can also be attained in construction, but that various influences reduce the rate of improvement, so that the time per unit will be reduced only to 90% rather than the 80% found in industry (UN ECE, 1963; UN, 1965). While these results are still valid, questions have been raised about their usefulness. The recent global slump in demand for new buildings has also reduced the occurrence of large series and repetition. It has remained common to plan repetitive operations at a uniform speed and time, without taking into account any acceleration due to repetition (Sebestyén, 1993).

The construction industry has also recently attempted to introduce strategic planning, but once again, the conditions specific to construction (primarily the dependence on random changes in demand) dampened enthusiasm.

During the second half of this century, much of the construction industry developed to the levels of modern industry. The work of Porter in particular found resonance. Porter himself illustrated his thesis on competitive advantage with the thermal market, in which fibreglass acquired a temporary advantage that quickly disappeared with the rapid emergence of Styrofoam and rock wool. The potential of Porter's ideas in application to the construction industry have been examined (van Bezooijen, 1991; Betts and Ofori, 1992: Pries, 1995). It has been said that the threat of new entrants (which was restricted in medieval times by the guilds) used to be considerable, but has now diminished slightly with the increased capital investment requirements in construction.

Competitive advantage due to exceptional products does not usually tend to be long-lasting in the construction industry because substitutes can be found relatively easily. Recent ideas of industrial management such as down-sizing, de-layering, flat organizational structures and re-engineering, have all been taken up by contractors.

Organization through integration

We now come to the specific problems of management in the construction industry, in which integration and co-operation is of extreme importance because of the great number of different processes used in building. The idea of covering as many of these processes as possible within one organization is attractive because production can then be organized as a single integrated system and there is a reduced dependency on other organizations. This is the so-called vertical integration, and was much favoured in the former Soviet Union and other countries with a centralized planned economy. Co-operation between independent companies was poor in the former USSR and so in order to avoid production stoppages because of delivery delays, firms built up vertical organizations, thus being able to supply construction sites from their own production or storage facilities as necessary. Such firms were called 'trusts' and had within their structure a number of construction companies, building materials manufacturing firms, units operating building machines, caterers, and suppliers of building materials. Construction trusts (corporations) usually had a staff of at least 10 000 or more. To make such complicated organizations function, a military-style management system called the 'dispatcher system' was developed with liaison officers. The person at the head of the trust was the director-general. His/her deputy, the technical deputy director-general, was in charge of the construction processes and was assisted by a staff of dispatchers, who were in turn supervised by a chief dispatcher working directly under the technical director, occasionally replacing him/her. Daily dispatcher meetings were held, usually on a multiconferencing basis. The technical director had or could have simultaneous telephone connections to all units so that in case of any problems, such as materials being out of stock, or machinery being broken down, s/he could take immediate action.

Although the technical equipment was unsophisticated (in some cases the company installed its own telephone network etc.), an amazingly efficient and effective management was often achieved, although the system required strong personalities at the top. From among the construction trusts, Zaporozhstroy may be regarded as having perfected the 'dispatcher system' to an advanced level. Zaporozhye, in present-day Ukraine, has a large metallurgical plant and a hydropower station.

The management style in the former Soviet Union exemplifies a pattern that is not too different from the requirements in the building industry, but the vertical integration has proved to be impractical because it is impossible to organize such differing activities efficiently. Horizontal integration on the other hand, meaning concentration of similar construction firms into one single organization, has not found much application in construction where, despite a certain level of concentration, a great number of firms remain independent.

Organization through co-operation

The lack of co-operation on the part of suppliers in centrally planned economies was an expression of the priority of production over consumption, of supply over demand. In such systems, shortages and delivery delays were a rule and co-operation was therefore not working well.

In countries with free market economies the supplier must accommodate the consumer, which necessitates a reliance on suppliers and sub-contractors by the main contractors. In Western economies, a high level of co-operation has increasingly replaced vertical integration, which used to be common. Construction companies concentrating on core activities require very exact compliance with their delivery needs. The 'just-in-time' philosophy and practice combines this with a policy of minimizing stocks, which improves financial yields and saves space on and around the building site. If vertical integration called for a military style of leadership, co-operation needs good information networks and transport services. This has been facilitated by the development of information technologies and telecommunications.

INFORMATION MANAGEMENT

MODELLING BUILDINGS: INFORMATION SERVING ALL PARTICIPANTS

Management in construction applies modern information technologies in the same way as do other industries. There are, however, two closely interrelated problems that are to some extent specific to building. The first is the modelling of buildings with the objective of computer-aided design (CAD). The second is devising information systems that can be used by various firms participating in the building process.

CAD technologies have modernized the design process. It has become quicker and cheaper, with better technical solutions, and at the same time the results are readily accessible to construction managers. Ideally, a CAD system should have interfaces to enable the various design specialists to use each other's design work and share a common data base. On the other hand, each design discipline is independent and complex in itself and most systems are therefore intended for use within one design sector only. It is desirable that the modelling of buildings or structures should satisfy the various design disciplines as well as the contractor and sub-contractors. Various tools have been developed to serve the integration of computer systems in general, and those in the construction industry in particular. Some achieve the objective of enabling a dialogue to take place between different users, including digital data exchange of information on drawings, which will eventually be replaced by digital information sets. These developments are not just restricted to construction; they are relevant to many branches of industry and are therefore progressing in a wider context.

The work on up-to-date product modelling and representation has been coupled with standardization, so that essentially uniform systems can be applied by different designers, manufacturers and contractors. One of the results of such work is the Standard for Exchange of Product Data (STEP). The Initial Graphics Exchange Specification (IGES), devised in the USA, has been combined with STEP to form the Product Data Exchange Specification (PDES) (Sadri and Kangari, 1993). Electronic Data Exchange (EDI) is one of several computer-based methods of sending and receiving (primarily standard format) documents directly through computers. UK EDICON in the UK and EU EDIBUILD in the EU oversee EDI developments in the building industry. ISO 10303, which is not restricted to construction, deals in general with product data representation and exchange. This should be the basis for models of buildings and civil engineering works, with the aim of producing standardized textual documents.

Together with the drawings, the most important design outputs are the bills of quantities and the specifications of the work to be carried out. Simultaneously these are inputs for the contractor. Long before computers, there were standard texts for specifications and model structuring for bills of quantities, but they usually served simply as a help to the designer or the quantity surveyor and did not have any mandatory character. In recent years there have been several attempts to produce such models for general application (Debras *et al.*, 1995; Alshawi and Underwood, 1996). UNIFORMAT II was devised at NIST (the National Institute of Standards and Technology) in the USA, as a result of studying some earlier classifications (Bowen, Charette and Marshall, 1992). Its purpose is to define six major 'groups of products' in the construction industry: buildings; roads and bridges; dams; tunnels; railroads; and other. For buildings it proposes six major 'group elements': substructure; shell; interiors; services; equipment; and furnishings (level 1). It defines the remaining group elements (17 in total) as level 2, and the 'individual elements' (a total of 49) as level 3. For example: within 'shell', one of the group elements is 'exterior closure', which has three individual elements:

'exterior walls, 'windows' and 'exterior doors'. It also categorizes building-related sitework and defines five group elements (e.g. site preparation), within which there are 22 individual elements (e.g. site clearing).

Another necessary classification concerns types of buildings or facilities, such as residential, educational buildings, etc. There are such classifications on a national basis in most countries as well as several international lists.

Considering the greatly differing traditions, changing technologies and manifold types of buildings and works, it is inconceivable for there to be a universal and global classification system, but some progress can be expected. The primary aim of any construction firm is to establish a complex information system for its own use, and many firms have succeeded in this. However, all have been faced with the problem that a construction firm is not a closed production unit; it has to co-operate with frequently changing partners including clients, designers, manufacturers and subcontractors. People have therefore been working for some time towards establishing the basis for such a common understanding. One of the classifications is the so-called *CIB Master List* (CIB, 1993) published by CIB, the International Council for Building Research, Studies and Documentation. This is an internationally agreed list of headings for the arrangement of information used in design, construction, operating, maintenance and repair of buildings and building services.

International agreement is advanced in the field of product information, i.e. the way information on materials, products, components and services should be structured. Most product information services now adhere to an agreed classification. A technical report (not a standard) has been published by ISO on classification requirements on information in the construction industry, which demonstrates that this is an area where progress can be expected in the near future (ISO TR 14177). The various classification systems agreed on an international basis constitute a platform for understanding between different organizations but do not provide any overall standard on structuring, storage and retrieval of information, which is still left to individual organizations. Nevertheless, the evolution described above has led to the Computer Integrated Construction (CIC) synthesizing product data management and interchange.

DATABASE MANAGEMENT AND CLIENT/SERVER SYSTEMS

Programmers used to store their data in files that were structured to suit their own particular application needs. It was difficult to compile and update information, and duplication caused redundancy and increased costs. Newly introduced data management systems have many advantages over file systems: reduced costs, shorter development time, and easier updating of information (Atre 1980, 1992; Bontempo and Saracco, 1995; Ruley *et al.*, 1995; Spencer, 1996).

Data management is now a key area of software technology and all software companies offer database management systems that manage data as a shared resource and enable users to group together with others to store and share information. Database management systems are available on a wide variety of computing platforms, from personal computers to large mainframes.

Medium or large companies employ individuals to administer or manage database management systems. Such companies often use hardware and software products from different vendors and use multiple database management systems, including different 'servers'. Within database management systems, distributed databases are available, accessible through appropriate middleware and gateways. The term 'middleware' is used for software that provides an application to some (often remote) service(s).

Along with the traditional programming languages (COBOL, FORTRAN, etc.) new object-oriented ones have appeared, such as Smalltalk and C++. Certain database management systems are closely tied to object-oriented programming languages. In 1995, Sun Microsystems launched Java, a new programming language designed to run on a network such as the Internet using 'applets', i.e. small programs devised for specific jobs. The concept of this new development is to transfer many of the tasks that are currently performed on personal computers to the network. This could ultimately result in cheaper 'network computers'.

The client/server database systems appeared in the 1980s. These split the traditional database management system into two, distributing tasks in such a way that one component (the client) requires services from the other (the server). The client/server systems are distributed systems, enabling the co-ordinated use of several computers of different makes at different locations (Niemann, 1995; von Thienen, 1995). Distributed database environments broaden the extent to which data can be shared. They allow autonomous database management systems to be connected through network facilities and to communicate with each other in managing and responding to requests from users at different locations. The replication or copy of data enables firms to maintain copies of the same information in different database management systems. This improves response time and the availability of data, serves as a backup database and simplifies system management. Copy management services are also known under the name of extractors, replication servers, snapshot facilities, or propagators.

The application of information technology by the construction industry has been examined repeatedly (Betts, 1995). Major construction companies have established their own information systems and also participate in networks. The multidisciplinary consultancy Ove Arup &

Partners, for example, runs a global network that links its 53 offices around the world via the Internet and Ethernet. Unix servers have replaced mainframes.

An efficient use of up-to-date computers and computer systems is a prerequisite for the transformation of construction into a modern industry.

PLANNING AND CONTROLLING PRODUCTION

GENERAL SURVEY: BAR CHARTS

The set of processes that ensure that production conforms to the final specification is called production control. This includes programming, scheduling, information processing, making and implementing decisions, control, accounting and reporting (Melles and Wamelink, 1993).

Planning, scheduling and control of production are important management responsibilities that used to be based on experience but for which a number of techniques are now available. The traditional tool for planning and scheduling is the bar chart, which shows processes, times, durations and dates. It can be used to control progress and to compare realizations with schedules (O'Neill, 1989). Due to their simplicity, bar charts are readily used by contractors. If a cost completion curve is superimposed over a bar chart, a 'lazy S' curve is seen. This provides a rather general tool for controlling progress.

ARROW DIAGRAMS

Newer techniques are based on graphs consisting of arrows and nodes. Arrow diagrams depict activities as arrows going to node points, which represent events. Precedence diagrams depict activities as nodes, while arrows are used to show the relationship between activities. Arrow diagrams are used more frequently than precedence diagrams. In its simplest form, the arrow diagram illustrates technological interrelationships (sequences) alone. For example, a smooth surface can be painted only after it has been prepared in some way. In this case, the arrow representing painting must be preceded by the arrow representing the preparation of the smooth surface. Arrow diagrams are used to illustrate the duration of individual activities and, based on this, to define the amount of time required for carrying out all activities. The basic technique for this is the critical path method (CPM). In order to prepare a CPM project schedule, three questions must be answered for every activity:

- What activity must immediately precede this activity?
- What activity must immediately follow this activity?
- What activity or activities may be performed simultaneously with this activity?

When the responses to these questions are available, the arrow diagram can be constructed and time scheduling is possible. The critical path is defined as the continuous sequence of activities that produces the minimum duration time for the whole process (Benson, 1970; Stevens, 1990; Callahan *et al.*, 1992). CPM is an excellent scheduling technique, but it does need to be thoroughly understood. Contractors often claim that it is laborious, time-consuming and frequently misunderstood by some. It is generally used for large projects, especially since computers have become commonplace. Its application is now spreading even among smaller contractors.

CPM has been developed further. One of its variants is PERT, the Project (Performance) Evaluation and Review Technique, which includes probabilities, i.e. it is a stochastic scheduling device. Some of the other variants are: the Project Control System, the Project Management System, the Integrated Civil Engineering System, and the Management Scheduling and Control System. PDM is the abbreviation of Precedence Diagramming Method, belonging to the second group of network diagrams. The Linear Scheduling Method (LSM), which is not based on the arrow technique, illustrates the progress of construction diagrammatically by comparing the time and location, or the sequence number, of repetitive units. In a high-rise building, the 'location' would be the different floors. In residential construction, progress is denoted by the completion of an individual house or certain parts of it. The progress made in each process (such as foundations, masonry, partitions, etc.) is represented by lines that follow each other at a distance. The lines may have a different slope, depending on the speed of the operation.

CPM, PERT, PDM, LSM and other similar techniques illustrate relationships that cannot be shown by a bar chart (O'Brien, 1984).

MATHEMATICAL PROGRAMMING

Mathematical programming is concerned with the extrapolation of a function over a set that is defined by linear or non-linear, equal or unequal constraints (Haftka and Kamat, 1985). Various types of technique have been developed under the name of mathematical programming. The most used type is the Linear Programming Technique (LPT), which was developed during the 1930s and used in the Second World War for planning maritime convoys across the Atlantic Ocean. Its most common applications are for determining optimal manufacturing or transport plans. In manufacturing, it is used to determine the optimal mix of production quantities of several products under constraints of limited production capacity and with the objective of determining the best production plan. Mathematically, this may mean finding a maximum or minimum value of a function. The most common transport problem is determining the quantities of goods to be transported from the various supply locations to the locations of consumption at the minimum costs.

In linear programming, as its name indicates, relations are linear. Linear programming has applications for architectural, engineering (e.g. structural design) and space allocation problems. In quadratic or other programming models linearity may not be a requirement. Non-linearly constrained problems may be formulated as linear programming problems, but caution must always be exercised to ensure that the approximation does not distort the character of the original problem. For investment and some other problems, the method of dynamic and integer programming has been developed (Burns *et al.*, 1996). For scheduling and mathematical programming techniques, algebraic (matrix calculus) methods and computer programs have been devised. For the optimization of decisions the game theory seems to provide assistance in some contexts, although it has found only sporadic application in construction practice (von Neumann and Morgenstern, 1994; Bacharach, 1976).

PROCUREMENT (CONTRACTING)

TRADITIONAL PROCUREMENT

Procurement, or contracting, is the formal arrangement by which the client has a building (or groups of buildings) designed and constructed (Masterman, 1992). In traditional procurement, the client employs independent professionals (architects, engineers, quantity surveyors) to design the building and then enters into a separate contract with a building contractor to construct it. In the UK, conventional procurement methods were used from the nineteenth century until 1945. Since then, clients, designers and contractors have experimented with various new methods (Masterman, 1992).

While traditional contracting can yield perfectly satisfactory results and is still much used, criticism has emerged over recent years that it does not always provide the optimum service to clients. The increasing specialization in construction sometimes results in confused lines of responsibilities and thus in a growing number of disputes, claims and conflicts. In order to reduce areas of conflict, new procurement methods have been developed and applied with various degrees of success.

The function of the designer and the contractor in the client–designer–contractor triangle have been clear enough for a long time, but attention has lately turned to the client. The construction of buildings is the principal business of some clients who are more or less permanently in that role. For others, constructing buildings is only a peripheral activity. Clients in the first category, who are usually developers, should be experts in the field. Those in the second category may be less experienced. A client, whether an individual or an organization, may or may not be the owner of the building (Barrett and Hoxley, 1993). The designer and the contractor have to accommodate the client. This begins with the preparation of the brief, which is an important document in making the building process a success.

DESIGN AND BUILD

New procurement methods can be categorized in various ways. One of the new methods is the 'design and build' (or 'design and construct') method (Hisatomi and Reismann, 1994), in which a designer prepares the basic design concept for the client but then the contractor, who takes over the design concept, is responsible for the detailed design and construction. This has also been called the 'bridging method' and 'novation design and building' (Akintoye, 1994a, 1994b). The 'turnkey method' and the 'package deal' can be either variants of design and build, or independent methods. In both, the contractor remains fully in charge for the complete design and construction. 'Package deal' is often used for the provision of standard or systems buildings.

In the 'design and manage' process, the contractor receives a fee for managing all aspects of planning, design and supervising the subcontractors. In the 'design, manage and construct' method, the contractor not only manages the construction but also carries out some of the construction work with his/her own staff. The term 'fast track construction' is used when the brief demands that construction begin before the design work has been completed. Thus design progresses parallel with construction.

MANAGEMENT CONSTRUCTION

'Management construction' is when a contractor is appointed to a construction project at the preconstruction stage and is paid a fee to manage and deliver the project. The fee is on a percentage basis and relates to the project's costs and fixed overheads. All the work is carried out by subcontractors (work package contractors), who are selected and appointed by the management contractor in consultation with the client and his/her professional advisers.

BUILD-OPERATE-TRANSFER

'Build-operate-transfer' (BOT) contracts are design, build and management contracts that include a contract for the operating by the contractor of the facilities to be built. This method has been increasingly applied to the realization of public facilities such as toll roads, bridges, water and sewer systems, airports, ports and prisons. In a BOT project, the public authority grants a promoter, sometimes known as a concessionaire, the right to construct, finance, operate and maintain a facility (Menheere and Bol, 1995).

CONSTRUCTION MANAGEMENT AND PROJECT MANAGEMENT

In construction management, which is a particular form of project management, the construction manager (a person or a firm) co-ordinates the actions of the client, designers, contractors and suppliers, and co-operates with the authorities. The construction manager acts as the client's agent, issuing contracts for a fee. Whereas construction management is restricted to construction, project management, which may be a temporary assignment or an independent profession, includes other activities aimed at realizing usually complex projects (Reiss, 1994). The managers may be construction experts or they may specialize in project management. Sometimes the project managers form a temporary business entity to realize a project.

International project management for large projects requires powerful and versatile project planning, communication, information processing, decision support and control techniques (Tuman Jr, 1984). Project management can be paid on either a lump-sum or fee plus costs basis (Levy, 1994).

RELATIONAL CONTRACTING

Relational contracting (also known as 'long-term partnering' or 'collaborative contracting') is another of the procurement methods that differ from the traditional. In the context of the construction industry, it entails a long-term affiliation between the contractor and the client. Naturally, this can only happen when the client has projects to be executed either continuously or repeatedly, and for this reason it is primarily practised by large organizations. Examples in the USA are associations between DuPont and Fluor Daniel, between Shell Oil and R.M. Parsons, and between Union Carbide and Bechtel (Alsagoff and McDermott, 1994). Relational contracting is also often used in Japan. Architects are usually not too enthusiastic about management contract forms that deprive them of their traditional position, but clients and contractors tend to favour the new methods (Chan, 1994).

DEFECT AND CONFLICT MANAGEMENT

DEFECT, DAMAGE AND FAILURE: CONFLICT MANAGEMENT

Quality management was described in Chapter 2 and durability and degradation of materials and structures was looked at in Chapter 5.

Construction (and design) firms should adopt a management system that is focused on minimizing accidents, if possible reducing them to zero (Levitt and Samuelson, 1993). But even with a culture of zero accidents and a leadership that is focused on safety, proper use and maintenance of equipment and quality management, defects may still occur and construction firms must be able to deal with them adequately (CIB, 1996).

The size of a risk depends on the probability of failure and the magnitude of the consequences of failure, and can be quantified by appropriate methods. The direct costs of the Chernobyl disaster were US$4–5 billion, the indirect costs amounted to US$20 billion and there were also many hidden costs.

Errors and omissions can lead to defects, some of which can result in damage. Serious defects and damage can cause failure of a building or its parts (Knocke, 1993). While damage usually entails a monetary loss, a mere defect does not. Damage is usually a cause of claim, but the legal definition of damage may preclude compensation for minor defects. Acknowledged good quality has a market value. Defects, damage, disputes and conflicts blemish the image of a contractor or designer. It is therefore desirable that such problems are settled as quickly as possible. This does not mean taking over the responsibility that properly belongs to others, but it is senseless to prolong a dispute if a conflict can be resolved at minimal or even no cost. Amicable dispute resolution, or out-of-court methods such as arbitration, are frequently sought options.

A new discipline called building pathology has taken on the knowledge about defects. Technical experts have evolved who specialize in analysing defects and recommending remedies. The non-specialized architect, engineer or builder should not, however, simply leave these matters to such experts. On the contrary, practitioners should increase their own understanding of the factors that affect durability. While it is impossible to eliminate defects completely, it is possible to make advance economic provision against damage and risks. There are various methods for this purpose.

CONDITION ASSESSMENT OF BUILDINGS AND DEFECT ANALYSIS

Systematic inspection, maintenance, repair and periodic condition surveys ensure that degradation is discovered early and appropriate actions are taken to prevent, arrest, or at least slow down such processes (Verhoef, 1988; Kondo, Kuno and Osawa, 1994; Nakamura, Tokaido and Sakai, 1994). Defects can be detected during inspection, and there are sometimes advance signs, but defects can also surface without warning. For managers of a large stock of buildings, condition inspection should be a planned and systematic activity. There are situations in which the condition of buildings must be assessed because certain common features have given cause for concern, e.g. after an earthquake, fire or explosion. Based on past experience, guidelines have been devised for the methodology of such investigations. The purpose of these assessments is to verify whether the structures will continue to function safely, economically and efficiently, or whether repair or demolition is called for.

In the UK, about 160 000 dwellings were built using various large panel construction systems after the Second World War. The Building Research Establishment investigated the structural adequacy and durability of these buildings and found that no large panel building exhibited signs of structural distress sufficient to give concern for the safety of the occupants, nor has it received any reports of a large panel building failing to sustain the loads required in service, including fire loading. At the same time, cases of cracking and spalling of concrete seemed likely to occur in increasing numbers, which could present a hazard from falling debris (BRE, 1991). Similar investigations into large panel system buildings have been carried out in other countries and formed the basis of repair programmes.

Some individuals and organizations have gained a good deal of experience of defects, including their analysis and methods of repair. The collected experience is sometimes stored in databases and/or published. Some experts specialize in certain types of defects, such as those caused by earthquakes, fire, noise, or heat and moisture problems (Salvadori, 1980; Levy and Salvadori, 1992; Hermans, 1995; Priestley, Seible and Calvi, 1996). Spectacular fires, earthquakes and collapses are always studied in great detail in order to define technical, legal and financial responsibility and to draw lessons for the future. One notorious event in 1968 was when a large panel building collapsed at Ronan Point in London after a gas explosion. This led to the identification of the 'progressive collapse' phenomenon and the requirement for codes to include appropriate design measures to prevent it. On 17 June, 1980, a walkway collapsed during the inauguration festivities of the Kansas City Regency Hotel, killing 114 people and injuring more than 200. The subsequent investigation showed that the original design of the connections had failed to satisfy the code and that the walkways would not have collapsed under the actual load had the contractor not changed the connections in the course of execution.

These catastrophic events are just two examples from the many actual and possible failures and defects. To identify and analyse them, various technical methods and instruments have been introduced, including field tests, laboratory tests and control calculations. Various diagnostic aids such as diagnostic charts and matrices, fault and diagnostic trees, expert systems and case-based systems have been developed (Watson and Abdullah, 1994). A new tool for inspecting the exterior condition of wall or roof surfaces is computer image processing (Martin *et al.*, 1988). Robots have also been developed for the inspection of wall surfaces. Thermography is used to find heat bridges and inequalities in heat insulation. Practical experience and theoretical research show that the transition of a structure from a satisfactory to an unsatisfactory condition may be either gradual or abrupt. The actual condition is sometimes not quite clear, and so expert opinion often differs.

MANAGEMENT OF BUILDINGS AND FACILITIES

A NEW PROFESSION IS BORN

After the Second World War, the main concern for most European countries was the serious shortage of buildings, and the construction industry concentrated on new buildings. This situation changed drastically around 1980, when the continually growing construction volume was halted or even reversed; demand became stagnant or diminished. On the other hand, the existing large stock of buildings required more maintenance, repair and renewal, and therefore careful management, which had to be organized by the owners of the buildings. The management of building assets includes continuous and periodic surveys of the stock's condition, planned maintenance, and execution of planned and emergency repairs, plus management of administrative and financial affairs. Ageing of the building stock causes deterioration in its condition that can usually be rectified by maintenance. In time, buildings become obsolete or ineffective, and decisions then have to be made about whether they should be renovated or demolished and replaced.

'Facilities management' is a new concept of building management that began in the USA and has now spread to other countries (Barrett, 1995). 'Facilities' are defined as buildings, grounds, utilities and equipment placed in buildings, such as elevators, heating systems, furniture, computers, medical equipment, transport machinery at airports, and so on (Regterschot, 1990). Facilities management co-ordinates functions that were previously managed by various departments or individuals. Its key goals are (Haugen, 1994a):

- to make optimal use of the facilities available and to improve their composition
- to minimize operating costs
- to contribute to higher productivity and effectiveness of organizations.

The facilities of an organization may be restricted to one single building, and this may be relatively simple, or sophisticated. The facilities may comprise a number of buildings at one location, such as a university campus or an airport, or they may consist of several buildings at different places, perhaps growing in number, as in the case of multinational companies. At the lower end, facilities management may not even require a full-time manager. At the other, facilities management may be in the hands of a large structured organization that accepts contracts for integrated or specialized (restricted) facility management. Some multinational corporations, such as General Motors, Ford, IBM, Philips, Royal Dutch/Shell, each have a total personnel of several hundred thousand and total assets of over US$100 billion. Facilities management, understandably, is a complex activity for such companies. This also explains the growing number of facility management companies, some of which are quite large. The company Johnson Controls IFM (Integrated Facility Management), for example, has a staff of 55 000.

In addition to the usual participants in building construction (i.e. clients, designers, contractors, occupants), others interested in facilities are interior decorators and furniture manufacturers.

FUNCTIONAL ACTIVITIES OF FACILITIES MANAGEMENT

The various functional activities of facilities management can be organized under four major management control units:

- property management
- facilities planning
- facilities operations and maintenance
- facilities support services.

Property management is concerned with real estate, defined as land, structures and equipment. It includes strategic property management, acquisition, disposal and operation of real estate, administration and possibly government relations.

The basic responsibilities of facilities planning are:

- policy-making for fixed assets
- co-ordinating construction and the use of spaces
- consulting on maintenance operations and user requirements.

The specific goals of maintenance and operations activities are:

- to optimize the performance capability of facilities
- to ensure that maintenance and operations are realized in the most effective way
- to implement programmes to conserve energy and other resources, reduce risks and hazards, and maintain the required quality of the facilities
- to manage the analysis and audit functions of maintenance and operations.

Facility support services take care of security, safety, telecommunications, traffic, parking, transportation, mail services and distribution functions.

THE PRACTICE OF FACILITIES MANAGEMENT

Building asset management must make decisions on how maintenance, repair and renewal should be carried out. This task can be executed by in-house staff, or contracted out on a one-off or permanent basis.

'Outsourcing' means the transfer of a task or tasks by the building management to some other organization, e.g. maintenance, cleaning, catering, HVAC operations, security, gardening, mail services, payroll and recruitment. The outsourcing of non-core activities that might otherwise overburden key staff has recently become more common (Magee, 1988).

Facilities management requires technical (architectural, engineering) and management (financial, administrative) skills. It also includes leadership functions for co-ordinating an organization's internal and external relations. Facilities managers are therefore recruited from various professions. As facilities management emerges as an independent profession, some courses have started on the subject, and national and international professional associations have been created. Two such associations are the International Facilities Management Association (IFMA) and the European Facilities Management Association (EuroFM). IFMA was the first and was established in the USA. Although it now has members outside the USA, its membership is primarily from North America. As its name implies, EuroFM is basically European.

SUMMARY

Over the past 100 years, management in industry has emerged as a scientific discipline, with many new ideas such as ensuring competitive advantage, down-sizing, de-layering, concentration on the core business and human aspects, and re-engineering. Management in construction, on the other hand, has always been based on experience and organizational talent. In the twentieth century, construction has borrowed various methods from industry, such as the critical path method. It also developed some specific management methods, such as procurement (contracting), defect and conflict management, and working with various forms of company alliances. Construction has begun to apply up-to-date information technologies, data management and client/server systems. Great efforts are being made to devise integrated information systems that can be used by different clients, designers, general contractors and subcontractors.

The term 'facility' is used to designate buildings together with the land, technical services and functional equipment of the user. 'Facility management' is a new field that is broadening the scope of management. The changes in management and information work are another factor transforming construction into a modern industry.

BIBLIOGRAPHY

Akintoye, A. (1994a) Design and build: a survey of construction contractors' views., *Construction Management and Economics*, **2**, 155–63.

Akintoye, A. (1994b) Design and build procurement method in the UK construction industry. In S. Rowlinson (ed.), *East Meets West*, CIB Publication 175, 1–10.

Alsagoff, S. A. and McDermott, P. (1994) Relational contracting: a prognosis for the UK construction industry? In S. Rowlinson (ed.), *East Meets West* CIB Publication 175, 11–19.

Alshawi, M. and Underwood, J. (1996) Applying object-oriented analysis to the integration of design and construction, *Automation in Construction*, May, 105–21.

Atre, S. (1980) *Data Base Structured Techniques for Design, Performance, and Management*, John Wiley & Sons.

Atre, S. (1992) *Distributed Databases, Cooperative Processing, and Networking*, McGraw-Hill Inc.

Bacharach, M. (1976) *Economics and the Theory of Games and Economic Behaviour*, Princeton University Press.

Barnes, R. M. (1968) *Motion and Time Study*, John Wiley & Sons.

Barrett, P. and Hoxley, M. (1993) The client-professional relationship. In *CIB W 65 Symposium Proceedings*, 15–22 September, 512–23.

Barrett, P. (1994) Motivational profiles for construction professionals. In *CIB W 65 Symposium Proceedings*, 641–51.

Barrett, P. (ed.), (1995) *Facilities Management towards Best Management*, Blackwell Science.

Benson, B. (1970) *Critical Path Methods in Building Construction*, Prentice-Hall.

Betts, M. and Ofori, G. (1992) Strategic planning for competitive advantage in construction. *Construction Management and Economics*, **10**. 511–32.

Betts, M. *et al.* (1995) *A Process-Based Study of an IT Research Research Work Plan*, University of Salford, Construct IT.

Bol, A. J. *et al.* (1995) *Case Studies*, TU Delft.

Bontempo, C. J. and Saracco, C. M. (1995) *Database Management Principles and Products*, Prentice Hall PTR.

Bowen, B., Charette, R. P., Marshall, H. E. (1992) UNIFORMAT II, *Recommended Classification for Building Elements and Related Sitework*, NIST Special Publication 841.

BRE (1991) *The Structural Adequacy and Durability of Large Panel System Dwellings*, Part 1 and Part 2.

Bresnen, M. (1990) *Organising Construction: Project Organisation and Matrix Management*, Routledge.

Burns, S. A. *et al.* (1996) The LP/IP hybrid method for construction times-cost trade-off analysis, *Construction Management and Economics*, May, 265–76.

Callahan, M. T., Quackenbush, D. G. and Rowing, J. E. (1992) *Construction Project Scheduling*, McGraw-Hill International.

Chan, A. P. C. (1994) Design and build procurement method in the UK construction industry. In S. Rowlinson (ed.), *East Meets West*, CIB Publication 175, 27–33.

Chan, K. W. and Lai, W. C. (1994) A comparison between growth in labour productivity in the construction industry and the economy, *Construction Management and Economics*, **12**, 183–5.

CIB (1993) *CIB Master List*, CIB Report Publication 18, Rotterdam.

CIB (1996) *CIB 196: The Origin, Incidence and Resolution of Conflict in Construction*, CIB Publication 196.

Coskunoglu, O. and Moore, A. W. (1987) *An Analysis of the Building, Renewal Problem*. USA-CERL Technical Report P-87/11.

Debras, Ph. *et al.* (1995) Elaboration des documents textuels associés à un projet de construction, *Cahiers du CSTB*, Cahier 2796, April.

Fabrycky, W. J. and Jorgensen, P. E. (1966) *Operations Economy: Industrial Applications of Operations Research*, Englewood Cliffs, NY, Prentice-Hall.

Gold, M., Campbell, A. and Alexander, M. (undated) *Corporate-Level Strategy: Creating Value in the Multibusiness Company*, Ashridge Strategic Management Centre.

Gordon, G. (1969) *System simulation*, Englewood Cliffs, NY, Prentice-Hall.

Haftka, R. T. and Kamat, M. P. (1985) *Elements of Structural Optimization*, Martinus Nijhoff Publishers.

Hall, A. D. (1962) *A Methodology for Systems Engineering*, Princeton, D. Van Nostrand Company.

Haugen, T. (1994a) Total build – an integrated approach to facilities management, FM in Scandinavia. In *Architectural Management: Practice and Research. Proceedings of CIB W 96 Symposium in Nottingham. UK, 17–18 September 1994*.

Haugen, T. (1994b) Linking design and construction to facilities management by information systems. In: *Architectural Management: Practice and Research. Proceedings of CIB W 96 Symposium in Nottingham, UK, 17–18 September 1994*.

Hermans, M. (1995) *Deterioration Characteristics of Building Components: A Data Collecting Model to Support Performance Management*. Doctoral Thesis, TU Eindhoven.

Herzberg, F., Mausner, B. and Snyderman, B. (1959) *The Motivation to Work*, John Wiley & Sons, New York.

Herzberg, F. (1966) *Work and the Nature of Man*, World Publishing Company, Cleveland.

Hillebrandt, P. M. (1990) Management of the building firm. In *Proceedings of CIB Symposium in Sydney, Australia, 14–21 March 1990*, Vol. 6, 1–10.

Hisatomi, Y., Reismann, W. (1994) Design and construct: trend, challenge, improvement?, *Structural Engineering International*, **3**, 177–82.

Kanter, R. M. (1985) *The Change Masters: Corporate Entrepreneurs at Work*, Unwin, London.

Kanter, R. M. (1990) *When Giants Learn to Dance*, Touchstone, New York.

Kanter, R. M. (1992) *The Challenge of Organizational Change: How Companies Experience It*, Free Press New York.

Knocke, J. (ed.), (1993) *Post-Construction Liability*, E&FN Spon.

Kondo, T., Kuno, M. and Osawa S. (1994) Improvement of inspection process efficiency in building's exterior maintenance. In *Strategies and Technologies for Maintenance and Modernisation of Building. Proceedings of CIB Symposium, Tokyo, Japan*, 471–8.

Lansley, P. (1987) Corporate strategy and survival in the UK construction industry, *Construction Management and Economics*, **5**, 141–55.

Levitt, R. E. and Samuelson, N. M. (1993) *Construction Safety Management*, John Wiley & Sons.

Levy, M. and Salvadori, M. (1992) *Why Buildings Fall Down*, WW Norton & Company, New York-London.

Levy, S. M. (1994) *Project Management in Construction*, McGraw-Hill.

Linder, M. (1994) *Projecting Capitalism: A History of the Internationalization of the Construction Industry* Greenwood Press.

Magee, G. H. (1988) *Facilities Maintenance Management*, Means R. S. Company, Kingston, Massachusetts.

Martin, J. W. *et al.* (1988) *An Automated Maintenance Management Program: Part I: Quantitative Assessment of the Exterior Condition of Metal Buildings and Roofing Systems via Computer Image Processing.* NBIR 88–3719 Publication, Gaithersburg, Maryland.

Maslow, A. H. (1943) A theory of human performance, *Psychological Review*, July, 370–96.

Maslow, A. H. (1968) *Toward a psychology of being*, Princeton, Van Nostrand Company.

Masterman, J. W. E. (1992) *An Introduction to Building Procurement Systems*, E & FN Spon.

Maynard, H. B. (1970) *Handbook of Modern Manufacturing Management*, McGraw-Hill Book Company, New York.

Maynard, H. B. (1973) *Industrial Engineering Handbook*, McGraw-Hill Book Company, New York.

Melles, B. and Wamelink, J. W. F. (1993) *Production Control in Construction*, Delft University Press, Delft.

Menheere, S. C. M. (ed.) and Bol, A. J. (1995) *Build-Operate-Transfer*, TU Delft (in Dutch).

Nakamura, S., Tokaido, S. and Sakai, S. (1994) Automatic diagnostic system for tiled wall structures. In *Strategies and Technologies for Maintenance and Modernisation of Building, Proceedings of CIB Symposium, Tokyo, Japan*, 651–8.

Newcombe, R. *et al.* (1990) *Construction Management*, 2 vols, Mitchell + CIOB.

Niemann, K. D. (1995) *Client/Server Architektur*, Verlag Vierweg.

O' Brien, J. J. (1984) *CPM in Construction Management*, McGraw-Hill Book Company.

O' Neill, J. J. (1989) *Management of Industrial Construction Projects*, Nichols Publishing, New York.

Peters, T. J. and Waterman, Jr. R. H. (1982) *In Search of Excellence*, Harper & Row, New York etc.

Porter M. (1979) How competitive forces shape strategy. In *Havard Business Review*, March-April 1979, 137–46.

Porter, M. E. (1980) *Competitive Strategy; Techniques for Analyzing Industries and Competitors*, Free Press, New York.

Porter, M. E. (1985) *Competitive Advantage; Creating and Sustaining Superior Performance*, Free Press New York.

Porter, M. E. (1986) *Competition in Global Industries*, Harvard Business School Press, Boston.

Pries, F. (1995) *Innovatie in de bouwnijverheid*, Doctoral Thesis, Rotterdam, in Dutch, with summary in English.

Priestley, M. J. N., Seible, F. and Calvi, G. M. (1996) *Seismic Design and Retrofit of Bridges*, John Wiley & Sons.

Regterschot, J. (1990) 'Facility management in changing organizations' building maintenance and modernization. In *Proceedings of International Symposium on Property Maintenance and Modernisation*, CIB W 70, Singapore.

Reiss, G. (1994) *Project Management Demystified*, E&FN Spon.

Ruley, J. D. *et al.* (1995) *Networking Windows NT 3.51*, John Wiley & Sons.

Sadri, S. L. and Kangari, R. (1993) Integrated information systems in construction: strategic technology. In *CIB W 65 Symposium Proceedings*, Vol. 1, 193–9.

Salvadori, M. (1980) *Why Buildings Stand Up*, W. W. Norton & Company, New York, London.

Sebestyén, G. (1993) Planning repetitive construction: comment, *Construction Management and Economics*, **11**, 487–8.

Spencer, K. L. (1996) *NT Server: Management and Control*, Prentice Hall.

Stevens, J. D. (1990) *Techniques for Construction Network Scheduling*, McGraw-Hill International.

Taylor, F. W. (1911) *The Principles of Scientific Management*, Harper & Brothers, New York.

Tuman J. Jr. (1984) Technological revolution in international project management, *IABSE Journal*, J-22/84.

UN (1965) *Effect of Repetition on Building Operations and Processes on Site*, United Nations, New York.

UN ECE (1963) *Cost, Repetition, Maintenance: Related Aspects of Building Prices*, UN ECE, Geneva.

van Bezooijen, P. F. (1991) *The Economic Strength of the Building and Construction Industry in the Netherlands*, CIB W82 Working Paper.

Verhoef, L. G. W. (ed.) (1988) *Soiling and Cleaning of Building Facades*, RILEM Report, Chapman & Hall.

von Neumann J. and Morgenstern, O. (1944) *The Theory of Games and Economic Behaviour*, Princeton University Press.

von Thienen, W. (1995) *Client/Server*, Verlag Vierweg.

Wagner, H. M. (1967) *Principles of Operations Research*, Englewood Cliffs, NY, Prentice Hall.

Watson, I. and Abdullah, S. (1994) Diagnosing building defects using case-based reasoning. In *Proceedings of CIB W70 Symposium Tokyo, University of Salford*, pp. 621–6.

Some spatial and social aspects 8

INTRODUCTION

Most agricultural or manufactured products are moved from the place of production to the place of consumption. By contrast, buildings and structures are bound to the ground. Cities are not just a conglomeration of buildings, they create the ambience and framework for social life. Much of the spatial and social aspects of construction lead into non-technological fields, but their impact on construction justifies a short discussion on their importance.

Most structures are constructed above ground. Construction therefore creates and rearranges the built environment and thus has a strong spatial aspect. In modern societies, most people live and work in buildings, move between buildings and communicate with each other from various distances in an environment that is largely created and recreated by construction. In earlier times, the spatial impact of buildings was restricted to their immediate surroundings. The expansion of built-up areas in cities was limited by the modes of transport of the time, e.g. walking, horseback, or horse-driven. With industrialization in the nineteenth century, the suburbs and their population of commuters began to grow. The use of cars and the introduction of suburban trains began to reduce the effect of distance. We are now experiencing further commuter expansion through air transport, high-speed trains and telecommunications. Electricity, oil, gas, water, and above all information can be swiftly transported several thousand kilometres. Places within continents and on different continents are linked by various networks.

All of this has affected the construction industry, which has now grown from a local or domestic craft into an international industry. Construction firms used to serve local needs almost exclusively. Regulations often protected local and domestic markets from external competition. Today, regionalization and globalization have resulted in

Fig. 8.1   Human community in attractive natural environment, Positano, Italy. *Source:* F. Pogány (1960) *Terek es utcák müvészete*, Müszaki Könyvkiadó, Budapest.

the expansion of the market. The possibility of working outside the home market is increased by the various forms of association between regional or global companies and local or domestic firms.

Throughout history, the objective of creating a stable urban community was often combined with the concept of the 'ideal city'. The concept of urban planning can be traced back to Plato and Aristotle, but conscious planning really only evolved around the end of the Middle Ages. In the fifteenth century, two Italian architects, Alberti and Filarete, prepared one of the first plans for a utopian future city, and many more followed, including one by Thomas More, published in 1516. Much later, a different type of utopia was proposed by Robert Owen, an English manufacturer. Such plans were usually based on ideas of social arrangements as well as geometric layout, but in practice life was seldom able to follow these plans.

By the twentieth century, the fundamental problems of housing were no longer technical but social ones. Although such problems also existed before, and were none the less acute, the twentieth century saw a change in the reaction of society to social injustice and housing needs. Increasingly, sociological research has embraced studies of life styles, analysis of time spent on various activities, participation of future occupants in design, assessment of dwelling alternatives, examination of the

Fig. 8.2　Human settlement with picturesquely cluttered buildings, Herrenberg, Schwarzwald, Germany. *Source:* F. Pogány (1960) *Terek es utcák müvészete*, Müszaki Könyvkiadó, Budapest.

housing needs of different groups (such as ethnic minorities, children, elderly people and people with disabilities), the relationship between dwellings and their occupants and the surrounding environment, and the composition and mix of families in neighbourhoods.

This increased interest in the social aspects of housing gave birth to 'housing research'. This discipline encompasses not only the technical/architectural problems but also the economic, financial and sociological problems of housing. The emergence of housing as part of sociological research established new links with the previously largely technical discipline of building research. In the USA, the so-called Chicago School of sociologists (R.E. Park, E.W. Burgess and others) studied the interrelationship of spatial arrangements and the functions of city districts, such as the core and the districts surrounding it. In the UK, the idea of Garden Cities and New Towns gave an impetus to such research.

Demographic matters have always influenced housing conditions and needs. The alarming population growth in eighteenth century England prompted Thomas Robert Malthus to publish his *Essay on the Principle of Population* in 1798, in which he predicted that natural population growth would surpass the food supply and recommended measures to reduce the birth rate. Malthus' theory was dismissed during the nineteenth century because of the strong belief in the power of science then prevailing, but has been resurrected in the twentieth century with the concept of growth limits and the need for sustainable development. Phenomena such as the decreasing size and changing composition of households, the ageing population, migration, segregation and desegregation, ethnic conflicts and others have also had an impact on housing, building and urban development. Increasing demographic and sociological problems have raised social awareness and called for responsibility from those engaged in the construction industry, the housing sector and city management, broadening the tasks of building, housing and urban research.

THE GLOBAL URBAN NETWORK

A GLOBAL SURVEY

Historically, a high birth rate was accompanied by a high mortality rate for both adults and infants. As a result, low natural growth meant that the world's population, estimated to be 250 million, 2000 years ago, increased only slowly until some 150 years ago. Growth accelerated in the eighteenth century, and the most recent population expansion started around 1950 as a result of a sharp reduction in mortality in developing countries, where the population growth is fastest. China's population, for example, has surpassed 1 thousand million, and India's is very close to it. This population growth was particularly fast in urban areas. In 1980, the world's urban population was 1 thousand million. The growth of cities should reflect increasing wealth, but sometimes it has been associated with poverty, social conflicts, unemployment and urban degradation. Four-fifths of the population in industrialized countries lives in cities. In developing countries, the urban population is still in the minority, but increasing fast. The economic importance of cities invariably exceeds their share of the population. As already mentioned, urbanization is fastest in the developing countries. The largest cities of the world are no longer New York and London, but Mexico City and São Paulo. In 1914, all the largest cities in the world were in industrialized countries; at the end of the 1980s, seven out of 10 were in developing countries and, according to estimates, within a few decades, Tokyo will be the only city among the world's 10 largest to be located in a present-day industrialized country.

Nevertheless, much of the world's population still lives in medium-sized and small settlements and in rural areas. In some cities in the less developed countries, population density exceeds that of cities in industrialized countries.

Despite hopes, the wealth gap between rich and poor countries persists. Despite the acknowledged imperfections of such indices as gross domestic product (GDP) and gross national product (GNP), these do reflect certain levels of economic development and wealth. The per capita indices of different countries range from over US$20 000 to below US$1000. Some countries have achieved healthy economic growth (particularly in South-East Asia and the Pacific region), but others have failed to grow, e.g. many African countries.

Bad economic conditions invariably lead to a reduction in the resources available for new construction, ultimately resulting in poor housing conditions, and giving families the impetus to emigrate. Domestic and international migration has become part of life in many countries. Across the world, the total number of migrants is near to 100 million, and their situation and future prospects are a cause for concern in many regions of the world. Gateway cities in Europe (such as Marseille, Paris, Amsterdam and Berlin) and on the west coast of the USA are particularly under pressure from immigration. Immigration can be a major component in formulating demand for construction (Sassen, 1994).

More than a thousand million people currently live and work in a degraded environment, without regular or adequate income, lacking acceptable shelter, clean water and rudimentary sanitation facilities. At the other end of the scale are the regions and cities that have become more affluent as a result of the progressing economy.

Finally, there has been much speculation about the future of working from home – so-called 'telecommuting' – and its impact on transport and other factors. The number of people working from home has increased in recent years in, for example, North America, but nowhere did the share of telecommuters as a proportion of the whole working population reach more than a few per cent. This trend therefore still has only a marginal impact on the most important aspects of urban life, although this may well change in the future.

URBAN PATTERN TRENDS

These days, medieval cities surrounded by walls and moats are just tourist attractions, nothing like our modern cities, which are open and linked by surface and air transport and telecommunications. Historical sites still attract people, but new functions can cause explosive growth, e.g. in tourist spots, technopoles, high-speed train stops and air hubs. New territorial units as growth corridors have also appeared.

Urban life and the development of cities have long been studied. In modern times cities have become standard-bearers of progress and also locations of conflicts. They continue to be studied by a great number of scholars and institutions (Newland, 1980; Brown and Jacobson, 1987). Previously, it was found that large centralized cities foster innovation and attract development. While this would seem still to hold some validity for some but not all central locations, network cities and growth corridors sometimes compete successfully with unicentric cities (Batten, 1992). Some cities, such as London, New York, Tokyo, Beijing, Moscow, São Paulo, Mexico City and Paris, have grown to the level of 'global cities' or 'Megalopolises' (Brotchie *et al.*, 1995). Others, such as Brussels, Frankfurt, Chicago, Milan and Amsterdam, are near to that level. There are a number of indicators that reflect the global character of a city. One of these is the number of large multinational companies that have located their headquarters there. In 1987, New York had 59 such companies , London 37, Tokyo 34, Paris 26, Chicago 18, Essen 18, Osaka 15, Los Angeles 14, Houston 11 and Pittsburg 10.

Countries, regions, cities, city centres and suburbs may develop, stagnate, or decline in different ways, and each is normally keen to ensure its own development. This leads to competition between the various territorial units of human settlement as they try to attract economic growth. Successful city marketing directly benefits landowners and commercial developers. Indirectly, it may also benefit the region and its inhabitants.

During the period of industrial (manufacturing) development, certain factors such as the location of raw materials and consumers, and transport conditions affected the growth or decline of regions. The classic theory of space allocation optimization found that the minimization of transport costs was of primary importance (Launhardt, 1882; Weber, 1929; Isard *et al.*, 1979). Later, the new mathematical methods of linear and dynamic programming were adapted for problems such as transport and investment costs, thereby serving as a basis for solving investment location problems. (At one time I myself devised new algorithms and computations for such problems for the creation of new prefabrication plants.)

These days, transport costs have become less important but a new universal theory on space location optimization is still awaited. Nevertheless, a number of factors that affect the choice of a site and hence the growth or decline of individual regions and cities have been identified. Since the Industrial Revolution, much of the urban growth that took place was a consequence of the development of manufacturing. Nowadays, at least in industrialized countries, employment in manufacturing is stagnating or declining, even if the volume of goods produced is stable. At the same time, manufacturing and commerce are using more product services such as advertising, consultancy, legal, finance and accountancy. Thus, services directly linked to business (also termed 'producer services') are growing fast in most developed countries. The society created by the consequent shift of employment has been termed 'post-industrial'. These changes began before the Second World War and have continued to grow since. In 1963, 35% of the labour force in the USA worked in goods production and 58% in services. By 1983, the figures had changed to 28%

and 68.5%, respectively. Similar changes occurred elsewhere, e.g. the UK, Germany and Japan (Brotchie, Hall and Newton, 1987).

The classification of a city may seem to be purely theoretical and without practical consequences, but a particular classification expresses the vitality or stagnation of a city, not at all a matter of indifference for the inhabitants of that city or the managers of its economy and government. The main classification indicators of a city are: its population and its change, the level of cultural life, and the presence of universities, airports, ports, important company headquarters, research, financial and information services, and press and publishing outlets. Another series of indicators has been identified for the classification of cities according to the quality of life they offer. These include indicators on criminality, general educational facilities and leisure possibilities.

A large number of trends has been identified as causing changes in the global urban network. One of these is the migration to regions with a better climate, which in the northern hemisphere usually means southwards. In Europe, the strengthening of the EU favours the central core over the peripheral regions where the disappearance of internal borders may therefore be favourable to such towns as Strasbourg and Aachen. The growing network of high-speed trains will favour the cities that are stops long these lines, as has been the case in Japan. It is not yet clear what impact the EU will have on cities such as Prague, Budapest and Frankfurt-on-Oder. Political changes such as the unification of Germany and the formation of new states from the former Yugoslavia, will inevitably affect the status of Berlin, Zagreb and Ljubljana.

THE TECHNOPOLES

The agglomeration of high-technology and R&D firms into one area is a phenomenon of recent decades. Silicon Valley in California was the first and best known, and it was followed by many others, such as Sophia Antipolis in the south of France, Tsukuba City in Japan and Hsinchu in Taiwan. Areas where such 'technopoles' or science cities emerge are rich in intellectual resources and create entrepreneurial and innovative environments. Several high-technology parks have expanded to become high-tech cities and later high-tech regions. Nevertheless, some highly developed regions do not seem to attract these firms in sufficient numbers, while others are more successful, such as in New York State where biotechnology firms are clustered.

Governments and municipalities are aware of the fact that high-tech firms contribute greatly to the modernization and affluence of their environment and are therefore keen to create favourable conditions to attract them. Technopoles, growth corridors and peripheral locations are generally much preferred by companies and supported by municipalities, but this raises problems for the city centres.

CITY CENTRES, SUBURBS AND GROWTH CORRIDORS

In highly developed countries, suburbs still grow faster than the city centres. Suburbs also seem to attract more economic activity, so that jobs are relocated from the metropolitan core to the periphery and beyond. City centres attempt to invest in new offices, hotels and hospitals in order to remain attractive. The competition of city centres and suburbs can be favourably synergic for both, or it can harm inner city development.

Commuting distances have tended to grow in recent decades. Most of the home to workplace journeys are centre-oriented, and metropolitan transport networks have developed with a hub-and-spoke pattern to serve commuters. As a consequence of the activities developing in the suburbs, suburb-to-suburb (intra-suburban) commuting is also growing, but this is, and will probably remain, small in relation to suburb-to-centre commuting. Despite the increasing distances, and the growth of single-occupant car commuting, commuting times in American cities have not increased much recently, generally averaging between 1.0 and 1.5 hours. Governments and local authorities are endeavouring to persuade commuters to switch to other forms of travel (multi-occupant car use, bicycle, bus, tram) but with only very limited success.

The inner cities in the industrialized countries are changing. They have either completely lost their residential function, or else have retained mainly low-income families as residents. At the same time, the city centre has been transformed into a place for shopping and services. Often the absence of local residents makes these centres unsafe after business hours. The structure of retailing also has an impact on cities. Open markets are still around in many parts of the world, but they are complemented by small shops, or in larger towns by high street shops and department stores. The most recent places for shopping are the suburban supermarkets (hypermarkets) and the shopping malls. Moreover, with the development of telecommunications, teleshopping has appeared.

Segregation and racial tension have taken hold of some North American cities in recent years, and this unrest has spread to some European towns. Technical measures in residential areas (such as fenced gardens, gates for cars to eliminate through-traffic, cul-de sacs, etc.) may be adopted, but the spread of crime and violence is best prevented by improving economic and social conditions.

Traditional cities had a clearly identifiable centre, surrounded by zones with equally well-defined functions. Modern American cities have developed along 'growth corridors' and the various functions have therefore become blurred. Larger metropolitan areas are tending to stagnate and even to decline, while smaller ones show the fastest rate of growth. Within larger urban areas, growth is moving away from the central areas to smaller, peripheral ones (Hall, 1985). Congestion, high land prices and rent levels in large cities have induced counter-urbanization (suburbanization, rurbanization, etc.) policies. In spite of this, cities seem to retain their functions and such trends may therefore prove to be of limited importance.

This brief survey demonstrates that patterns of growth and decline in the world's cities do not follow one single law, but that there are complex forces at work in the process that change in time and space.

INFRASTRUCTURE

In this book, the word 'infrastructure' is meant to include highways, roads, railways, tramlines, airports, water, gas and oil supply networks, solid waste and waste water treatment and disposal, electric power distribution, telecommunications and other similar municipal, metropolitan, regional or global services. Although there are very sophisticated infrastructure systems in several industrial countries, most of the world's population lives with inadequate transport, electricity, water and sanitation services.

The movement of people, materials, commodities and services constitutes the metabolism of cities and human society. The technical backbone for this is the municipal, national or global infrastructure, which has acquired increasing importance to the construction industry, and which now requires a great deal more experience and knowledge than was needed previously. When most of these facilities were first built, they were operated by governments, municipalities and various public or semi-public bodies. Recently, many have been privatized.

In order to mobilize private capital, infrastructure investments also develop as 'build-own-operate' (BOO) and 'Build-own-transfer' (BOT). There is a widespread wish to see improvements in infrastructure services in both the public and private sectors. It is to be hoped that conditions will improve, and that sooner or later resources will be made available so that the construction industry can satisfy the huge pent-up demand.

SURFACE AND UNDERGROUND TRANSPORT

In Chapter 1, we traced the development of the roads and railways from their beginnings up to the first half of the twentieth century. Here we consider the development since 1945.

The USA led the way to universal car ownership. In 1955, there were already 315 passenger cars per 1000 population in the USA, while there were 74 per 1000 in France, 71 per 1000 in the UK, and only 2 per 1000 in Japan. By 1985 the these figures had increased to 490 per 1000 in the USA, 415 in France, 387 in the UK, and 421 in Japan. Since then, ownership density has increased still further so that on average there is now more than one car per household in most industrialized countries (although obviously in fact some families own several cars while others don't own one at all).

This increased use of cars and other vehicular transport has led to large-scale highway construction which is now an extremely mechanized branch of the construction industry. The use of cars has also had an impact on several other aspects of modern life, including the need for repair garages, petrol stations and car parks. As a consequence, increasing amounts of land are occupied by moving or stationary vehicles or buildings connected with the development of the oil-extracting, petrochemical and car manufacturing industries. The design of roads has been enhanced by various structures, e.g. motorways, dual-carriageways, junctions, roundabouts and double-decker expressways. The enthusiasm for the car has been somewhat dampened by new problems in road transport such as congestion, escalation of oil prices and concern for the environment (Buchanan *et al.*, 1963). It would be unrealistic to try to stop the development of road transport, but attempts are being made to develop smaller cars (ultralight, narrow-lane, urban cars and subcars) with a higher fuel efficiency and to introduce alternative forms of transport.

For some time the nineteenth century was considered to be the century of railway construction and the twentieth to be the century of roads and road transport, but recently efforts have been made to switch some cargo from road transport to the railways or river, maritime and air transport. This has increased the demand for constructions of various sorts needed by these alternative transport sectors.

The construction of underground railway lines began in London. The first line in continental Europe was built in Budapest in 1895. Work started on the Moscow underground in 1932, and there are now about 50 large towns and cities worldwide with an underground railway network. The street-car or tramway is now also experiencing a renaissance in many cities.

With the modernization of railways, these too are receiving attention again. The speed of rail transport is increasing, the newest generation being the high-speed trains (HST). Such trains require better, stronger rail lines and transform the pattern of connections by making fewer stops along their routes. Steam locomotives are gradually disappearing and being replaced by oil or electric traction. Some steam railways are preserved as tourist attractions, however (Ransom, 1973). Japan built the first high-speed railway, the Tokaido Shinkansen line between Tokyo and Osaka, on which train speeds exceed 200 km per hour. It was opened in 1964 and was later followed by other high-speed lines: the Sanyo line, opened in 1975, and the Tohoku and Joetsu lines, opened in 1982. By 1985, the latter two had been extended to Tokyo. In Europe, Paris and Lyons were the first cities to be connected by a high-speed train (known in French as the *train à grande vitesse*, TGV). It can travel up to 275 km per hour. In the 1990s, such lines were extended or built in Japan and France, and other countries began preparations for similar services. The first international network of TGV services is the so-called PBKAL network, comprising nine high-speed rail connections between Paris, Brussels, Cologne, Amsterdam and London. Eurostar is the high-speed train service that has connected London, Paris and Brussels via the Channel Tunnel since 1994. The tunnel cost £11 thousand million (US$17 billion) to construct, more than double the original estimate. Since the first high-speed railway lines were built in Japan and France, the cities served by those links have developed faster than those not served by them.

It is possible to achieve high train speeds with the use of magnetic levitation (maglev) technology. Two variants have been developed: one in Germany, using an attraction system; and one in Japan with a repulsion system. Both could operate at speeds of 400–500 km per hour, but magnetic trains need special tracks, which makes approaching city centres more costly. In Europe, the first magnetic railway line will be built between Berlin and Hamburg at a cost of US$6 thousand million. It is planned that it will operate at a maximum speed of 425 km per hour. In Japan, a maglev line will be built between Tokyo and Osaka to relieve the saturated Tokaido Shinkansen. It will follow a different route from the latter. Once again, it is expected that cities served by maglev lines will develop faster than others.

Depending on the distances covered and the speed of the service, high-speed trains can successfully compete with air travel. The USA, Japan, Korea, China and Taiwan are all planning new high-speed railway lines. The 1300 km long Beijing–Shanghai rail link is estimated to cost more than US$11 billion. An even more ambitious project is proposed to link Beijing and Kowloon, a distance of 2400 km. The project would require the construction of 500 bridges and 126 tunnels and could keep 130 000 workers busy for some time. According to recent information, the Beijing–Hong Kong railroad has been completed but not yet as a high-speed link.

A new idea for future high-speed rail links is to put them underground. The trains would be able to travel at a speed of around 500 km per hour, would save land, conserve energy and be highly economical (Nijkamp and Perrels, 1991). Plans for such trains to pass under Paris and the Alps have been prepared (CSTB, 1994).

Bridges and tunnels are an essential part of certain lines and they have recently been constructed with imposing lengths and spans. Long bridges and tunnels, such as Japan's 54 km long Seikan tunnel, of which 16 km is under water, or the Channel Tunnel, have changed spatial relations and distances. Microtunnels are service tunnels with a small internal diameter. They are built (and also inspected and repaired) partly by trenchless construction and unmanned mechanical methods such as pipe-jacking (Stein, Möllers and Bielicki, 1989; CSTB, 1992). Well over 1 million kilometres of microtunnels are built in the world each year, in addition to the millions of service connections to houses, which provide work to many construction firms.

Following the construction of undersea links between the islands of Japan, and between England and France, Denmark embarked on a connection between the islands of Sjælland and Fyn. It will be 18 km in length and will include the longest span suspension bridge in Europe, with 260 m high pylons. Another immense project is the connection of the Japanese islands of Honshu and Shikoku by three arteries, two of which will contain railway lines. In total, 27 bridges will be built, one of which will be the Akashi–Kaikyo suspension bridge mentioned in chapters 3 and 6.

To raise the productivity of transport, the use of containers was developed, offering the ability to transfer containers from one type of transport to another. This led to the establishment of container ports. For bulk goods (coal, ore, etc.) and oil and gas, highly mechanized transfer methods have been developed and the scale of operations (the size of tankers etc.) greatly increased.

Transport has become an important sector within national and global economies and is now served by sophisticated information technology.

AIR TRAFFIC

The world's air traffic has greatly increased recently and is set to continue to grow. The world's largest airports are listed in Table 8.1, together with the number of passengers in 1993. If the number of international passengers only is counted, London Heathrow heads the list, followed by Frankfurt, Hong Kong, Paris Charles de Gaulle and New York Kennedy.

Kennedy Airport is now 40 years old and is due to be drastically renewed and modernized at a cost of US$4.3 thousand million. New big airports are Tokyo's Narita and Osaka's Kansai. The latter was built on an

Table 8.1   World's largest airports (passenger numbers, 1993)

Chicago O'Hare	65 million
San Francisco	62 million
Dallas/Fort Worth	50 million
Los Angeles	48 million
Atlanta	48 million
London Heathrow	48 million
Tokyo Haneda	42 million
Frankfurt	32 million
Miami	29 million
New York Kennedy	27 million
Newark	27 million
Phoenix	26 million
Paris Charles de Gaulle	25 million
Hong Kong	25 million

artificial island, 5 km out in Osaka Bay. The new Hong Kong Chek Lap Kok Airport and related projects form the largest single public works currently under way in the world. It is being built on a 5 × 3.5 km artificial island and will be linked to central Hong Kong by a 34 km rail and road connection using a 1377 m long main span suspension bridge and tunnels. The total cost is budgeted at over US$20 thousand million. More than half the world's dredging fleet came to Hong Kong for the land reclamation work. Consisting of a consortium from six countries, the fleet dredged up 150 million m³ of clay and mud.

WATER ENGINEERING STRUCTURES

Waterways are used for shipping, irrigation, flood prevention and, recently, for electric power generation. As a result, several large rivers, river basins and estuaries e.g. the Rhine, Nile, Amazon have changed and their future is a problem for hydraulic engineering. Transportation on smaller rivers and canals has lost some of its earlier importance, although there are attempts to revive it (Ransom, 1979). On the other hand, maritime and large river transport has grown and many ports, such as Rotterdam, Antwerp, Yokohama, Hong Kong and Singapore have been greatly enlarged as a result (Dolman and van Ettinger, 1990).

Dams are barriers built across rivers or estuaries to control the flow of water or to collect and retain water for other uses. The simplest dams are the earth- and rock-fill structures. More labour-intensive dams are the solid masonry gravity, the solid masonry arch and the arch-gravity dams (e.g. the Hoover Dam). Projects on rivers and coasts usually have a combined purpose: flood prevention, shipping, energy generation and irrigation. The Three Gorges Dam on the Yangtze River in China will be 100 m high when it is finished early in the next century, with a total electricity generation capacity of 18 000 MW, eight times that of the Aswan Dam on the Nile (Pearce, 1995). Large dams are perhaps the most voluminous structures. Most of the world's highest dams were built after 1945 with the exception of the Hoover Dam across the Colorado River in Nevada, which was built in 1936 at a height of 221 m. The environmental impact of large dams is often controversial, and more attention will be devoted to this in future. Some of the highest dams are listed in Table 8.2.

Most dams are of medium size. In 1990, there were more than 36 000 dams over 15 m high in the countries that supplied data. Those with the most were, in descending order, China (19 000), the USA (5000), Japan (2000) and India (1000). The total number of dams of all sizes in the world probably exceeds 500 000. There are also many embankments, the two largest being in Argentina on the Parana River at Chapeton, 300 million m³ and at Pati, 240 million m³.

Fig. 8.3 Hisayoshi Dam: interrelation of nature and man-made structure, Ohbayashi, Japan. *Source:* Courtesy of Company Ohbayashi.

Following the disastrous floods in The Netherlands in 1953, the Delta Project was launched and is now completed. One last storm surge-barrier was built across the Nieuwe Waterweg with two box-shaped arch-gates, each 203 m long and 22 m high which swing closed to stop the flow of water.

Although they are mainly useful, dams and dikes sometimes have an adverse environmental effect. Some of the problems are: water eutrophization, increasing salt concentration, decline of fish reproduction, prevention of fish migration, accumulation or loss of sedimentation, groundwater level changes, weather effects, impact on fauna and flora, etc. Consequently, it is now an absolute requirement to study the proba-

Table 8.2 World's highest dams since 1945 (height, completion date)

Rogun, Vaksh River, Tadzhikistan, earth fill dam (335 m, 1987)
Nourek, Vaksh River, Tadzhikistan, earth fill with clay core (317 m, 1980)
Grande Dixence, Dixence River Valais, Switzerland, concrete gravity dam (285 m, 1962)
Inguri, Inguru River, Georgia, concrete arch dam (272 m, 1980)
Sayany Yenisey River, Siberia, Russia, composite arch and gravity dam (245 m, 1980)

ble impact of all environment-related projects in great detail before beginning them.

WATER SUPPLY AND WASTE DISPOSAL

More than half the earth's surface is covered by water, of which most is salt water; only 2.5% of the total is fresh water. The worldwide distribution of water is unequal. In wet, lightly populated countries such as Canada, per capita water resources amount to more than 100 000 m³ per year. In dry countries, such as Saudi Arabia, Israel and Libya, the per capita water resources total fewer than 1000 m³ per year. There is now a water shortage in several countries and this is likely to be further aggravated in the future. In Libya, a 4000 km long water supply pipeline has been built at great cost to bring water from underground aquifers in the Sahara to Benghazi on the Mediterranean coast. It was heralded as the 'Great Universal Project' for the twenty-first century.

Among the urban poor of the developing countries, fewer than 30% of households are connected to a water supply and fewer than 20% have access to adequate sanitation. In the cities of developing countries, 25% of the population depend on water vendors and polluted open streams for their drinking water. Overuse of groundwater has resulted in severe land subsidence in Mexico City, Bangkok, Houston and Venice. Some areas of Mexico City have subsided by as much as 9 m. In such countries, polluted water is responsible for 80% of diseases and 33% of deaths; 1.5% of children die before the age of 5 years from diarrhoea caused by polluted drinking water. Over 2 million tonnes of human excrement is produced daily in cities around the world. Less than 2% of it is adequately treated, the rest is discharged directly into water courses. Waterborne diseases account for more than 4 million infant and child deaths per year in developing countries.

The supply of water sanitation, and solid and liquid waste disposal require large investments. According to a study by Brown and Jacobson (1987), the average urban resident in the USA uses approximately 568 l of water and generates 454 l of sewage per day. Where adequate infrastructure exists, household waste water is usually treated in municipal plants, although more waste water is often produced than there is capacity for its treatment. The waste water of individual households or a group of households can be disposed of through small 'autonomous' plants. Unfortunately, in many countries too many households let their waste water flow into the ground untreated, thereby contaminating the soil.

In some places it has been the practice to separate the supply of drinking and non-drinking water, thereby reducing the volume of water needing to undergo more costly quality treatments and standards. Recycling of used water is practised to a limited degree (see also Chapter 5).

These glimpses into the problems of infrastructure demonstrate the immense tasks that construction has had and will continue to have in responding to various requirements.

INFORMATION AND GLOBAL COMMUNICATION

Computing, telecommunications and television converge into the 'Information Superhighway'. The various strands of this 'electronic highway' embrace the entire world economy, creating the 'information society'.

The primary information sector participates directly in the market for information services, such as mail, telegraph, telephone, telex, fax, radio and television services. The secondary information sector comprises information work in all sectors of human life and is sometimes called the 'in-house' sector. Many organizations now contract out to the primary information sector former in-house work such as book-keeping and salary administration. On the other hand, some formerly centralized services, such as mobile telephones, have become decentralized.

In developed countries, jobs in manufacturing are decreasing; the number of jobs in goods-handling services may stagnate or decrease, but the number of jobs in the information services are steadily growing. Information can be moved by telex, analogue or digital fax, interactive videotext and some other newer means. Telex is being superseded by fax and electronic mail (e-mail), i.e. direct communication between computers. Both the latter are expanding at present.

Cities with good information services are being strengthened; places with poor information bases are being left behind. Certain synergystic benefits exist in urban business centres with many information-hungry organizations. The City of London or New York's Manhattan continue to be prime locations for firms such as banks, law firms, and insurance and advertising companies. Firms with various high-tech profiles locate to the science parks or technopoles not only because of the presence of the modern information infrastructure, but also because there they can attract excellent ambitious professionals.

PERCEPTION OF THE ENVIRONMENT

The environment is a space shaped by both nature and human intervention. Natural space-shaping events are vulcanic outbursts, floods, erosion, precipitation and drought. Human space-shaping activities are construction, agriculture, mining and regulation of waterways. Construction introduces edifices (buildings etc.) that either blend into nature or seek to harmonize with it through the conscious contrast of artificial shapes with the natural world.

There have been attempts to establish a theory on and a catalogue of periods of space-shaping construction. According to one theory (Giedion, 1941), the first period lasted approximately until the building of Rome's Pantheon and was characterized by sculptural objects and volumes (e.g. the pyramid) placed in limitless space. The second period lasted up to the end of the eighteenth century, and was characterized by hollowed-out spaces and circumscribed interior spaces. The third period started with the nineteenth century and contained elements of both the first and the second stages. Such theories may lead away from construction practice towards the philosophy of architecture (Hall, 1966; Venturi, 1966; Norberg-Schulz, 1971; Canter, 1974; Rapoport, 1977; Krier, 1979).

People's reactions to their environment, including the built environment, are a consequence of how they perceive their environment within buildings, looking at buildings or moving around in cities. Consequently, throughout the ages, the great designers consciously or instinctively wished to evoke feelings of fear, awe, respect, appeal, or other pleasant or unpleasant feelings. The study of the impact of built surroundings on people has become a branch of psychology called environmental psychology or the science of the perception of the environment. But it is not yet an integral part of building science. The relationships between building research and environmental psychology are few and require expansion. At present, professional associations of psychology rather than building research organizations are the leading exponents in this area. (On the international level there is the International Association for the Study of People and their Physical Surroundings, IAPS.) As well as dealing with human perceptions of the natural and built environments, environmental psychology is also concerned with the interrelation of nature and buildings, and the function of trees, vegetation, water surfaces, hills, etc. in the human perception.

While it is difficult to establish a general theory on the perception of the (built) environment, some of the practical implications of technological progress are obvious. The psychological impact of buildings constantly changed in the past with the appearance of new styles. The new elements that result from technological progress are certainly substantial and affect human perceptions in new ways. The tall buildings, long-span bridges, long tunnels, large space coverings, light glazed façades and high atria of the modern world are all new for us and cause new types of sensation. Industrialization and prefabrication change the appearance of buildings by giving up small dimensions (of bricks, tiles, stones) in favour of the larger scale of the prefabricated components. The perception of the built environment includes our relationship with the internal spaces of buildings as well as with the environment on streets and in cities in general. When moving in or around buildings, but also in an unbuilt environment, one memorizes certain surrounding elements, i.e. a mental map is being made. Such maps may be based on previous experience, on drawings studied beforehand, or on information about what to expect. In shaping the environment, one ambition may be to give us assistance in making these mental maps.

The perception of space is fundamental to our ability to estimate distance, height, depth and width. The visual impression may assist or mislead one when estimating lengths and sizes.

Cities, their existing building stock, new constructions, and the repair and renewal of existing buildings should all contribute to the satisfaction of people. This is often expressed as the 'quality of life', of which economic conditions are just one component. Others are social and cultural components, such as housing, family and health conditions, political stability, criminality, and the potential for leisure activities. Various studies have analysed and synthesized these components.

SUMMARY

The technological, technical and economic trends in construction can only be understood in the context of social and spatial conditions.

Population and macroeconomic phenomena provide the overall background to the fluctuations of demand in construction, housing, urban expansion and renewal. Local, national, regional and global projects of various forms of transport, infrastructure and telecommunication networks occupy the construction industry more and more. Many new developments are concentrated in new areas: technopoles, growth corridors, transport hubs and areas of tourism.

The design of buildings and human settlements takes account of the results of sociological and psychological studies, e.g. the participation of future occupants in the design process, and studying the human perception of the environment.

The construction industry is involved in the broader context of urban and regional planning, and in the evolution of human society, including the newly emerging 'information society'.

BIBLIOGRAPHY

Batten, D. F. (1992) Network cities, infrastructure and variable returns to scale. Paper submitted to the 4th World Congress of the Regional Science Association, Palma da Mallorca, May 1992.

Brotchie, J. F., Hall, P. and Newton, P. W. (1987) *The Spatial Impact of Technological Change*, Croom Helm.

Brotchie, J. *et al.* (1995) *Cities in Competition*, Longman, Australia.

Brown, L. R. and Jacobson, J. L. (1987) *The Future of Urbanization: Facing the Ecological and Economic Constraints*, Worldwatch Paper 77, May 1987.

Buchanan, C. B. *et al.* (1963) *Trcffic in Towns*, HMSO, London.

Canter, D. (1974) *Psychology for Architects*, Architectural Science Series, Applied Science Publishers, London.

Canter, D. and Lee, T. (1974) *Psychology and Built Environment*, Architectural Press, London.

CSTB (1992) Réseaux d'Assainissement, *CSTB Magazine*, **60**, December, 3–8.

CSTB (1994) Ecole: La Traversée de Paris à 30 mètres sous terre, *CSTB Magazine*, **73**, April, 30–1.

Dolman, A. J. and van Ettinger, J. (eds.) (1990) *Ports as Nodal Points in a Global Transport System*, Pergamon Press.

Giedion, S. (1941) *Space, Time and Architecture*, Harvard University Press, Cambridge, Mass.

Hall, E. (1966) *The Hidden Dimension*, Anchor Books, Doubleday, New York.

Hall, P. (1985) The world and Europe. In J. Brotchie *et al.*, *The Future of Urban Form*, Croom Helm and Nichols Publishing Company.

Isard, W. *et al.* (1979) *Spatial Dynamics and Optimal Space-Time Development*, North-Holland Publishing Company.

Krier, R. (1979) *Urban Space*, Academy Edition, London.

Launhardt, (1882) Die Bestimmung des zweckmässigsten Standortes einer gewerblichen Anlage, *Zeitschrift des Vereines Deutscher Ingenieure*, Band XXVI, Heft 3.

Newland, K. (1980) *City Limits: Emerging Constraints on Urban Growth*, Worldwatch Paper 38, August.

Nijkamp, P. and Perrels, A. (1991) New transport systems in Europe: a strategic exploration. In J. Brotchie *et al.*, *Cities of the 21st Century*, Longman Cheshire; Halsted Press, 49–61.

Norberg-Schulz, C. (1971) *Existence, Space and Architecture*, Praeger Publishers, New York.

Pearce, F. (1995) The biggest dam in the world, *New Scientist*, 28 January 1995, 25–9.

Ransom, P. J. G. (1973) *Railways Revived*, Faber & Faber.

Ransom, P. J. G. (1979) *The Archeology of Canals*, World's Work Ltd.

Rapoport, A. (1977) *Human Aspects of Urban Form*, Pergamon Press.

Sassen, S. (1994) International migration and the post-industrial city, *The Urban Age*, Spring, 3–5.

Stein, D., Möllers, K. and Bielicki, R. (1989) *Microtunneling*, Ernst & Sohn.

Venturi, R. (1966) *Complexity and Contradiction in Architecture*, The Museum of Modern Art, Papers on Architecture 1, Garden City, New York, Doubleday.

Weber, A. (1929) *Theory of Location of Industries*, University of Chicago Press, Chicago.

A global survey: the future

9

THE ECONOMIC AND SOCIAL ENVIRONMENT

The future of construction will very much depend on the economic and social environment that surrounds it. At present, there is an enormous gap between the most advanced and the most backward economies in the world. It can be envisaged that economic progress will develop further in more regions, as has been the case recently in South-East Asia and the countries of the Pacific Rim. This would strengthen economic globalization and the growth of the world market.

Various studies have postulated that the problems due to economic development (demand for more energy, raw materials and land, population growth, protection of the environment) can be solved over the course of the next few generations (Kahn, Brown and Martel, 1977). Despite major deficiencies, such as poverty, housing shortages, lack of clean water, sanitation and so on, much progress has in fact already been achieved and more can be expected. Growth rates will probably be reduced, however. New technologies will contribute in a positive way to such trends.

The global population, which was 3.7 billion (thousand million) in 1970, 5.3 billion in 1990, may be around 8.2 billion by 2025 (Allen *et al.*, 1992; Documents of Habitat 2, UN Conference in Istanbul, Turkey, 3–14 June 1996). The population of the more developed regions may grow to 1.4 billion by 2025 (from 1.1 billion in 1970), and that of the less developed regions may reach 6.8 billion (from 2.6 billion in 1970). The population of industrialized countries will grow mainly through immigration. Population will grow fast in the developing countries at first, but a slowdown is expected later. Coping with the economic, social and cultural consequences of this will challenge these societies.

The percentage of the world's population that lives in cities was 37% in 1970 and may be more than 60% by 2025. In the more developed regions, 67% of people lived an urban existence in 1970, and this may reach 78% in 2025. In the less developed regions, the urban population accounted for 25% of the total in 1970 and may reach 57% in 2025. By then there will be 33 'megacities', each with a population exceeding 8 million, and 27 others each with a population exceeding 10 million; 23 of these latter will be in developing countries with the possible exceptions of New York, Los Angeles, Tokyo and Osaka. There will be more than 500 cities with a population in excess of 1 million.

Urbanization has reached a high level in industrialized countries, and in developing countries the cities will continue to grow. Some, such as São Paulo, Mexico City, and Calcutta, will be larger than any of the cities in developed countries except Tokyo. The structure of the population, economy and occupation will continue to change.

Employment in agriculture, mining and traditional industrial sectors will continue to decline. By contrast, modern industries, such as biotechnology, telecommunications, distribution and services, will grow. Information technologies, in particular, will saturate all aspects of life. People will work shorter weeks, and this extra leisure time will help the development of leisure sectors including tourism. An increased lifespan will increase the importance of health care and modern medical advances.

Breakthroughs in energy consumption must materialize. These, together with the creation of a new type of car, should help to reduce dependence on oil and gas and increase energy generation from renewable sources. Science and technology will continue to advance and bring affluence to many people.

Mankind would be assured of a bright future if the progress mentioned above could be achieved without major conflict. However, it can hardly be expected that economic and social conditions will be improved without some unrest. The idea of an ideal and peaceful future has suffered a setback. We must be prepared to face a future containing disasters, such as natural ones (earthquakes, floods, hurricanes) and man-made ones (wars, violence, criminality). Human activities will no doubt continue to cause unintentional and unforeseen catastrophes such as global warming, deforestation and industrial accidents, but it is to be hoped that society will be able to restrain its powers of destruction. Knowledge has been accumulated that will enable us to counter natural and man-made disasters. The construction industry itself has acquired experience in such actions, e.g. in designing earthquake-resistant buildings, providing safeguards against progressive collapse, and protecting buildings and their occupants from extremes of temperature, wind, rain and floods.

Inherent in a positive attitude towards the future is a belief in economic development and technical progress, particularly in the extension of such progress to regions that are currently less developed. This has posed a challenge for some time, and it has so far not been sufficiently or successfully tackled.

One urgent task to be addressed for the future is the requirement for sustainability. This is discussed later in this chapter.

Predicting the future may lead to erroneous conclusions. Even great scientists can misread the future and have done so on many occasions (Nicholls, 1991). According to an old Arab proverb, 'He who predicts the future lies, even if he tells the truth', and examples of incorrect assumptions about the future are abundant (Schwartz, 1991). With this in mind we shall be cautious about predictions and also about identifying evolution and progress, which are certainly inseparable. However, it is also certain that technical advances do not in themselves bring happiness to mankind. These then are the basic assumptions that enable us to look at the future of the construction industry. Several reports have attempted to identify the trends of the construction industry's future, and they can be referred to for more details (CIB, 1996).

THE CHANGING CONSTRUCTION INDUSTRY

Under the circumstances described above there will be a large volume of construction work to be carried out. The nature of this work may change, however: much more will be aimed at maintenance and renovation and new construction will diminish.

The future structure of the industry is unlikely to be that much different from the present one: a great number of small and medium-sized contractors will carry out small and local projects and a smaller number of large, partly multinational, firms will undertake the larger projects. The globalization of the construction industry will continue, but the spatial distribution may change in time. Trade contacts and financial and capital markets are bound to become more global. Progress in communications and information technology will enable construction to proceed successfully in different countries simultaneously, facilitated by various forms of alliances between global and local firms. Competition between engineering and construction firms will continue, and each will seek competitive advantages, one of the most highly valued of which will be specialist knowledge. A study in the USA examined the opinions of international engineering and construction firms about the impact of specific factors on competitiveness and found that knowledge-related factors were ranked higher than technology-related ones. The top three factors were project management expertise, reputation of the firm and financial packaging capability (Moavenzadeh, 1989). It can be expected that the importance of technology and knowledge-related factors will increase.

Technical progress, including industrialization, mechanization, prefabrication and the use of new materials, components and equipment will continue. Construction will no doubt become more capital-intensive. The development of technical services in buildings and specialization of construction crafts will continue. As a consequence, the cost share of the external envelope of buildings will become smaller. Even this external shell may not remain in the field of traditional crafts (masonry), but become a task for industrial specialists (curtain wall and glazing contractors). Specialization will increase the number of subcontractors, and increase the share of the work that they take. This process will also transform many traditional contractors into project managers. Construction firms will have to face a changing clientele, partly as a consequence of privatization, partly because of the increased professionalism of clients.

THE FUTURE TASKS OF CONSTRUCTION

HOUSING AND CITY RENEWAL

Population growth provides an obvious demand for new housing, but demand also stems from the fact that the existing building stock is inadequate, both from a quantitative and a qualitative aspect.

Poverty and low income render people homeless or force them into housing that is not really acceptable. At present, the gap between the housing conditions of the more affluent and the most destitute is still increasing. This progress has to be reversed. It is not realistic to hope for the housing standards enjoyed by the most affluent for everyone, but substantially better conditions is a realistic objective. A decent shelter is often unaffordable for families on low incomes. The affordability gap may be closed by eliminating poverty and, in the meantime, by reducing it and expanding housing assistance programmes for those on low-incomes (Howenstine, 1994).

It is still uncertain whether owner-occupiers will continue to have privileges or not. The strengthening of the private sector would indicate deregulation both in the owner-occupied and rented housing sectors. Social trends will affect demand: fewer babies, longer lives, high levels of cohabitation, divorce and separation rates, more young and elderly people wishing to live independently, and migration. In the more developed regions, the future dwelling will evolve from the present 'smart' homes comprising energy conserving envelopes and equipment, integrated control and telecommunications services. Creating conditions favourable to human health will be an important factor in selecting the building materials and design solutions for new housing (Allen *et al.*, 1992).

Construction will be affected by changes in social conditions. Sociology will concentrate on the urban problems of poverty, financing of housing and municipal life, segregation, social mobility, safety, land, shelter, governance, environment and sustainability (Hamm, 1995). The improvement of housing conditions is linked to the improvement of communal buildings such as schools, hospitals, offices, and cultural and leisure facilities. These form the cities, and sooner or later the renewal of existing cities will also have to be undertaken. The office of the future, for

Fig. 9.1   Hotel Sofitel Tokyo, Japan: modern materials and design produce imaginative forms, Obayashi, Japan. *Source:* Courtesy of the Obayashi Corporation.

Fig. 9.2 Human being in natural environment. *Source:* Publication by Swedish building research organization.

example, will be established in energy-efficient buildings with integrated individual workstations at which the user can control his/her personal environment, and smart glazing, control devices and technical services will be provided in the floor cavity, allowing flexibility to rearrange spaces (Davidson, 1991).

BUILDINGS AND CIVIL ENGINEERING

This section lists some tasks for the future. It is a hypothetical list and it is quite uncertain which, if any, of the items on it will materialize. Its purpose is merely to demonstrate the huge needs and desires that already exist.

An enormous amount of construction will be devoted to the elimination of the housing shortage and the rehabilitation of decayed cities. Such work will consist of both small and large projects. In the developing countries, about 600 million new dwellings need to be built. Large-scale construction will modernize cities and update municipal services. A number of megaprojects are already in sight:

- New railway lines
  - high-speed lines in several countries
  - linking Russia's trans Siberian with the Canadian–Pacific, 7200 km
- New long crossings under difficult conditions
  - crossing the Straits of Gibraltar (the latest version is a 28 km long train tunnel between Tarifa and Tangier with a maximum depth of 400 m under sea level)
  - tunnel under the Bosporus to connect Europe with Asia
  - tunnel under or 80 km long bridge over the Bering Strait to link Russia with Alaska
  - tunnel under the Pyrenees to link France and Spain
  - tunnel under the Alps to link Lyons with Turin
  - tunnels under both Paris and Berlin
  - tunnel under the Alps to link Germany with Italy
  - 3 km long-span bridge from Italy across the Strait of Messina to Sicily; (an alternative is a submerged composite steel-concrete tunnel with a flat elliptical cross-section
  - a 16 km crossing of the Øresund between Copenhagen and Malmö (this may be begun soon and completed within five years (Lundhus and Braestrup, 1995))
  - a 20 km crossing of the Fehmarnbelt to link Lolland Island (Denmark) and Germany
- Land reclamation and flood protection
  - land reclamation in Japan and Monaco
  - protection against floods, tsunamis and eventual sea level increases in The Netherlands and Bangladesh

   – storm surge barrier to protect Venice (three sections with flop-
     gates, preliminary cost estimated to be US$1.8 thousand million).

Some future large civil engineering projects were mentioned in Chapter
8, e.g. the planned railway line in China. High-speed railways, roads,
tunnels, dams, bridges, urban underground railways, sewerage networks, undersea pipelines and cable lines are all potential future civil
engineering programmes.

   In the category of buildings, the high-technology element will become
more important:

- super-tall buildings (800–2000 m)
- super-long-span roofs (400–600 m)
- new major airports
- power stations for new types of energy
- nuclear physics megaprojects
- advanced offices, hotels, hospitals (Loring, 1995)
- industrial facilities for high-tech industries (telecommunications, bio-
  genetics).

In order to be able to address such demands realistically, the design and
actual construction must work on a modern scientific basis. The knowledge component will therefore be increasingly important as the following
section illustrates.

BUILDING RESEARCH

Research would not be necessary if one could foresee its outcome, thus it
is possible only to sketch in the fields in which efforts should be concentrated and give a general definition of goals (Lemer, 1992). We also omit
the question of how much should be devoted to building research
(Sebestyén, 1983). Suffice it to say that the construction industry has
woken up to the benefits of research and will no doubt wish to devote
adequate resources to it to allow work on new and improved materials,
components, and equipment, with an emphasis on the environmental
impact, to continue. Research will also further refine design methods by
exploring in more depth the phenomena of earthquakes, wind, heat and
moisture, noise, light and electric and electromagnetic fields. Building
research will establish close links with various human and social science
sectors, such as biology, hygiene, health, physiology, psychology and
sociology. This should result in more defined performance requirements,
codes and standards.

   Modern management and information methods will be increasingly
applied. More attention will be devoted to safety and security in buildings, cities and construction sites, to the prevention of violence, crime and

vandalism, and to the personal health and well being of people. A higher technical level of design and execution of buildings and civil engineering works should be accompanied by acceptable quality, economic efficiency, protection of the environment, and conservation of energy and other natural resources including land, all with a view to sustainable development.

Research in the future is based on the finance that is approved today, and so it is not surprising that a number of programmes for future research have either already been approved or are under consideration. Some of the main projects proposed by such programmes are listed below.

The European Union (EU) has a running involvement in supporting research and development projects in construction (Bazin *et al.*, 1993).

Not long ago, the US National Institute of Standards and Technology rated the following four research areas as having highest priority:

- the relationship of indoor air quality to energy consumption
- validation of fire models and design models
- high-performance concrete in buildings
- extreme wind resistance in design and construction.

Other research institutes are also defining, and from time to time revising, their lists of top priority research. In 1994, the USA Civil Engineering Research Foundation (CERF) prepared a 10-year plan for deploying high-performance materials and systems (CERF, 1994). It defines six areas of improvement:

- reduction in project delivery time
- reduction in operation, maintenance and energy costs
- increase in productivity and facility comfort
- reduction in occupancy-related illnesses and injuries
- reduction of waste and pollution
- greater durability and flexibility.

The plan defines the research needed on high-performance concrete, hot mix asphalt, masonry, steel, wood, aluminium, composites, coatings and roofing materials.

A plan formulated by a team headed by K. Dekker and submitted for approval to the Directorate-General DG XII of the EU, proposes five projects to address the major technology gaps:

- consumer-oriented building
- environmentally-oriented construction
- complex building and civil engineering structures
- use of new technology and systems to improve international competitiveness
- urban infrastructures: integrated urban systems for the movement of goods, services and people.

This plan defined further research needs in the areas of design, materials, and manufacturing and construction technologies.

Advisory Committee 6 of the European Convention for Constructional Steelwork (ECCS) has published its research priorities in the field of design, composite structures, light gauge steel, fabrication and erection, connections, fire resistance and structural materials (ECCS, 1995). Selected examples of the research topics they highlighted are listed below:

- calculation methods should be further developed, particularly on the influence of second order theory, buckling and torsional-flexural buckling
- design methods for cold-formed steel sections and frames should be simplified
- additional research is proposed on semi-automated connections, use of cast-steel joints, blind-bolting and flow-drilled connections in hollow sections and in the use of direct tension indicating devices.

Toma *et al.* (1993) and ENBRI (1990) also list the areas that research is needed in, the former concentrate on cold-formed steel in tall buildings, while the latter considers more general problems adding: '... the stronger the R&D effort of a sector, the better its image'. Naturally, this is only true if the body of research actually reflects real needs.

In its corporate plan for 1996–98, the UK-based Construction Industry Research and Information Association (CIRIA) listed the following issues as being of highest priority:

- improving the process of construction
- improving the performance of what is constructed
- improving the management of risk and the contribution made by construction to the environment.

It recommended research projects on:

- productivity and management
- technology, materials and environment
- safety and site management
- the ground and water.

Professor H. Hens of the Catholic University of Leuven, Belgium, considers the following building physics research areas to be the most important (Hens, personal communication, 1995):

- combined heat, air and moisture transport: modelling, testing, translation into performances and practice
- hygrothermal load and durability (stochastic approach)
- introduction of performances
- environmental impact of buildings and sustainability

- developing better models on heat and moisture transfer, energy, comfort, acoustics, lighting
- integration of knowledge in the subdomains of building physics, in correlation with HVAC and building construction.

These examples amply demonstrate that construction is still a long way from solving all its problems. Indeed, as the industry progresses, it continually encounters new areas that require research. Work on these will enable the industry to solve its problems in more reliable and economic ways.

Building research will continue to take place in building research institutes, universities, and organizations of industry and design. International contacts in research and development will increase and become more efficient. Building research will have to become more science-oriented, but it must also be practice-oriented, the two being not contradictory but complementary (Coulter, 1991). Governments have traditionally played an important role in establishing and financing building research institutions, but this is now changing. As industries become privatized, and as many public services are gradually taken over by private capital, the building research institutes will increasingly work for private clients.

Studies have repeatedly demonstrated that most of the progress in industry and construction has its origin in invention, innovation and research (Seaden, 1995). This ensures that the building industry will continue to have an interest in building research. At the same time, the tasks of standardization and codes will retain public interest in research.

The traditional objective of technical progress and the methods used to measure economic effectiveness are changing. While the ambition to raise productivity and thereby reduce the demand for labour remains, high unemployment rates compel countries to introduce measures to ensure employment opportunities. The conservation of energy and the sustainability of economic development become new goals.

A SUSTAINABLE FUTURE

Throughout history there has been an almost universal perception that the earth was large enough and rich enough to sustain human life, the flora and the fauna. Indeed, man's main preoccupation was to extract more of what the earth seemed to contain in such abundance. The growth of the world's population, the acceleration of technical development and increases in various forms of consumption did not present a cause for concern until relatively recently. While there were early warnings, for example by Malthus, that resources were limited and could become insufficient, these warnings were dismissed because it was thought that science and technology, then both developing, would be able to increase, maintain or substitute supplies. By the middle of the twentieth century, however, doubts were being expressed, and concern later increased greatly. The number of species of animals and plants that were threatened with extinction increased. Renewable natural resources such as forests and fish were in danger of depletion. It became obvious that important non-renewable resources such as coal, oil and gas would last for only a limited period.

Out of these anxieties about the future of life on our planet grew the movement to protect the environment. When the book *Limits to Growth* (Forester and Meadows, 1972) was published, it acquired international fame as the Meadows Report. It contrasted world economic growth with the world's resources, and concluded that many of these resources would be exhausted in the not too distant future, in some cases within 100 years or so. The book caused controversy and debate, and although many agreed, there was also much opposition, underpinned by the discovery of new oil and gas reserves. Twenty-five years on, it has become universally acknowledged (with some reservations, see De Jong, 1995 and others) that the Meadows Report raised a serious problem that cannot be ignored: technological progress cannot be expected to ensure sustainability, including safeguarding resources and protecting the environment, without some massive initiatives, e.g. control of population growth and support for the use of renewable energy forms.

Despite the difficulty in defining sustainable development, governments are in agreement that this would be desirable and should be pursued as far as possible. The World Commission on the Environment and Development suggested a definition in the so-called Brundtland Report in 1987:

> Sustainable development is the development that meets the needs of the present without compromising the ability of future generations to meet their own needs.

This means that it is our obligation to leave sufficient resources for future generations to have a quality of life similar to ours.

Sustainability requires resources to be conserved, the environment to be protected and a healthy environment to be maintained (Kibert, 1994). The main resources to be conserved are the life, land and raw materials, including energy, water and air. A healthy environment comprises both the outdoor and indoor environment. Sustainability will not be reached simply by renouncing technical progress and reducing consumption levels. From the very beginning, sustainability has been understood to be not purely defensive, i.e. it is more than merely a movement to reduce the depletion of resources. The concept has been extended to take in sustainable development. This, however, was soon recognized as contradictory because it was questioned whether development could continue indefinitely. On the other hand, to halt or reduce growth would be regarded as socially unacceptable at present. In any case, it would not in itself achieve sustainability. Only stronger measures can achieve this, and such measures are not yet available.

The negative environmental impact of growth has increased during the past 20 years. There is no willingness, either in the developed north or in the less developed south, to give up growth, and anyway even zero-growth would not achieve sustainability. Technologies that ensure sustainability must be found very soon or grave and forceful events will compel humans to see the ecological realities. Nevertheless, even if sustainability cannot be ensured, we still have to strive to come as close to it as possible.

An increasing number of firms are beginning to discern sustainability as a source of competitive advantage. Movements and slogans like 'Build Green' have appeared. There is nothing inherently wrong in this, so long as it embraces more than just commercial posturing.

Prior to the call for sustainability, economic optimization served as the selection mechanism between competing alternatives. Well established methods exist to determine the economic impact of various technology alternatives. These take account of initial (investment) cost, running (operating) cost, maintenance, repair, replacement, salvage cost and value, i.e. life-cycle cost. In such calculations the discount technique is used in order to sum up values and amounts. Adjustment for inflation and other time-dependent factors can be incorporated into such calculations. Comparisons are fairly straightforward if the benefits (results, yields, value for the use) are identical. Various conversion techniques can be used to eliminate differences in benefits and make the alternatives comparable. The idea of extending such calculations to environmental problems, however, revealed instead how inadequate the methodologies were for such purposes. When discounted to the present, influences that will exert their effect in the long-term – in 100 years or more – show such a reduced importance as to be unacceptable. With its discounting system, cost-benefit arithmetic makes costs occurring far in the future too small and insignificant for comprehension in the present. Using reduced discount rates for remote costs introduces an element of arbitrariness and thus negates its value as a solid methodology. The same applies to the proposal to add to present costs a theoretical discounted future expenditure for restoring environmental damage, which anyway is not always possible, e.g. in the case of the extinction of a species.

Some economists suggest that environmental and sustainability problems should not be forced into the cost–benefit calculation framework at all. Instead, they argue, it should be accepted that these problems require moral and political decisions to be taken. A combination of these two ways of addressing the problems would be for the state to levy tax on materials and technologies that have an adverse impact on sustainability.

With such additional artificial advantage, environmentally sound solutions would become competitive. Unfortunately, there is a lack of enthusiam for measures that would require global agreements and that cannot be derived from any solid calculations.

Solow (1993), an American economist, has proposed another concept. He argues that some of the proceeds from the exploitation and depletion of non-renewable resources should be invested in other assets, which could include human or physical capital (e.g. education and factories), to maintain productive capacity. The concept of 'sustainable income' is thereby introduced.

Another concept is that of tradeable entitlements (Barrett, 1992; Rose, 1992; Tietenberg, 1992; UNCTAD, 1995). There is already some experimental application of this in California where tradeable levels for nitrogen oxide emissions have been introduced in order to fight ozone concentration in the air. The same principle could be applied to carbon dioxide emissions to fight against climate warming or to reduce waste production. No international agreement of this kind is in sight however, as the individual interests of different countries are still too divergent.

Classical and neoclassical economic theory need to be substantially revised in order to serve sustainability. Among others things, this could mean that the current national income and wealth calculations would have to include fiscal quantification of changes in environmental resources, and environmental indicators would have to be introduced to current economic statistics.

For the construction industry, there are some self-evident areas in which it can serve the cause of sustainability. For example, 'green' buildings should not (Halliday, 1993; Spence and Mulligan, 1995):

- endanger the health of occupants or others
- cause unnecessary damage to the natural environment
- consume an excessive amount of energy or other resources
- use materials from threatened species.

Sustainability could have a broader impact on construction. It could certainly be questioned whether any new construction on land hitherto not used for construction could not be avoided, and whether one should not rather opt for the renewal of the existing stock on land already in use. Some scientists go even further and claim that mankind has a deep genetic emotional need to affiliate with the rest of the living world. This is the 'biophilia hypothesis' (Wilson and Kellert, 1993), which claims that as life becomes increasingly urban, it is leading to indifference, or even hostility, to a mindset that could encourage destruction and degradation of the natural world. Although not supported by concrete evidence, many claim that the biophilia hypothesis strengthens the argument for sustainability.

The idea of sustainability ultimately advocates that major catastrophes endangering human life should be prevented. Scientific progress has already enhanced our ability to prevent or reduce the harmful effects of certain natural disasters, such as floods, hurricanes, earthquakes and fires, but at the same time, human activities have increased the potential severity of such calamities: the earth is now so much more densely populated than before that the chances of a natural disaster occurring in an unpopulated area, and therefore being of little concern, have been much reduced. Over the past 30 years, the costs of natural disasters have escalated substantially. The construction industry, among others, may itself contribute to disasters if the consequences of certain actions are not foreseen. Naturally, it is our duty to reduce the probability of natural disasters, but some will always occur, either because we could not foresee them, or because our abilities were insufficient to combat them, e.g. a collision with a large meteorite. In any event, engineering knowledge has an obligation to increase our ability to fight off natural disasters.

Steps to mitigate disasters comprise measures of prevention, reduction and recovery, with various combinations in each of the three main groups (Davenport, 1992). Industrial activities can be the cause of accidents or contamination of the air, water and soil. Efforts have increased to eliminate or reduce such effects, but they are unlikely to disappear altogether, which means that the earth will increasingly become an artificial environment. Unfortunately, engineering knowledge has no means to prevent such purely human catastrophes as wars. However, it can assist in reducing their impact, although we should not forget that it also contributes to increasing destruction by improving weaponry.

Sustainability joins other global concerns by having established projects and institutions on both national and international levels. The United Nations (UN) has founded the Commission on Sustainable Development and the Interagency Committee on Sustainable Development.

A KNOWLEDGE-BASED FUTURE

It is by now a commonplace that the future will be knowledge-based. Richness in natural resources is favourable but does not guarantee affluence. The message in this is that the standard-bearers of progress will be those who master the most recent knowledge, or, better yet, those who are themselves creating new knowledge. The message is also that progress will be based on high-level computer applications, telecommunications and combinations of these to produce powerful tools, thus giving an edge over less advanced competitors. This has a very special connotation for the construction industry. Some parts of the activities of building will continue to be of a vernacular character for a long time.

Small, local contractors will survive and cater for small local projects. They may use modern materials and processes but, basically, they will do what has been practised in building since ancient times. Some building activities will not even need a small contractor: people will execute the work themselves on a do-it-yourself basis. Construction, however, will become increasingly occupied with much more sophisticated tasks, which it will solve with more science- or knowledge-based processes. This sector will not only realize individual projects, among them some whose size will surpass anything known until now, but it will also have a much broader responsibility. Construction (and building) will bear some responsibility for a sustainable development, for shaping and reshaping our environment in such a way that it leads towards a better, healthier, socially more balanced and affluent life.

This is not to say that construction should meddle in politics. The power of construction should not, and will not, be based on political power; it will be based on knowledge. The combined knowledge of both specialists and generalists will be necessary. Members of the profession must master the various disciplines, structural design, building technology, building services, and so on, to a high level. There will also be a need for people to work with representatives of a large number of other disciplines, those in hygiene, health, psychology, social sciences, and biology, for example. Construction will retain some of the characteristics of an ancient craft, but at the same time it will be transformed into a modern industry that will have a leading task in human society in both quantitative and qualitative terms. Naturally, this has to be translated into education and training – basic, advanced, postgraduate and continuous. The range of construction tasks and those working on them will broaden enormously. Education and training will have to be adapted accordingly.

These features demonstrate that construction has a potentially bright future and that it should, once again, be a sector that attracts the young because of the great opportunities for creative work it offers. This should give those involved in the industry grounds for pride as well as humility.

SUMMARY

Our ability to foresee the future of human society is limited. Nevertheless, we can be certain that construction will face considerable demands, which, along with the more traditional products, will comprise new buildings and structures, a number of megaprojects and maintenance and repair of our current built environment. Building research will also continue, and regionalization and globalization will probably eliminate unnecessary duplication. The contributions to research made by designers, manufacturers, contractors and educators will be maintained and, perhaps, be more fully integrated with the activities of traditional research institutes.

A new requirement is sustainability. For the construction industry, this entails conservation of energy and other natural resources (including land) and an increased use of renewable resources. The classic methods of welfare/utilitarian economics (the discount technique and cost–benefit analysis) cannot ensure sustainability. New economic methods and indicators such as the introduction of the 'green national economy', the balance of natural resources, and tradeable emissions, will be necessary, not only to measure and promote sustainability, but also to protect the environment.

The future of the construction industry will be affected by the changes in society and the developments towards an information/knowledge-based society.

While construction will continue to progress towards being a 'high-tech' industry, some of its traditional and vernacular features will be retained. Construction will have to compete with other economic sectors for a fair share of the finite financial resources and, in order to succeed, it will have to develop its technology and improve productivity still further.

In conclusion on the future, I would like to express my agreement with the following two statements by Kahn, Brown and Martel (1977) (pp. 7 and 8):

Although the possibilities of overcrowding, famine, resource scarcity, pollution and poverty cannot be dismissed, they should be seen as temporary or regional phenomena that society must deal with rather than as the inevitable fate of man.

... [economic] growth is likely to continue for many generations, though at gradually decreasing rates ...

Under such future circumstances, the construction industry will be an ever more important sector of the economy and society.

BIBLIOGRAPHY

Allen, W. A. *et al.* (1992) *A Global Strategy for Housing in the Third Millenium*, E&FN Spon.

Barrett, S. (1992) *Transfers and the Gains from Trading Carbon Emission Entitlements in a Global Warming Treaty*, UNCTAD.

Bazin, M. *et al.* (1993) Analyse stratégique en science et technologie, *Cahiers du CSTB*, Cahier 2643, April 1993.

Building Services (1994) The future world of advanced houses, *Building Services, CIBSE Journal*, **16**(7) 26–9.

Built Environment (1995) *Hazards in the built environment*, **21**, (2/3).

CERF (1994) *Materials for Tomorrows Infrastructure: A Ten-Year Plan for Deploying High Performance Construction Materials and Systems*, Civil Engineering Research Foundation (CERF), Washington, DC, USA.

CIB (1996) *Future Organisation of the Building Process*, CIB Report W82.

Coulter, C. (1991) The role of education in meeting the research demands of the 21st century. In *Proceedings of Conference, University of Florida, Gainesville, Florida*, 35–45.

Davenport, A. G. (1992) Natural disaster reduction through structural quality, In *Post-Congress Report of IABSE*, 1–6 March 1992, 55–66.

Davidson, P. J. (1991) The energy efficient office of the future. *Building Services, CIBSE Journal*, **13**(2), 53.

de Jong, T. M. (1995) The existing environmental perception inhibits contemplating effective solutions to the ecological crisis. In *Future Buildings Forum*, Proceedings of IEA Workshop, Lake Constance (CH) 15–17 May 1995.

ECCS (1995) *Research and Development Promoting Steel Structures*, (ECCS) Advisory Committee 6, Structural Design and Research, European Convention for Constructional Steelwork.

ENBRI (1990) *Construction Research Needs in Europe*, Publication of the European Network of Building Research Institutes (ENBRI), Luxembourg.

Forester, J., Meadows D. *et al.* (1972) *Limits to Growth*, Universe Books, New York.

Halliday, S. (1993) *Ecological Villages*, CIB W82 Working Paper, Brussels.

Hamm, B. (1995) New trends in urban social science, *Innovation: The European Journal of Social Sciences*, June, 133–54.

Hill, R. C. *et al.* (1994) A framework for the attainment of sustainable construction, *Proceedings of Conference on Sustainable Construction*, 6–9 November 1994.

Howenstine, E. J. (1994) Homeless prevention, *International Journal on Urban Policy*, **11**(2) 83–5.

Kahn, H., Brown, W. and Martel, L. (1977) *The Next 200 Years*, Associated Business Programmes.

Kibert, Ch.J. (ed.) (1994) *Sustainable Construction*, Proceedings of CIB TG 16 Conference, Tampa, Florida, USA, 6–9 November 1994.

Lemer, A. C. (1992) Construction research for the 21st century, *Building Research and Information*, **1**, 28–34.

Loring, J. R. (1995) The 21st century office building – how 'Smart' will it be? In L. S. Beedle (ed.-in-chief), and D. Rice (ed.), *Habitat and the High-Rise: Tradition and Innovation*, Proceedings of the 5th World Congress, 791–8.

Lundhus, P. and Braestrup, M. W. (1995) The Oresund link between Denmark and Sweden, *Structural Engineering International*, November, **5** (4), 224–6.

Moavenzadeh, F. (1989) *A Strategic Response to a Changing Engineering and Construction Market*, Paper for the World Economic Forum, Engineering and Construction Forum, April 1989, Japan.

Nicholls, M. (1991) The perils of prediction, *New Scientist*, 21/28 December 1991, 63–4.

Rose, A. (1992) *Equity Considerations of Tradeable Entitlements*, UNCTAD.

Schwartz, P. (1991) *The Art of the Long View*, Doubleday Currency.

Seaden, G. (1995) *Economics of Technology Development for the Construction Industry*, Paper for the CIB Congress in Amsterdam, May 1995.

Sebestyén, G. (1983) *Measurement, Accounting and Taxation for Research and Development: Volume and Support of Construction R&D*, Report to the Board of CIB.

Sebestyén, G. *et al.* (1992) *Measurement and Evaluation of Construction Research*, CIB Report, Publication 147, Rotterdam.

Solow, R. (1993) *An Almost Practical Step to Sustainability*, Reviewed in *Resources for the Future*, Washington D.C.

Spence, R. and Mulligan, H. (1995) Sustainable development and the construction industry, *Habitat International*, **19** (3), 279–92.

Tietenberg, T. (1992) *Relevant Experience with Tradeable Entitlements*, UNCTAD.

Tisdell, C. A. (1991) *Economics of Environmental Conservation*, Elsevier.

Toma, T. (ed.) *et al.* (1993) *Cold-Formed Steel in Tall Buildings*, McGraw-Hill Inc.

UN World Conference on Population (1994) *Papers of the Conference*, Cairo, Egypt, September 1994.

UNCTAD (1995) *Controlling Carbon Dioxide Emissions: the Tradeable System.* UN, Geneva.

Wilson, E. O. and Kellert, S. R. (1993) *The Biophilia Hypothesis*, Island Press/Shearwater Books.

Appendix: chronology of inventions, innovations and innovative buildings from the end of the eighteenth century

Year or Period	Description
1772	Cast-iron interior columns, St Anne's Church, Liverpool, England
1776–9	Cast-iron arch bridge over the Severn River, Coalbrookdale, Shropshire, England, span 30 m, designed by Abraham Darby III (and Pritchard)
1792	Warm air central heating, Belper textile mill, William Strutt
1792–3	First multistorey building with floors supported by iron columns, calico mill, Derby, England
1802	Steam heating, Matthew Boulton and John Watt
Early 1800s	Introduction of gas lighting, water pipes and cast-iron radiators
1814	Power-driven circular saw appears in USA
1814	Craigellachie Bridge over the River Spey, Scotland, span 45 m, cast-iron arch, designed by Thomas Telford
1819	Early atria and arcade at Burlington Arcade, London, designed by S. Ware.
1823	The principle of heat pumps discovered by S. Carnot, France

1824	The invention of artificial (Portland) cement, by Joseph Aspdin, England
1824	First steel suspension bridge, Tournon, River Rhône, France, designed by Marc and Camille Seguin (brothers)
1825	First public railway to use steam from the outset, Stockton to Darlington, UK
1826	Menai Bridge, one of the early steel chain bridges, designed by Thomas Telford, the world's longest-spanning structure at that time
1830	The first public passenger mainline railway, Liverpool to Manchester, UK
1830s	Mechanical steam digger (shovel) appears in the USA
1830	Appearance of machine-made nail
1834	First modern aqueduct, Old Croton, New York
1835	Place de la Concorde, Paris, paved with asphalt
1835	First compression refrigeration machinery, Perkins, USA
1839	Excavator patent granted to W.S. Otis, USA
1841	Wallpaper printed by machine in continuous lengths, C. and J. Potter
1841	Riveted wrought-iron girders in road bridge, Glasgow
1843	Thames Tunnel near City of London (Wapping to Rotherhithe) completed by Sir Marc Isambard Brunel
1843	Hamburg, Germany, first important municipality to construct a sanitary sewer system
1850–70	Introduction of steel to replace iron
1851	First major prefabricated and site-assembled iron structure at Crystal Palace, London, architects John Paxton and Charles Fox
1854, 1977	Reinforced concrete patented by Wilkinson and (separately) Joseph Monier
1854	Elisha Graves Otis demonstrates the effectiveness of safety ratchets for elevators at New York exposition
1855	First steel suspension railway bridge across the Niagara Gorge, span 250 m, designed by John Roebling
1855	First direct steam ram
1856	New steel-making process invented by Henry Bessemer
1857	First modern urban sewage treatment system built, Brooklyn, New York
1857	The installation of the first hydraulic passenger elevator installed in New York
1857–71	Construction of the Mont Cenis Tunnel, linking France and Italy, length 12.8 km, the first under the Alps, with the use of compressed air drills from 1860
1859	Steam dragline excavator patented by Couvreux

1860–69	Construction of the Suez Canal begins, Ferdinand de Lesseps
1861	Linus Yale invents the pin-tumbler cylinder lock
1863	The first part of the London Underground opened
1864	François Coignet builds concrete shell church, Le Vesinet, France
1866	Invention of linoleum flooring
1866	Hyatt brothers and Parkes develop the first thermoplastics
1867	Henry Bessemer's steel making process improved by Wilhelm Siemens
1871	Great fire in Chicago
1872	Hydraulic elevator comes into use
1872–81	Construction of the 16.3 km long St Gotthard Tunnel under the Alps, the first major tunnelling application of nitroglycerine
1874	First major steel bridge completed in USA, over Mississippi River, St Louis, spans of 153 m, 159 m and 153 m, designed by James Eads
1874	William Baldwin patents a radiator consisting of pipes screwed into a cast iron base, USA
1874	Parmalee invents the fusible link automatic sprinkler
1875	Blasting gelatine invented by Alfred Nobel
1875	The first excavator produced outside USA; Ruston, Proctor & Burton, England
1877	Arched and trussed steel Pia Maria Bridge over the Douro River, Portugal, span 160 m, designed by Gustave Eiffel
1878–9	Incandescant (charcoal filament) lamp: Thomas Edison in New York, Sir Joseph Swan in London (20 years earlier); Edison introduces lamp with screw socket
1879	Firth of Forth, Scotland, trussed railway bridge, span 521 m
1880s	Construction of gas supply network begins in the USA
1880–1900	Rolled steel production begins; first steel-framed buildings and skyscrapers in Chicago
1880–1904	Continuous production of glass-sheet from molten glass
1882	Thomas Edison constructs the first electrical power station in New York
1882	Start of the modern lacquer and varnish industry
1883	Electromechanic thermostat patented, Warren Johnson, USA
1883	Brooklyn Bridge, East River, New York, first suspension bridge, first use of hard-drawn steel wire cables and steel deck structure, span 486 m, J. Roebling & Son

1883–4	Home Insurance Building, Chicago, the first skyscraper in the modern sense, built with masonry walls and half steel, half cast iron structure, architect William Le Baron Jenney
1884	Arched and trussed steel Garabit Viaduct over the Truyère River, France, span 165 m, designed by Gustave Eiffel
1884	The first major architectural application of aluminium: Washington Monument, Washington DC.
1886–9	Tacoma Building, Chicago, 12 storeys, partial steel skeleton, designed by Holabird & Roche (this and the Home Insurance Building were demolished in the early 1930s)
1887	First electric elevator installed
1888	Charles Otis (son of Elisha Graves Otis) invents improved safety elevator brake
1889	Gustave Eiffel wins exhibition competition with his tower design for Paris, height 300 m
1890	Steel cantilever bridge over the Firth of Forth, Scotland, span 513 m, then the world's longest, designed by Benjamin Baker
1891	Rand-McNally Building, nine storeys, first all-steel framed building
1891	Chicago, Monadnock Building, 16-storey building with masonry walls, designed by John W. Root
1894	First reinforced concrete bridge, Viggen, Switzerland, designed by François Hennebique
1896	St Paul high-rise building, New York, height 95 m
1896–1910	Introduction of tubular steel scaffolding
1896	The first underground urban railway line in mainland Europe opened in Budapest
1897–8	Park Row Building, New York, height 115 m, world's tallest from 1900–8
1898	Construction the Paris Métro (underground) begins
1898	Gypsum partition tile developed
1898–1906 and 1912–21	Simplon Tunnel, Alps, twin single-line railway tunnel, length 19.8 km
1899	Bridge over Vienne River, Châtellerault, France, span of central arch 50 m, longest-spanning reinforced concrete bridge in the nineteenth century, designed by François Hennebique
1900–22	The gradual introduction of air conditioning: Carrier's first fully air-conditioned building is a theatre in Los Angeles
Early 1900s	Invention of various stainless steel alloys were: Harry Brearly (England), Elwood Haynes (USA), Edward Maurer and Benno Strauss (Germany)

1901	Invention of vacuum cleaner by H.C. Booth
1901	Rohm awarded doctorate for his thesis on acrylate polymers
1903	The first one-piece coupler for tubular steel scaffolding patented by Edward Wilding
1903	Elisabeth Bridge, River Danube, Budapest, one of the last major chain suspension bridges with eyebar members, span 290 m
1904	Ourthe Bridge, Liège, Belgium, arched reinforced concrete bridge, span 55 m
1904	Fourcault process for drawing a continuous band of glass vertically patented
1904–14	Construction of the Panama Canal
1905	Libbey-Owens process for drawing glass horizontally patented
1905	Slipform technology introduced for tall cylindrical concrete structures, Philadelphia, USA
1905	Plywood invented by Hetzer
1906	Kuhn and Loeb Bank, New York, suspended ceiling to conceal mechanical equipment
1906	Cramer uses sprayed chilled water to clean and cool air and calls the method 'air conditioning'
1906	Carrier controls humidity in air, and patents the dew-point control
1908	Singer Building, New York, height 184 m, world's tallest from 1907–9
1909	AEG Turbine Hall, Berlin, Germany, early reinforced concrete building
1909	Michigan Tunnel, Detroit, USA, first major submerged tunnel with steel sections
1909	Metropolitan Life Building, New York, height 213 m, world's tallest from 1909–13
1909	Leo Baekeland discovers and patents (1916) bakelite, the first synthetic (phenolformaldehyde) resin with commercial possibilities
1910	Giesshübel warehouse, Zurich, Switzerland, beamless concrete slab supported by column mushroom capitals, designed by Robert Maillart
1911	Fagus Factory Building, Germany, early reinforced concrete industrial building, designed by W. Gropius and A. Meyer
1913	Jahrhunderthalle, Breslau, Germany (now Wroclaw, Poland), ribbed reinforced concrete dome, diameter 65 m, designed by Max Berg

1913	Woolworth Building, New York, height 241 m, world's tallest from 1913–29
1914–20	Central heating boilers become common
1916	Le Corbusier erects the first concrete framed villa (house) at Chaux de Fonds, Switzerland
1916	The Hell Gate Bridge over the East River, New York, steel, world's longest-spanning arch (293 m) when completed, designed by Gustav Lilienthal
1919	The Bauhaus institution established in Weimar, Germany, moved in 1925 to Dessau and later to Berlin
Early 1920s	Inception of mobile homes in the USA
1920s	Urea resins developed for bonding of laminates (Formica); alkyd paints begin to replace oil paints; introduction of thermostats and sprinklers
1921–2	Schindler-Chase house, Kings Road, Hollywood, USA, storey high pre-cast concrete slabs, designed by Rudolph Schindler
1922	W. Bauersfeld and F. Dischinger take out patents on thin shell concrete roof systems, later to be called Zeiss–Dywidag system
1925	Tour d'Orientation, Grenoble, France, 100 m high concrete transmission tower, designed by Auguste Perret
1925	Timber lamella system for barrel vaults introduced in the USA by Kievitt
1926	Asphalt floor tiles appear
1927	The first reinforced concrete dome designed using the membrane theory, planetarium in Jena, Germany; span:thickness ratio = 420:1
1927–36	Organic glass (Plexiglass) developed by Rohm (Rohm and Haas)
1928	Milam Building, San Antonio, first fully air-conditioned office building
1928–36	Marie Eugène Freyssinet introduces prestressing wires into hardened concrete (first patent on prestressed concrete: USA, 1888)
1929	The Market Hall, Leipzig, Germany, 76 m span polygonal reinforced concrete domes, weight one-third of the Breslau dome in 1913
1929	Industrial research on styrene and polystyrene initiated in Germany
1929–30	Chrysler building, New York, height 319 m, world's tallest from 1929–31
1930s	The development of synthetic resin adhesives to be used for the manufacture of plywoods and veneers

1930s	Chlorofluorocarbons (CFCs) introduced for refrigeration equipment by Thomas Midgley Jr and Henley
1930–50	Application of welding for high-rise steel building structures
1930	The Salginatobel Bridge near Schiers, Switzerland, hollow-box three-hinged reinforced concrete arch, span 88 m, designed by Robert Maillart
1930	Elorn Bridge, Plougastel, France, three hollow-box reinforced concrete arches, self-supporting, centring floated in, span 186.4 m, designed by Marie Eugène Freyssinet
1931	First synthetic rubber – Neoprene – produced by Wallace Carothers for the Du Pont Company, USA, which was awarded the patent
1931	102-storey Empire State Building, New York, steel, height 381 m, world's tallest from 1931–71, architects Shreve, Lamb and Harmon Associates
1931	George Washington Bridge, Hudson River, between New Jersey and New York, steel suspension, span 1067 m, twice the span of any previous suspension bridge, designed by Othmar Ammann
1931	The Bayonne Bridge, Kill van Kull channel, between Bayonne and Staten Island, New York, its 496 m span steel arch was the world's longest when finished, designed by Othmar Ammann
1932	Giovanni Berta Stadium, Florence, reinforced concrete structure, designed by Pier Luigi Nervi
1932	Construction of the Moscow underground railway begins
1933	Styrene-butadiene rubber (Buna-S) introduced
1933	Crawford devised commercial synthesis for methyl methacrylate
1933	Algeciras Market Hall, reinforced concrete dome and cylindrical vaults, designed by Eduardo Torroja
1934	First commercial production of Perspex
1935	Madrid Zarzuela Hippodrome (racecourse), reinforced concrete cantilevered hyperboloid roof, designed by Eduardo Torroja
1935	Owens-Corning develops fibreglass wool insulation bat
1935	The Diesel ram introduced (Delmag)
mid-1930s	Introduction of heat pump by General Electric
1936	Hoover Dam, Colorado River, Nevada, concrete arch dam, height 221 m
1936	Hershey Stadium, USA, reinforced concrete rib supported barrel vault, span 68 m
1936	Burgess Acousti–Vent, first acoustic ceiling

1937	Golden Gate Bridge, San Francisco, cable suspension bridge, span 1281 m
1937	Polyurethanes first produced
1938	Fluorescent lamp made commercially available by General Electric
1938	Decorative laminates in colour gain popularity
1938	Pre-stressed concrete bridge, Oelde, Germany, span 33 m
1938–9	Maison du Peuple building, Clichy, France, Jean Prouvé as consultant designs double convex steel sheet panels with springs
1939	E. Hoyer patents the pre-stressing of wires prior to concreting
1939–42	The Esla Arch Bridge, Spain, reinforced concrete arch, span 210 m, designed by Eduardo Torroja
1939	The Bronx–Whitestone Bridge over the East River, New York, steel suspension, span 690 m, designed by Othmar Ammann
1940	Collapse of the Tacoma Narrows Suspension Bridge due to wind flutter
1940	US Gypsum develops rock wool
1941	Epoxy resin surface coatings developed
1942	MERO lattice grid system appears in Germany, system owner Max Mengeringhausen
1942	Maastunnel, Rotterdam, first major submerged tunnel with concrete sections
1945	Dow Chemical develops styrene foam
1945	The development of polyethylene, later used for vapour barriers
1945–8	Temporary housing programme in the UK, 157 000 houses erected (ARCON, Aluminium Bungalow, Uni-Seco and others)
1946	Dymaxion Dwelling Machine, Wichita, Kansas, USA, central mast, roof dome, aluminium cladding, continuous Plexiglass window, designed by Richard Buckminster Fuller (initiated in 1927)
1946	Fibreglass strengthened by epoxy resins
1946	Vinyl floor tile introduced
1946	The Luzancy Bridge over the Marne River, France, pre-stressed concrete, span 55 m, designed by Marie Eugène Freyssinet
1947	Standardized suspended ceiling systems
1947	Rapid City, South Dakota, USA, aircraft hangar, reinforced concrete shell, span 104 m
Late 1940s	Introduction of particleboard

1948	Exhibition Hall, Turin, Italy, 79 m span reinforced concrete barrel with pre-cast ribs, designed by Pier Luigi Nervi
1949	Operation of Lustron Home factory at Columbus, Ohio, USA, wall and roof panels porcelain enamel steel sheet, (closed in 1950)
1949	Le Havre, France, first large-scale reinforced concrete large-panel residential construction, system Camus
1950	First large scale production of Teflon (polytetraflouro-ethylene = p.t.f.e.)
1950s	Foamed plastics and curtain walls developed
1950s	Large span concrete shells developed with span:thickness ratio up to 1700:1
1951	Dome of Discovery, UK, aluminium, diameter 104 m
1951–5	Stuttgart, Germany, one of the first reinforced concrete transmission towers with a viewing platform and tower restaurant, structural proposal F. Leonhardt, architect E. Heinle
1952	Pilkington float glass process invented: molten glass poured on a bed of liquid tin and drawn continuously
1953	Ford plant, Detroit, Richard Buckminster Fuller geodesic dome, diameter 28 m
1953	Raleigh, USA, cable net suspended roof supported by two inclined intersecting concrete arches
1953–5	Lijnbaan, Rotterdam, large car-free shopping centre, architects J.H van der Broek and J.B. Bakema
1954	US patent 2 682 235 for geodesic dome, Richard Buckminster Fuller (applied 1951)
mid-1950s	First air-supported domes ('radomes') in the USA
1955	First all-plastic house exhibited in Paris, designers Schein, Coulon & Magnant
1956	Underground trains on tyres, Paris
1956–9	Seagram Building, New York, architect Mies van der Rohe (and Philip Johnson), one of the first tall buildings with a modernist approach (curtain wall etc.)
1956–62	TWA Terminal, Kennedy Airport, New York, swinging arches, designed by Eero Saarinen
1957	The Consortium of Local Authorities Special Programme (CLASP) is created
1957	Honolulu, the first Kaiser, aluminium panel geodesic dome, diameter 44 m
1957	Monsanto House of the Future, glassfibre-reinforced polyester shells with multiple honeycomb cores, designed by Hamilton & Goody

1957	Mackinac Straits Bridge, Michigan, USA, span 1158 m
1957–8	The world's largest reinforced concrete dome assembled of pre-cast units: CNIT, La Defense, Paris, span 206 m; engineer N. Esquillan
1957–1960	Sport Palace (Palazzo and Palazzetto), Rome, reinforced concrete domes with two-way rib systems, designed by Pier Luigi Nervi
1958	Xochimilco restaurant, 42 m diameter roof, an eight-petalled flower, thin reinforced concrete paraboloids, deigned by Felix Candela
1959	Baton Rouge, USA, geodesic dome, diameter 117 m, hexagonal steel panels supported by exterior pipe framework
1959	Severin Bridge across the River Rhine, Cologne, main span 302 m, cable-stayed steel bridge, one pylon asymmetrically placed, cables in central plane
1959	Polycarbonates come on to the market
1959–67	Ostankino TV Tower, Moscow, height 539 m
1959–73	Sydney Opera House, reinforced concrete 'sail' roof, Jörn Utzon architect, structure Ove Arup
1960s	Invention of screwable metal stud, screw gun, self-drilling and self-tapping screws; gypsum board becomes widespread; patent for the concept of placing insulation above a roofing membrane ('inverted roof'), USA; Du Pont, USA, develops Kevlar, an organic (aromatic polyamide) fibre
1961	First architectural application of weathering steel in John Deere office building at Moline, Illinois, architect Eero Saarinen
1962	US patent 3 063 521 on tensegrity structures granted to Richard Buckminster Fuller (applied 1959)
1962	Toronto Dome, Canada, triodetic structure, diameters 180 m, retractable roof
1962	Grande Dixence, Valais, Switzerland, concrete gravity dam, 285 m high
1963	Maison de la Radio, Paris, hung tall glass panes, St Gobain
1964	The first weathering steel bridge, Detroit, Michigan
1964	Two Marina City residential towers, Chicago, designed by Bertrand Goldberg
1964	Verrazano Narrows Bridge, New York City, suspension, span 1298 m, designed by Othmar Ammann
1964	The Reichenau Bridge over the River Rhine, Reichenau, Switzerland, 100 m span reinforced concrete arch stiffened by pre-stressed concrete hollow-box deck girder, designed by Christian Menn

1964	Parramatta Bridge, Gladesville, Sydney, Australia, arched reinforced concrete bridge, span 305 m
1966–72	Munich Olympic Stadium, square tensile acrylic glass roof sheets with cable net, designed by Frei Otto, G. Behnisch and J. Joedicke
1966–82	Epcot Center, Orlando, Florida, USA, geodesic dome with external cladding triangular aluminium panels, diameter 165 m
1967	Regency Hyatt, Atlanta, Georgia, first modern hotel atrium (John Portman)
1967	Montreal Expo, Canada: (a) US Pavilion, geodesic tensegrity (octahedral truss) dome, designed by Richard Buckminster Fuller; (b) German Pavilion, tensile fabric roof freely suspended on cable net, designed by Frei Otto
1968	First double-decker elevator installed in the Time Life Building, Chicago, 30 storeys (earlier unsuccessful experiments in New York in 1932)
1968	US architect Ezra Ehrenkrantz describes the US Californian School Construction Systems Development (SCSD) and his own work at a London conference
1968	16 May, Ronan Point, London, progressive collapse of a large-panel building due to gas explosion on the 18th floor
1969–70	John Hancock Building, Chicago, braced 'trussed' tube structure, height 344 m, designed by Skidmore, Owings & Merrill, architect Bruce Graham, engineer Fazlur Khan
1970	David Geiger, USA, develops a soft, flexible, inflated fabric roof for the Osaka World Fair
1970s	Reflective coated glass
1970s	Tallest steel mast, Warsaw, Poland, five rigs, height 642.50 m
1971–5	Superdome (covered stadium), New Orleans, USA, diameter 204 m
1971–7	Centre Pompidou building, Paris, mechanical equipment exposed in ornamental fashion, architects Renzo Piano and Richard Rogers
1971	The first fully hydraulic excavator in excess of 100 t, Poclain, France
1971	Ostankino Television Tower, Moscow, 539 m high
1972	British NODUS space lattice system introduced
1972–88	Seikan undersea railway tunnel connecting Japanese islands of Honshu and Hokkaido, length 54 km, world's longest
1973–6	CN Tower, Toronto, height 553 m
1973	Bosporus Bridge, Istanbul, suspension, span 1074 m

1973	Twin Towers of the 110-storey World Trade Center, New York, framed-tube steel structure, height 417 m, world's tallest from 1971–4, designered by Minoru Yamasaki & Associates and Emery Roth & Sons
1974	Sears Tower, Chicago, bundled-tube steel structure, height 443 m, world's tallest from 1974–97, designed by Skidmore, Owings & Merrill, structural design by Fazlur Khan
1975	Pontiac Stadium, Michigan, the world's largest air-supported roof using PTFE (Teflon) coated glass fibre fabric
1975	Saint Nazaire, France, cable-stayed bridge, span 465 m
1976	New River Gorge, West Virginia, USA, steel arch bridge, span 518 m
1978	The world's largest hydraulic excavator, Demag
1978–86	Lloyd's building, London, central atrium, architect Sir Richard Rogers
1979	Covent Garden Market reconstruction, London
1980	Ganter Bridge, Simplon Road, Switzerland, main span 174 m, highest column 150 m, pre-stressed cables embedded in triangular concrete walls above the roadway, designed by Christian Menn
1980	Nourek, Vaksh River, Tajikistan, earth fill with clay core dam, 317 m high; Inguri, Inguri River, Georgia, concrete arch dam, 272 m high; Sayany, Yenisey River, Siberia, Russian Federation, composite arch and gravity dam, 245 m high
1981	The introduction of the TGV (high speed rail link) between Paris and Lyons, 260 km/h
1981	Humber Bridge, Hull, England, suspension, span 1410 m, pylon height 152 m
1981	Haj Terminal, Jeddah, Saudi Arabia, largest fabric roof to date
1982	Maglev shuttle begins operation at Birmingham International Airport, UK
1983	Barrios de Luna, Spain, cable-stayed bridge, span 440 m
1985	Riyadh Stadium, Saudi Arabia, fabric roof, span 247 m, designed, by H. Berger
1985	Marriott Marquis Hotel, New York, atrium over 46 storeys high, architect John Portman
1986	Hongkong and Shanghai Bank, Hong Kong, height 179 m, floors suspended in groups, 93 000 aluminium panels and computer-controlled mirrors used to beam sunlight into the building, architect Norman Foster Associates, engineer Ove Arup & Partners

1986	City of Science and Industry, La Villette, Paris, structural glazing façades; designer Adrien Fainsilber, RFR, main contractor: CFEM
1986	Marriott Marquis Hotel, Atlanta, Georgia, high atrium with a decorative design by John Portman
1986	Broadgate, London, completed, fast-track construction, designers Arup Associates
1987	Musée d'Orsay, Paris, former railway station converted into museums, designed by ADP/Aulenti
1987	Montreal Stadium, cable structure, retractable fabric roof
1987	Baha'i Temple, Delhi, reinforced concrete shells based on lotus, symbol of purity in India
1987	Rogun, Vaksh River, Tajikistan, earth fill dam, 335 m high (highest in the world to date)
1987–9	Yamousoukro, Côte d'Ivoire, church 190 m long, 156 m high
1988	Bank of China building, Hong Kong, steel structure, height 315 m, architect I.M. Pei & Partners, structural engineer Robertson, Fowler & Associates
1988	Nordstrom Store, San Francisco, California, first curved escalator flights outside Japan, in atrium
1989	Le Grand Louvre glass pyramid, Paris, designed by I.M. Pei
1989	Doncaster Dome, UK, largest European leisure facility under one roof
1990	Modified TGV (Atlantique) sets world speed record for locomotives, 515 km/h
1990	Bercy Charenton Shopping Centre, atrium, designed by Renzo Piano
1992	Georgia Dome, USA, hypartensegrity cable dome with fabric roofing, 240 × 192 m three-dimensional space truss exposed on façade, architect I.M. Pei, engineer: Robertson, Levy
1993–1998	Kuala Lumpur, Malaysia, Petronas Towers, height 450 m, core plus cylindrical perimeter frame, mixed steel plus concrete structure, high-strength concrete, world's tallest from 1997, architect Cesar Pelli
1994	Le Havre, Normandy, France, cable-stayed bridge, span 856 m
1994	Channel Tunnel (between UK and France), length 51 km of which 38 km is under water level.
1995	Komatsu 930E, world's largest truck (mining and heavy construction) is built in Japan, length 15.34 m, width 8.1 m, working load 315 t

| 1997 (planned completion) | Tsing Ma Bridge, Hong Kong, suspension, main span 1377 m, the longest span for combined road and rail use |
| 1998 (planned completion) | Akashi Bridge, Japan, suspension, centre span 2022 m, longest in the world to date |

Name Index

Author Index

Subject Index